Crisis of Command
in the Army of
the Potomac

Crisis of Command in the Army of the Potomac

Sheridan's Search for an Effective General

Jay W. Simson

McFarland & Company, Inc., Publishers
Jefferson, North Carolina, and London

LIBRARY OF CONGRESS CATALOGUING-IN-PUBLICATION DATA

Simson, Jay W., 1953–
Crisis of command in the Army of the Potomac : Sheridan's search for an effective general / Jay W. Simson.
p.   cm.
Includes bibliographical references and index.

ISBN 978-0-7864-3653-8
softcover : 50# alkaline paper ∞

1. United States. Army of the Potomac — History.   2. United States. Army of the Potomac — Officers.   3. Sheridan, Philip Henry, 1831–1888 — Military leadership.   4. Averell, William Woods, 1832–1900 — Military leadership.   5. Torbert, Alfred Thomas Archimedes, 1833–1880 — Military leadership.   6. Warren, Gouverneur Kemble, 1830–1882 — Military leadership.   7. Mackenzie, Ranald Slidell, 1840–1889 — Military leadership.   8. Generals — United States — History — 19th century.   9. Command of troops — History — 19th century.   10. United States — History — Civil War, 1861–1865 — Campaigns.   I. Title.
E470.2.S56   2008   973.7'33 — dc22   2008017038

British Library cataloguing data are available

©2008 Jay W. Simson. All rights reserved

No part of this book may be reproduced or transmitted in any form or by any means, electronic or mechanical, including photocopying or recording, or by any information storage and retrieval system, without permission in writing from the publisher.

On the cover: General Philip H. Sheridan © 2007 Corbis Images; The Army of the Potomac Marching up Pennsylvania Avenue © 2007 Pictures Now

Manufactured in the United States of America

McFarland & Company, Inc., Publishers
Box 611, Jefferson, North Carolina 28640
www.mcfarlandpub.com

Table of Contents

Introduction and Acknowledgments   *1*
Prologue: Sheridan Takes Command   *5*

Part I: William Woods Averell
The Man Who Preferred Mountains

1. Averell's Background   *19*
2. The Battle of Kelly's Ford   *24*
3. The Chancellorsville Campaign   *29*
4. Redemption in the Mountains   *37*
5. Averell and Sheridan   *41*
6. Fisher's Hill   *48*
7. Sheridan Sacks Averell   *53*

Part II: Alfred Thomas Archimedes Torbert
The Man Who Was Promoted Too Far

8. Commissioned by Both Sides   *61*
9. Torbert in the Overland Campaign and at Trevilian Station   *68*
10. Chief of Cavalry   *74*
11. Failure at Milford   *79*
12. Hesitation at Tom's Brook   *84*
13. The Battle of Cedar Creek   *89*
14. Flunking the Final Exam at Gordonsville   *97*

Part III: Gouverneur Kemble Warren
The Man Who Suffered from Combat Fatigue

15. The Master Engineer, Cartographer and Teacher   *105*
16. Showing the Spark at Second Manassas/Bull Run   *111*
17. The Hero at Chancellorsville and Gettysburg   *118*
18. A Strong Performance at Bristoe Station   *125*
19. Moral Courage at Mine Run   *129*
20. The Long Hard Grind of the Overland Campaign   *137*
21. On the Road to Five Forks   *149*
22. Broken Hero at the Fatal Victory of Five Forks   *154*
23. The Court of Inquiry   *161*

Part IV: Ranald Slidell Mackenzie
The Man Who Proved the Rule

24. The Most Promising Young Officer in the Army *171*
25. The Perpetual Punisher *176*
26. Mackenzie at Five Forks *181*
27. The Pursuit to Appomattox *187*
28. The Most Tragic One of Them All *192*
29. Sheridan's Troubleshooter *201*

Epilogue:
The Method Behind Sheridan's Madness *211*

Notes *223*

Bibliography *227*

Index *233*

Introduction and Acknowledgments

Crisis of Command in the Army of the Potomac at its most basic level is an examination of the two very different and contrasting styles of command that were represented in the Union's Army of the Potomac during the American Civil War. One of these was the style of command that was established when the Army of the Potomac was created by its first commander, George B. McClellan, and the other was the new style of command that came out of the West when Ulysses S. Grant was summoned to take charge of the Union's military effort and to bring the war to a successful conclusion.

On its most direct level this is accomplished through an examination of the Civil War careers of William W. Averell, Alfred T.A. Torbert, Gouverneur K. Warren, and Ranald S. Mackenzie. Indirectly the book is also a study of Philip Henry Sheridan's military abilities and personality, both positive and negative. He could also be called the fifth major person featured in the book, since on at least one level it is the story about the interaction between Sheridan and Averell, between Sheridan and Torbert, between Sheridan and Warren, and above all else between Sheridan and Mackenzie.

On another level it is also about the indirect interaction between two people who at different times held the same two jobs simultaneously, General-in-Chief of the Armies of the United States and (the actual or de facto) commander of the Army of the Potomac. These two men were George B. McClellan and Ulysses S. Grant. McClellan was the man who failed and Grant was the man who succeeded and the main difference between them lay in their almost totally different styles of command. It was McClellan's style of command, which permeated the high command of the Army of the Potomac, that was primarily responsible for lengthening the war. It was Grant's style of command that was primarily responsible for ending it.

From its very beginning the American Civil War was a total war fought for total ends. Either the Southern Confederacy would win its independence or the Union government would prevent it from doing so. Although the war was fought for total ends from the beginning, until the ascendancy of Grant in late 1863 and early 1864 only limited means were actually used. Lincoln and Grant understood that a war being fought for total ends required total means. This was an insight that eluded the men who formed the original command structure of the Army of the Potomac. They were gentlemen, by their own definition, almost to a man, and it has been already noted that their gentlemanly way of war was practically guaranteed to lengthen the conflict not bring it to any sort of a conclusion.

This realization also did not elude William T. Sherman, who took over from Grant in the Western Theatre of Operations. And it most certainly did not elude Sheridan, who provided the spearhead that brought eventual victory in the Eastern Theatre of Operations against Robert E. Lee and his Army of Northern Virginia. Although the American Civil War by this time had been mostly won by the Union in the Western Theatre, it could still have been lost by the Union in the Eastern Theatre if Lee had succeeded in drawing out the stalemate that existed in the spring and summer of 1864 in both the Eastern and Western theatres, before Farragut seized control of Mobile Bay, before Sherman's conquest of Atlanta, before Sheridan's triple victories in the Shenandoah Valley, and while the Siege of Petersburg continued without an apparent end in sight.

In the process, Sheridan demonstrated that while he was not a loveable person (due primarily to his hot temper) and he did not have an unblemished character (as shown by the fact that he was not above manipulating his superiors, most especially Grant) he did have the drive and the ruthless determination to get the job done. Generally if you disappointed Sheridan you were gone and that was more or less what happened to Averell, Torbert and Warren. But, if you did what needed to be done when it needed to be done and could use your own initiative to build upon the orders given to you (like Mackenzie) then you were just the kind of subordinate that Sheridan was looking for.

What *Crisis of Command* is not intended to be is a history of the end of the American Civil War. It is also not intended to be a mere collection of biographies of William Woods Averell, Alfred Thomas Archimedes Torbert, Gouverneur Kemble Warren, and Ranald Slidell Mackenzie, although it does contain much material that is historical and much material that is biographical concerning these men and their contributions— their successes, and in some cases their failures— in the final six months of the American Civil War.

What you are about to read is one of the little-known stories of the American Civil War. This is primarily the story of three men, none of whom were incompetents, none of whom were even mediocrities, and the contrast between them and a fourth man who proved to be everything that they were not and yet who was still a tragic figure in his own right.

The tragedy for the three found wanting was that if the demands that were made upon them had been kept within their personal limitations they could have met them. But, circumstances— or their superiors—forced each of them to go beyond their limitations; and when they failed— or were perceived to have failed— they were discarded one by one by someone who would prove himself to be one of the single most ruthless and determined generals of the entire war.

The fourth man, Ranald S. Mackenzie, The Man Who Proved the Rule, was a man who had very few limitations, at least as a soldier. He proved himself to be an extremely effective cavalry commander and his small cavalry division made great contributions during the Battle of Five Forks and the ensuing Appomattox Campaign that succeeded in bringing the war to something of a spectacular ending, at least in the Eastern Theatre of Operations in Virginia. Then when the war ended Mackenzie continued his contributions to the United States Army— and even to the United States as a whole— when he became Sheridan's troubleshooter upon the frontier and probably the most important, most successful, and the very best of the five major Indian fighting military commanders who served on the Western frontier.

His, however, were the limitations of a human being, and for over 20 years Mackenzie forced himself to the edge of those limitations and beyond them and then, at the very pinnacle of his career, he collapsed and as a result is today almost totally unknown and forgotten.

It can also be said (to paraphrase) that success has a thousand authors and failure has none. While in this particular endeavor there has been only one author, there have been a number of persons without whose assistance this project could not have been accomplished.

First and foremost among them has been my wife, Lynn. She has assisted me in every way possible, particularly with my research, without which I could not even have started this project, much less completed it. She has also supported me even though history is not her passion.

Assistance in preparing some of the maps has been provided by my daughter, Terry, who has considerably more talent in this area than I do.

Eric Wittenberg of Columbus, Ohio, and Greg Biggs of Clarksville, Tennessee, have also been very supportive. Eric is an attorney, an author, and a historian — having extensively written about Sheridan and the rise of the Union cavalry. Greg is a recognized Civil War flag expert and all-around Civil War enthusiast. Together they are partners in Ironclad Publishing, a small publishing house that specializes in books about the American Civil War.

"I think it's a tremendous idea," Eric e-mailed me when I first broached the idea for this book to him, and he has been a rock of support and encouragement, providing a sounding board whenever I felt that I needed one. I shared with him many of the interesting tidbits I discovered along the way while researching this book. Greg, for his part, was a great help with that research.

I have also found myself to be in agreement with many of the conclusions that Eric has reached concerning "Little Phil" — up to a point. However, beyond that point I do not choose to go. For I still believe that Sheridan belongs in the pantheon of Union military leaders who brought an end to the American Civil War.

I would also like to recognize the assistance provided by Chris Calkins of Petersburg, Virginia, who is chief of interpretation for the Petersburg National Battlefield and is employed by the National Park Service. He has been of considerable help to me, particularly when it came to obtaining information from the transcripts of the court of inquiry into the conduct of Maj. Gen. G.K. Warren at the Battle of Five Forks. Several chapters of this book were based directly upon information provided by Chris that most directly had a bearing on the testimony of Joshua L. Chamberlain and Ranald S. Mackenzie and upon the conclusions and findings of the court of inquiry.

John Carr, Van Wert County Brumback Library director, and his staff deserve considerable thanks for all of their assistance in the research and writing of this book. Without their assistance it probably would not have been written, or at least it would not resemble its current form. To editorialize for just a moment this is one reason why communities must support their public libraries, particularly when shortsighted politicians in the state legislature act stupidly and fail to meet their responsibilities. On the state level nothing should have a higher priority than education and there can be no adequate support for education without adequate support for libraries.

Photographs and maps for this project were obtained through the Library of Congress, whose Website and personnel were of considerable assistance. It was through the Library of Congress that I came upon the work of Robert Knox Sneden (1832–1918), who created a number of maps of various battlefields either at the time the engagements occurred or shortly thereafter.

In addition, I must also mention the eHistory Internet Website maintained by Ohio State University, since it provides online the complete *Official Records of the Union and Confederate Armies during the War of the Rebellion* and therefore it is probably one of the single most important research resources available to just about any student or historian of the American Civil War. Having this resource available through the Internet was invaluable in so many different ways providing, as it did, primary source material.

Finally, I would also like to say a special word of thanks to Susan Burchfield, PS, MS, of Van Wert, who is a licensed professional clinical counselor, for the assistance she provided when she allowed me to pick her brains concerning a theory regarding one of the subjects of this book. I simply wanted to know if my theory was plausible. She told me in effect that not only was it plausible it was highly plausible.

Prologue
Sheridan Takes Command

It was the fourth spring of the American Civil War when a new wind blew into Washington, D.C., from the West, signaling the arrival of Ulysses S. Grant on the central stage of the war. It was only during the previous winter (1863–1864) that the Union had finally established a modern high command system, which would not be equaled in Europe until the advent of the Prussian General Staff (in 1866). Still, it would take one more full year to bring about the final collapse of the Southern Confederacy.

Alas, it was a command system that, once the war was over, would be dismantled and would not be effectively replaced until the advent of World War II.

In 1861 the Union was woefully unprepared to fight any kind of war. The army was tiny (consisting of 16,000 men, hardly enough to even adequately police the Indians); there were few good modern weapons, no officers trained in the higher art of war, and a completely and totally inadequate and archaic system of high command. Armies could be and would be raised and modern weapons manufactured or purchased abroad relatively quickly. But only time, battles, and blunders could provide the experience necessary to train generals (more or less on the job) and develop a modern command system.

* * *

When the war began there was no one who was capable of administrating or of commanding a large army.[1] Only Winfield F. Scott and John E. Wool (of the Union generals at the beginning of war) had any experience in handling large bodies of troops; they were both old men on the very edge of retirement and due to physical limitations they were not up to the rigors of field command.

Scott, at 75 years of age and tipping the scale at over 300 pounds, was physically unable to take to the field and Wool was even older than Scott, although less physically infirm. Outside of Scott and Wool (who were mostly self-educated) no one in the military on either side of the American Civil War really knew much about the history and theory of warfare. There was no school in the United States that taught it (not even West Point, the Virginia Military Institute, or the Citadel in Charleston, South Carolina). The U.S. Military Academy at West Point instead taught engineering, fortifications, and mathematics. Cadets learned a little about strategy and tactics but next to nothing about leading troops in battle, staff work, or administration. Their experience after graduating from West Point usually dealt with Indian fighting (which provided them with some experience of leading troops in combat but only on an extremely small scale), building forts, and various civil engineering projects (such as badly needed flood control along the Mississippi River).

One of the greatest ironies was the fact that both Northern and Southern generals were fighting within their own country yet they usually had no idea about where they were going or how they were to get there. This was due to the fact that there were few accurate maps—military or otherwise. As a matter of fact, the Army of the Potomac did not even obtain an accurate map of Northern Virginia, its primary area of operations, until 1863. (Two of the best generals of the war, Thomas J. Jackson for the Confederacy, and Philip H. Sheridan for the Union, got around this particular problem by personally selecting two of the best topographical engineers and cartographers available — Jedediah Hotchkiss for Jackson and John R. Meigs for Sheridan — and adding them to their staffs to specifically draw them the maps they needed.)

However, one thing the war soon demonstrated was that one did not need to have a military background in order to be a war director. Abraham Lincoln had been a civilian all of his life, except for 90 days militia service in a very minor Indian war where he saw no military action at all. Jefferson Davis, on the other hand, was a graduate of West Point, a combat veteran and regimental commander of the Mexican War, in addition to being a former secretary of war (possibly one of the best secretaries of war to serve prior to the American Civil War). Yet Lincoln became a great war president while Davis was, at best, only a mediocre one.

Lincoln, by the power of his mind alone, with no prior training or experience, became a competent strategist, seeing the big picture practically from the very beginning of the war. His sole objective was to restore the Union. He immediately realized that this could only be done by force, therefore, the Union must take the offensive, destroy the Confederate armies in the field, and destroy the very ability of the Southern Confederacy to make war; not really attempt to conquer Southern territory. Such a conquest would only be a by-product of his grand strategy. Lincoln's strategic thinking was both sound and, for a rank amateur, frankly astonishing. Lincoln never delegated his authority or deferred his judgment to others when it came to choosing generals. But he was always willing — if he considered a general to be able and competent — to defer to that general's opinion concerning the framing and direction of strategic operations. Although on occasion accused of micromanaging the war he did so only when forced to do so by circumstances or by his generals.

* * *

Lincoln and Congress eventually created a modern system of high command during the winter of 1863–1864 when they institutionalized the lessons learned from three years of general failure (or at least stalemate) in the East and general success in the West. What Congress authorized Lincoln set into operation.

Grant was central to the entire scheme to reorganize the military high command and was the choice of Lincoln, of Congress, and of the Northern people. For Grant, at least by the time of the aftermath of the Battle of Shiloh, had reached the same general conclusions as had Lincoln concerning the best way to conduct the war. Thus when Grant came east he was prepared to accept Lincoln's three fundamental concepts or commandments for the conduct of the war.[2] These included:

Major General Philip H. Sheridan as he appeared while in command of the Cavalry Corps, Army of the Potomac, and the Army of the Shenandoah (Library of Congress).

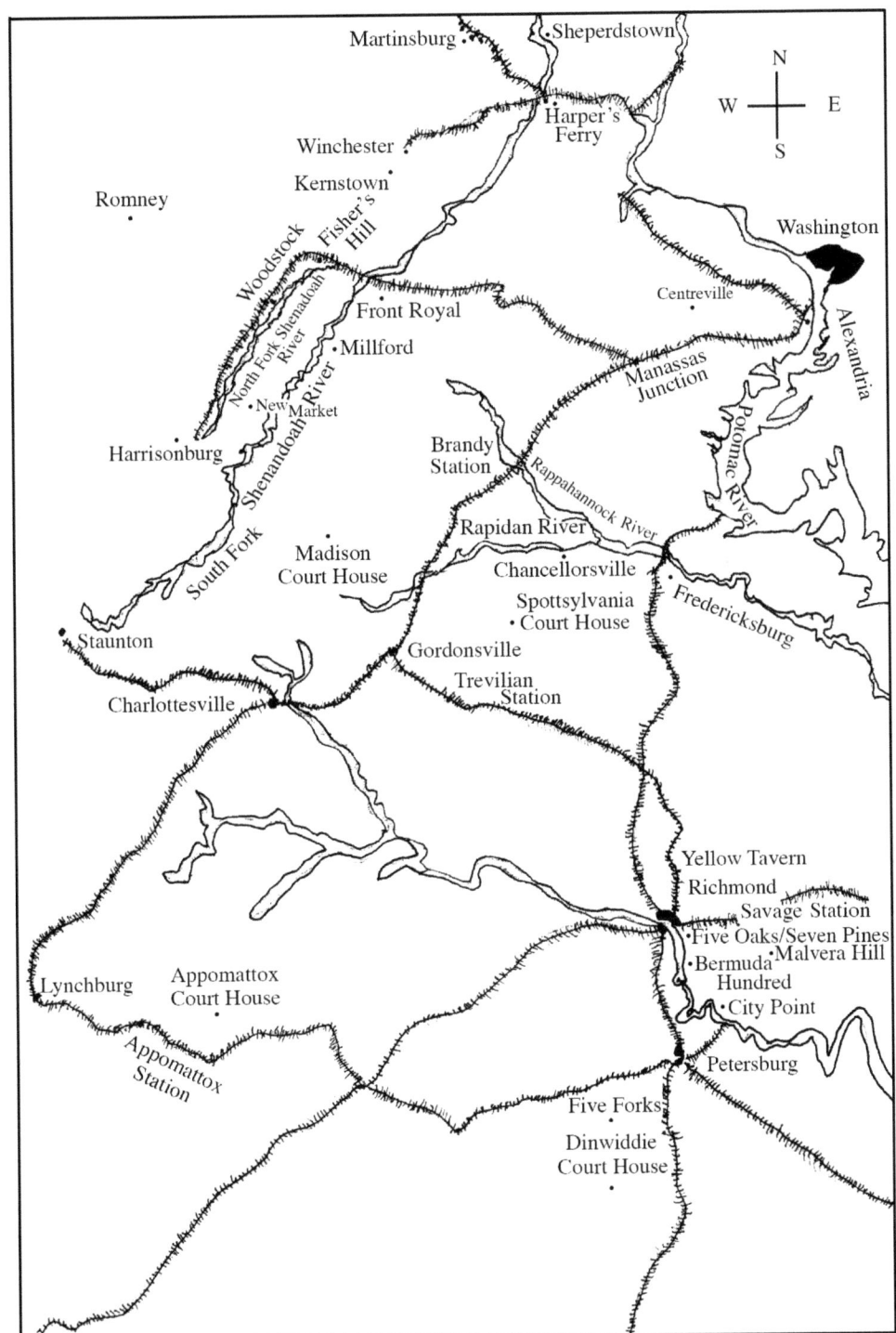

The 1864 and 1865 campaigns of U.S. Grant and Philip H. Sheridan in the Shenandoah Valley and Central Virginia are depicted above. This map can also be used to follow most of the other campaigns of the Army of the Potomac and the Army of Northern Virginia with the exception of the Gettysburg Campaign and W.W. Averell's raids in West Virginia. Of particular interest are the Shenandoah and Overland campaigns of 1864 as well as the Appomattox Campaign of March 26 through April 9, 1865 (Library of Congress).

1. The destruction of the Confederate armies, for as long as they remained in the field the Southern Confederacy lived. Once they were removed the Southern Confederacy would die.
2. Political generals had to be tolerated and even given important commands in order to bolster Lincoln's support in Congress and among the political machinery within the Northern states. Grant would tolerate them until their disasters became so apparent that he could get rid of them without ruffling Lincoln's political arrangements.
3. The national capital, Washington, D.C., had to be protected at all costs. Any threat to the capital had to be taken seriously regardless of developments elsewhere, for to lose control of the capital — as Lincoln and Grant well realized — even if only for a short time could lead to the Northern people's repudiation of the war itself.

Congress started the ball rolling late in February 1864, when it passed a bill reviving the rank of lieutenant general and authorizing Lincoln to fill the appointment from among the present major generals of the regular army. It was understood that the new lieutenant general, as the highest-ranking general in the army, would become the general-in-chief, since he was authorized — under the direction of the president — to assume command of the Armies of the United States. In the previous history of the United States only two men had ever held this rank or these responsibilities: George Washington, by permanent appointment of the Continental Congress, and Winfield Scott, by brevet (or honorary rank) and presidential appointment.

Grant was the only viable candidate, and Lincoln was eager to make the appointment; however, there was one stumbling block: the question of Grant's own political ambitions and whether he would challenge Lincoln for reelection in 1864. Grant received the commission and the appointment after he reassured Lincoln that he had no desire to be a political candidate for anything and since he was a soldier he had no business uttering any political views until after the war was over.

The other conditions Grant had to accept to receive the appointment were confirmed by Alfred Pleasonton and Fitz John Porter.[3] Pleasonton claimed that he had once been offered command of the Army of the Potomac provided that:

1. The war must not be ended until the South was crushed.
2. Slavery was abolished.
3. Lincoln was reelected.

Porter, when told that Pleasonton claimed to have been offered command of the Army of the Potomac but had refused the price and that Grant had accepted the terms, disbelieved that Pleasonton had ever been offered command of the army, but he (Porter) understood that those were the terms under which command of the Army of the Potomac was offered.

Grant accepted the commission and the appointment with the understanding that his headquarters would be in the field and not in Washington. Henry Halleck, then serving as general-in-chief, stepped down in favor of Grant and was named to be Grant's chief of staff in Washington. Although his friend William T. Sherman had urged Grant to stay far away from Washington, Grant decided that he would have to remain in the East for several reasons:

1. All political pressures were centered in Washington and he was the only person who could withstand such pressures upon military operations.
2. It was likely that Lincoln wanted Grant close at hand.
3. It was in truth the logical place for him to be.

Although Grant was willing to stay in the East, he was not willing to stay within the political atmosphere of Washington. His only other option was to maintain his headquarters with the primary army in the field: the Army of the Potomac. Although Grant kept the army's current commander, George G. Meade, in place he, and not Meade, would direct its strategy and at times even its tactics.

It was Halleck, as chief of staff in Washington, who actually made the scheme (outside of the Army of the Potomac with Grant directly overseeing Meade) work as well as it did. He provided the liaison between Lincoln and Grant; and between Grant and the other field army commanders fighting the war. Halleck communicated military ideas to civilians and civilian ideas to soldiers in such a way as to make them both understand what he was talking about. Because of Halleck, Lincoln and Grant never misunderstood each other.

* * *

On the other hand, the Confederate States of America never adopted a modern system of high command, let alone a grand strategy, and it showed.[4] The primary problem was that Jefferson Davis, the Confederate president, felt that he could do it all, alone. In his own person he tried to fill the roles that Lincoln, Stanton, Halleck, and Grant filled for the North. Davis tried to be commander-in-chief, secretary of war, chief of staff, and general-in-chief all rolled into one. In point of fact it was far too much for any one man to do.

The closest the Southern Confederacy got to a modern command system was when the Confederate Congress, just prior to the final collapse, forced Davis to name Lee as his general-in-chief and to name a serving general, John C. Breckinridge, as secretary of war. Breckinridge, who had served as vice president before the war and had been one of the failed candidates in 1860 for the presidency, was both an adroit politician and a reasonably competent general officer. Unfortunately, by the time these changes finally occurred it was far too late for them to have any real effect upon the course of the war.

Davis also had troubled relationships with his top generals. He and Joseph E. Johnston couldn't get along to the point that they were expending just about as much energy in fighting each other as they were in fighting the Union. Lee and Davis have been said to have had a wonderful partnership, but the partnership may have been nothing more than a mask for Lee's ability to manipulate Davis. Braxton Bragg could have been a quite acceptable general except that Davis never allowed him to select his own subordinates (and in fact Lee and Davis used the Western Theatre of Operations as a dumping ground for "failed" generals), and most notoriously saddling him with Leonidas K. Polk (who was both incompetent and a crony of Davis). The working relationship between Davis and P.G.T. Beauregard always seemed to be based on mutual loathing, yet it worked, to a degree, because Beauregard believed in the American constitutional tradition that the military must submit to the civilian authority. Finally, in John Bell Hood, Davis found a general he liked. Unfortunately, the problem with Hood—who was an extremely capable brigade and division commander—was that he just was not competent at the corps and army level, which Hood proceeded to amply demonstrate when Davis attempted to do what God had failed to do—make an army commander out of him.

For these and other reasons, while Davis well realized that the Western Theatre of Operations needed a clear, unified, workable command system, he was never able to establish one.

* * *

Grant eventually demonstrated that he was superior to Lee as a general, because the American Civil War was a modern war and Grant had a modern mind, which Lee did not. Lee looked to the past in war in the same way that the Southern Confederacy looked to the past in spirit. Lee's staff, for instance, was not a planning staff (remaining more or less only a secretarial one), with Lee choosing to do for himself what his staff should have been doing for him. Lee did it this way, because this was the traditional way war was conducted. Grant's staff, although it, too, tended to leave much to be desired, was, on the other hand, an organization of experts in the various phases of strategic planning, which in the final analysis helped rather than hindered Grant.

Since Grant had a modern mindset, what was realistic to him was often what Lee considered to be barbaric and therefore anathema. Lee, the most Southern of Southern gentlemen (like the many Union officers who were also Northern gentlemen), saw war as a conflict between armies. Grant knew that it was actually a conflict between societies.

* * *

Despite fears that Grant would pack the eastern armies with new generals chosen from among his western cronies, Grant brought only three generals East with him. They were Philip H. Sheridan (whose aggressiveness in the assault upon Missionary Ridge during the battles for Chattanooga had greatly impressed Grant), William F. Smith (who had originally served in the Army of the Potomac and had also impressed Grant with his engineering expertise), and James H. Wilson (a recent graduate of West Point and an engineer on Grant's staff who had particularly distinguished himself during the Vicksburg Campaign).

Of the three, Grant had determined that Sheridan would command his cavalry, Smith would command a corps in the Army of the James (until his great blunder at Petersburg), and Wilson would first head the War Department's Cavalry Bureau, command a division of Sheridan's cavalry, and eventually return to the West and be the only Union commander to ever defeat Confederate Lt. Gen. Nathan Bedford Forrest in open battle. (In point of fact, Wilson against Forrest would be much more a Johnny-come-lately than Sheridan would ever be against J.E.B. Stuart and his successors, Wade Hampton and Fitzhugh Lee. By the time Wilson bested Forrest it was so late in the war that even the "Wizard of the Saddle" could do nothing against Wilson and the blitzkrieg tactics of what was in effect his mounted army.)

Although Grant would eventually fire Smith and allow Wilson to be transferred back west, he would be unstinting in his support of Sheridan to the point that he would ignore certain aspects of Sheridan's behavior up to and including outright insubordination, something that would puzzle at least one modern historian of the American Civil War. Grant first met Sheridan in 1862 and was impressed. In 1863 he would watch as the Army of the Cumberland, which included Sheridan's division, took Missionary Ridge in a frontal assault that appeared suicidal and, in the aftermath of the battle, without orders and on his own initiative, attempted the only pursuit of the fleeing Confederate army.

Following the death of Sheridan, General Joshua Lawrence Chamberlain (the only man ever to be promoted on the field of battle by Grant, and after the war a political ally of Grant) was asked just why Grant took such an interest in Sheridan.[5]

"His fighting qualities," Chamberlain responded, without hesitation. "He would fight— always. He was not an engineer. He did not entrench. He was a terrible fighter. His character was so different from Grant's that he [Grant] admired him and tried to make him what he was not—to the injustice of other men."

Grant realized that Sheridan, along with William T. Sherman, shared his basic concept of how to win the war—to grind away at the Southern Confederacy until it finally collapsed. He also realized that outside of Abraham Lincoln they were the only ones, in and out of the government, and in and out of the army, who did. The four of them would support each other and protect each other from their critics, be they political or military.

* * *

Grant's win-the-war strategy called for a coordinated offensive on all fronts, which was designed to exhaust the Confederacy and make it impossible for any one theatre to weaken itself to bolster another.[6] This had been an important strategy for the Confederates. It had allowed for the Confederate concentration of troops to fight the battle of Shiloh, the periodic reinforcement of Gen. Robert E. Lee's Army of Northern Virginia, and the reinforcement of Gen. Braxton Bragg's Army of Tennessee just prior to the last large scale Confederate victory at the Battle of Chickamauga.

The essence of Grant's strategy was as follows:

1. Grant, accompanying the Army of the Potomac, would press into the defenses of Richmond and thus deny the room to maneuver that Lee had used to hold off attackers since 1862.
2. Maj. Gen. William T. Sherman, taking over for Grant in the Western Theatre of Operations, would drive for Atlanta. Once he had taken Atlanta his next move would be determined by circumstances. What Sherman would do was to march to the sea, taking Savannah as an 1864 Christmas present for President Lincoln. Then he would disdain going into winter quarters and turn north to drive through the Carolinas, completing the fragmentation of the Southern Confederacy and eventually, possibly, even trapping Lee between his and Grant's armies.
3. Maj. Gen. Nathaniel Banks was to move up the Red River and disrupt operations within the Confederate Trans-Mississippi Department, primarily to keep its forces occupied.
4. Eventually land forces were supposed to be provided by Banks to cooperate with Rear Adm. David G. Farragut for an assault upon the last major Confederate port on the Gulf of Mexico at Mobile, Alabama, and from there to open up the Confederacy's soft underbelly to assault.
5. Smaller armies were to cooperate with Grant's offensive against Lee. Maj. Gen. Benjamin Butler and his Army of the James was to move up the Virginia peninsula once again, while Maj. Gen. Franz Siegel and his Army of West Virginia was to move into the Shenandoah Valley.

They did not all have to succeed. As Grant planned it, each would help the other. Only Grant or Sherman had to succeed in their primary efforts and the Southern Confederacy would be brought to its knees.

Confederate President Jefferson Davis realized that fact. He also realized that the forces he had available were inadequate, but that had always been the case.[7] In order to counter Grant's strategy he had to keep Lee in Virginia to protect Richmond. After the disasters at the battles of Franklin and Nashville, General Joseph E. Johnston and his remnants from the Army of Tennessee and various garrison forces had to face Sherman. Davis was confident that General Edmund Kirby Smith could deal with Banks in the Trans-Mississippi, and to protect the Shenandoah Davis had sent Breckinridge, who in point of fact turned out to be an inspired choice.

Kirby Smith did handle Banks, stopping him cold. Banks almost lost the entire Union river gunboat fleet to the receding waters of the Red River. In addition, Banks' failure also dried up the troops that Admiral Farragut needed to use against Mobile. So the admiral went ahead without them and in the August 5, 1864, Battle of Mobile Bay secured control of that waterway and closed the port of Mobile without actually seizing the city. But, it would never be the base for a drive against the soft underbelly of the Confederacy that Grant had originally envisaged. Breckinridge drove Siegle back at the Battle of New Market and Butler managed to get himself stalled at Bermuda Hundred by Beauregard.

Although it took a while, Sherman did finally succeed in taking Atlanta and it was the victory needed for Grant's strategy to succeed. Grant himself was fought into a stalemate and siege at Petersburg, while Maj. Gen. David Hunter replaced Siegle and was ordered to burn out the Shenandoah Valley, which he failed to do due to Lee's response, dispatching Lt. Gen. Jubal Early and his II Corps from the Army of Northern Virginia at Petersburg to the Shenandoah Valley.

Lee's primary purpose in 1864 — in response to Grant's strategy — was to seek the exhaustion of the Northern leadership and then the Northern people's patience with the continuation of the war.[8] Except for the united front provided by Grant and Lincoln, he might have succeeded.

After the bloody losses in the Overland Campaign that had climaxed at Cold Harbor, Grant, by his crossing of the James River, had outmaneuvered Lee. It was true that except for William F. Smith's hesitation Grant might have been able to storm the Petersburg lines before Lee could arrive. But the public did not realize these facts for what they were: confirmation that the South was doomed — under Grant's strategic plan of assault from the north, east, and west, simultaneously — just as long as the North persevered.

What they knew was that Grant's campaign of relentless assaults upon Lee had failed, or at least had not succeeded, that the casualty lists were getting longer every day and there seemed to be no end in sight. Therefore, what the Northern public did not realize was that the Southern Confederacy was becoming totally and completely exhausted.[9]

Just after the Siege of Petersburg began, Lee attempted his final masterstroke, sending Lt. Gen. Jubal Early and his II Corps (what had been Stonewall Jackson's command, until his death) to join Breckinridge in the Shenandoah Valley. Early then launched the final invasion of the North in the East, a gigantic raid aimed at Washington, D.C. Although he did not enter the Union capital (knowing he could never hold it), Early did scare everyone in it, including the Union government. In addition, he frightened Hunter enough to cause Hunter to drop everything and fall back into West Virginia, and then, when the raid was over and Hunter pursued Early and his army on their return back to the Shenandoah Valley, Early turned and almost effortlessly threw back the pursuit at the Second Battle of Kernstown.

Lincoln trusted Grant, and Grant failed to panic. Lee's attack upon the morale of the Northern leadership failed. But his assault on the morale of the Northern people came close to succeeding.

Lincoln was able to survive the crisis, in part by having made emancipation one of the Union's war aims, which created within the North a reserve of enthusiasm upon which Lincoln was able to draw at need.[10] He had also created a unity of command, he supported his chosen general, and he left to that general the actual military conduct of the war. This was demonstrated when, in the midst of Early's invasion, Grant asked Lincoln if he wanted him to come to Washington, Lincoln replied: "What I think is that you should provide to retain your hold where you are, certainly, and bring the rest with you personally and make a vigorous effort to destroy the enemy's force in this vicinity. I think that there is really a fair chance to do this if the movement is prompt. That is what I think upon your suggestion, and it is not an order."

Grant did not go to Washington. Instead he consolidated four separate departments (the Middle Department, the Department of West Virginia, the Department of Washington, and the Department of the Susquehanna) to create the Middle Military Division, and placed Maj. Gen. Philip H. Sheridan in charge on August 7, 1864, thus putting into motion the 1864 Shenandoah Valley Campaign. During that campaign Sheridan defeated Early and destroyed one of the few remaining sources of relatively easily obtained supplies for Lee's army. This combined with Farragut's victory at Mobile Bay and Sherman's capture of Atlanta to assure Lincoln's reelection on November 8, 1864, and the final failure of Lee's campaign against the morale of the Northern people.

Sheridan would also, between September 23, 1864, and April 1, 1865, during the last six months of the American Civil War, relieve three Union generals of their commands. The controversy over the relief of one of them, Gouverneur K. Warren, which would occur at the very end of the war, would go on to endure for the next 17 years.

Aside from Warren the generals effectively fired by Sheridan would include Bvt. Maj. Gen. William W. Averell and Bvt. Maj. Gen. Alfred T.A. Torbert. Thus, they would become the Man Who Suffered from Combat Fatigue (Warren), the Man Who Preferred Mountains (Averell), and the Man Who Was Promoted Too Far (Torbert).

By relieving each of them of their commands, Sheridan would show that an entirely new standard of competence was now being demanded along with the establishment of a new command style for the eastern armies—most particularly the Army of the Potomac—which occurred with the advent of Grant and Sheridan.

The command style of the Army of the Potomac, which was instituted by General George B. McClellan when he created the army, was fatally flawed. It was originally conceived that the war would be relatively short and would be fought and commanded by gentlemen. Many of the officers and members of the Army of the Potomac's high command were part of what was then called the "new gentry elite," the Americanized version of the old colonial gentry, which was descended from English aristocratic traditions.[11]

In the South the "gentry" remained very much a social class, although basically an open one. But in the North the conditions of the New World and the Industrial Revolution had succeeded in changing the nature of the "gentry" from a social class maintained on a hereditary basis to a mass of individuals with shared characteristics. Members of this very loose elite grouping consisted largely of professionals in all fields who subscribed to a distinct code of values, which esteemed honor and reputation over material gain and anticipated an eventual rise of its members to high and honored places in society as the natural order of things.

It was in fact a kind of social Darwinism, survival and the assured advancement of the best and the fittest. Thus the Northern gentleman was at once comfortable among all social classes and was aware of his leadership role, with success being the product of self-discipline and restraint.

If one wants to prolong a war, then a command style based upon this ideal is the way to go about it, because total war—which was what the American Civil War had been from the very beginning (although outside of Lincoln and Grant this was not recognized until about 1863)—was not, is not, and has never been a gentlemanly endeavor. At the bottom, war is a brutal, bitter process, devoid of gentlemanly glory, glamour, or grandeur. It is very much a matter of we won, they lost, and that's the way we wanted it to be. The problem during the American Civil War was that gentlemen simply could not in general (although there were exceptions) be ruthless enough to do what was necessary to actually win the war.

Of the commanders of the Army of the Potomac, McClellan, Burnside (who was incompetent at this level and knew it, but unfortunately nobody believed him), and Meade were all gentlemen. Pope doesn't really count, since he commanded another army entirely (the Army of Virginia), and he was no gentleman, which caused him to be despised by his contemporaries within the Army of the Potomac, and which in part helped lead to his failure at the Second Battle of Manassas/Bull Run, another of the great controversies of the American Civil War, which resulted in what one author has called an American Dreyfuss Affair. Nor was Hooker a gentleman, but he was surprisingly competent as well as being something of a gifted strategist. His failure was a personal one, a failure of nerve; it was not a systemic one.

George Gordon Meade was a typical Northern military gentleman. Due to his class-conscious impulses as part of the "gentry" he was skeptical of the volunteer soldier. As part of the New World gentry and its ethical standards Meade stayed aloof from the cliques and intrigues within the command structure of the Army of the Potomac. Although he could be critical of McClellan as a general, Meade was neither pro– nor anti–McClellan. He never climbed upon the "dump Burnside" bandwagon after the Fredericksburg catastrophe or the "Mud March" fiasco. He also refused to associate himself with the anti–Hooker cabal after Chancellorsville.

However, he could and did make enemies — such as Dan Butterfield, whom Meade inherited from Hooker as chief of staff — along with many newspaper reporters and editors. (As soon as possible Meade would replace Butterfield as chief of staff with A.A. Humphreys.) Like Sherman he distrusted the reporters and the editors; newspapers, he believed (correctly), tapped into (what he saw as the great, dark, and practically Satanic power of) mass opinion. Thus, his enemies among the press ignored Meade as much as possible and emphasized Grant and Sheridan to Meade's detriment and helped cause much of his contributions to the outcome of the war to be quickly and quietly forgotten.

Although he could be critical of McClellan, that did not mean that he and "Little Mac" did not share certain points of view concerning tactical management and leadership. Like McClellan, Meade had little faith in his cavalry and they both tended to disperse their cavalry to carry out secondary goals. This policy Meade continued until Grant and Sheridan forced him to change it. McClellan and Meade both had an instinctive orientation away from offensive operations in favor of defensive operations. Finally, they shared a style of command that was consistent more with resource management than with front line leadership.

In comparison, neither Grant nor Sheridan were what could be considered gentlemen. Grant was a common man without any of the social graces which were important to Meade. Grant's bonds — unlike Meade's — were not with those guided by a similar code of behavior (certain of Grant's military and later political appointments would demonstrate that he tended therefore to be a rather poor judge of character), but with kindred spirits, whatever their behavior. Grant shared with such men an understanding compounded by shared perceptions, certain strengths of character, and personal loyalties. Meade's world operated on unspoken but accepted codes. Grant's world, on the other hand, was much more wide open. It operated from Grant's personal sense of justice and probity, which could allow him to admit that he could be, and was, wrong upon some occasions. Grant realized that war touched everyone, no matter what their social level. Meade, like most American gentlemen, viewed war solely as a "conflict between men in uniform," while Grant knew that it really was a conflict of peoples. Grant, in addition, was a lifelong failure in everything, except war and his relationship with his wife, Julia.

Sheridan, on the other hand, was in effect an economic Irish refugee (at least his parents were), with a huge chip on his shoulder — directed against the "quality" or "gentry" both North and South. What Grant and Sheridan shared was ruthlessness and a determination to get the job done, no matter what the obstacles they encountered — physical, personal, or otherwise. This ruthless drive could lead to injustices. The biggest example of this has to be the relief of Warren, the credit or the blame for which must be shared by both Grant and Sheridan. Neither man was ever able to bring himself to admit to the possibility that in this particular instance, given the actual facts of the matter (rather than what they perceived those facts to be), they might have been wrong.

An interview with Chamberlain, after Sheridan's death, took note of this[12]:

> "It was cruel the way he [Sheridan] treated Warren," was the comment made to Chamberlain.
> "Yes," Chamberlain responded.
> "I intended to ask him why he did not let up on Warren."
> "Did you ask him?"
> "No."
> "He told me he would have let up on Warren," Chamberlain revealed, "but he said, 'Warren is such an Indian that he will not meet me halfway. He wants me to go down on my knees to him — and I won't do it.'"
> "I believe it broke Warren's heart."
> "Yes, Warren died of a broken heart."

Of the other two generals that were relieved by Sheridan, Averell and Torbert, both were examples of the "gentlemanly" mindset that permeated the high command in the Eastern Theatre of Operations, especially that of the Army of the Potomac. Sheridan was too ruthless to be able to work with Averell within his limitations, so he was eventually gone. Torbert, although he was also a gentleman, though of a more Southern school since he was from Delaware, could be ruthless (as demonstrated by his execution of six guerrillas under the command of Colonel John S. Mosby at Front Royal, Virginia), but he was also a perfect example of the Peter Principle in action during the American Civil War. Torbert was a competent brigade, and even division, commander; however, he required too much supervision to be truly competent as a corps commander. Ironically, Sheridan showed much more patience with Torbert than he ever did with Averell or than he would with Warren, allowing Torbert to disappoint him three times before Sheridan quietly (and with very little fuss or muss) got rid of him.

If Averell, Torbert, and Warren were the antithesis of what Sheridan was looking for and demanding in a subordinate then a fourth general, Brig. Gen. Ranald S. Mackenzie had the right stuff and would become The Man Who Proved The Rule. Mackenzie, by his personal background, could definitely be classed with the gentlemen — since his father was a well-known naval officer and author. However, his father's disgrace (due to what became known as the "*Somers* Affair") probably had something to do with what he became, for he had the ruthlessness and the killer's instinct that Sheridan (and Grant) were always looking for; he would embody the new standard, which was being demanded, in that he was ruthless when it came to attaining victory (a quality Mackenzie demonstrated not only during the American Civil War but also during the Indian Wars on the frontier that followed it). Mackenzie also had the single ability that was most sought after by Sheridan, that of being able to use his orders as the foundation for his own initiative.

After the war he would do something that none of the other three probably would have dared even to contemplate. With just an emphatic wink and a nod from Sheridan, he ignored an international boundary (the Mexican border) while pursuing raiding Apaches or Mexican bandits. He did this not once but several times, and his actions eliminated what had been a sanctuary which allowed the Apaches and others (both Indians and non–Indians) to drag out their resistance to both the U.S. and Mexican governments. Because he was the type of subordinate commander that Sheridan favored he would join George C. Crook, Wesley Merritt, George A. Custer, and Nelson A. Miles as one of Sheridan's primary Indian fighting frontier commanders after the war.

But Mackenzie became something more than any of them. He was Sheridan's personal troubleshooter. If you look at the history of the Indian Wars and you want to find out where the biggest headaches for the army were located, just find Mackenzie. He would be there dealing with and solving the problem, whatever the problem was. It didn't matter if it was Southern Cheyennes, Southern Arapahoes, Comanches and Kiowas riding rough shod over half of Texas; Sioux, Northern Cheyennes, and Northern Arapahoes who had to be put down in the aftermath of the Battle of the Little Big Horn; Apaches running wild in Arizona, New Mexico and Texas; or an uprising of Utes in Colorado.

All three reliefs would be more or less controversial (and in the case of Warren there would eventually be a court of inquiry), with some historians declaring at least two of them (those of Averell and Warren) as being, in effect, totally unnecessary. In fact, Sheridan had ordered the relief of both Averell and Warren during fits of anger and temper, while having been granted the express authority — in both cases — to do so by Grant.

Even before the American Civil War, Sheridan's temper had been legendary in the United States Army. While he was at West Point, Sheridan was forced to repeat an entire year at the military academy following an incident which occurred on the parade ground. Sheridan had become enraged due to his mistaken perception about the way an order from a Virginia upperclassman, William Terrell, had been given to him and he actually was about to attack Terrell with his bayoneted rifle, stopping just short of impaling his fellow cadet upon it. (In short, it was the "he looked at me funny" excuse.) At the beginning of the war Terrell, although he was from Virginia, had decided to remain with the Union. He and Sheridan were to become personally reconciled just before Terrell was killed during the 1862 Battle of Perryville where Sheridan first distinguished himself while in command of an infantry division in Don Carlos Buell's Army of the Cumberland.

If an officer or a soldier failed to perform his duty, or even failed to display Sheridan's zeal for combat, the general's wrath was formidable.[13] Warren had so irritated Grant — with his attitude and behavior — since he had assumed command of the Armies of the United States, that Grant had given Sheridan the unsolicited authority to remove Warren just prior to the Battle of Five Forks. Warren's sins in this instance were that Sheridan perceived that he moved his troops into position for the battle too slowly and that he displayed a quiet calm in the face of the enemy, which Sheridan interpreted as apathy.

But it is doubtful that Sheridan cared what historians might think, although he did use his memoirs to vociferously defend his actions. However unpleasant Sheridan may have been in person he exhibited two traits that were essential to winning the war, and which placed him among the Grant-Sherman-Sheridan triumvirate of Northern heroes of the American Civil War.

First, he was one of the great battlefield commanders of the American Civil War. His American Civil War career, as a general rule, proved the adage that no battle plan survives contact with the enemy. Sheridan's genius lay in his ability to pick up the pieces in the middle of battle and to improvise his way to victory. Ironically, the only battle plan he ever adopted that did work as originally planned was the brainstorm of someone else, his old friend from West Point, George C. Crook. Crook would never forgive Sheridan for seeming to take credit for the battle plan that he had proposed, and which Sheridan used, to win the Battle of Fisher's Hill.

His greatest triumph, the Battle of Cedar Creek, began with a disaster when his Army of the Shenandoah was routed while he was returning from a strategy conference in Washington, D.C. Sheridan rode from Winchester to Cedar Creek, rallying his soldiers as he went. Once he arrived on the battlefield he took that army, which had been totally defeated and demoralized in the morning, and led it to an overwhelming victory in the late afternoon and early evening of that same day. This is an achievement matched by no other general, North or South.

Second, he was ruthless enough to drive for total victory. Sheridan had a killer's instinct to go for the jugular, which most other Union generals lacked, and he let nothing whatsoever stand in his way.

PART I

William Woods Averell

The Man Who Preferred Mountains

Brevet Major General of Volunteers William Woods Averell, who was The Man Who Preferred Mountains. He was the first of the three generals to be sacked by Sheridan in the final six months of the war (Library of Congress).

1

Averell's Background

William Woods Averell was one of the most controversial generals ever to wear Union blue in the American Civil War. Generally he was competent, yet time after time he either failed or was not as successful as he should have been.

His biggest fault may have been a simple inability to peer through the fog of war and be able to understand what was going on. He did not work well under close supervision. The reason may have been his inability to cope with confusing orders as would be best demonstrated during the Stoneman Raid, which occurred during Joseph Hooker's Chancellorsville Campaign.

In the aftermath of that debacle Averell would be sent to the mountains of West Virginia, where he found his niche. Here Averell shone as a commander, perhaps because the nature of the terrain meant that he tended to be cut off from higher authority and the oftentimes contradictory, incomplete, or inadequate orders, which happened to be the bane of most subordinate military commanders during the American Civil War. What superiors he had were unable to stay in close contact with him and create the confusion that he in particular was totally unable to deal with.

The same problem would reappear when he came under the command of Philip H. Sheridan and made a request for clarification of his status, which permanently damaged his working relationship with Sheridan. In all probability Sheridan already had some doubts due to what happened during the Chancellorsville Campaign and the Second Battle of Kernstown—which occurred shortly before Sheridan was given command of the Middle Military Division and its new Army of the Shenandoah—and which was witnessed at close hand by George C. Crook, who had been a close friend of Sheridan's ever since their time together at West Point.

A career cavalryman, Averell was dashing and likeable, and he would prove himself to be a commander of some daring who would win for the Army of the Potomac's cavalry its first sizeable action against J.E.B. Stuart's Confederate cavalry at the Battle of Kelly's Ford.

He also, however, seemed to be somewhat tentative when operating as part of a larger force. He would eventually be relieved of command twice for the same reason, once by Joseph Hooker in the aftermath of the Chancellorsville Campaign, and once by Philip H. Sheridan following the Battle of Fisher's Hill. Both Hooker and Sheridan would get rid of him for what they perceived to be his lack of aggressiveness.

Averell, who was born in Cameron, New York, on November 5, 1832, looked the part of a dashing cavalryman. Like Stuart, Lee's cavalry commander, Averell was fond of music and played the guitar. Between the Chancellorsville Campaign in the spring of 1863 and Sheridan's Shenandoah Valley Campaign in the late summer and fall of 1864, he had earned the respect and even the admiration of the soldiers he led in the mountains of West Virginia, yet he failed at times to simply live up to his promise.

After his graduation from West Point in 1855, at the age of 22 and in the lower third of his class, he was eventually assigned to the frontier, joining the Regiment of Mounted Rifles as a second lieutenant. Initially he was assigned to the cavalry school at Jefferson Barracks, St. Louis, Missouri, but was then transferred to Carlisle Barracks, Pennsylvania, where he served as adjutant to the post commander. In 1857 he was transferred to New Mexico, where he found the customs and people strange, but enjoyable. During this period the Navajos, Kiowas, and Zunis kept him busy dealing with raids, and in 1858 he suffered a severe leg wound in an Indian attack along the Rio Puerco. This forced his return to his home in Bath, New York, for an extended convalescent leave. During the later stages of the secession crisis he was finally able to return to duty, but he was still a second lieutenant at the outbreak of the war, not being promoted to first lieutenant until May 14, 1861.

His first action of the war was to be set off on a wild journey with secret dispatches intended for Union troops in Arkansas and the Indian Territory (modern day Oklahoma). Eventually he was transferred east and served as a staff officer and did provost duty in Washington, D.C. As a staff officer, he fought at the First Battle of Manassas/Bull Run and on August 23, 1861, he was appointed colonel and commander of the 3rd Pennsylvania Cavalry Regiment. He served creditably during General George B. McClellan's Peninsula Campaign commanding his regiment and later a small provisional cavalry brigade of two regiments, which served as the Army of the Potomac's rear guard when McClellan retreated from Malvern Hill to Harrison's Landing following the Seven Days' Battles.

Between July and September 1862, Averell commanded the First Brigade, Cavalry Division, Army of the Potomac, being promoted to brigadier general, United States Volunteers, on September 26, 1862. He commanded this brigade during the Antietam Campaign.

Averell was introduced to the frustrations of being a Union cavalry commander the following month while he was commanding a small cavalry brigade when Stuart raided the Chambersburg, Pennsylvania, area on October 9–10, 1862. Unfortunately, Averell was diverted by another Confederate cavalry force under John Imboden and he wired a request for orders as to which Confederate cavalry force to chase. Averell did not receive orders to chase Stuart until late on October 10. Unfortunately the pursuit was not well managed and he was led astray by rumors in Maryland and Pennsylvania that Stuart was headed west and thereupon Averell veered west, not returning to the Potomac until October 13, well after Stuart had returned to Virginia. After a 200-mile ride he never really came close to catching Stuart.

During the debacle at Fredericksburg he commanded the Cavalry Brigade, Centre Grand Division, Army of the Potomac. Averell and his men performed creditably during that campaign and then Averell's big chance occurred when Joseph Hooker took over command of the Army of the Potomac and decided that he would attempt to make something out of his cavalry. In fact Hooker would become the father of the Cavalry Corps, Army of the Potomac.

By 1863 there had been four top military commanders in the Eastern Theatre of the war. Irvin McDowell had led the first hastily raised levies to defeat at the First Battle of Manassas/Bull Run, George B. McClellan had created the Army of the Potomac and had failed at the Seven Days,' John Pope with the Army of Virginia (along with some troops from the Army of the Potomac) had been humbled at the Second Battle of Manassas/Bull Run, McClellan (although he had never been officially removed from command of the Army of the Potomac) had been brought back to reorganize the army and then to oppose Lee's first invasion of the North during the Maryland Campaign (where he fought Lee to a bloody draw at the Battle of Antietam/Sharpsburg and then allowed him to escape), and then it was Burnside's turn, who accomplished absolutely nothing with the immensely bloody debacle of Fredericksburg and his almost comical "Mud March."

Now it was the turn of Joseph Hooker.

Hooker was chosen by Lincoln to head the Army of the Potomac primarily because of his demonstrated talents as a corps commander and despite the fact that he had advocated the appointment of a military dictator to take over the reins of government in this emergency. Lincoln also chose to disregard Hooker's penchant for self-aggrandizement and the shameless way in which he had sought Burnside's removal and his own promotion. Lincoln's choice was also questioned because Hooker was given to swaggering, boasting, erratic behavior, self-delusion, excessive ambition, and (as the Chancellorsville Campaign would reveal) wavering in a crisis.

In point of fact, Hooker soon proved himself to be a remarkably able choice, although many officers within the Army of the Potomac thought that his headquarters was a den of iniquity. (Hooker lent his name to both a straight shot of whisky and to the euphemism by which prostitutes are still known today.) However, he still managed to restore the morale of the Army of the Potomac, which as a result of Fredericksburg and Burnside's Mud March had sunk to its lowest level of the entire war.

In effect Hooker first reestablished, and then left to his successors, the veteran army that Meade would use first to win the Battle of Gettysburg and then Grant, Meade, and Sheridan would use to bring the war itself to a successful conclusion in the Eastern Theatre of Operations. Finally, Hooker would give the cavalry of the Army of the Potomac the final push it needed to become the extremely effective force it was to be in the hands of Philip H. Sheridan by the end of the war.

Before Hooker took the cavalry in hand it could not compare with its Confederate opponents. The contempt felt by the Confederate cavalry for their Union counterparts was well deserved, and the bungling way in which it was handled by practically all Union commanders, up until the advent of Hooker and even afterwards in some cases, truly defies belief.

In addition, at the beginning of the conflict Union cavalrymen were mounted on substandard horses supplied by corrupt contractors. In contrast Confederate cavalry at the beginning of the war was usually mounted upon the very best blooded stock available, which was provided by the rank and file themselves, who under the Confederate system or non-system provided their own mounts. Edwin M. Stanton, when he eventually took over the War Department from Simon Cameron (who Lincoln pointed out would not stoop to stealing a red hot stove), eliminated many, but not all, of the corrupt contractors by the time the Union troopers had managed to learn how to ride their horses.

In addition, the Confederate cavalry was just entering its period of decline, due primarily to the fact that it had no practical remount system. By the spring of 1863 there was an acute shortage of horses in the Army of Northern Virginia. Even worse was the shortage of fodder to feed what horses were available. At the same time the volunteer Union cavalry trooper had by a process of evolution changed from a civilian who often lacked the most elementary riding and fighting skills to an efficient trooper adept at both dismounted and mounted combat.[1] The first year and a half of the war for both Union cavalry officers and their men had been primarily a very painful learning experience. They had to discover pretty much for themselves both what needed to be done and just how to do it.

At that time, it was a given that it took about a year and a half to two years to properly train a raw cavalry recruit (much longer than it did to train an infantry recruit) and transform him into an effective cavalryman. Since most Northern farm boys know what a chore it was to take care of a horse, most of them served in the infantry. Ironically, most Northern cavalry was recruited from among city boys, who had no idea at all about what they were getting into.

The big advantage of the Southern cavalry was that they did not have to be taught how to ride a horse before they could do anything else. Most of the Southern cavalry was recruited from among the South's agrarian gentry. They were men who generally learned to ride almost before they had learned to walk. In addition, their leaders were among the best cavalry commanders of the entire war. Men like J.E.B. Stuart, Wade Hampton, Matthew C. Butler, Thomas L. Rosser, and Thomas Munford, in the Eastern Theatre of Operations.

As they developed their skills the Northern cavalry also began to bring definition to their purpose and their eventual mission. At Hooker's direction the cavalry of the Army of the Potomac was for the first time concentrated into a corps organization consisting of its own divisions and brigades. Before this, part of the cavalry might be concentrated in a sort of reserve division while the rest of it — usually in regiment or sometimes brigade strength — was scattered among the various infantry divisions and corps in order to perform only limited reconnaissance and screening duties.

In their new organization, being massed in brigades and divisions (and supported by light horse artillery) they would become (by the end of the war) extremely effective against both mounted and dismounted opponents.[2]

The war basically demanded that the Union cavalry learn how to deal with a foe similar to themselves, in difficult terrain, and whose troopers were initially better at riding and fighting. Confederate cavalry tactics ranged from J.E.B. Stuart's primarily traditional actions, to the unconventional tactics of the untaught and native military genius of Nathan Bedford Forrest, to the hit and run guerrilla and partisan ranger tactics of John S. Mosby and others.

The Union cavalry's response was to combine traditional European cavalry tactics with American dismounted tactics developed upon the frontier, to in effect become a true "dragoon" who was specifically suited to combat his Confederate opposite number.[3] Dragoons have been around about as long as there has been cavalry, and a dragoon is a soldier who is equally adept at both mounted and dismounted fighting. Therefore, the mounted charge still remained a tactic that was definitely used in conjunction with dismounted combat.

In effect, what the Union had developed was a super-dragoon, whose firepower (particularly with breech-loading and repeating carbines) gave him some of the striking power of massed infantry on the ground while remaining a real cavalryman on horseback. In addition, the story of the Union cavalry also suggests that the Union went about creating its cavalry force backwards.

Rationally, what should have been done was to decide what the mission of the cavalry actually was going to be, then to answer the basic tactical questions before going ahead and raising a large mounted force. Instead, immediately upon the advent of the war, "cavalry" regiments were raised, equipped with whatever was immediately at hand, then inconsistently trained. There was no real defined mission, and the tactical questions were left completely unanswered.

After Hooker created the Cavalry Corps, the next question was who was to command it. First-rate cavalry commanders were in short supply. Hooker's choice was George Stoneman (who was placed in command of the Cavalry Corps on February 12, 1863), and on the same day Averell was named to command the Second Division, Cavalry Corps, under Stoneman. The problem with the new Cavalry Corps commander (and effective chief of cavalry) was that, while Stoneman was a veteran cavalry officer, he lacked the dash, determination and zest for battle that characterized what was expected of a cavalry commander. In addition, Stomenan was overly prudent and conservative, slow moving and cautious, and was prone to overestimate obstacles. Stoneman, however, was at least conscientious and did his best, although his best had a tendency of falling short of what was required. Stoneman and Hooker were both believers in the tactic of the cavalry raid. However, Stoneman's cavalry raids never seemed to achieve any of the hoped for results. Stoneman was a native New Yorker and had graduated from West Point in 1846. Before the war he had first been posted to the dragoons and then to the cavalry. At the beginning of the war Stoneman was a captain in the 1st U.S. Cavalry Regiment, a rank he had held since 1855. (Before the American Civil War the U.S. Army had five cavalry regiments, which included: the 1st U.S. Dragoons Regiment, the 2nd U.S. Dragoons Regiment, the Regiment of Mounted Rifles, the 1st U.S. Cavalry Regiment, and the 2nd U.S. Cavalry Regiment. The 3rd U.S. Cavalry Regiment was raised immediately upon the start of the war. On August 3, 1861, these regiments were redesignated as the 1st U.S. Cavalry Regiment (1st Dragoons), 2nd U.S. Cavalry Regiment (2nd Dragoons), 3rd U.S. Cavalry Regiment (Mounted Rifles), 4th U.S. Cavalry Regiment (1st Cavalry), 5th U.S. Cavalry Regiment (2nd Cavalry), and 6th U.S. Cavalry Regiment (3rd Cavalry.)

Stoneman had led a mixed cavalry-infantry force during McClellan's Peninsula Campaign and the Seven Days.' During the rest of the summer he commanded the Army of the Potomac's Cavalry Division (being promoted to the rank of brigadier general, U.S. Volunteers) and then, for the Maryland Campaign, commanded the First Division, III Corps, which had been left behind to garrison Washington, D.C. He commanded III Corps between October 30, 1862, and February 5, 1863 (during the Battle of Fredericksburg), being advanced to the rank of major general, U.S. Volunteers. Hooker tapped Stoneman to command the newly formed Cavalry Corps probably because he already had experience as a corps commander and he had been a cavalry officer since the beginning of his military career, so the assumption was that he knew something about cavalry. But, all in all, despite Stoneman's possible shortcomings as a cavalry commander, since the cavalry was finally unified there was at least a chance for it to be able, and to be allowed, to do its real job, oppose the Confederate cavalry of J.E.B. Stuart.

2

The Battle of Kelly's Ford

Concentrating the cavalry, and naming a commander for the new corps, did not solve all of the problems. Stoneman — and his division commanders, Averell, David M. Gregg, and Alfred Pleasonton (each division consisting of two brigades) — soon found that the cavalry's main job, screening the Army of the Potomac, was practically impossible, due primarily to the terrain that was currently occupied by the Army of the Potomac.

In order to screen the Army of the Potomac the Cavalry Corps was forced to maintain and patrol a line of outposts that was at least 100 miles long. This line of outposts ran through broken country, dense woods, and was crisscrossed by winding lanes (they could hardly be called roads and were more like pathways) most of which were so obscure that only a native of the area had any idea of where they were or of how to find them. The problem was that these people had strong Southern sympathies and considered the Union troops to be invading barbarians, thus the people provided an informal, highly successful and effective intelligence network (consisting of men, women and children) for Robert E. Lee's Army of Northern Virginia. They provided whatever information they had to Stuart's cavalry scouts, who constantly roamed the area between the two armies; and even, upon occasion (in point of fact, rather frequent occasion), penetrated the Union army's lines.

One form of entertainment for the Confederate cavalry consisted of having small groups of troopers slip unnoticed across the Rappahannock River and then gather at some remote farm, forming larger raiding parties; these raiding parties would then be guided by local residents to the Army of the Potomac's vidette (for cavalry) and picket (for infantry) outposts. The Southern raiders, once in position, would descend upon these tiny outposts, smash them, take prisoners, and then get clean away before Stoneman's headquarters knew anything was going on. Pursuit of the raiders was generally an exercise in futility.

As a result, the men and horses of Stoneman's Cavalry Corps were being worn out by simply doing outpost duty, which, due to circumstances beyond their (or anyone else's) control, simply could not be done effectively in the first place. In addition, those infantrymen and cavalrymen manning the outposts were so jittery (for good reason) that their reports were almost totally unreliable.

In addition, Stuart and his cavalry conducted several large-scale raids. One of the largest occurred on Christmas Eve 1862, before Hooker took over the Army of the Potomac and reorganized the cavalry. The purpose of the raid was to gather intelligence, but Stuart, who had a healthy sense of humor, had some fun too. He captured a telegraph station about 15 miles from Washington, D.C., manned it with his own telegrapher and sent a wire to the Union quartermaster general, Montgomery C. Meigs, to complain about the quality of mules Meigs was sending to the Union army to be captured by Stuart's cavalry.

The other major Confederate cavalry raid occurred when Fitzhugh Lee — a nephew of Robert E. Lee, one of Averell's West Point classmates and one of Stuart's brigade commanders, took over Culpepper Court House on the Union side of the Rappahannock River and held the upper part of the river for most of the winter of 1862-1863.

Lee and his Army of Northern Virginia had its own troubles, however. Lee had to play a waiting game, since it was becoming harder, but not impossible, for him to get good information about what the Army of the Potomac was up to. Ever since Hooker had consolidated his

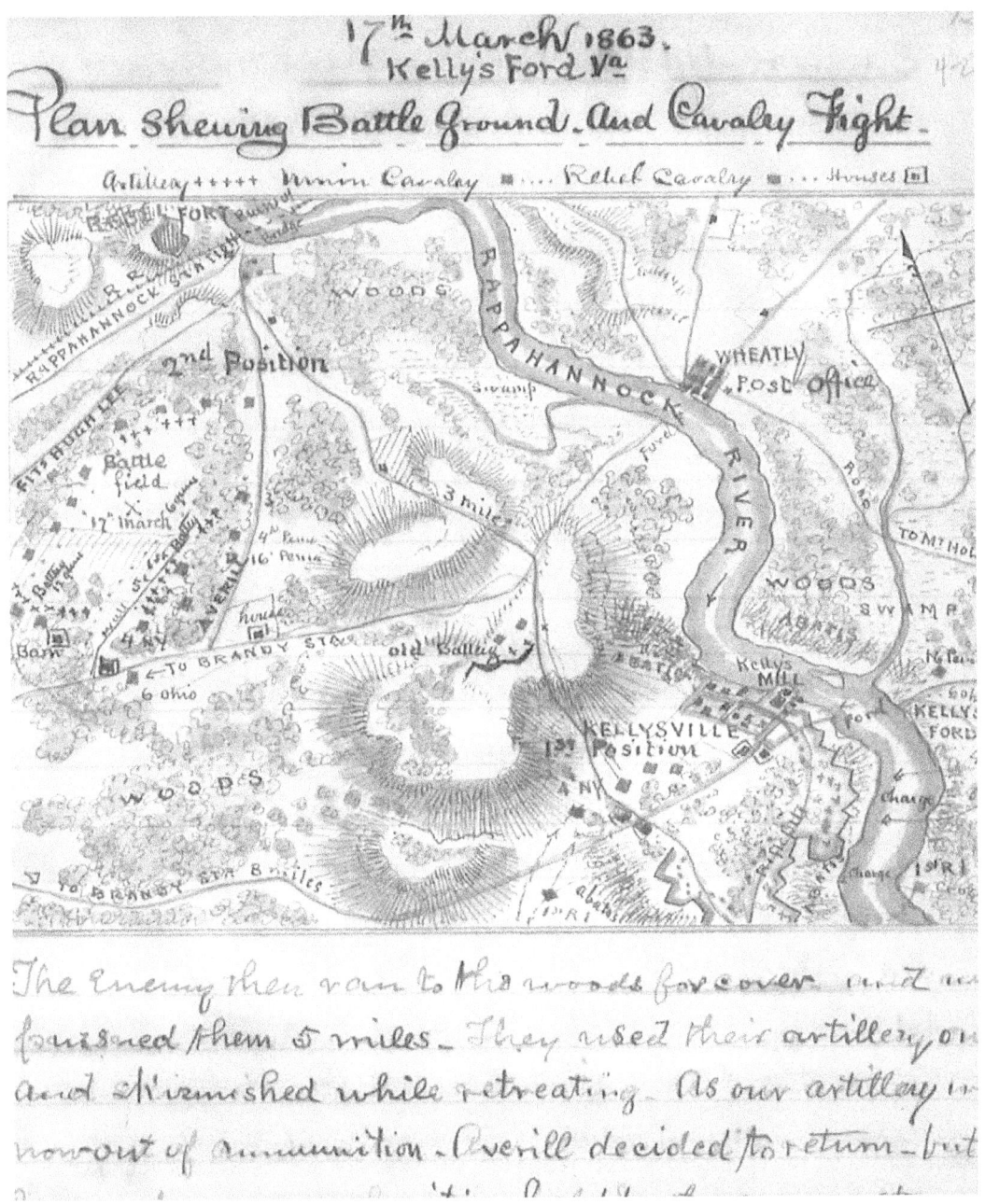

The Battle of Kelly's Ford, fought on March 17, 1863, marked the day when the cavalry of the Army of the Potomac reached parity with the cavalry of the Army of Northern Virginia. Union Brig. Gen. Williams Woods Averell faced off against Confederate Brig. Gen. Fitzhugh Lee (Library of Congress).

cavalry into an autonomous corps Stuart was finding it more difficult to roam at will behind Union lines.

There were no more rides around the Army of the Potomac (which Stuart had done twice during McClellan's tenure), although Stuart would make one more attempt at this tactic later that summer during the Gettysburg Campaign, which would end in abject failure, with Stuart remaining out of contact with Lee during one of the most important weeks of the war. Stuart would not rejoin Lee until the Battle of Gettysburg had actually been under way for almost two full days, during which Lee had been left practically blind and deaf as far as reliable intelligence about the Army of the Potomac was concerned.

Averell eventually realized that there was only one way to keep J.E.B. Stuart and his Confederate cavalry out of the Army of the Potomac's lines. That was to attack Stuart on his own home ground and keep him so busy trying to defend himself that he wouldn't have time for excursions into the Union lines. Philip H. Sheridan, when he eventually inherited Stoneman's job about a year later, instantly realized this fact, which led to his Richmond Raid (during the Battle of Spotsylvania) and the death of Stuart in the Battle of Yellow Tavern.

Averell also had a personal motive, a little more or less friendly rivalry with his one time West Point classmate and friend, Fitzhugh Lee. While raiding Union outposts, Fitzhugh Lee would from time to time taunt Averell personally by sending him messages asking when his cavalry was ever going to amount to anything. Then on February 25, 1863, just 13 days after Averell assumed command of his division, he was embarrassed when Fitzhugh Lee and a small force of Confederate cavalry captured about 150 of his men during one of his smaller raids. Finally Fitzhugh Lee invited Averell to come across the Rappahannock River and pay him a little visit, asking Averell to be sure to bring along some coffee. That was the last straw.

Averell went to Hooker and asked if he could take his cavalry division across the Rappahannock River and go looking for a fight. Since this happened to fit in with Hooker's own ideas, Hooker had no objections. On March 17, 1863 (St. Patrick's Day), Averell led his division (about 3,000 cavalrymen) across the Rappahannock River at Kelly's Ford. The official objective was that Averell would move on to Culpepper Court House and raid and destroy what he could of the Orange & Alexandria Railroad. The unofficial, and more important, objective (at least to Averell) was finding and whipping Fitzhugh Lee.

From the beginning of the raid Averell was cautious. What passed for Union military intelligence — something that Hooker would also go far to correct when he established an official intelligence unit for the Army of the Potomac called the Office of Military Information — credited Fitzhugh Lee with having several times the number of effective troopers than he actually did have. Fitzhugh Lee had only about 800 effectives currently on hand probably due to the shortage of horses the Army of Northern Virginia suffered from and the difficulty in locating and procuring remounts. In fact, Stuart (who at this time officially commanded four brigades of cavalry) had only Fitzhugh Lee's brigade and the brigade of W.H.F. "Rooney" Lee, a son of Robert E. Lee, immediately at hand. His other two brigades had been wintering away from the Army of Northern Virginia where scarce fodder for their horses could be more easily obtained. Together the two brigades Stuart retained with the Army of Northern Virginia had about 3,000 men, but less than half of them were still mounted.

As spring was about to arrive Brig. Gen. W.E. "Grumble" Jones and his brigade of Stuart's cavalry, along with the Shenandoah Valley cavalry brigade of Brig. Gen. John Imboden, were at this particular time planning and preparing to launch a major raid from the Shenandoah Valley into West Virginia, seeking livestock. (This raid would become very important to Averell's future following the Chancellorsville Campaign.) Stuart's fourth brigade, under Wade Hampton, was located much farther to the south with two infantry divisions from James Longstreet's I Corps.

The Confederate government in Richmond, recognizing the emergency, sent out a call for horses from Texas and the Deep South. In addition, more cavalry units were ordered to report to Stuart, but these actions did not begin to take effect until after the Chancellorsville Campaign had ended at the beginning of May. By the time of the Gettysburg Campaign that summer Stuart's Cavalry Division, Army of Northern Virginia, would be increased to six brigades with a seventh (that of Imoden) also being available but not officially part of Stuart's Cavalry Division.

Eventually, after the Gettysburg Campaign, Stuart's cavalry would be reorganized into a corps consisting of two divisions (each consisting of three brigades), one under the command of Fitzhugh Lee and the other under the command of Wade Hampton. After Stuart's death, Hampton would eventually assume command of the corps. (During the last months of the war Hampton, recovering from a wound in his native South Carolina, would find himself being the chief opposition to Sherman's march through the Carolinas, and command of Lee's cavalry would more or less descend upon Fitzhugh Lee — after he recovered from the wound he received at the Third Battle of Winchester — as the senior division commander.)

All went well for Averell until, above Warrenton, Maj. John S. Mosby (commander of the 43rd Virginia Battalion of Partisan Rangers) and about 29 of his men began harassing Averell's column so badly that Averell detached 900 men to ride flank and rear guard on his column. Making Averell split his column may not have been Mosby's intention. He had already captured one Union general out of his own headquarters and he may have been seeking at this time to force the complete breakdown of Averell's division by offering himself as the target for a wild goose chase. Mosby was not known as the Gray Ghost for nothing.

Averell, no wild bull of the woods he, did not take the bait. Continuing his raid, Averell without much effort brushed aside Confederate pickets and went looking for his West Point classmate, after watering and feeding his horses. He found him and his brigade, but Fitzhugh Lee struck first, sending two pitifully weak regiments to attack and scatter Averell's advance guard, which they did. Then Averell led his main body through the scattered advanced guard, forcing the Confederate cavalry back for a mile or so before Fitzhugh Lee reached his horse artillery where he made his stand and, with that artillery support, counterattacked. Given his superiority of numbers (since quantity has a quality all of its own), with little effort Averell's men drove off the counterattack.

It was now that one of Averell's basic weaknesses, his lack of a killer's instinct, showed itself. Averell could have, if he had renewed his assault, completely routed the lone Confederate cavalry brigade facing him and then he could have moved on and destroyed their camp before moving on to his final objective, the railroad. What happened next may have been influenced in part by the staunch resistance of Fitzhugh Lee's cavalry brigade; after all, the Confederate cavalry was still near the top of its reputation if not its fighting form. As Averell was preparing to renew his assault, just at the wrong time, he suffered an attack of caution. Confederate prisoners (not a particularly reliable source for raw information) told Averell that Stuart and reinforcements had arrived. They were half right. Stuart (who had been nearby for the purpose of sitting on a court-martial board) personally was on the field, however, except for his staff he was alone. Stuart had not brought any reinforcements with him. (Stuart had, however, been accompanied onto the field by Maj. John Pelham, a particularly daring and well-known horse artillery commander, who had absolutely no business whatsoever being in the middle of a cavalry melee without his horse artillery battalion. But Pelham — who was nearby wooing a young lady — also was one of those irrepressible Southern cavaliers, and he was mortally wounded at Kelly's Ford and died at the home of the girl he had been courting. All in all, it caused at least one veteran trooper to say, "Yankee cavalry taking the initiative, John Pelham dead! The war in Virginia is beginning to grow old.") In addition, Averell was further informed that Confederate infantry was on the way. This also was untrue.

Instead of renewing his own assault, Averell decided that the bird in the hand was better than the two in the bush and that it might be the better part of valor to rest upon his laurels. He had after all successfully carried the fighting to Stuart's own back yard. Averell, therefore, pulled back across the Rappahannock River. But before recrossing the river Averell left something behind for his friend, Fitzhugh Lee: a bag of coffee and a note that read, "Dear Fitz: Here's your coffee. Here's your visit. How do you like it? (Signed) William W. Averell."

Averell's men were proud of themselves and Averell himself was thoroughly satisfied with his day's work. However, Hooker was not! When he considered what Averell could have accomplished during his foray across the Rappahannock River, Hooker became considerably disgruntled. He had expected something more out of Averell when he had requested permission to go across the Rappahannock. He, Hooker, had wanted something more out of this raid than to simply raise the morale of his own cavalry. Hooker's response was an angry letter to Averell. In this letter he wrote sharply that Averell had had a sweeping victory in the palm of his hand and that he had thrown it away due to nothing more threatening than "imaginary apprehensions!"

To a certain extent Hooker was right. Averell had penetrated less than two miles into Fitzhugh Lee's territory. However, aside from the death of Pelham, the Confederate cavalry had suffered considerable other casualties, dead and wounded, with a third of them having been taken prisoner. In addition, 150 almost irreplaceable Confederate cavalry horses had been killed or wounded. This was a particularly heavy blow to a cavalry command that was already nearly dismounted.

Stuart himself realized that the times were changing. Averell's Union cavalry had not only stood and fought, they had demonstrated that they knew how to ride, too. Although Stuart did not come out and say that the Union cavalry was becoming more and more professional as time went on, he certainly implied it in his report to General Lee, after the fight at Kelly's Ford.

Despite its lack of real results, the Battle of Kelly's Ford was always considered by the Union cavalrymen who fought there to be their first solid combat success against the Confederate cavalry; and with this success upon the battlefield under their belts, Averell's Northern cavalrymen were beginning to feel that they could face Stuart's Southern cavalry on a more or less even basis.

The mere fact that Union cavalry had entered territory controlled by Confederate cavalry — and had performed quite well once they got there — was recognized by themselves, by their fellow infantry and artillery soldiers of the Army of the Potomac, and even by the army's leadership, who were all forced to stopped asking (at least for the time being), "Whoever saw a dead cavalryman?"

3

The Chancellorsville Campaign

Joseph Hooker was full of confidence.

Hooker felt that he knew how to go after Robert E. Lee and his Army of Northern Virginia without doing the same old "hey diddle diddle and straight up the middle" into the face of strong Confederate defenses that had been part of the defeat at the Second Battle of Manassas/Bull Run, and that had led to the debacle at Fredericksville and the equally immense casualties suffered at Antietam/Sharpsburg, although that battle had been counted as a draw.

In addition, Hooker had an asset that his predecessors had lacked (and that he was prepared to take to the bank)—a unified Cavalry Corps whose morale was rising, thanks to William W. Averell's foray across the Rappahannock River at Kelly's Ford, although that had been ultimately disappointing, due primarily to a little too much caution on Averell's part.

By the spring of 1863 Hooker's cavalry had learned how to ride, had learned how to fight, and was now largely supplied with superior weaponry (breech-loading carbines), which had improved his cavalry's firepower over that of the Confederate cavalry (which was primarily equipped with muzzle loading shoulder arms) by a factor of at least four to one. (A trained and experienced soldier during the American Civil War armed with a muzzle-loading rifle musket or carbine could fire, at the most, three aimed shots per minute. The same soldier, equipped with a breech-loading rifle or carbine, could fire at least 12 aimed shots per minute.)

Basically, what Hooker intended to do was to pry Lee's army out of its fortified lines and make it fight out in the open. (This too would be one of Grant's objectives in the 1864 Overland Campaign, which was not fully successful, and the 1865 Appomattox Campaign, which was.) And, at least at first, he intended to use Stoneman and Averell, and their cavalry, as his pry-bar. His original plan was a model of maneuver. The problem was that Lee, although outnumbered at this time by the Army of the Potomac, by a factor of at least two to one (55,000 to 130,000), occupied a line of fieldworks that was all but impregnable. Hooker had to cross the Rappahannock River, which was at flood stage due to the spring thaw and rains. However, upstream, above Fredericksburg, there were the shallow Bank's Ford and United States Ford, further west.

Hooker figured that if he could reach those fords undetected he might be able to overwhelm what Confederate troops were guarding them, cross the river, and force Lee to turn and face him without the advantage of his fieldworks and with the disadvantage of maneuvering against an opponent twice his strength. In addition, Hooker intended to move against Lee's communications by sending most of Stoneman's Cavalry Corps into his rear.

Stoneman was to take his cavalry far up the Rappahannock River, cross it, swing south until he reached the Virginia Central Railroad, then turn east and head for Hanover Station, which was thought to be Lee's principal supply depot. If this were to be accomplished, Hooker believed, it would force Lee to withdraw from his fieldworks. This would be the signal for Hooker to cross the Rappahannock River with his army, and with Stoneman and his cavalry in front of him Lee would be unable to move with any speed and there would be a big battle.

One of the reasons that Hooker outnumbered Lee so badly was that James Longstreet and two divisions of his corps (along with Wade Hampton's brigade of J.E.B. Stuart's cavalry division) had been detached from the Army of Northern Virginia to guard against Union raiders in the Suffolk area, below Richmond. What Hooker intended to do during his big battle was to push Lee's army into the defenses of Richmond, where he would be besieged and eventually forced to surrender. (Once again this was the same general objective that Grant would achieve with his Overland Campaign.) On paper it was an excellent plan, and except for Stoneman, it might very well have succeeded.

Hooker put his plan into motion on April 13, 1863. Stoneman's cavalry was to cross the river, according to the orders issued by Hooker, "for the purpose of turning the enemy's position on his left, throwing the cavalry between him and Richmond, isolating him from his supplies, checking his retreat, and inflicting every possible injury, which will tend to his discomfort and retreat." These particular orders further said, "If you [Stoneman] cannot cut off [the enemy's] column in large slices, the general desires that you not fail to take small ones. Let your watchword be fight, fight, fight, bearing in mind that time is as valuable to the general as rebel carcasses." It turned out, however, that Stoneman's watchword was wait, wait, wait.

One brigade of Stoneman's cavalry, consisting entirely of regulars under Brig. Gen. John Buford, managed to get across the river immediately to give Stoneman the capability of moving against the vital crossing points from both sides of the river simultaneously. When this brigade crossed the river Confederate pickets immediately raised the alarm, and when the main body of Stoneman's cavalry arrived at the chosen crossing points of Beverly Ford and Rappahannock Bridge, Stoneman found both places were strongly held on the Confederate side of the river. And Stoneman paused.

This is something that Sheridan probably would not have done.[1] One major historian was adamant in declaring that Stoneman could have easily forced his way across, particularly since Buford's Reserve Brigade, which was already across the river, could have taken the defenders on the flank.[2] But Stoneman decided to wait until everything was ready before making the attempt.

And then it started to rain, and rain, and rain, and rain.

Soon the river, in Stoneman's estimation, had become impossible to cross due to the rising water, although Buford's brigade that had already gotten across the river was withdrawn to Stoneman's side of the river without difficulty.

Fighting Joe Hooker (who earned his nom de guerre due to a misunderstood newspaper heading), when he found out what was going on, was definitely not happy. Although outraged, Hooker told Stoneman to wait where he was until the rain stopped. When it did not stop, Hooker actually came up with a better plan.

The genesis of the new plan occurred when Averell was able to report that Kelly's Ford (where just over a month previously he had met and held his own against the Confederate cavalry of Fitzhugh Lee), 15 miles above the junction of the Rappahannock and Rapidan rivers and about a mile above United States Ford, was both unfortified and comparatively shallow. Once the water levels of the Rappahannock River finally fell it could be forded by men on foot and by horses drawing wagons and artillery. Kelly's Ford was also far enough from Lee's left to cause Hooker to hope that half of his army could reach it undetected. At the same time, the other half would mass at Bank's Ford and United States Ford in order to give Lee the impression that it was Hooker's main body that was about to make a major assault there.

After crossing at Kelly's Ford, Hooker's flanking force—by making a second crossing, this time of the Rapidan River—could move into the heavily wooded area, known as the Wilderness (and the site of the first major battle of Grant's Overland Campaign the next year), and then move under cover of the trees into Lee's rear. As this force advanced, Hooker intended for it to uncover both Bank's Ford and United States Ford, shortening his communications and placing the two halves of his Army of the Potomac within supporting range of each other, should there be any emergencies. In addition, the high ground at Bank's Ford also dominated Lee's position behind Fredericksburg. If Hooker's new plan succeeded, Lee would be forced to come out and fight upon open ground against a vastly superior Union force. The plan was nothing if not daring.

Hooker figured that he had enough of an advantage in numbers that he could safely divide his Army of the Potomac in the face of Lee's Army of Northern Virginia. Each half of Hooker's army would still outnumber the entire force that Lee had available, due to the earlier detachment of Longstreet and his two infantry divisions along with Jones' and Hampton's brigades of cavalry. Hooker began his new offensive 13 days after Stoneman disappointed him.

On April 26, 1863, V Corps, XI Corps and XII Corps, with General John Slocum of XII Corps in overall command, were ordered to march to Kelly's Ford the following day and to be ready to cross the Rappahannock River by 4:00 P.M. on April 28. Slocum's troops were then to move south to the Rapidan River and cross it at Ely's Ford and Germanna Ford, pass through the Wilderness, and decend into the open ground at Chancellorsville, 10 miles west of Lee's left flank.

Meanwhile, II Corps—minus John Gibbon's division, which was in plain view of the Confederates on Marye's Heights at Fredericksburg and thus dared not to make a move because of possibly alerting the Confederates that something was going on—was to move out at dawn on April 29, 1863, to a position behind Bank's Ford, ready to move across a pontoon bridge once Slocum's force had flushed Lee out of his positions. Opposite Lee were I Corps, III Corps, and VI Corps, all under the command of General John Sedgwick (VI Corps); they were to move down the riverbank opposite Fredericksburg, where Union forces had crossed the river in December 1862 for the Battle of Fredericksburg. Once his three infantry corps (and their supporting artillery) arrived, Sedgwick was to establish a bridgehead on the west bank in full view of Lee's army. This was intended to distract Lee from worrying about his vulnerable rear and confuse him about where Hooker would actually be attacking.

Stoneman, with all but one brigade of his Cavalry Corps, was supposed to increase Lee's confusion by conducting a raid aimed at the Virginia Central Railroad and following the Richmond, Fredericksburg & Potomac Railroad east to place his cavalry between Lee's army and Richmond should Lee seek to evade the jaws of Hooker's planned pincers movement by retreating on the Confederate capital.

The major apparent defect of this plan was that, by detaching Stoneman with all but one brigade of his cavalry to strike at Lee's communications, Hooker was going to leave himself practically blind to Lee's movements since he was retaining only one brigade of cavalry (under the direction of Alfred Pleasonton whose other brigade would be accompanying Stoneman) and thus would lose the intelligence gathering capabilities provided by the cavalry. (However, the Confederates were at least similarly handicapped by the fact that Stuart still had only two grossly undersized cavalry brigades available. However, Stuart would successfully accomplish his mission of providing Lee with the intelligence he needed to make the necessary decisions in what would become Lee's ultimate battlefield masterpiece.)

Hooker's plan both looked good on paper and appeared to work well in reality. Slocum moved out and was joined by Hooker at Chancellorsville on April 30, 1863. At this point Hooker's attention to detail, strict secrecy, and marching discipline, and Sedgwick's demonstration opposite Lee's army at Fredericksburg had all combined in what was the successful completion of one of the finest maneuvers ever to be conducted during the entire American Civil War.

Instead of putting 10,000 cavalry in Lee's rear (which had been his intention under his original plan), Hooker had successfully placed 70,000 infantry, with artillery support, there. Where

Hooker had originally intended to force Lee to pull back into the defenses of Richmond, he now intended to destroy Lee's army outright and if successful possibly end the war with a single blow. But, once he had gotten into this position, Hooker paused, thus giving Lee the opportunity to do unto Hooker what Hooker had intended to do unto him, and to do it first.

Stoneman at least began well enough in his second start (although he again allowed too many delays), apparently fully intending to follow his orders. If he had done so—and had properly disrupted the tracks and bridges of the Virginia Central Railroad and the Richmond, Fredericksburg & Potomac Railroad—Lee's supply situation would soon have become impossible. However, Stoneman did not do that. He had a different idea instead.

Hooker's final communiqué instructed Stoneman to cross the river by 8:00 A.M. April 29, if not sooner. Although the order had been anticipated for days and Stoneman should have been ready for it, he was demonstrating once again the fatal flaw of the Army of the Potomac. He failed to position his command at the crossing until late on the morning of April 29. Only after a lengthy reconnaissance did Averell cross at or near Kelly's Ford at about 3:00 P.M., at least seven hours later than Stoneman's orders had dictated. The last of Stoneman's cavalry did not cross until nearly two more hours had passed.

Once across the river, Stoneman stopped, laid out his maps, and called in his brigade and division commanders to tell them what they were to do and where they were to go. This was something that should have been done long before he ever crossed the river. Stoneman had decided to send Averell with about half of his cavalry to keep the Confederate cavalry at a safe distance, but he failed to detail the full extent of what he wanted Averell to do. Thus he allowed one of Averell's major weaknesses, his inability to peer through the fog of war (usually, like now, created by his own superiors), to immediately come to the forefront.

Averell understood that he was to reach the Orange & Alexandria Railroad depot at Brandy Station, six miles above Culpepper Court House, by nightfall. There he was to communicate with Stoneman via nearby Stevensburg. Unless Stoneman modified his orders he was to proceed to Culpepper Court House and drive W.H.F. (Rooney) Lee's Confederate cavalry brigade as far as Rapidan Station.

Beyond this, Averell had no idea what Stoneman intended him to do. Hooker, who knew of Stoneman's intention to divide the cavalry, had intended that the cavalry be reunited at some point along the Pamunkey River, where they might oppose the expected retreat of Lee's Army of Northern Virginia. It is not known whether or not Stoneman informed Averell of Hooker's intentions, but, from his actions, as far as Averell apparently knew he was supposed to operate independently indefinitely.

Then within half an hour of leaving Stoneman, Averell encountered one of Rooney Lee's regiments, which delayed and harassed Averell's entire division as it advanced, for the next five hours. Then Averell received false information that Stuart and four brigades of cavalry were waiting at Brandy Station; then later reports had Stuart moving to Stevensburg, which caused Averell to bypass that area and was probably a factor in his not rejoining Stoneman.

Averell departed from Brandy Station the following morning, reaching Culpepper Court House about noon. After dispersing some of Rooney Lee's cavalry, Averell remained in Culpepper Court House for several hours destroying Confederate foodstuffs and rooting through captured mail sacks. A dispatch found in a mail sack indicated that Stonewall Jackson and his corps had assembled at Gordonsville, 25 miles to the south. Averell did not move until a dispatch from Stoneman arrived at 6:30 P.M. directing him to drive Rooney Lee's command toward Rapidan Station. Averell pushed south past Cedar Mountain and at 8:00 P.M. ran into two of Rooney Lee's regiments opposite the depot. Averell pulled back and in the morning found the entire Confederate force dug in around the south bank of the Rapidan River. Averell than consumed the better part of a day deciding what to do. After burning a bridge to strand Averell and his division on the north bank of the river, the Confederate force slipped away to chase Stoneman, who was reported to be creating havoc near Richmond. Averell stayed above the Rapidan for another 24 hours, wrecking bridges and telegraph lines near Rapidan Station. In response to a general recall order from Hooker on May 2, Averell left the area.

Stoneman took the rest of the cavalry and proceeded to ride down the line of the Virginia Central Railroad. He explained his intentions to his subordinate officers as follows: "We have been dropped in this region of the country, like a shell, and I intend to burst it in every direction, expecting each piece or fragment will do as much harm and will create nearly as much terror as would result from sending the whole shell, and thus magnify our small force into overwhelming numbers." The problem was that this was not what Hooker had ordered.

There was then nothing, at this particular part in the campaign, which would have prevented Stoneman from marching his cavalry into Lee's immediate rear. As a matter of fact, just about all of Lee's supply wagons were then at Guiney's Station, 18 miles south of Chancellorsville, in the care of a relatively small guard force. Stoneman could have taken his entire cavalry there and destroyed everything, including all of the accumulated supplies for Lee's army. If Stoneman had done this, he might very well have forced Lee and his army to make the kind of desperate retreat that Hooker wanted.

Instead, Stoneman broke his command up into smaller raiding parties (as part of the "bursting shell" analogy). This tactic did cause a great deal of alarm in Richmond (and prevented Longstreet from rejoining Lee with his two infantry divisions and Hampton's cavalry brigade), but not in Lee's headquarters.

Lee was informed that Sedgwick and his half of Hooker's army were massing at Franklin's Crossing and were establishing their bridgehead on both. Lee in response ordered Jackson to move up his corps and notified the Confederate War Department in Richmond to inform Longstreet to be prepared to move his two infantry divisions and Hampton's cavalry brigade north to rejoin the Army of Northern Virginia.

Then Stuart's cavalry reported Slocum's crossing of the river at Kelly's Ford and, later, that they were heading towards Ely's Ford and Germanna Ford. Realizing that Union troops were between him and Stuart, Lee ordered Stuart to head east and join him, although this would uncover Lee's own supply and communication lines, leaving them vulnerable to Union cavalry attacks by Stoneman and Averell. Lee supposed that Slocum was trying to get into his rear, and this was confirmed when another message arrived reporting that the Union troops had crossed the Rapidan.

When Stoneman had crossed the Rappahannock to begin his raid, Stuart (who still had only the brigades of Fitzhugh Lee and Rooney Lee available) ordered Rooney Lee and his weak brigade to harass Stoneman and keep him out of any important ammunition or railroad depots. Stuart took Fitzhugh Lee's brigade and spread it thinly along Hooker's right front and right flank. By doing so Stuart accomplished all three of his major objectives:

1. Providing information about Hooker's movements to Lee.
2. Keeping information about Lee from reaching Hooker.
3. Helping to protect the flank of Lee's army.

As reports from Stuart reached Lee, Maj. Gen. Richard H. Anderson and two brigades of his division were ordered to move from United States Ford to Chancellorsville, where he would join the rest of his division to counter the Union move around Lee's left flank. Anderson was not strong enough to stop Slocum, but he could buy Lee some time.

Lee realized that this Union flanking force could drive deeper into his rear areas and get between him and Richmond. He thereupon decided to strike first while leaving only a skeleton force to hold his current position; this job was given to Jubal Early's infantry division reinforced by a brigade from McLaw's division and the reserve artillery. This would give Lee about 45,000 troops to oppose Slocum while Early and 10,000 troops would be responsible for holding off Sedgwick.

This was not what Hooker had expected Lee to do.

Jackson had some volunteers pretend to desert and be captured by Hooker's pickets. They were coached to tell the fairy tale that Longstreet and his two divisions had returned, bringing Hampton and his cavalry brigade with them. Then a cavalry regiment, from the brigade Hooker had retained, got itself surrounded and confused in the strange country of the Wilderness, where it was soundly beaten by a portion of Fitzhugh Lee's brigade. They reported to Hooker that they had run into strong cavalry resistance where it shouldn't be, Hooker having assumed that Stuart would send all of his cavalry after Stoneman. However, since Stuart's cavalry was to the west, Hooker assumed that the force, which had scattered that regiment of his cavalry, was Hampton's brigade screening a strong force of infantry, which could only be Longstreet and his two divisions. In response, Hooker had Sedgwick detach III Corps and send it to reinforce his position in the Wilderness.

The next morning, April 30, Hooker's troops on the south and east reported heavy fighting. Hooker believed that somehow Lee had done the impossible and had closed in on three sides of his 70,000 man flanking force. Thus Hooker must have realized that instead of retreating to the south that Lee was going to strike north. Hooker immediately went on the defensive and had his men building fieldworks. However, except for the Wilderness itself, there were no natural features on his western front to protect his vulnerable right flank.

Lee and Jackson realized that Hooker thought that he was flanked on three sides when in fact his troops were only in contact with reconnaissance probes from Stuart's cavalry and from Lee and Jackson's infantry.

By 11:00 A.M. on May 1, elements of both armies had collided within the Wilderness. Although Hooker considerably outnumbered Lee he allowed himself to be fought to a standstill instead of forcing Lee back into the open ground where Hooker wanted him to be. The fighting that day demonstrated that, while Hooker had originally outmaneuvered Lee, Hooker in turn had allowed Lee to outmaneuver him. Until the battle began in the Wilderness, Hooker, a poker player of great skill (turning one of his vices into a virtue), had played his hand well until the stakes became so high that he folded.[3] In effect, while not a coward, Hooker lacked the moral courage to move when he actually had Lee's army in the palm of his hand.

Lee and Jackson met at sundown. Both of them were eager to attack and discussed ways to do so. Then Stuart arrived with news that his cavalry had discovered that Hooker's right flank was hanging "in the air" upon the Orange Plank Road. Checking their maps, Lee traced a route for Jackson, which ran two miles west of Catherine Furnace then turned further south before veering northwest to the Orange Plank Road. What now needed to be done was to find the roads and trails that would allow such a movement to be accomplished.

At dawn, May 2, 1863, when word arrived from Stuart that a covered approach to Hooker's right flank at Chancellorsville had been found, it was decided that Jackson would take his entire II Corps to the left (minus Early and his division), leaving Lee and only 15,000 troops (the other three divisions belonging to Longstreet's I Corps) to face Hooker. Lee was about to take the greatest risk of his entire military career. Although the maneuver was completely successful it was a close-run thing, since Jackson's approach was soon detected and a number of warnings were sent to Hooker's headquarters where, in the end, nothing was done.

At 9:00 A.M. a courier from III Corps commander Maj. Gen. Daniel Sickles, an old crony of Hooker's, had arrived at Hooker's headquarters. Sickles reported sighting a huge Confederate column moving south of Catherine Furnace, in Sickles' front, before it disappeared into the woods. Hooker jumped to the conclusion, after consulting a map, that Lee was retreating. Hooker did take the precaution of alerting Oliver O. Howard, commanding XI Corps on his extreme right, in case Lee was up to something. Howard then informed Hooker that he had also detected the mysterious Confederate column and that he, Howard, was taking precautions.

This was where the lack of Union cavalry apparently became important.[4] Since there was only one brigade available to patrol the many roads and trails that wound through the Wilderness and since Howard's message had allayed Hooker's concerns, he ordered Sedgwick to prepare to strike at Early. Then at 3:00 P.M. Sickles reported capturing Confederate soldiers and wagons, but he had not regained sight of the huge Confederate column in the woods.

Although Hooker convinced himself that Lee was in full retreat he kept getting warnings that the Confederates were massing for an attack upon XI Corps at Hooker's extreme right.

The precautions that Howard had mentioned to Hooker had consisted of refusing his flank, slightly, and positioning a single section of artillery (two field guns) to repulse an attack. Howard also did nothing to close or cover a half-mile gap between his XI Corps and Slocum's XII Corps, the next corps in line. Howard was not too concerned about a Confederate attack, since he considered the woods—that were hiding Jackson's men—to be impenetrable.

Meanwhile, as Stonewall Jackson and his corps approached Hooker's right flank, Jackson realized that he might not have enough daylight to do the job. His progress through the woods was considerably slower than he had expected. Eventually Jackson reached Fitzhugh Lee's cavalry brigade, which was keeping an eye on the Union army's vulnerable flank. The cavalry showed Jackson the exact location of his objective but it still took another three hours for him to get his corps into position to attack. Jackson gave the order to attack at 5:15 P.M., when only about 90 minutes of daylight remained.

Jackson struck XI Corps—on Hooker's extreme right flank, and the Union XI Corps division on that extreme flank disintegrated—and shortly thereafter, Hooker's right flank essentially ceased to exist. Hooker did not find out what was happening until the first fugitives managed to reach his headquarters at the Chancellor House. Hooker ordered a division from III Corps to shore up his right. When Sickles found out about the disaster he pulled back into a defensive position with the rest of III Corps but blundered about in the dark as Union artillery stabilized the situation. Eventually, Sickles got his two divisions back inside Union lines, with a detachment holding the vital high ground at Hazel Grove (which, as a matter of fact, happened to overlook the entire Union position at Chancellorsville).

After darkness fell Jackson tried to continue the attack in the dark. He was conducting a personal reconnaissance when, while returning to his lines, he was wounded by his own men. He died a few days later, and Stuart took command of Jackson's Corps. The next day, May 3, Stuart resumed the offensive. That same morning, Hooker received reinforcements when I Corps (sent by Sedgwick) reached him, but made no effort to regain the initiative and ordered III Corps to abandon the high ground it held at Hazel Grove. Stuart immediately seized it, placed his artillery there, and proceeded to pound the Union positions to pieces. (Even more confusion resulted when Hooker was stunned while leaning against a pillar at the Chancellor House, his headquarters, which was struck by a Confederate cannonball.)

Sedgwick saved the army by attacking Early in accordance with orders he had received from Hooker at 9:00 P.M. May 1. This forced Lee to detach McLaws' Division to reinforce Early. On May 4, Hooker remained on the defensive, and Lee decided to attack Sedgwick, but he had withdrawn back over the Rappahannock. Early and Lee then joined with the intention of again attempting to attack Sedgwick, who managed to disengage as darkness approached. Lee then planned to attack Hooker again on May 6, but in a council of war held during the night of May 5-6, Hooker decided to retreat. That night Hooker withdrew his artillery and then at first light his infantry.

Averell, meanwhile, had reached Hooker's headquarters on May 4, and 12 days later Hooker relieved him. Hooker was incensed that Averell had dawdled so long after Rooney Lee had eluded him. Not only that, Averell's casualty list indicated that his force had hardly been engaged at all during the raid. Averell was ordered to Washington in disgrace, which almost ended his career.

Hooker also castigated Stoneman for his own actions, or lack of them, as well as for allowing Averell to go astray. Hooker assigned no value to Stoneman's Raid whatsoever and sacked Stoneman on May 22, 1863, replacing him with Pleasonton, who had become something of a rival to Stoneman. (After the Chancellorsville Campaign the Cavalry Corps, now under Pleasonton, would be reorganized into two divisions, each consisting of three brigades, under Gregg and John Buford. Just before Gettysburg a third division of two brigades would be added to it from the Washington, D.C., garrison.)

In effect Hooker had made Stoneman and Averell the scapegoats for his own shortcomings at Chancellorsville, although it had actually been Hooker's own failures that had made Stoneman's Raid an entirely pointless affair. (Stoneman would eventually be named to head the War Department's newly established Cavalry Bureau, an assignment, as it turned out, where his talents were most effectively utilized. His return to field command in 1864 — with Sherman's armies moving against Atlanta — would once again be disappointing, to say the least.)

While it has been accepted by many historians that the lack of cavalry at Chancellorsville had led to Hooker's defeat, this conventional wisdom has been challenged by more recent historians who maintain that the conventional wisdom is lacking in validity, which fails, among other things, to take into account the fact that the terrain at Chancellorsville was not favorable to cavalry, and that Jackson's movement was spotted and reported a number of times by the troops of Howard's XI Corps and Sickles' III Corps, with the sightings being entirely ignored once the information had been transmitted to Hooker's headquarters.[5] And the cavalry that was present with Hooker, the brigade under the direction of Pleasonton, did help to slow Jackson's attack.

Thus, this revision contends that Hooker's defeat actually owed little to the absence of Stoneman's cavalry and considerably more to Hooker's own ineptness and loss of nerve, along with the superb performance provided by Lee and Jackson in their final collaboration. The Battle of Chancellorsville would soon be justifiably called Lee's Masterpiece.[6]

4

Redemption in the Mountains

When Joseph Hooker relieved Averell of his command on May 16, 1863, he left a final insult ringing in Averell's ears: "I could excuse General Averell if I could anywhere discover in his operations a desire to find and engage the enemy." Hooker charged Averell with disregarding his orders and said Averell was guilty of culpable indifference and inactivity. Averell immediately asked for a court of inquiry but never got one.

But Averell took his removal like a man and reported as ordered to Washington, D.C.[1] Almost immediately he was sent to Philadelphia to serve as a mustering officer. Then on May 23, 1863, just when it looked like his military career was over, he was sent to the mountains of West Virginia to replace failed Brig. Gen. Benjamin Roberts in command of the 4th Separate Brigade, VIII Corps, Middle Department. While it was thought by many historians that either it was decided to ignore Hooker's condemnation or it was felt that Averell couldn't do any worse than Roberts, what had actually happened was that Maj. Gen. Robert Schenck, Middle Department commander, was badly in need of competent commanders and requested that Averell be assigned to replace Roberts.

(At about the same time as the Chancellorsville Campaign was being conducted Confederate cavalry under John Imboden and W.E. "Grumble" Jones were raiding West Virginia seeking livestock to help feed Lee's army and to help alleviate the Army of Northern Virginia's critical shortage of horses. Roberts and the 4th Separate Brigade totally failed to protect West Virginia from the raiders. As a matter of fact, Roberts, who was exercising an independent combat command for the first — and last — time, panicked and ran from the mere hint that the raiders were approaching his headquarters. Upon his immediate relief of his duties, Roberts was sent to a noncombat post in the west. Since his previous assignment had been as John Pope's inspector general and he had played a prominent role in the court-martial of Fitz John Porter, there may have been at least some Union officers who thought that the entire affair in West Virginia was merely a matter of poetic justice.)

The assignment was Averell's redemption. In West Virginia he was much less of a public figure than he had been in his days with the Army of the Potomac, and he received the chance to demonstrate that he was still a competent commander, within his limitations. His failures had come, and would continue to come, when he was under fairly close supervision upon level ground.[2] On the other hand, when he was in command of an autonomous, or at least semi-independent, force in mountainous country he was to all intents and purposes invincible.

Between then and his final relief by Sheridan on September 23, 1864, Averell continued to command his brigade when it was moved to the Department of West Virginia on June 26, 1863. In December 1863 he was named to command what was now the Fourth Division of the same department (his brigade having been reinforced to division size and status) and finally received command of the Second Cavalry Division of the same department (basically the same outfit but under a new designation), which he generally competently commanded until his second and final relief.

The 4th Separate Brigade, when Averell became its commander, consisted of infantry which had been kicked around so hard and so often by the Confederates that it had no faith in itself or its superiors. The first objective that Averell had was to lick the brigade into shape, building it into a solid and extremely capable command. Once Averell assumed command, the first thing he did was to mount as much of the brigade as possible, turning it into mounted infantry in order to increase his mobility. This was an expedient used by a number of commanders during the war. These troops remained infantry, using their horses, and sometimes mules, for transportation only. Once they reached the battlefield they would dismount and fight entirely on foot. (One of the most famous of these mounted infantry units was Wilder's Lightning Brigade, which served with the Army of the Cumberland. The brigade commander, to increase his brigade's effectiveness, first mounted it with captured or confiscated horses; and then at his own expense he rearmed it entirely with Spencer repeating rifles. He made an arrangement with his bank to take out a loan with his men, under which they would repay him out of their army pay, which they did — even though each Spencer rifle cost about $200, the equivalent of a year's pay or more, which came to $156 for each of the privates at $13 a month.)

Once he had his brigade mounted, Averell, in August, November and December, led major raids against Confederate positions, seeking to influence events in both Virginia and Tennessee. The first raid was not a success, primarily due to Averell's unfamiliarity with the region and his troops' lack of familiarity with the horses upon which they were now mounted. Although the raid had not reached its main objective at Lewisburg, Virginia, there were some positive results, and the men of the 4th Separate Brigade began to gain confidence in both themselves and their commander.

Averell tried again, with a second raid aimed at Lewisburg, which this time was a complete and overwhelming success. Averell handled his command skillfully in the broken and wooded countryside, overcoming stout resistance. He can be faulted for only one decision. Instead of vigorously chasing his defeated opponents, Averell waited for reinforcements, which were supposed to cut the Confederates off and which did not arrive.

His third raid began on December 8, 1863, and demonstrated that as long as he was in the mountains he could even cope well with winter weather. His target was the Virginia & Tennessee Railroad, which he hoped to disrupt badly enough to hinder Confederate operations in the area of Knoxville, Tennessee. The entire operation was plagued with difficulties. Two planned diversions failed to distract Confederate troops, which were able to concentrate against Averell's advance. Then the weather turned increasingly bad, becoming even more of an obstacle than the Confederate troops contesting his movements.

Through it all, Averell kept his men on the move. He entered Selma, Virginia, on December 16 and destroyed the railroad, local facilities, and supplies, along with five bridges, several culverts, and some lengths of track. After a full day of frenzied activity, Averell withdrew his soldiers from the area late in the afternoon and headed for home. The return was made on little used roads and trails. Although 121 men from his rearguard were captured, Averell's main body managed to elude several thousand Confederate troops under the command of then Maj. Gen. Jubal Early who were scouring the countryside for them. As Averell eventually put it, "Early was late." All in all, this raid was probably the most successful operation ever conducted by Averell and did much to restore his reputation after Chancellorsville.

Then in December of 1863 his command was reinforced and was redesignated as the Fourth Division, Department of West Virginia. The Department of West Virginia itself was reorganized in March 1864 and Averell and his division eventually came under the command of Maj. Gen. Franz Siegel. Averell established his headquarters in Martinsburg, Virginia, in the lower, or northern, end of the Shenandoah Valley and conducted several small raids that harassed Confederate forces in the Shenandoah Valley and disrupted Confederate railroads in the area. Later

4—Redemption in the Mountains

in the spring of 1864, Averell and a portion of his division were transferred to the Kanawha Valley, where his command was reinforced back to division strength and was thereupon redesignated as the Second Cavalry Division, Department of West Virginia.

Averell told his own story about this next period in a series of official reports, which he sent to the adjutant general of the army, and which were dated October 25, 1864, from his home in Bath, New York. Included were reports of his expedition to Wytheville and destruction of the Tennessee Railroad, operations during General Hunter's expedition to Lynchburg, Virginia, an account of an engagement with General Stephen D. Ramseur's infantry division on July 20, 1864, of operations with the Army of West Virginia, of the fight at Moorefield on August 7, 1864, and of his operations with the Middle Military Division through to his relief by Sheridan on September 23, 1864.

"All of these reports," Averell wrote in his cover letter to the adjutant general, "have been sent through the proper channels, but, owing to the fact that I was relieved of the command of my division on the 23rd of September, I have the honor to ask the attention of the Department to these reports in the connected form in which they are presented, in order that a just opinion may be formed of my conduct since the opening of the spring campaign."

Averell wrote in his reports that the opening of the spring campaigning season in 1864 found him at Martinsburg and by April 20, 1864, his division was on its way to Beverly to join an expedition that was soon abandoned. Afterwards, Averell and 1,000 of his men were ordered back to the Kanawha Valley, where they were joined by the 2nd West Virginia Cavalry, 3rd West Virginia Cavalry and the 34th Ohio Mounted Infantry. With this force he went over the mountains to the Tennessee Railroad, fought a severe engagement on May 10 and destroyed the railroad from New River to Lafayette and came back to Lewisburg.

In June 1864, Averell and his division went across the Alleghanies to Staunton, Virginia, where he joined Maj. Gen. David Hunter's expedition, which was moving against Lynchburg, Virginia. Neither Hunter nor Averell distinguished themselves, with Hunter blaming Averell, who found himself continuing in his role of convenient scapegoat. After the failure of that expedition, Averell returned to the Kanawha Valley once again and moved around the Shenandoah and up to Winchester.

At Winchester his cavalry joined infantry under Brig. Gen. George C. Crook, defeating Ramseur's infantry division, which was part of Jubal Early's Valley District Army. Averell, however, once again came up short during the Second Battle of Kernstown in the aftermath of Confederate Lt. Gen. Jubal Early's raid upon Washington, D.C.

The Army of West Virginia, consisting of two small VIII Corps divisions under the command of General Crook and Averell's cavalry division, was in pursuit of Early's army. Crook planned a flanking attack and waited for Averell and his cavalry, which had been sent around the Confederate right. But Averell dawdled and before he was in position Crook's infantry was caught in a double envelopment, with Confederate Maj. Gen. Stephen Dodson Ramseur's division swinging around the right and Maj. Gen. John C. Breckinridge's division attacking on the left. Under vicious fire from both flanks, Crook's line began to fold. Averell observed the attack, but to Crook's disgust he simply led his troopers to the safety of the rear, towards Winchester.

In his official reports, Averell barely mentioned the incident and the whole Second Battle of Kernstown, simply noting, "Early and his united Valley Army forced Crook and the Army of West Virginia to fall back to Maryland," where Averell bivouacked at Hagerstown.

Just after this repulse, Confederate cavalry under Brig. Gen. John McCausland raided Chambersburg, Pennsylvania, burning the town to the ground when it failed to provide the ransom demanded by McCausland. Averell and his division were dispatched to chase the raiders down; however, Averell failed to offer any real threat to the Confederate cavalry until they were back in their own home territory. Averell explained his apparent failure by noting that since

May his cavalry division had marched at least 1,400 miles without being provided with any remounts or even having any halts long enough to have their horses reshod. Averell himself, during this period, appeared to be sluggish in his movements and possibly even mentally weary. Averell noted in his reports, however, that he had pursued McCausland for 135 miles, attacking him at McConnellsburg. When news of this latest failure, occurring on top of the Second Battle of Kernstown, was brought to the attention of Lt. Gen. Ulysses S. Grant, he suggested that Averell should possibly be relieved. Grant apparently issued what was an optional order to that effect.

Before that could happen, however, on August 7, 1864, the same day that Sheridan assumed command of the Middle Military Division and its Army of the Shenandoah, Averell's cavalry division caught McCausland and Bradley Johnson's Confederate cavalry brigades near Moorefield and broke them up, capturing over 400 prisoners. Averell accomplished this feat with the same worn out horses (apparently by now at least reshod) that were unable to catch McCausland in Pennsylvania and Maryland.

Averell, after his triumph at Moorefield (which in all likelihood saved him for the time being from Grant's optional order approving his relief, an option which Sheridan would eventually carry out a little over a month later in the aftermath of the Battle of Fisher's Hill), had just returned to Hagerstown, on August 8, 1864, when he received the following telegram from Sheridan:

> Harpers Ferry, August 7, 1864.
> Brigadier-General Averell:
>
> Concentrate your cavalry command at Hancock and join me by the shortest and most practicable route.
>
> P.H. Sheridan
> Major-General

Sheridan was one of the new type of military commanders, like Grant and Sherman, who had recently come into prominence. Averell belonged to the old school that had emphasized training, preparation, and caution. The new school, as represented by Sheridan, demanded sacrifice, decisiveness, and success. Perhaps it was simply inevitable that Averell and Sheridan would clash.

5

Averell and Sheridan

On the same day that Averell received his orders from Sheridan to concentrate his division at Hancock and then to join Sheridan as soon as possible, Sheridan issued the following orders, which were apparently sent to Averell (and which he apparently believed were for his information, only):

> General Orders No. 4
> Headquarters Middle Military Division
> Harper's Ferry, W.Va, August 8, 1864
>
> 1. Brig. Gen. A.T.A. Torbert, First Division, Cavalry Corps, Army of the Potomac, is hereby announced as chief of cavalry for the Middle Military Division. Commanders of the Middle, Susquehanna, and Washington Departments will at once render returns of the cavalry force, and where stationed in their respective departments.
>
> By command of Maj. Gen. Sheridan:
> E.B. Parsons
> Assistant Adjutant General

The orders made no mention at all of the cavalry within the Department of West Virginia (which included Averell's command and that of Alfred Duffie), which was also officially a part of the Middle Military Division. (It also gave command of Torbert's First Cavalry Division, Cavalry Corps, Army of the Potomac, to Wesley Merritt as senior officer present.) In addition, Averell was senior to Torbert and, under normal army procedures, which Sheridan did not choose to follow, would have been entitled to and most likely would have otherwise been given command of the cavalry as the senior officer present.

As a matter of fact, Averell and Torbert knew each other quite well, having been West Point classmates and apparently rivals while at the academy.[1]

In choosing Torbert over Averell as chief of cavalry Sheridan was most likely influenced by Grant's orders that stated in part: "Do not hesitate to give commands to officers in whom you repose confidence, without regards to claims of others on account of rank. If you deem Torbert the best man to command the cavalry, place him in command and give Averell some other command or relieve him from the expedition and order him to report to General Hunter. What we want is prompt and active movements after the enemy, in accordance with instructions you already have."

As Grant may have foreseen, an exchange of messages between Averell and Sheridan and between Averell and Torbert reveal that relations between Averell and the high command of the Middle Military Division were strained from practically the very beginning. This strained relationship could well have been, and as a matter of fact most likely was, one of the background, and behind the scenes, circumstances that eventually led to Sheridan's relief of Averell.

Averell in his official reports stated that he concentrated his division at Hancock and on August 14 reached Martinsburg on his way to join Sheridan, who was then at Cedar Creek. At

Martinsburg, Averell received new orders to rest and refit his division for field duty. Except through his own scouts, Averell noted that he was unable to obtain any information about Sheridan's subsequent movements until August 18.

Then on August 19 he received the following dispatch:

> Headquarters Middle Military Division
> Berryville, August 18, 1864 — 5:30 A.M.
> [Received at 11:00 A.M. August 19]
>
> General:
> I am directed by the major general commanding to inform you that our cavalry under Torbert at Winchester have fallen back to Summit Point. The general directs that you move your command to the north side of the Potomac, if necessary, and cover the country from Williamsport to Sharpsburg.
>
> Very respectfully, your obedient servant,
> James W. Forsyth,
> Lieutenant Colonel and Chief of Staff

In addition, Averell also received orders from Torbert, as chief of cavalry, which actually arrived first. They stated as follows:

> Headquarters Cavalry, Middle Military Division
> August 17, 1864
> [Received at 2:30 A.M. August 18]
> Brig. Gen. Averell
> Commanding Second Division
>
> General:
> Winchester is evacuated tonight. Fall back towards Charlestown. The enemy are here in strong force.
>
> By command of Brig. Gen. Torbert
> M.A. Reno
> Captain and Chief of Staff

(Reno, who would eventually receive command of the 12th Pennsylvania Cavalry Regiment just before the end of the war, would be the same Reno who would be George A. Custer's second in command at the Battle of the Little Big Horn on June 25, 1876, against the Sioux, Northern Cheyenne and Northern Arapaho.)

Starting for Charlestown, Averell received verbal orders through Torbert to go to Smithfield instead. Averell changed direction to proceed to Smithfield when he was overtaken by the order (repeated) of Sheridan's to cover the Potomac River crossings, and if necessary to cross to the north side of the Potomac.

"To cover from Cherry Run to Harper's Ferry," Averell wrote in his reports, "with a division of cavalry operating on the south side of the river, it is necessary to take post at or near Martinsburg and establish a picket line from Mill's Gap, in North Mountain, across the Valley to Charlestown. If unable to maintain that line it is best to guard the fords on the north side of the river."

Averell wrote there was nothing in the instructions received from Sheridan which contemplated the occupation of Martinsburg by Averell's division. Averell, therefore, moved to Shepardstown on the evening of August 18 and picketed the river as well as possible. On the morning of August 20, Averell received new orders from Sheridan as follows:

> Headquarters Middle Military Division
> In the Field. August 19, 1864 — 10:00 P.M.
> [Received the morning of August 20]
> Brig. Gen. William W. Averell
> Commanding Cavalry Division

General:

The major general commanding directs that if you can that you employ loyal citizens of Williamsport and vicinity to give you information in the case of an advance or attempt on the part of the enemy to cross the Potomac. In fact, the general rather desires that the enemy should cross; all that he wants is early information of the character and number of troops that pass over. All citizens that you may employ you will be authorized to pay a fair compensation to for all information given.

I am, general, very respectfully, &c.,
James W. Forsyth
Lieutenant Colonel and Chief of Staff

In order that Early's Confederates should have the opportunity to make the crossing, and that the observations Sheridan wanted could be made, Averell moved his division across the river to Fair Play, Maryland, and placed his pickets from Cherry Run to Antietam Furnace, which satisfied all the conditions of the instructions received from Sheridan. Averell then proceeded to open what can only be called a can of worms.

Not only was Averell senior to Torbert he also had never been informed that he was officially under Torbert's orders, since the announcement of Torbert's appointment as chief of cavalry for the Middle Military Division had not specifically included the cavalry serving in the Department of West Virginia (the two cavalry divisions under Duffie and Averell). Therefore, having received what Averell perceived to be improper orders since Averell did not consider himself to be under Torbert's command as chief of cavalry, when he received direct orders from Torbert on August 19 Averell decided to seek clarification and sent the following communication to Sheridan's chief of staff:

Headquarters Second Cavalry Division,
Department of West Virginia,
Shepardstown, August 19, 1864
Lt. Col. J.W. Forsyth,
Chief of Staff, Middle Military Division

Colonel:

I have received orders from General Torbert regarding the return of some men of General Duffie's division, now serving with mine, and also requiring returns, &c. As I received no order placing me under General Torbert's command, and as my commission is senior to his, I do not think it proper to obey his orders until I am shown by some law or order that it is proper that my rank be ignored. The only general orders I have received regarding the organization of the cavalry of the Middle Military Division did not include the cavalry of the Department of West Virginia. I trust that you will understand that my only motive in declining to obey the orders of a junior is dictated by a sense of duty to myself and from no disrespect to General Torbert or others. Will you be good enough to instruct me, if I am wrong, at your earliest convenience?

I enclose a return of my command; the rearming and remounting of a portion is going on at Hagerstown. The latest news I hear of the enemy is that he placed a strong infantry picket north of Winchester last evening, upon the road to Martinsburg. He had also about 400 cavalry at that point. As I have been unable to hear anything of the cavalry of Ramseur I apprehend a demonstration upon our flanks or some other points in West Virginia. I have sent some good scouts upon that flank, and have requested Maj. Gen. Kelley, at Cumberland, to send scouts to Romney and Moorefield. I hardly think the enemy has any business upon your eastern flank at present. I shall be glad to be informed of any news or movements. My pickets are undisturbed at Martinsburg and other points southwest of that place. I have sent three parties to ascertain as exactly as possible the force of the enemy in the Valley, and gain some indications of his designs.

Respectfully, &c.,
William W. Averell
Brigadier General

In response to this communication, Averell on August 23, apparently somewhat to his surprise, received a very heated answer to his query about the propriety of Torbert giving him orders:

> Headquarters Middle Military Division
> Halltown, Va., August 23, 1864 — 2 P.M.
> Brig. Gen. W.W. Averell
> Commanding Cavalry Division
>
> General:
>
> The major general commanding directs that you report without delay to Brig. Gen. A.T.A. Torbert, chief of cavalry, Middle Military Division. All orders received by you from him will be obeyed and respected accordingly.
>
> Very respectfully, your obedient servant,
> James W. Forsyth
> Lieutenant Colonel and Chief of Staff

Two days earlier, on the morning of August 21, Averell received the following dispatch:

> Headquarters Middle Military Division
> In the Field, August 20, 1864 — 8:30 P.M.
> [Received at 8:00 A.M. August 21]
> Brig. Gen. W.W. Averell,
> Commanding Cavalry Division
>
> General:
>
> I do not know why you moved your cavalry from Shepherdstown. If there was a necessity, it was not known to me, and you have not informed me. Your scouts report nothing at Martinsburg or for four miles beyond in the direction of Winchester. Report to me at once where you are and why you moved from Shepherdstown.
>
> Very respectfully, your obedient servant,
> P.H. Sheridan
> Major General

Averell maintained that this message both amazed and pained him, as it showed an undue readiness on the part of Sheridan to find faults in Averell's official conduct. In reply Averell sent the following message to Sheridan:

> Headquarters Second Cavalry Division,
> Department of West Virginia,
> Fair Play, Md., August 21, 1864 — 8:30 A.M.
> Maj. Gen. P.H. Sheridan,
> Commanding Middle Military Division,
>
> General:
>
> I have received your note of 8:30 P.M. yesterday, stating that I had not informed you why my cavalry was moved from Sheperdstown, &c. In reply, I beg leave to state that I sent a report yesterday morning of the movement to you, and that it was made to carry out your desires and in compliance with instructions received from you. There was no necessity in the shape of an enemy, but it was necessary that your orders should be complied with. I received information from you that General Torbert's cavalry had been compelled to fall back at Summit Point, and directions to fall back to the north side of the Potomac if necessary, covering the crossings. I awaited the necessity, which came in the orders from the chief of cavalry to fall back from Martinsburg to Charlestown, on the way there to proceed to Smithfield, and a few minutes afterward a repetition of your order to cover the crossings of the Potomac, crossing it if necessary, and again, yesterday morning an order from you in which these words occur:
> "In fact, the general rather desires that the enemy should cross; all he wants is early information of the character and number of the troops that pass over."
> Now in order that the enemy might do as you desired, it was necessary that I should cross to this side, where the observations you required could be made. The instructions received from your headquarters since I was ordered to stop at Martinsburg on my way to join you have not involved a chance to fight, but their uniform tenor has been to keep my division from the front, and also to give it some opportunity to remount. The position I now occupy at Fair Play, with my pickets from Cherry Run to Antietam Furnace, satisfies the conditions of your instructions better than any other except Martinsburg, which I was directed to leave, and no other place has been

directed in your orders. The reports of my own scouts, to which you refer, conflicted with those received from your headquarters, that 4,000 to 5,000 of the enemy's cavalry were moving in my direction. The remounting of my division is progressing as rapidly as horses can be procured. I have yet over 600 dismounted men. I regret exceedingly that there be any misunderstanding regarding the position of my division, as my only desire is to do with it the greatest possible good to the cause and render the most assistance to you.

> Respectfully, your obedient servant,
> William W. Averell.
> Brigadier General

Averell noted that the correctness of his dispositions was shown on August 26 when the enemy attempted to force a crossing with their entire cavalry, supported by a division of infantry and artillery. Averell prevented the crossing without incurring heavy casualties, although he complained that his action received no expression of approval from Sheridan. Believing that the Confederates were withdrawing from the vicinity of Winchester, Averell recrossed the Potomac on August 28 and advanced to Hainesville, and on August 29 to Martinsburg, driving the enemy's pickets four miles beyond Martinsburg. Averell then established a picket line across the valley.

An advance by a force of Confederate infantry, cavalry, and artillery on August 31 caused Averell to retreat to Falling Waters. Believing this advance to be merely a screen for a Confederate retreat, Averell again advanced on September 2, without meeting any serious opposition until he reached Bunker Hill, about 10 miles from Martinsburg, where Averell attacked Lunsford Lomax's Confederate cavalry division and routed it.

On September 3, Lomax counterattacked but was beaten back and was driven to within five miles of Winchester, where Averell's troopers met Confederate infantry. On September 4, 5, 6, and 7, Averell repeatedly pressed the Confederates until it was ascertained that they did not intend any further movement up the valley. All information gained was promptly transmitted to Sheridan's headquarters. Averell wrote in his collected reports that he believed that it was upon the receipt of this information that Sheridan's army left Harper's Ferry and made the advance, which resulted in the Third Battle of Winchester/Opequon Creek.

All of this activity, Averell wrote, was made in compliance with instructions received from Sheridan as follows:

> Headquarters Middle Military Division,
> September 4, 1864—4:20 P.M.
> Brig. Gen. W.W. Averell,
> Commanding Cavalry Division,
>
> General:
> General Torbert came back from the Front Royal pike last night; reports no rebel troops have left the Valley. Last night Kershaw attacked Crook on the Berryville pike, about dark, and was handsomely repulsed, some 360 killed, wounded, and prisoners. The enemy's force appears this evening to be concentrated at or about the Berryville ford of the Opequon. I want you to cover the Smithfield road from Bunker Hill, if possible, and to push up the Valley so far as it is prudent. Whenever you have an opportunity attack the enemy.
>
> Very respectfully,
> P.H. Sheridan
> Major General, Commanding

However, according to Averell these operations were the subject of covert "animadversions," or unfavorable comments, at Sheridan's headquarters and Averell was informed that the manner in which they were represented to Grant had induced the issuance of an optional order to relieve him from his command. "Actuated solely by a desire to render the greatest possible service with my division, I cannot conjecture the grounds upon which my motives and reputation were permitted to suffer reproach," Averell wrote. (If Averell's information was accurate this was the second optional order from Grant permitting the possible relief of Averell, since Grant had issued a similar order after having been informed of Averell's poor performance during the Second Battle of Kernstown. It is not known whether a second optional order was actually issued or whether Averell confused it with the original optional order for his relief that was issued by General Grant.)

On September 8, following orders from Torbert, Averell moved the main body of his division across the Opequon to Leetown, picketing the valley with one brigade until September 10, when it was driven back to Martinsburg by a Confederate infantry division. On September 13, Averell was ordered by Sheridan to conduct a reconnaissance to Bunker Hill, Geraldstown, and Pughtown. The enemy's cavalry were driven to beyond Bunker Hill and his infantry was located. On September 14, Averell returned to Leetown, remaining quiet, but kept both vigilant videttes and active scouting parties out, until September 18, when the enemy, under Early in person, advanced a division of infantry, with a brigade of cavalry and an artillery battalion, supported by a second infantry division at Bunker Hill, to Martinsburg, driving Averell's First Brigade across Opequon Creek.

Averell at 5:00 A.M. September 19, in accordance with instructions received from Torbert, began his portion of the Third Battle of Winchester/Opequon Creek by moving across Opequon Creek to Darkesville and from there to Bunker Hill, driving Confederate cavalry videttes back steadily. Eventually there was a determined stand made by the Confederate cavalry at Bunker Hill, which stubbornly resisted the advance of Averell's division to Stevenson's Depot, five miles north of Winchester. At this point, Averell noticed heavy firing occurring to his left and rear.

He found that this was Torbert, attempting to cross Opequon Creek with Wesley Merritt's First Cavalry Division. Averell could also hear distant musketry to the south and he promptly attacked the enemy opposing the advance of George A. Custer's Michigan Cavalry Brigade of Merritt's division. This allowed Custer's brigade to cross the creek and form on Averell's left. From here Averell's division shifted entirely to the west side of the pike, and as it advanced, the line of battle to the left, consisting of Merritt's First Cavalry Division, had an opportunity to form. (Although Averell does not mention it in his collected reports the two divisions were under the direct command and supervision of Torbert.)

Averell's division continued to advance, driving the Confederates before it, to within three miles of Winchester, until at 2:30 P.M. the Confederates presented a strong line about a mile in front of the town, which Averell immediately attacked with his division. Averell's troops swept away the portion of the Confederate line west of the pike, capturing a cannon, seizing the heights west of Winchester, and penetrating the town itself.

Custer's brigade suddenly gave way, according to Averell's reports, which opened Averell's left flank to attack. The Confederates promptly did so with infantry and artillery but failed to force Averell's division away from the gains it had made. Averell's further advance was delayed due to Confederate resistance until about 3:00 P.M., when Crook attacked the opposite flank of the Confederate army with his Army of West Virginia/VIII Corps troops, which cinched the victory.

It had been the assault of Averell and Merritt's cavalry divisions that had broken the Confederate lines at Winchester in conjunction with Crook's attack, and as a result Early's army was driven from the field in full retreat.

West of the town of Winchester, broken ground intersected by deep ditches and high embankments gave Early the chance to save his left flank. The Union cavalry on that ground (Brig. Gen. James H. Wilson's Third Cavalry Division) was opposed by stubborn infantry and well handled artillery and therefore could make only slow progress, but as evening fell the advancing Union infantry came to Averell's assistance. "Throughout the whole engagement," Averell wrote proudly in his collected reports, "my division was not broken or thrown into disorder and was constantly in the advance."

The defeated Confederate Valley District Army spent the night of September 19-20, 1864, in full retreat until they reached the natural fortress, which was Fisher's Hill, arriving there at about daybreak on September 20. Early chose to make his stand at Fisher's Hill, judging it to be the only place where he could make a stand with any hope of arresting Sheridan's progress.

6

Fisher's Hill

Fisher's Hill, Early's refuge that confronted Sheridan's victorious troops, was a natural fortress that in effect barred the entrance to the upper Shenandoah Valley. It was positioned up against Masanutten Mountain on the east and Little North Mountain on the west. It was a steep, rocky bluff, which extended nearly four miles and was cut by a number of ravines. At the time of the American Civil War it also included several woodlots. In addition, Tumbling Run, a brook of fast moving water, ran along its base and into the North Fork of the Shenandoah River.

The previous month, Early had skillfully used Fisher's Hill to hold off Sheridan's army in its first advance up the Shenandoah Valley. Now, following the casualties that his army had just suffered at Winchester, Early no longer had sufficient infantry to adequately man this huge natural fortress. He would try to make up for this lack with dismounted cavalry, but those troops were not fitted for such a task.

Since Sheridan, after the victory at Winchester, still had some 35,000 troops (compared to Early's total of just over 10,000 men), he was not about to be inhibited by Fisher's Hill in the same way he had been in August. Furthermore, Sheridan knew that Fisher's Hill was simply too large for Early and his small number of troops to effectively hold it. That didn't mean that Early wasn't going to try.

In deploying what troops he did have, Early solidly anchored his right flank where the bluff was at its steepest. In addition, he was aided by the fact that the North Fork of the Shenandoah River confined the area of attack, making this flank particularly unassailable. Finally there was located in this area a triple peak formation, the Three Sisters. This natural rock formation stood 1,365 feet and towered above the valley's floor, making a natural watch-tower from which the movement of any Union troops attempting to attack this portion of Early's lines would have been immediately visible.

Early positioned the remainder of his troops along the heights.[1] Lunsford Lomax and his division of cavalry, except for one brigade placed on the far right in the area of the Three Sisters, was positioned to hold Early's left. The remainder of Early's cavalry, a division of two brigades under Brig. Gen. Williams C. Wickham, was not present since it was detached with the particular mission of protecting and keeping open Early's escape route. (This was actually Maj. Gen. Fitzhugh Lee's cavalry division, which was under the temporary command of Wickham, since Fitzhugh Lee had been seriously wounded during the Third Battle of Winchester and would not resume command until prior to the Battle of Five Forks and the resulting Appomattox Campaign that led to the final surrender of Robert E. Lee's Army of Northern Virginia.)

Lomax's two available brigades of cavalry were dismounted, being deployed on low ground and upon a "hog-backed" ridge that ran parallel to Fisher's Hill. Unfortunately, these troopers were undermanned, poorly armed, and seriously demoralized.[2] In the year since Chancellorsville and Gettysburg the Union cavalry was generally and increasingly armed with Spencer repeating carbines and rifles, although a few units probably still carried various single-shot breech-loading carbines. Confederate cavalry, while it had a few breechloaders, was still mainly equipped with muzzle-loading carbines and cut down muzzle-loading infantry rifles.

The repeaters gave the Union cavalry even more of a firepower advantage than the breechloaders had, since, equipped as they were with extra pre-loaded tubal magazines for their Spencers, they could fire up to 21 aimed shots a minute, compared to 12 for breechloaders and only three for muzzle-loaders.

Sheridan was in no hurry, particularly since Fisher's Hill was too rugged for a frontal assault. As his troops moved into position and bivouacked on the valley floor, Sheridan made a personal reconnaissance seeking some way to crack this especially hard shelled nut. Deciding to pick his subordinates' brains for any ideas that they might have, on the evening of September 20 Sheridan called a council of war. Usually Sheridan avoided such things like the plague, since they were prone to provide a commander with an excuse for doing the timid thing when it was generally bold action that was required.

Those attending were his infantry corps commanders and included Maj. Gen. Horatio G. Wright (VI Corps), Maj. Gen. William H. Emory (XIX Corps), and Brig. Gen. George C. Crook (Army of West Virginia/VIII Corps). They were immediately unanimous in rejecting a frontal attack. They also rejected the next option Sheridan proposed, that of hitting Early's right flank, where his position was at its strongest, since any attacking force would be forced to form in plain sight where it could be seen by Early's lookouts upon the Three Sisters. Among other problems were the facts that any attacking force would first have to cross the North Fork of the Shenandoah River, from there attack up a sheer bluff, and from there straight up a mountainside. This was generally recognized as being impossible.

Crook, who had also made a personal reconnaissance of Fisher's Hill, provided a possible solution. He suggested turning Early's left flank, held by Lomax and his dismounted cavalry. Wright and Emory opposed the idea, but Sheridan could see that it had possibilities. Sheridan and Crook had been friends ever since their days at West Point, and although their friendship would later cool and ultimately end (primarily because Sheridan would later claim credit for this and other ideas first proposed by Crook), Sheridan trusted Crook's judgment, and Crook's two division commanders, Col. Joseph Thoburn and Col. Rutherford B. Hayes, were summoned to the council.

Crook, who sometimes had trouble expressing his ideas, used Hayes (who in 1876 would be win a closely contested election to become the 19th President of the United States) as his salesman to convince Wright and Emory of the general feasibility of his proposal. From there, once Sheridan had accepted Crook's proposal, the discussion turned into a planning session.

The resulting battle plan depended on two things—surprise and the ability to move Crook's troops (who were chosen to make the assault since it was, after all, Crook's idea) without their being noticed by Confederate lookouts that Early had undoubtedly posted on the Three Sisters.

Therefore, it was decided that Crook's Army of West Virginia/VIII Corps troops would remain hidden all day on September 21, 1864, and then would make a night march to get into position. Sheridan also instructed Torbert to take two brigades (Custer's Michigan Brigade and Col. Charles R. Lowell's Reserve Brigade) of Merritt's First Cavalry Division and join the two brigades of Wilson's Third Cavalry Division at Front Royal, Virginia, where Wilson was keeping Wickham and his Confederate cavalry division occupied. Wilson had been directed by Torbert on September 20, 1864, to take his division and find a "good position" between Front Royal and Cedarville, and had collided with Wickham on Crooked Run and had driven him across the North Fork of the Shenandoah River. That done, Wilson had bivouacked for the night, attacking Wickham again the following morning.

Once Torbert had united Merritt's and Wilson's commands, these four brigades of cavalry were instructed to sweep up the Luray Valley, cross the Massanutten Mountains at New Market

Gap and form a barrier across the Shenandoah Valley and thus block Early's line of retreat. They would form the anvil against which Sheridan and the rest of the army would hammer the Confederate Valley District Army into surrender. Averell and his cavalry division, along with one brigade from Merritt's division (under Thomas Devin), would be retained with Sheridan's main body. Sheridan expected that Averell and Devin, with three brigades of cavalry, could handle any pursuit, in addition to having Averell's division screen Crook's advance as he made his final approach to Lomax's position. (However, Sheridan neglected to communicate this expectation to Averell, possibly because he considered it too obvious to mention.) Crook was scheduled to make his attack on September 22 and, if Torbert held up his end, it would all be over by September 23.

The plan got underway when Merritt, accompanied by Torbert, moved out at 5:00 A.M. on September 21. The men of VI Corps and XIX Corps rose at sunrise, cooked their breakfasts, and relaxed. Their job would come later. Crook's two small infantry divisions remained hidden north of Cedar Creek as Sheridan and Wright resumed their personal scouting of the Confederate positions on Fisher's Hill looking for any last minute problems. Mostly, Early's troops went to work strengthening their positions by building fieldworks. Occasionally a cannon might fire or there might be the sound of musketry as the two armies continued probing away at each other.

Then shortly before noon, things began to happen, as VI Corps and XIX Corps formed up into marching columns, with VI Corps swinging around Strasbourg. The move was immediately seen and reported to Early by the lookouts on the Three Sisters, which in turn sparked Confederate artillery fire and additional fire from Confederate sharpshooters. The VI Corps continued moving until about 4:00 P.M., when its soldiers were halted just west of the Manassas Gap Railroad; then XIX Corps was deployed to the immediate left of VI Corps. The troops of both corps were pointed directly at the heights of Fisher's Hill.

When they came under Confederate artillery fire from Fisher's Hill, Sheridan ordered them to seize Flint Hill, a knoll that would give Sheridan an unobstructed view of Fisher's Hill. After three assaults Flint Hill was seized, by which time it was past sundown and the Union line formed by VI Corps and XIX Corps stretched for two miles in front of the Confederate positions along Fisher's Hill.

During the night, Sheridan's troops were kept busy. The capture of Flint Hill caused Sheridan to shift VI Corps to the west, which, due to the broken ground and the scattered woodlots, took most of the night to complete. This also required a similar realignment by XIX Corps that had been ordered for first light, but which actually began at 4:30 A.M. It was also during the night that Crook's two small infantry divisions left their place of concealment and began moving, crossing Cedar Creek. They had spent the entire day hidden in the woods, and advanced shortly after dark into another woodlot north of Hupp's Hill, a mile from Strasbourg, whereupon Crook's troops rested.

By the time the sun rose on September 22, 1864, Sheridan had deployed the five infantry divisions from VI and XIX Corps nosily and visibly in front of Fisher's Hill. The ruse worked and Early waited for Sheridan's obvious attack with decreasing confidence. By late afternoon, Early concluded that his force was simply not strong enough to resist a "determined assault" and ordered the beginning of preparations for a withdrawal after dark.

First light also brought renewed skirmishing. Early's Confederates had spent the night sleeping on the ground they held between Sheridan's troops and Tumbling Run, taking advantage of each and every terrain feature. As a diversion, Sheridan had VI Corps and XIX Corps begin to apply pressure to the main Confederate line, while Crook marched his infantry to Little North Mountain where the bulk of Lomax's dismounted cavalry were positioned. The skirmishing against Early's primary position escalated at about midday in order to spread the illusion that Sheridan was about to attempt a frontal attack.

At about the same time, knowing that his lines were very thin and could be outflanked, Early issued the orders for his troops to prepare to make their withdrawal once it became dark. Early had correctly surmised Sheridan's general intentions, what little good it did him, since he had no idea exactly when—and exactly where—Sheridan's main blow would fall.

Early issued his orders for the planned withdrawal sometime between 2:00 P.M. and 3:00 P.M., about the time Crook's troops reached the base of Little North Mountain, north of the Confederate left flank. Crook had personally led the march since it had begun. By the time his command reached the Back Road at St. Stephen's Church, about a mile and a half from Lomax's position, Averell and his cavalry division had formed a screen between the church and Lomax's dismounted cavalry. Averell had been skirmishing with Lomax since early morning, holding his attention. Crook conferred with Averell, requesting support from one of Averell's brigades when the assault began. The other brigade would protect Crook's troops from attacks by Confederate guerrillas and secure any Confederate troops or equipment captured during the assault.[3]

Crook had Thoburn and Hayes form their troops into two columns and then continued on his way up and along the mountain. Their route passed through a clear area, which for the first time exposed the advancing Union troops to the Confederate defenders. As Confederate artillery and pickets opened fire upon the two advancing Union infantry divisions they stumbled into the Confederates' reserve picket, which fled. The main body of Lomax's dismounted cavalry, if they even suspected what was about to happen, made no attempt to meet this unexpected threat.

Crook halted his troops about 200 yards behind the picket post, faced them east, brought Thoburn's division into line upon the left of Hayes' division, and began their attack at about 4:00 P.M. Crook's troops swept down the east slope of Little North Mountain, moving as fast as possible in the rough terrain and shattering Lomax's dismounted cavalry upon impact. Lomax's men sprinted for their horses or disappeared into the wooded areas to the south.

Confederate Maj. Gen. Stephen Dodson Ramseur, commanding the infantry division to the right of Lomax, reacted quickly. He pulled out a brigade to a ridge paralleling Crook's advance and with artillery support managed to temporarily slow Crook's troops. But, Ramseur's brigade was unable to stem the tide and was eventually forced from its position.

Ramseur thereupon pulled out another brigade and sent it towards the sound of the guns. However, it got lost and could act only as part of the rear guard as Early moved into full retreat. This allowed Hayes' division to enfilade Ramseur's retiring first brigade; it had enough and was soon scattering across the countryside. The Confederate artillery conducted a fighting retreat covering the infantry, and three North Carolina regiments managed to momentarily stop Crook, but the rest of the Confederate line was collapsing under a frontal attack by VI Corps and XIX Corps.

Crook's dusk attack, rolling up as it did the thin line of dismounted cavalry, was the same maneuver, which had won for Sheridan the battle three days earlier at Winchester; yet it took the Confederates completely by surprise. "Had the heavens opened and we'd been seen descending from the clouds," according to one Union officer, "no greater consternation would have been created." In moments Crook's left connected with the right flank of VI Corps and the combined Union troops swarmed over Early's breastworks.

The entire Confederate position had been engulfed, reducing Early's army to complete and total confusion as the entire line west of the Valley Pike collapsed. Although some Confederate units managed to retain their organization and cohesion, most of them ran from the field in a stampede that continued for miles. Although a rear guard was patched together near Mount Prospect, the Confederate rout continued through the night.

"The mischief could not be repaired," Early admitted grudgingly. For the second time in three days his army had been routed. He had lost a total of 1,200 men, mostly as prisoners, along with at least 20 cannon. What was left of his army was now in danger of total destruction.

Sheridan's army, however, had been almost as disorganized by its victory as Early's army had been by its defeat. An organized pursuit took time to form due to jumbled units, impromptu victory celebrations, rain, and simple darkness. When the pursuit was finally organized it was led by XIX Corps, followed by VI Corps, while Crook's Army of West Virginia/VIII Corps troops, exhausted from carrying the brunt of the fighting, stayed behind guarding prisoners and bivouacking on the battlefield.

Sheridan expected that Averell, with his division of cavalry, along with Devin's brigade that Torbert had left behind, would be pressing the pursuit. However, Averell remained under the mistaken belief that his job was merely to collect prisoners and spoils from the battlefield.

All that night the Union troops hounded Early's shattered brigades as they moved southward. "Run, boys, run!" Sheridan ordered his men as he led them up the Valley Pike. "Don't wait to form! Don't let them stop!" When some soldiers protested that they were too tired, exhausted and fatigued to continue, Sheridan responded, "If you can't run, then holler!"

Five miles from Fisher's Hill, the Confederates placed two guns on some high ground and attempted to hold their pursuers back but were soon overwhelmed. Among those Confederates killed in the rout was Lt. Col. Alexander S. (Sandy) Pendleton who had been chief of staff to Stonewall Jackson, Richard Ewell and now Jubal Early. His father, Brig. Gen. William Pendleton, was Lee's titular chief of artillery.

The vanguard of Sheridan's pursuing army reached Woodstock, nine miles from Fisher's Hill, at 3:30 A.M. on September 23, 1864, with Sheridan and his staff arriving at 5:30 A.M., roughly dawn. Sheridan believed that he had Early and his army right where he wanted them—caught between VI Corps and XIX Corps with Averell's and Devin's cavalry on one side and Torbert's cavalry, which Sheridan believed should have crossed New Market Gap by then, on the other.

Sheridan waited for word from Torbert, but when it arrived, it was not what he expected or wanted to hear.

7

Sheridan Sacks Averell

As first light dawned on September 23, 1864, Sheridan, after more than a month of dilatory marching up and down the Shenandoah Valley, in the space of 96 hours had won two major victories. He felt that he had Early and his Valley District Army in the palm of his hand, but he was about to discover that, due to the failings of two of his subordinates, the bird was just about to fly the coop.

With his main body, Sheridan had pried Early out of his natural fortress at Fisher's Hill. He had detached his chief of cavalry, Torbert, with elements of two cavalry divisions on an end run. He intended for Torbert to block Early's escape route up the Luray Valley, hold the Confederate Valley District Army in place until the infantry of VI Corps and XIX Corps could arrive, and force that entire army to surrender. (In effect these were the same tactics that would be used by Sheridan after the Battle of Five Forks on April 1, 1865, to eventually force the surrender of Lee's Army of Northern Virginia on April 9, 1865.) In addition, Sheridan thought that Averell and his cavalry division was in hot pursuit of Early, although Sheridan was not then, and had not been the previous night, in communication with Averell.

Then came the news that Torbert had been bluffed out of the Luray Valley by Williams C. Wickham's Confederate cavalry division, which was about half the size of Torbert's own cavalry force. Due to Torbert's failure, Sheridan expected Averell's reinforced division to redouble the speed of its pursuit. Sheridan attempted to dispatch orders to Averell to that effect but he could not be found. At noon, Averell and his troops trotted into Woodstock. It was only then that Sheridan learned that instead of joining in the pursuit Averell had gone into camp at Fisher's Hill on the previous evening, leaving the pursuit entirely to the infantry and Devin's brigade.

Averell wrote in his collected reports that after the battle his division was not entirely assembled, after detaching a brigade to protect Crook's rear from guerrillas while collecting prisoners and booty from the battlefield, until after midnight. "The sounds of battle had died away on my left and rear with the daylight," Averell wrote, "and a darkness succeeded through which it was difficult to find the way. Trains of ambulances, ammunition wagons, with guards and stragglers, were constantly coming up, requiring directions as to their destination. No information was received from the left and no instructions came from the major general commanding [Sheridan] or anyone else." (In point of fact, since Torbert was away on his Luray Valley Expedition there was no one else but Sheridan who could give commands to Averell's cavalry; in effect, Averell was primarily on his own, and, confused by Sheridan's lack of precise instructions as to what he was to do next, he failed entirely to make use of his own initiative, thus earning a great big black mark in Sheridan's little black book.)

Averell wrote that he sent a staff officer to obtain information. That staff officer returned and reported that operations had been concluded on the left and that the army was at a halt. Sheridan expected that Averell would pursue what was obviously a beaten opponent. It would have been the same thing that Sheridan tried to do in the aftermath of the tremendous victory at Missionary Ridge, where after the battle he had reorganized his own division on his own initiative, without orders, and led it in pursuit of Confederate General Braxton Bragg's army until stalled by the rear guard that had been patched together by Maj. Gen. Patrick Cleiburne and his infantry division. Instead, Averell did nothing and simply bivouacked for the night.

In his collected reports Averell noted that he pushed on over a rough country road, sending scouting parties out to the left to communicate with the troops on the left. During this time Averell received a message from General Crook stating that he "had done exactly right" and, if no orders had yet been received, to move on. When he arrived at Woodstock, Averell found Sheridan already there.

When he arrived at Sheridan's headquarters he was told by Sheridan (Averell wrote) that he had made a mistake by not pursuing the enemy the night before. In his collected reports Averell then recounted the confrontation that eventually led to his being removed from command of his division. "He did not ask if I had pursued him or seemed to care about knowing what had occupied me," Averell wrote. "I replied that I had received no information or instructions for me. He stated that he could not find me. I asked him if he had tried, to which he made no reply, but stated that the rebel army was a perfect mob, which would run away upon the firing of a single gun, and he desired that I go and put in my cavalry. I assured him that I had never hesitated to put it in when there was any chance for success. The tone, manner, and words of the major general commanding [Sheridan] indicated and implied dissatisfaction." (All in all this was probably one of the greatest understatements of the entire American Civil War.)

At this particular time the main problem was that Averell simply did not, could not, believe that Early's army was quite as demoralized as Sheridan indicated and, in addition, Averell had not made, and would not make, any effort in particular to go ahead and find out. "I did not entertain the opinion," he wrote, "that the rebel army was a mob. The loss of his guns at Fisher's Hill had been the result of the flank movement, but his loss in men had been inconsiderable, and his troops had been too well handled and his stragglers too few to justify in my mind an opinion that he was totally demoralized."

After his confrontation with Sheridan, Averell proceeded down the pike from Woodstock to within two miles of Mount Jackson, where he found Devin and his cavalry brigade engaging a superior Confederate force that was making a stand there. (Devin had done what Sheridan had expected that Averell would do, pursue the enemy as soon as it became apparent that they were in full retreat.) Averell said that he put his division in line and drove the enemy beyond the town. He wrote that on the heights beyond the town the enemy could be plainly seen in bivouac, while a division of Confederate infantry with artillery support marched down and engaged Averell. According to Averell, this Confederate position was naturally strong and had been strengthened with fieldworks. Averell wrote that the Confederates were fully on the alert and could have held that position against five times his force. (By that particular time, this was probably true but might not have been true if Averell had in fact conducted the pursuit the previous night that Sheridan had expected from him. Due to the failures of Torbert and Averell, Sheridan may well have thought that the curse of the Army of the Potomac had struck again and decided to make an example of the very next person who committed what he, Sheridan, perceived to be the very next screw-up.)

Then a signal officer reported to Averell that a Confederate brigade or division was moving around his right. Averell's left rested upon the river and behind him was an almost impassable creek, over which his troopers had managed to build a bridge. Averell immediately reported the situation to Sheridan.

Shortly afterwards, Averell (who had just received a promotion to brevet major general of volunteers for his actions at the Third Battle of Winchester/Opequon Creek) received the following dispatch from Sheridan:

Headquarters Middle Military Division,
Woodstock, Va., September 23, 1864

Bvt. Maj. Gen. Averell:
Your report and report of signal officer received. I do not want you to let the enemy bluff you or your command, and I want you to distinctly understand this note. I do not advise rashness, but I do desire resolution and actual fighting, with necessary casualties, before you retire. There must now be no backing or filling by you, without a superior force of the enemy actually engaging you.

P.H. Sheridan
Major General, Commanding

Upon receipt of this message from Sheridan, Averell held his position until dark, reporting the strength and the position of the Confederates to Sheridan. Averell placed a strong line of videttes close to the enemy and then, instead of making an assault (as Sheridan had directed), he moved his division back across the creek where water and forage could be obtained, and where his division could rest until morning. At 11:00 P.M. Averell received the following orders from Sheridan:

Special Orders No. 41.
Headquarters Middle Military Division,
September 23, 1864.

1. Bvt. Maj. Gen. W.W. Averell, commanding Second Cavalry Division, Department of West Virginia, is relieved from duty with that command and will at once proceed to Wheeling, W.Va., there to await orders from these headquarters or higher authority. General Averell will only take with him his personal staff. Col. William H. Powell, 2nd West Virginia Cavalry, is assigned to the command of the Second Cavalry Division, Department of West Virginia, until otherwise ordered.

By command of Maj. Gen. Sheridan:
C. Kingsbury, Jr.
Assistant Adjutant General

Averell wrote in his final collected reports:

An officer who has served the government for nine years, who has suffered from wounds in battle, cannot without any assigned cause or pretext be suddenly relieved from the command of a division whose record tells nothing but success and victories without having his sensibilities outraged and his reputation jeopardized. It is natural that the War Department should ask the wherefore for such action, and it is proper that I should state as explicitly as possible the reasons so far as they are known to me.

I have evidence that it was determined to relieve me to make Brig. Gen. Torbert chief of cavalry before Maj. Gen. Sheridan assumed command of the Middle Military Division. My success at Moorefield, achieved with an exhausted division against twice its numbers, probably caused a hesitation at my removal. The note of Maj. Gen. Sheridan, dated August 20, exhibits his readiness to avail himself of any pretext to censure me, and his reply to my explanation shows how completely his purpose was baffled.

Maj. Gen. Sheridan illegally assumed the prerogative of the President of the United States and ordered me to report to a junior officer on the 23rd of August without any just cause. While I had the entire country upon the right flank of the army to guard up to the 19th of September and had the orders of the major general commanding [Sheridan] to attack the enemy whenever I had the opportunity, my successes were barely mentioned, my activity was covertly censured, and an unjust impression was permitted to rest in the mind of the General-in-Chief [Grant] to the extent of causing him to send an optional order for my relief.

It was, I believe, admitted on the 19th of September, on both sides, that our cavalry attack was the key to the victory which we won, and I think it was obvious that the success of that attack, as to time and place, was mainly attributable to the exertions of my division, yet although I was the ranking officer of cavalry making the attack the mention of my name in the dispatches was studiously avoided.

[Averell in his collected reports completely and conveniently ignored the fact that the movement of his own division and that of Merritt's division in the decisive cavalry attack that culminated in the victory at the Third Battle of Winchester/Opequon Creek were under the direction of Torbert as chief of cavalry; he also makes no mention that he was immediately given a brevet promotion to the rank of major general of volunteers specifically for his contributions to the victory at Winchester.]

Finally, the angry and discourteous note of the 23rd [September 23, 1864] was addressed to me to give the pretext implied therein a quasi establishment in history, and before time was given me to reply the order was issued, which trampling upon my record and upon all military courtesy and justice, consigned me to the ignominy of idleness.

Sheridan of course did not see it that way. In his memoirs Sheridan noted that he had stopped at Woodstock, sending Devin's cavalry brigade to press the Confederates and if possible prevent them from halting long enough to reorganize. Sheridan wrote that notwithstanding Devin's efforts the Confederates managed to assemble a considerable force to resist him. Since Devin was too weak to attack this force he waited for Averell. Sheridan had informed Devin that Averell would be hurried to him as soon as possible because Sheridan thought that Averell must be close at hand. (Sheridan's mistaken belief in the closeness of Averell's cavalry division to Devin's cavalry brigade was due to Sheridan's expectation that Averell was participating in, if not leading, the pursuit of Early's Army from Fisher's Hill.)

It turned out that Averell was not nearby and, without any good reason that Sheridan could ascertain, had not taken any part in the pursuit of Early's defeated army, that instead he had gone into bivouac for the night and had left the pursuit almost entirely to the infantry.

According to Sheridan it was nearly noon before Averell arrived and a great deal of precious time had been lost. Sheridan admitted that he and Averell had some hot words, although he did not go into the detail that Averell did. However, hoping that Averell "would retrieve his 'mistake' of the night before," Sheridan directed Averell to proceed at once, join Devin and close with the enemy. Sheridan noted that Averell reached Devin at about 3:00 P.M., just as Devin was "pushing the Confederates so energetically that they were abandoning Mount Jackson." However, Sheridan wrote, Averell failed to accomplish anything.

When Sheridan learned of Averell's intention to withdraw he sent him the note stating that he "desired resolution and actual fighting, with necessary casualties before you retire." Sheridan wrote in his memoirs that shortly thereafter he was informed that Averell had withdrawn: "I then decided to relieve him of command of his division, which I did, ordering him to Wheeling."

Sheridan further commented in his memoirs:

> The removal of Averell was but the culmination of events extending back to the time I assumed command of the Middle Military Division. At the outset, General Grant, fearing discord on account of Averell's ranking Torbert, authorized me to relieve [Averell] ... but I hoped if any trouble of this sort arose, it could be allayed, or at least repressed, during the campaign against Early, since the different commands would often have to act separately.... But Averell's dissatisfaction began to show itself almost immediately after his arrival at Martinsburg, on the 14th of August, and, except when he was conducting some independent expedition, had been manifested on all occasions since.
>
> The failure of Averell to press the enemy the evening of the 23rd [September 23, 1864] gave Early time to collect his scattered forces and take up a position on the east side of the North Fork of the Shenandoah River, his left resting upon the west side of that stream at Rude's Hill, a commanding point about two miles south of Mount Jackson.

When Sheridan attempted to attack, Early, in a leapfrogging retreat, moved up the valley to New Market, where he finally eluded contact.

Sheridan's action in relieving him shattered Averell as nothing else succeeded in doing. For the rest of his life he would try to refute what had happened and sought evidence to substantiate

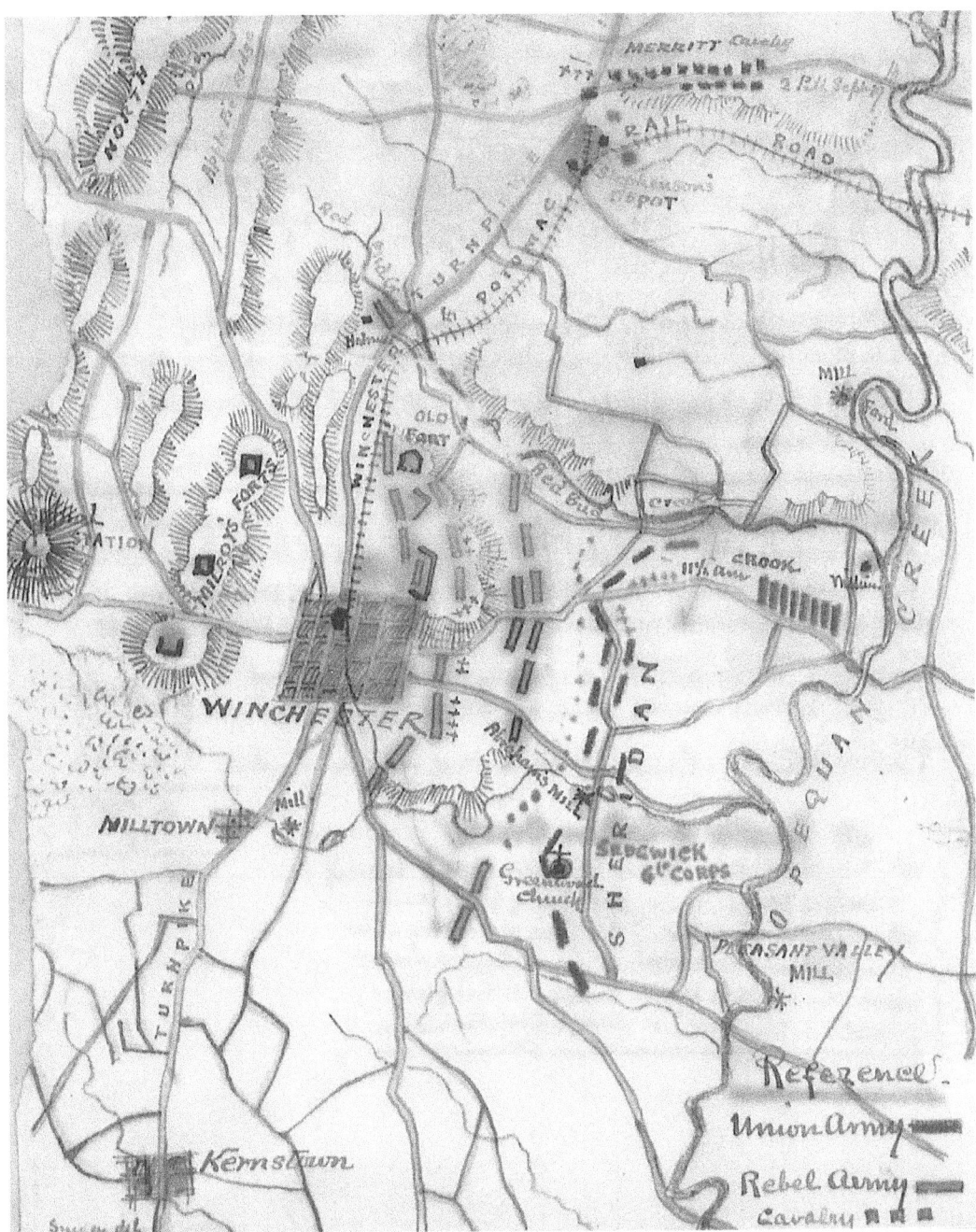

The Third Battle of Winchester, Virginia, on September 19, 1863, was the first of the victories won by Philip H. Sheridan in the Shenandoah Valley. Unlike Confederate Lt. Gen. Jubal A. Early, who had to win only once, Sheridan had to win all the time (Library of Congress).

his belief that his removal had been politically rather than militarily motivated, since he was a lifelong Democrat. The entire incident galled Averell more and more as he got older and reflected upon his military service during the American Civil War, and he believed that his record and reputation had been indelibly blemished by this incident.

Sheridan's orders had not only removed Averell from command, they had also directed him to go to Wheeling, West Virginia, and stay there, where he would be out of Sheridan's sight, out of Sheridan's army, and out of Sheridan's war.

At Averell's request the orders were moderated so that he could return to his home at Bath, New York, to recuperate from both injuries and illness that had afflicted him while on active duty. On March 13, 1865, he was awarded with a promotion to the rank of brevet major general, U.S. Army, for the war. Averell did not participate any further in the war and on May 18, 1865, he quietly resigned both his regular and volunteer commissions.

After the war, Averell was named by President Andrew Johnson to be U.S. consul general to Canada from 1866 to 1869, and was removed when Grant, a Republican, became president, since Averell was a Democrat. Shortly thereafter, Averell becoming both an inventor and a businessman, went into the asphalt business, asphalt having recently been developed as a road paving material.

In 1888, when a Democrat (Grover Cleveland) finally occupied the White House, Averell was quietly reinstated in the army by a special act of Congress and was placed upon the retired list. Averell's return to the army had been the culmination of his dogged and continuous effort to seek retribution for his removal by Sheridan, who died of a massive heart attack on August 5, 1888, after an illness that had lasted for several months. The reinstatement brought with it an appointment as assistant inspector general of soldiers' homes.

His duties included traveling to these hospitals to evaluate conditions for the care and treatment of Union veterans of the American Civil War, writing detailed reports of his findings, and struggling for appropriations to keep the homes running. He held this post until he resigned in 1898. He died two years later, on February 3, 1900, in Bath.

"If he had not fallen afoul of Grant and Sheridan, Averell might have completed the war and could have been noted as an average commander, sometimes failing, sometimes succeeding. After all, such men make up a large part of any army."[1]

PART II

Alfred Thomas Archimedes Torbert

The Man Who Was Promoted Too Far

Brevet Major General of Volunteers Alfred Thomas Archimedes Torbert, who was The Man Who Was Promoted Too Far. Torbert was the perfect example of the Peter Principle in action during the American Civil War (Library of Congress).

8

Commissioned by Both Sides

As the American Civil War began, Alfred T.A. Torbert had the distinction of being a commissioned officer on both sides. Torbert, who was from Delaware, graduated from West Point in 1855 and saw service against the Seminoles on the frontier and in the anti–Mormon Campaign led by Albert S. Johnston in Utah Territory.

He was born on July 1, 1833, in Georgetown, Delaware. Since his graduation from West Point he had been a second lieutenant assigned to the 5th U.S. Infantry Regiment, finally being promoted to first lieutenant on February 25, 1861, just before the war began in April when the Confederates in Charleston Harbor opened fired upon Fort Sumter. By the time he became a general he was a tall, scowling, brown–Dundrearied-whiskered man whose uniform was almost as outlandish as George Armstrong Custer's (although it elicited far less comment), consisting as it did of a sailor shirt with an embroidered star on each of the points of the collar, a star-embroidered jumper, bell-bottom trousers, and a star-studded fedora. In his personal habits, influenced greatly by his father, Torbert attended church by choice, and neither drank nor used intemperate language. However, he also displayed a fun-loving nature and he had a broad sense of humor.

At West Point one of his classmates was William W. Averell and their antipathy during the war (at least on the part of Averell) could possibly be traced all the way back to the competitive atmosphere at West Point, where a cadet's class ranking determined whether or not that individual cadet received a choice of service upon graduation. Averell and Torbert, during their years at West Point, were always very close to each other in class ranking, with Torbert usually a place or two higher than Averell and with Averell generally receiving many more demerits than Torbert.[1]

In addition, Torbert throughout his life sought to be a gentleman, a Southern gentleman. Therefore, he was correct in his dealings with other officers, solicitous in his relations to women, deeply religious, and intensely loyal to the Union.

Averell for one, in his jealously of Torbert, saw Torbert's singleness of purpose as ingenuous. He described Torbert in his partial autobiography, *Ten Years in the Saddle*, as "an amiable industrious man who would cheerfully attempt many things that others could easily do, and was not only not depressed by failure, but seemed not to realize that he had not succeeded."

During the final stages of the secession crisis, Torbert had been on leave while still an infantry officer in the United States Army when he was appointed, to his considerable surprise, to an artillery lieutenancy in the Provisional Army of the Confederate States, which he had no difficulty in deciding not to accept. The confusion probably was due to the fact that Torbert was a native of Delaware, which was both a border state and officially a slave state, although Delaware was a slave state in name only since it was without very many slaves. Due to economic forces slavery had just about died out in Delaware, which did not mean that the population of the state did not include a considerable number of Southern sympathizers. However, for any number of reasons, secession was simply not in the cards for Delaware, or for Torbert, for that matter.

Torbert returned to duty on April 17, 1861, less than a week after the bombardment of Fort Sumter, and was assigned to recruiting duty in New Jersey. During the next five months he apparently made friends and influenced some very important people within the state, because he was appointed colonel of the 1st New Jersey Infantry Regiment on September 16, 1861. (Torbert's greatest political friend throughout the war would be Robert F. Stockton, adjutant general of New Jersey, whose enthusiasm far outweighed his expertise and talents in raising and equipping troops and on whom Torbert by his assistance made a great and deep impression. As a matter of fact, it was Stockton's recommendation that won for Torbert his colonelcy.) The regiment was already serving near Washington and had participated in the First Battle of Manassas/Bull Run the previous July. Torbert was at first reluctant to accept a commission in a volunteer regiment because he recognized the simple fact that any rank he attained in the volunteers would be only temporary and evaporate once the war was over.[2]

Torbert led his veterans (having already been in combat, they counted as such) to the Peninsula, where he saw action at Yorktown and during the Seven Days. Moving back North he was named commander of the First Brigade, First Division, VI Corps, Army of the Potomac, on August 29, 1862. He remained in command of the brigade, except for various leaves of absences, until March 25, 1864.

His brigade participated, as a supporting unit, during the later portion of the Second Battle of Manassas/Bull Run. During the Maryland Campaign that followed on the heels of Second Manassas he was wounded at South Mountain and went on to fight at the battles of Antietam/Sharpsburg, Fredericksburg and Gettysburg (completely missing Hooker's Chancellorsville Campaign) and being promoted to the rank of brigadier general, U.S. Volunteers, on November 29, 1862.

The last corps to arrive at Gettysburg was VI Corps, reaching the battlefield at about 4:30 P.M. on July 2. As such, it became Meade's ace in the hole. It was the only sizeable unit on either side that by the end of the third day of the battle had not been fully engaged. The rest of the units on both sides had been literally fought to exhaustion. After Pickett's Charge had been repulsed on July 3, Lee had waited in his position on Seminary Ridge in vain for Meade to do something, anything, before Lee finally turned south and headed for home back in Virginia.

Even then Meade failed to vigorously pursue Lee, although the cavalry, specifically Brig. Gen. Hugh Judson Kilpatrick's Third Cavalry Division, had managed to catch up with Lee at Falling Waters — where Lee was waiting for the water level of the Potomac River to drop low enough so that the Army of Northern Virginia could cross over to the Virginia side.

This was the reason that at Gettysburg Torbert's brigade was hardly engaged, suffering only 11 casualties, all of them being wounded. Yet Torbert still managed to receive a brevet for his services during the battle. After Gettysburg, Torbert served in both the Bristoe Station and Mine Run operations. He was promoted to the command of the division of which his brigade formed a part on March 25, 1864, as part of the reorganization of the Army of the Potomac; however, he only retained the command for 16 days, until April 10, 1864, when he was suddenly shifted from the infantry, where he had served his entire army career, to take command of the First Division, Cavalry Corps, Army of the Potomac, under Sheridan.

In addition, Torbert, although acknowledged as being "as brave as a lion" and a "magnificent horseman," had been transferred to the Cavalry Corps solely as a compromise in order to resolve the question of how to plug what was the single remaining hole in the Cavalry Corps command structure.

Up to then, Torbert had served the Union army capably and well, but now, with his sudden transfer to the cavalry and his eventual advancement to what amounted to corps command, he may well have become a victim of the "Peter Principle" in that he was transferred and promoted beyond the level of his competence. He served best in a subordinate position as either a brigade or possibly a divisional commander, where he was able to look to guidance from a superior officer. Unfortunately, command of what amounted to a corps was simply too much for him and he was to be a dismal failure whenever he was given an independent command or assignment.

Even then, Philip Henry Sheridan, a man not noted for patience with the human frailties of others, would prove himself to be remarkably patient with Torbert, allowing Torbert three failures—three strikes—before he very quietly got rid of him. There have been some historians who have seen favoritism in Sheridan's unusual behavior (for him) towards Torbert, although there seems to be some evidence that they were not really all that close. Although they were at West Point together it was only for one year. (As a matter of fact, Torbert and his classmate William W. Averell both graduated from West Point in 1855; Sheridan himself had graduated from the military academy in 1853 and when the war started Sheridan was still a second lieutenant. Originally, Sheridan served as a quartermaster, where he learned the value of logistics; then he was made a cavalry regimental commander and was given command of a small cavalry brigade before receiving command of an infantry division, under what could only be called somewhat odd circumstances.)

Torbert graduated from West Point two years after Sheridan. However, during Torbert's first, or plebe, year Sheridan was not at West Point, having been suspended for a year. The next year Sheridan was a first classman while Torbert and Averell were both fourth classmen, and although all three were now upperclassmen and would have definitely known each other that did not mean that they would have necessarily mixed together to any great degree, especially given Sheridan's antithesis to gentlemen, particularly Southern gentlemen.

Torbert's sudden transfer to the cavalry had much to do with the upheavals, which had marked the coming of both Grant and Sheridan to the Army of the Potomac and which threatened to undo at the highest levels the parity with the Confederate cavalry which had been achieved by 1863.

The parity reached by the Union cavalry with their Confederate opponents within the Eastern Theatre of Operations had occurred in part due to the evolution of the Union cavalry trooper into an effective soldier and to the reforms and reorganization initiated during the winter and early spring of 1863 when Joseph Hooker took command of the Army of the Potomac. Although the first commander of the unified Cavalry Corps, George Stoneman, had been something of a misfire, its second commander, Maj. Gen. Alfred Pleasanton, had been determined to make something out of the cavalry of the Army of the Potomac.

Pleasanton succeeded, for the Cavalry Corps had been vital to the victory at Gettysburg. Unfortunately, it had also been in action practically nonstop ever since, and was worn down to a "frazzle." Then in the spring of 1864 the command structure of the Army of the Potomac's Cavalry Corps was thrown into chaos as a result of the Kilpatrick-Dahlgren Raid on Richmond.

Kilpatrick adopted a plan originally proposed by a Union spy in Richmond (one Elizabeth Van Lew) to raid the Confederate capital and free Union POW's being held in various Confederate prisons and prisoner of war camps in and around Richmond.[3] The raid was a complete and total fiasco and papers found on the body of Col. Ulrich Dahlgren, Kilpatrick's second in command, indicated that there were also plans as part of the raid to murder Jefferson Davis and his entire cabinet and then set fire to Richmond in order to cover the retreat. (The spy, Van Lew, managed to rescue Col. Dahlgren's body out from under the collective nose of the Confederates and return it to Dahlgren's family.)

Kilpatrick was relieved of his command. But his career was saved when General William T. Sherman asked for him. "I know Kilpatrick is a hell of a damned fool," Sherman is reported to have growled to those who found his choice of a cavalry commander unusual, to say the least, "but I want just that sort of a man to command my cavalry on this expedition." Kilpatrick commanded a cavalry division during Sherman's Atlanta Campaign and was Sherman's chief of cavalry during his March to the Sea and his March Through the Carolinas, which helped to bring the war to an end.

In addition, Pleasonton, the Cavalry Corps commander, was relieved of his command, although he had opposed the raid due to army politics. Army of the Potomac commander Maj. Gen. George G. Meade had also opposed the raid until he saw which way the political wind was blowing, since the raid had the support of President Lincoln and Secretary of War Edwin M. Stanton. Besides, Meade did not care for Pleasonton due to some unfortunate testimony before the Joint Congressional Committee on the Conduct of the War.

Aside from this, Pleasonton had trouble getting along with the former head of the Cavalry Bureau, George Stoneman, his predecessor in command of the Cavalry Corps, and the new head of Cavalry Bureau, Brig. Gen. James H. Wilson, who was a protégé of the new general-in-chief, Lt. Gen. Ulysses S. Grant. To both Stoneman and Wilson, Pleasonton constantly complained about the quality of the remounts issued to his corps.

Wilson had graduated in 1860, first in his class, from West Point, and his first assignment had been as a topographical engineer in Oregon, where he remained until July 1861. He then served as an engineer on Grant's staff. Wilson had distinguished himself during the Vicksburg Campaign and for engineering duties at Chattanooga just prior to the assault upon Missionary Ridge. These had resulted in his being promoted to the rank of brigadier general of volunteers in the fall of 1863. He actually preceded Grant to the East when he was brought to Washington after Stoneman was reassigned to a combat command in the Western Theatre; Wilson took over as his temporary replacement at the Cavalry Bureau and became in effect a military bureaucrat.

When Wilson (who was known to his two principal subordinates, who were both colonels and somewhat older than he was, as "our young whiz-bang") read a study, originally commissioned by Stoneman, which showed that the horses issued to Pleasonton's Cavalry Corps were breaking down and wearing out because they were not being properly cared for by the troopers, Wilson dug in his heels and Pleasonton was soon on his way to a new job in Missouri. In addition, Wilson (who had never commanded troops in combat before) badly wanted a combat command.

As a sort of harbinger for all this turmoil in the Cavalry Corps high command, John Buford, the hard-hitting commander of the First Cavalry Division, had died on December 16, 1863. Although it is not known exactly what killed him, the symptoms indicate that the most likely cause was typhus, pneumonia, rheumatism, exhaustion, or some combination of them all. The primary cause was the conditions of his service and the zeal with which he performed his duty.[4]

On November 7, 1863, during the Mine Run Campaign, Buford had embarked on his final ride, leading his division across the Hazel River; from there he directed it toward Culpepper Court House. However, on November 21 he was forced by his soon to be fatal illness to quit the field. In his last hours before he died Buford was attended by his aide—Capt. Myles Keogh, who was to die with George A. Custer upon the Little Big Horn battlefield. Becoming delirious, Buford's final words were, "Put guards on all the roads, and don't let the men run to the rear."

With Pleasonton and Kilpatrick gone and Buford dead, there remained only David M. Gregg, Second Cavalry Division commander, to take over if a new commander was to be named from within the Cavalry Corps. Although a competent enough commander, Gregg was not considered nearly aggressive enough for command of the corps.

Soon after arriving in Washington, Grant had discussed his concerns about the Army of the Potomac's cavalry with President Lincoln, noting in his memoirs "the little that has been accomplished by the cavalry so far in the war, and the belief that it was capable of accomplishing much more under a thorough leader. I said that I wanted the very best man in the army for that command."

Henry Halleck — formerly general-in-chief and now chief of staff in Washington and Sheridan's mentor ever since he had helped Halleck clean up the mess he had inherited in St. Louis after he had succeeded John C. Fremont in command there early in the war — had a suggestion: "How would Sheridan do?" "The very man I want," Grant replied.

President Lincoln wanted to give Grant, his chosen military commander, everything he reasonably could. Therefore, he approved Grant's plan for the reorganization of the Cavalry Corps, Army of the Potomac, and although he was not certain of the choice (Lincoln was not particularly impressed with Sheridan at their first meeting) he did agree to the appointment of the man Grant wanted to head the cavalry, Philip H. Sheridan.

Grant's choice of Sheridan was probably influenced by Sheridan's actions in the assault upon Missionary Ridge during the battles for Chattanooga. It was here that Sheridan demonstrated for Grant his relentless style of fighting, when he not only led his infantry division to the top of Missionary Ridge he also was the only officer to reorganize his troops to pursue the fleeing Confederate Army of Tennessee throughout the night. In addition, Grant had soon realized that Sheridan shared his vision about how the war could be brought to an end. Therefore, he supported Sheridan even when his conduct bordered on insubordination and even crossed the line into insubordination. As Sheridan himself admitted after the war,[5] "I was the first to find out that the army was the Confederacy. Now you take those fat property owners and make them poor, they would quickly drop on their marrowbones and cry for peace. I look upon death as a maximum punishment, and I think it is better to take those fat property holders and to make them poor rather than to kill the young men in the field. They did not suffer and as long as they did not they were perfectly content to stay home and in comfort, and sick us at one another as long as they were safe." (In point of fact, that is what Sheridan would do in the Shenandoah Valley and what William T. Sherman did in his March to the Sea in Georgia and his March Through the Carolinas.)[6]

It was not only the Cavalry Corps that was being reorganized. On March 25, 1864, Meade reorganized the entire Army of the Potomac. Based upon his experiences during the Bristoe Station and Mine Run operations, Meade had come to the conclusion that he could have better command control with just three corps instead of the five corps into which the army's infantry was then organized. Therefore, he retained II Corps, V Corps and VI Corps, while amalgamating the units of I Corps and III Corps into the other three army corps.

March 25 was also the day that Pleasonton got the axe. It was apparently Grant who suggested the choice of Wilson to take over Kilpatrick's Third Cavalry Division and Sheridan agreed, making the appointment. Although Sheridan noted in his memoirs that he had asked for Wilson to be appointed to command the Third Cavalry Division he also wrote that General Grant thought highly of Wilson and expected much from his mental and physical ability. However this caused problems, because the two brigade commanders within the Third Cavalry Division, George A. Custer and Henry E. Davies, were both senior to Wilson. In addition, Custer felt that his service of over nine months in command of the Michigan Cavalry Brigade entitled him to the command. To say that James H. Wilson was not one of Custer's favorite persons would have been a definite understatement.

It was therefore decided to exchange Custer and his entire brigade from the Third Cavalry Division for a brigade from the First Cavalry Division. It was also decided to transfer Davies from command of his brigade in the Third Cavalry Division to command of a brigade in David M. Gregg's Second Cavalry Division. This eliminated the problem of seniority, since the commanders of both of the brigades now forming the Third Cavalry Division were colonels.

Although the command problem had been solved in the Third Cavalry Division there was now a new command problem in the First Cavalry Division. Custer and Wesley Merritt — who had been in temporary command of the division since the death of Buford — had both been commissioned as brigadier generals on the same day, although Merritt was considered to be the senior. The problem was that Custer and Merritt were rivals (a fact that Torbert would make considerable use of during his tenure in command of the First Cavalry Division and later the Cavalry Corps) and neither Sheridan nor Grant wanted friction in the First Cavalry Division any more than they had in the Third Cavalry Division. In addition, both Merritt and Custer were seen as Pleasonton's protégés. (However, it would not be very long before they would both be counted among Sheridan's protégés. Other eventual protégés of Sheridan would include Nelson A. Miles and Ranald S. Mackenzie, who would both come to Sheridan's attention rather late in the war.)

Therefore, it was decided that neither one of them could command the division. Torbert, however, was not named to command the division by Sheridan. Instead Torbert received the appointment from Meade, in the aftermath of his reorganization of the army, as something of a compromise candidate, and he was duly transferred from his infantry division in VI Corps, which he had commanded for only about two weeks, to assume command of the First Cavalry Division in order to bring a final solution to this particular problem.

The news that Sheridan had been named to command the Cavalry Corps was not accepted enthusiastically at first. Davies noted that "when the orders appeared that announced the appointment of General Sheridan they were not received with much cordiality.... It was not known that he had ever served with or in command of cavalry, and the prejudice that has always existed and will always exist among mounted troops against being placed under the orders of an officer whose experience has been obtained in other arms of the service, affected to some extent his reception by his new command."

Sheridan and Custer met for the first time on April 15, 1864. Custer had returned to the army on April 14 from his honeymoon, which had been interrupted when he had been tapped to command a scratch force whose job it was to create a diversion for the Kilpatrick-Dahlgren Richmond Raid. Custer did everything he was supposed to do and Meade, for one, called his effort "an almost perfect cavalry raid." It had not been his fault that the Confederates had refused to take the bait and chase him instead of Kilpatrick. Therefore, none of the fecal matter that hit the rotary impeller concerning the raid spilled over onto Custer.

Custer, for one, was troubled by Pleasonton's removal from command of the Cavalry Corps. Although Custer believed that he deserved command of a division he realized that without Pleasonton he was not going to get it, yet. He was also disturbed by a rumor that he was to be transferred out of the Michigan Cavalry Brigade to another command. It was only at this meeting that Custer was actually informed, by Sheridan, about how the Cavalry Corps was to be reorganized.

Custer, to everyone's immense relief, accepted the situation; in reality there was hardly anything else he could have done. "Everything is arranged satisfactorily now," he said after his meeting with Sheridan. He considered Torbert "an old and intimate friend of mine and a very worthy gentlemen." Sheridan and Torbert also stroked Custer's ego by telling him (what may in actuality have been only the simple truth) that his brigade was unmatched in the Army of the Potomac.[7] "I have the finest and best brigade of cavalry in the entire army, I am laboring to make it better still," Custer had proclaimed happily.

For all practical purposes the Cavalry Corps that was poised to participate in Grant's Overland Campaign was starting practically from scratch. The individual troopers may have known what they were supposed to do but it remained to be seen if the new high command of the Cavalry Corps did.

The corps commander and two out of three of the division commanders were brand new to their jobs. Although Sheridan did have some cavalry experience, he had been commanding an infantry division in the Army of the Cumberland since just before the Battle of Perryville in 1862. Torbert had command experience at mostly the brigade level, although he had absolutely no cavalry experience. Wilson not only had no cavalry experience he had absolutely no combat command experience whatsoever. Whether or not Sheridan and his new division commanders and the one remaining veteran cavalry commander, David McMurtie Gregg, could manage to pull at all together remained to be seen.

9

Torbert in the Overland Campaign and at Trevilian Station

As Grant's Overland Campaign of 1864 got underway, Torbert and the First Cavalry Division were tasked with guarding the Army of the Potomac's 4,000-wagon baggage and supply train. Then on May 7, Tobert became ill and had to turn command of the division over to Wesley Merritt.

What Torbert was suffering from was a pilonidal cyst, a congenital condition in which an abscess formed at the base of his spine that periodically became infected, which made riding a horse excruciatingly painful. The problem could relieved only by lancing it and allowing it to drain. However, although it could thus be successfully treated, without modern antibiotics there was no guarantee that the problem would not return. Not wanting to miss the campaign, Torbert had remained with the army as long as he could bear the agony.

Torbert was gone for 18 days before resuming command of his division on May 25, just about in time to participate in Sheridan's second raid and the battles of Trevilian Station, Haw's Shop and Cold Harbor. Thus he entirely missed the Battle of Yellow Tavern that had culminated Sheridan's first raid while in command of the Cavalry Corps, Army of the Potomac. The target had been Richmond but the objective was J.E.B. Stuart, who was mortally wounded and died a few days later, and his cavalry. Lee after Stuart's death was in a quandary as to who to put in charge of his cavalry, so he had the two division commanders, Wade Hampton and Fitzhugh Lee, report directly to him, at least for the time being.

The problem was that Hampton was senior to Fitzhugh Lee, who was General Robert E. Lee's nephew, by virtue of the fact that his commission as a brigadier general was dated a month prior to Fitzhugh Lee's, and when they were both promoted to major general, Hampton's name had been listed first. This was such a narrow margin that Fitzhugh Lee apparently did not consider it to be a margin at all. In addition, there was also personal bad blood between Hampton and Williams C. Wickham, one of Fitzhugh Lee's brigade commanders, because Hampton blamed Wickham for the death of his brother, Lt. Col. Frank Hampton, which had occurred during the First Battle of Brandy Station at the beginning of the Gettysburg Campaign the previous year.

Lee's decision not to make a decision created a new set of problems since there was now no clear chain of command for the cavalry of the Army of Northern Virginia. In turn, when Fitzhugh Lee chose more and more during June 1864 to act upon his own initiative it had the tendency to exacerbate the problem.

When Robert E. Lee's son, W.H.F. "Rooney" Lee, who had been a prisoner of war, was exchanged in March 1864 he was promoted to major general. A new cavalry division was formed for him by taking a brigade from each of Fitzhugh Lee's division and Hampton's division. Now there were three more or less autonomous division commanders. In addition, just after the battle of Yellow Tavern, a new brigade of cavalry had been added to Hampton's division when Brig. Gen. Matthew C. Butler's South Carolina cavalry brigade was transferred from Charleston.

On the evening of May 26, 1864, having found the road to Richmond blocked by Lee's army at the Wilderness and Spotsylvania, Grant tried once again to extend his flank to slip around Lee's army. Sheridan, with Torbert's First Cavalry Division, led the way across the Pamunkey River at Hanover Town Ford on the morning of May 28. Sheridan also had with him Gregg's Second Cavalry Division, and Brig. Gen. D.A. Russell's infantry division of VI Corps was supporting him. Lee, however, had anticipated Grant's move and had two of his divisions of cavalry (Wade Hampton and Rooney Lee's) under Hampton, as senior officer present, waiting and prepared to fight dismounted at Haw's Shop. (Fitzhugh Lee's division remained with the army.)

Neither Lee nor Grant were really sure what the other was doing, so both Hampton and Sheridan proceeded to conduct a reconnaissance. Hampton's purpose was to seek the real position of Grant's infantry. Sheridan was ordered to reconnoiter in the direction of Mechanicsville in order to determine if a strong Confederate force was located there. Gregg's Second Cavalry Division was sent out in that direction. Once the Pamunkey River crossing had been secured by Russell's infantry, Gregg's division was to be followed by Torbert's First Cavalry Division.

By 10:00 A.M. May 28, Gregg and his division had reached Haw's Shop, named after the smithy located there. Discovering an important road junction, Gregg halted his division until reinforcements could arrive. Gregg sent out videttes that in turn collided with Hampton's reconnaissance force. While this was going on Hampton dismounted his main force and established a line of light fieldworks on either side of the road.[1]

Gregg was soon testing this line, dismounting four regiments and ordering them to attack on foot,

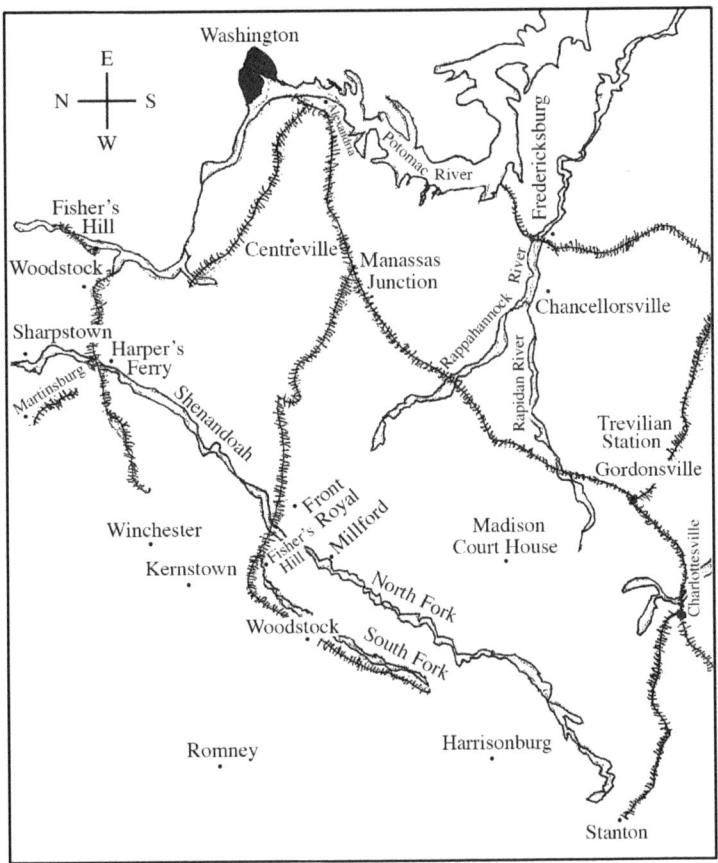

The Shenandoah Valley and Northern Virginia are depicted above. This map can be utilized to follow Union and Confederate movements during most of the Overland Campaign, along with Jubal Early's Raid on Washington and the entirety of Philip H. Sheridan's Shenandoah Valley Campaign of 1864 (Library of Congress).

and soon the two forces were delivering a blistering volume of fire against each other that wore on for the next six hours. Hampton eventually learned from some prisoners he had taken that the cavalry had Union infantry behind them on the south side of the Pamunkey River in direct supporting distance.

This was what Hampton had been seeking to find out with his reconnaissance. Seeing no purpose in continuing the fight, Hampton thereupon ordered an immediate withdrawal. It was then that Custer's Michigan Cavalry Brigade from Torbert's First Cavalry Division arrived. Custer dismounted his troopers and deployed them behind Gregg's division and they joined Gregg's men on the firing line as they opened up a gap in their lines to let his brigade advance. Custer's entire brigade was armed with Spencer repeaters and it was their added weight of fire that gave Sheridan's cavalry a decided advantage.

Feeling the fire from Hampton's troopers slackening as they obeyed his withdrawal order, Custer aligned his troopers in a column of platoons and attacked, hitting the Confederate lines just as Wickham's brigade was withdrawing and causing Wickham's troopers to break, creating a gap between Thomas L. Rosser's Laurel Brigade and two of Butler's rookie South Carolina cavalry regiments that were taking the brunt of the assault. Rosser's veterans withdrew, but the two South Carolina regiments, being rookies, did not know when to retreat and thus were flanked and suffered heavily. There was hand-to-hand fighting when Custer's brigade — joined by the men of Gregg's division — began penetrating the Confederate lines.

A number of the South Carolinians were surrounded and forced to surrender as Hampton pulled the rookies out of the line to keep them from being annihilated. Hampton eventually succeeded in pulling his men back and the Union cavalry was too exhausted and hampered by its own losses to pursue. After a hard day fighting, the Union cavalry had gained nothing except the field.

From there both sides headed for Cold Harbor (which consisted of two hamlets, Old Cold Harbor and New Cold Harbor), with the Confederates winning the race when Fitzhugh Lee's cavalry got there first. Torbert drove to within a mile of Old Cold Harbor on May 30, then on May 31, 1864, Merritt and Custer's brigades made a head-on attack, while Devin's brigade was to hit the Confederate flank. Devin failed, which exasperated Torbert, while Custer's 1st Michigan made a mounted attack late that afternoon just as the dismounted Confederate cavalry were pulling back to their infantry supports. These troops, thinking that a rout was in progress, turned and ran, leaving Sheridan holding Old Cold Harbor. Once he had it, Sheridan soon decided to abandon the place because he learned that Lee's entire army was approaching. When he received orders to hold his ground instead, Sheridan rapidly turned around and then held his ground until relieved by VI Corps. Sheridan, his two cavalry divisions, and VI Corps were thus left occupying Old Cold Harbor while the advanced elements of the Confederate army occupied New Cold Harbor.

During the night of June 1–2, the remainder of the two armies arrived and they both dug in. Ever since the Overland Campaign had begun, it had been one long hard grind, with battle after battle occurring and no rest for either side. Longstreet had been wounded during the Battle of the Wilderness and had been succeeded by Maj. Gen. Richard H. Anderson. Lee's two unwounded corps commanders, Richard Ewell and A.P. Hill, both broke down due to illness and the strain, with Ewell being permanently replaced by Jubal Early, while Lee himself fell ill for about a week. Ewell then took command of the Richmond garrison.

Grant pondered his next move. Sliding over to the left once again would lead the army to the Chickahominy River, where McClellan had come to grief in 1862, and which if successful would drive Lee into the defenses of Richmond. Grant wanted to end the war of attrition whose two to one loss rate in favor of Lee was straining Northern morale. If on the other hand Grant attacked, and if his men moved forward with confidence and were successful, he could drive

Lee's army into the Chickahominy River and maybe, just maybe, annihilate it. In addition, Grant believed that the endless grind had already whipped Lee's army. Therefore, he ordered a frontal assault on the Confederate positions at New Cold Harbor to take place at dawn on June 3, 1864.

However, Lee's army was far from whipped, and Grant's own troops did not move forward with confidence, only with resignation. By the time it was over, Grant had lost 7,000 men while inflicting only 1,500 casualties on Lee. It was the worst day for the Army of the Potomac since Fredericksburg.

Due to the debacle at Cold Harbor, Grant decided to change his strategy. His plan now was to cross the James River and move against the crucial railroad nexus at Petersburg, 25 miles south of Richmond. If he could capture Petersburg, while David Hunter and his small Union army in the Shenandoah Valley took Lynchburg or Charlottesville or both, Lee's army would be completely cut off from its sources of supply and have only three options—come out into the open and fight, flee, or surrender.

Grant decided to use his cavalry in a new raid aimed primarily at diverting Lee's attention away from his movement south to cross the James River. (This turned out to be the only objective to be actually achieved by the raid.) Sheridan's other objectives would be the important railroad junction at Charlottesville; once that was taken and destroyed Grant wanted Sheridan to join Hunter and his Lynchburg expedition in the vicinity of Charlottesville. This combined force could then march east and join Grant at Petersburg. Grant also hoped that this combined operation would see the destruction of the railroad junction at Gordonsville along with the James River Canal and the Virginia Central Railroad after Hunter and Sheridan joined forces.[2]

Hunter, for his part, was informed that the destruction of the canal and the railroad were of the highest importance. It was intended that Hunter was to advance upon Lynchburg and take it in a single day and then turn east. If, however, Hunter did not receive his new orders until his expedition was already in the Shenandoah Valley between Staunton and Lynchburg, under these new orders he was to turn east until he struck the Lynchburg branch of the Virginia Central Railroad. Hunter was then to move eastward, along the railroad, destroying it as he moved until he affected the junction with Sheridan.

Wilson's Third Cavalry Division would remain with the main body of the Army of the Potomac so that there would be some Union cavalry available to screen the movement across the James River; in addition, Sheridan gave orders for all his dismounted troopers to report to Wilson. Sheridan broke camp on June 7, taking the First and Second Cavalry divisions with him.

Sheridan intended, following the north bank of the North Anna River, to strike the railroad at Trevilian Station, 28 miles due east of Charlottesville. Hampton and Fitzhugh Lee, with their cavalry divisions, were dispatched in pursuit, actually reaching Trevilian Station before Sheridan on June 11. Sheridan sent Torbert and Merritt towards the station. Hampton was also in motion, planning to strike at Clayton's Store, an important crossroads three miles northeast of Trevilian Station, where Sheridan had bivouacked his troopers on June 10.

Sheridan and Hampton had each planned to strike first thing in the morning but Sheridan moved first, hitting Hampton at 6:30 A.M. with Merritt's and Devin's brigades of Torbert's First Cavalry Division, while keeping Gregg and his Second Cavalry Division standing back en echelon to the left.

Meanwhile, under Sheridan's orders, Custer had taken his Michigan Cavalry Brigade around the Confederate right, screened by a thick stand of woods. Hampton, planning a dismounted attack at Clayton's Store, had left 800 lightly guarded horses, artillery caissons, supply wagons, and ambulances at the station. When Custer saw this he sent his 5th Michigan Cavalry Regiment charging into the conglomeration. In a matter of minutes that regiment was snatching up all the horses, prisoners, and supplies it could grab, and then it began pursuing the fugitives north to Gordonsville, when Fitzhugh Lee, riding towards the sound of the guns, hit Custer from the east, separating him from the 5th Michigan. Hampton, realizing what was happening, rapidly disengaged a portion of his forces—Brig. Gen. Thomas L. Rosser and the Laurel Brigade—opposing Sheridan and sent it back to Trevilian Station.

As a result of Hampton's quick response Custer was left cut off and surrounded. Rosser and his Laurel Brigade were pressing Custer's Michigan Cavalry Brigade from the front and the right while Fitzhugh Lee and his division were attacking his left and rear. Custer and his entire brigade were facing total destruction and possibly surrender. Of course, the Confederates had by now recaptured everything that had been captured from them by the 5th Michigan at the beginning of the fight. The 5th Michigan itself was scattered and a number of its troopers were taken prisoner, while the remnants of the regiment rejoined Custer when and as they could. Some portions of the 5th Michigan would not rejoin the Michigan Cavalry Brigade until after the battle.

Custer realized that he would simply have to hold on until Sheridan, with Torbert and Gregg, managed to cut their way through to Trevilian Station. He took his brigade and positioned it in a circle on the open ground to which it had been driven. In effect this was Custer's first last stand.[3]

The fighting swirled for hours while Custer wondered just where the heck were Sheridan, Torbert and Gregg. At the same time, they were wondering where Custer was. Torbert and Sheridan knew that Custer was in action, but what they did not know was exactly where. Eventually growing weary of the standoff, Sheridan dispatched a brigade of Gregg's division to attack and ordered Torbert to cut his way through to Custer while another of Gregg's brigades moved around Louisa Court House and forced Rosser to let go of Custer's rear.

As Rosser and Fitzhugh Lee moved off, Custer reformed his 7th Michigan Cavalry Regiment, which pursued and recaptured most of Custer's wagons, which he had lost earlier in the fight due to the cowardly and incompetent actions of the officer who was in charge of the brigade's baggage train.

Who actually won at Trevilian Station has been disputed ever since, particularly as Hampton and Sheridan both claimed victory. However, by getting between Sheridan and Gordonsville, Hampton prevented Sheridan from moving further west. In addition, Sheridan claimed in his memoirs that he had learned that Hunter was no longer headed for Charlottesville but was moving up the Shenandoah Valley.[4] Another factor was that Sheridan's troopers had expended much of their ammunition. Although Sheridan's cavalry could live off the land and thereby feed themselves and their horses, there was no way to replenish their ammunition supplies. In addition, there was also the large number of wounded to deal with.

Sheridan claimed that his decision to abandon the raid had been due to the lack of ammunition and the fact that Hunter was no longer moving on Charlottesville as he had been ordered to do, and instead was moving in the opposite direction towards Lynchburg. The final factor, according to Sheridan, was the rumor that reinforcements of infantry from Ewell's corps were being sent to Hampton and Fitzhugh Lee. (These rumors were instigated by Lee's attempt to relieve the Siege of Petersburg by sending Ewell's successor, newly promoted Lt. Gen. Jubal Early, and II Corps, Army of Northern Virginia, to the Shenandoah Valley to reinforce the Valley District Army there; Lee's actions had in part been in response to the defeat and death of the previous Valley District commander, Brig. Gen. W.E. "Grumble" Jones, and also in response to Sheridan's raid.)

Sheridan decided that he could not safely continue his advance and therefore he broke off the raid after disrupting the railroad between Trevilian Station and Louisa Court House, and returned to the Army of the Potomac, arriving near Petersburg on June 25.[5]

Although Sheridan had failed in achieving all but one of his objectives, Lee never did tumble to the fact that Grant was shifting his army to Petersburg until it was almost too late, well after elements of the Army of the James and the Army of the Potomac arrived at Petersburg, thus fulfilling the only item on the list of objectives that Grant really required that Sheridan do.

Robert E. Lee certainly agreed with Hampton that it was a victory, for shortly thereafter he officially named Wade Hampton his new chief of cavalry. However, Hampton, like Stuart, remained a major general, never raising to the rank of lieutenant general that was generally the rank of a corps commander in the Provisional Army of the Confederate States.

10

Chief of Cavalry

The day before Sheridan arrived at Petersburg, Lt. Col. Henry Pleasants, 48th Pennsylvania Infantry Regiment, presented his plan for digging a mine and blowing up a portion of the Confederate works at Petersburg to provide a gap through which the Army of the Potomac could advance and take the vital railroad junction. Maj. Gen. Ambrose E. Burnside, commanding IX Corps (of which Pleasant's 48th Pennsylvania was a part), both liked and approved the plan. But Meade and Grant never officially acted upon it. Pleasants, however, did not wait for official approval from Army of the Potomac headquarters, and began work on the mine on June 25. (Although the mine project did not have official approval, no one in authority interfered with it because it gave the soldiers something with which to occupy their time as the siege wore on.)

The mine was detonated at 5:16 A.M. July 30, 1864, killing close to 300 Confederate soldiers outright. However, the assault was bungled (due primarily to interference from Meade and the fact that the commander of what was eventually to become the assault division was drunk, incompetent, and a coward) and nothing was accomplished except for another considerably long casualty list in what became known as the Battle of the Crater.

It was also during July that that the new commander of the Confederate Valley District, Lt. Gen. Jubal Early, conducted his Washington Raid, which threatened the Union capital itself. It was the Union response to this raid that resulted in the Shenandoah Valley Campaign of 1864.

Torbert, in his report on the campaign, wrote that he was ordered on July 30 to take his First Cavalry Division, which was then encamped at Lee's Mill, and move to City Point so that the entire command could be embarked to move by water to Washington, D.C. By August 9, 1864, the division had been concentrated at Harper's Ferry. Torbert had preceded his division, arriving on the evening of August 8, where he reported to Sheridan, who the previous day had been made commander of the new Middle Military Division. It was at this meeting that Sheridan appointed Torbert to be his chief of cavalry for the Middle Military Division and to take command of the cavalry of the Army of the Shenandoah in the field. In effect Torbert would command Sheridan's Provisional Cavalry Corps.

There were those, however, who wondered if Torbert was up to the demands of corps command. One of these was Capt. George B. Sanford, a former aide to the late John Buford, whom Torbert had inherited upon assuming command of what had been Buford's First Cavalry Division. Sanford described Torbert as a "dashing, handsome fellow ... a beautiful horseman, and as brave as a lion; but his abilities were hardly equal to such large commands."

Aside from Torbert's own First Cavalry Division, which was placed under the command of Brig. Gen. Wesley Merritt, the cavalry of the Middle Military Division also consisted of the First and Second Cavalry divisions, Department of West Virginia, that were under the command of Alfred Duffie and W.W. Averell respectively.

Normally, command of the cavalry should have gone to Averell as senior officer present.

However, Torbert had been his chief subordinate for the past five months and Sheridan had seen Torbert in action during such conflicts as Haw's Shop, Cold Harbor and Trevelian Station, where Torbert (being under close supervision by Sheridan) had performed well. As a matter of fact, Sheridan never stated why he had picked Torbert to be his chief of cavalry. Possible reasons included:

1. Sheridan may simply have wanted to have his cavalry commanded by an officer with whom he was familiar since he had never before served with Averell.
2. He may have been sending a message that with Sheridan in command things were going to be different.
3. It is possible that Sheridan had heard from his friend George C. Crook, and others, that Averell had not performed well at the Second Battle of Kernstown.
4. Hooker's relief of Averell, after the Chancellorsville Campaign, and his stated reasons for that relief might have influenced him.
5. All of the above.

At the time, Duffie's First Cavalry Division, Department of West Virginia, was at Hancock, Maryland, while Averell's Second Cavalry Division, Department of West Virginia, was at Cumberland, Maryland. Both of these divisions were immediately ordered to join Sheridan's army by the shortest practicable route. In addition, a new cavalry brigade was formed and placed under the command of Col. Charles R. Lowell. It joined the First, Second and Reserve Brigades of the First Cavalry Division as the Third Brigade. The original three brigades of the division were placed on the army's left flank at Berryville, while Lowell's brigade was placed on the right flank at Summit Point. (The rest of the Army of the Shenandoah consisted of VI Corps that had been drawn from the Army of the Potomac, XIX Corps that had been sent from the Gulf of Mexico to reinforce Grant, and the Army of West Virginia/VIII Corps, which was already on the scene.)

The very first thing, however, that Sheridan had done, even before he summoned Torbert to announce his advancement to chief of cavalry, according to his memoirs, had been to closet himself with 2nd Lt. John R. Meigs, a recent graduate of West Point and his new topographical engineer, who began preparing a series of maps. Meigs was familiar with every important road and stream and all points worthy of note west of the Blue Ridge, and was particularly well equipped with knowledge of the Shenandoah Valley, even down to location of the farmhouses. He clearly pointed out the configurations of the valley, indicating the strongest points for Confederate defense, at the same time illustrating, scientifically and forcibly, the particular disadvantages under which all of Sheridan's predecessors had operated and labored.

During the first movement of Sheridan's Army of the Shenandoah up the valley, which began on August 10, Torbert recorded in his report that Merritt's First Cavalry Division was in a large skirmish near Newtown on August 12, in which it met and threw back the rear guard of Early's Confederate Valley District Army.

On August 15, Duffie and his division reported personally to Torbert and were ordered to Berryville, while Averell reported the arrival of his division at Martinsburg. Averell was ordered to remain at Martinsburg for the time being. On the same day, Merritt, with Custer and Devin's brigades, moved over to the Front Royal and Winchester Pike and the next day were attacked by two brigades of infantry and one of cavalry with artillery support. Merritt moved out, met the attack, and totally routed the Confederates, driving them across the Shenandoah River.

Then, on August 17, orders were issued to fall back. On the same day, Brig. Gen. James H. Wilson's Third Cavalry Division, Cavalry Corps, Army of the Potomac, reported to Torbert at Winchester, having been ordered to reinforce Sheridan's cavalry. (Grant and Meade retained one division of the cavalry corps—David M. Gregg's Second Cavalry Division—to remain at

Petersburg.) The Army of the Shenandoah moved back down the valley, being covered by Torbert's cavalry, skirmishing with Early's advance guard as they went.

During this time, Torbert noted, orders were sent to Averell for him to move his division to Charlestown. Sheridan then ordered Averell, according to Torbert's report, to move in the direction of Shepardstown and cover the fords across the Potomac River. Torbert reported that by the morning of August 18 Wilson arrived at Summit Point and took position on the right of the infantry and was in communication with Averell on his right, in the vicinity of Smithfield; Merritt was in the vicinity of Berryville; and Duffie had been ordered to Charlestown.

The retreat was continued to Halltown on August 22. Merritt moved to Shepardstown, Wilson moved back to Halltown, Duffie moved to Point of Rocks, Maryland, and crossed over to Harper's Ferry, and Averell had crossed the Potomac and was at Fair Play, Maryland, watching the Potomac River crossings. (Torbert in his report made absolutely no mention whatsoever of having any problems with Averell due to the seniority question. Torbert also does not mention Sheridan's irritation with Averell's move across the Potomac River, even though Averell's written orders from Sheridan had allowed Averell this option.)

For the next two days the cavalry remained in its positions and then, on August 25, Torbert led Merritt and Wilson's cavalry divisions on a reconnaissance, where his two divisions successfully engaged a Confederate infantry division that was on its way to Shepardstown, before having Merritt return to Halltown. Wilson was sent across the Potomac, through Harper's Ferry, to Boonsborough, Maryland. Duffie's division was then ordered to Cumberland, Maryland, where it would be remounted.

Sheridan then began another movement up the Shenandoah Valley, until by September 5 his army was in the vicinity of Winchester, where it remained until the Third Battle of Winchester/Opequon Creek, which was fought on September 19. By this time the units that had formed Lowell's Third Brigade, First Cavalry Division, had been mostly detached and Lowell's own 2nd Massachusetts Cavalry Regiment had joined the Reserve Brigade, which then came under his command.

During this period Sheridan had been informed by Averell that his scouting parties north of Winchester had determined that two of Early's infantry divisions were on their way to Martinsburg, 20 miles away. Early had left his other two infantry divisions at Winchester. It was Early's intention to disrupt repairs to the Baltimore & Ohio Railroad. However, this movement opened up the possibility that Sheridan, if he moved fast enough, could attack and destroy the entire Valley District Army piecemeal before it could be reconcentrated. Early was saved, however, by an intercepted telegram stating that Grant had just completed a meeting with Sheridan. Early immediately realized that this could only mean that Sheridan was about to go on the offensive, whereupon Early took the two divisions that were with him and hurried back to Winchester.

On September 19, Sheridan issued orders for a complicated series of infantry and cavalry maneuvers designed to achieve a double envelopment of Early's entire Valley District Army. The VI Corps and XIX Corps would attack Ramseur's isolated infantry division east of Winchester; the Army of West Virginia/VIII Corps would follow Wilson's Third Cavalry Division southward around Early's right flank. Torbert, with the rest of the cavalry (Merritt's and Averell's divisions), was to swing northward, around Early's left flank, striking his rear above Winchester. If Early attempted to escape down the Valley Pike, Crook would stop him. The entire plan depended upon speed and surprise rather than numbers.

The one thing that Sheridan, unfortunately, did not take into account as he planned his battle was the innate slowness of the Army of the Potomac, as represented by VI Corps. In addition, the terrain around Winchester did not lend itself to large-scale troop movements. VI Corps and XIX Corps had to use the Berryville Pike, which ran through a two-mile long canyon and thick, bushy, woods before entering a cleared plateau, two miles east of Winchester. Paralleling the road were Red Bud Run to the north and Abraham Creek to the south, both of which emptied into Opequon Creek.

Wilson's Third Cavalry Division would have to force a crossing over Opequon Creek, clear the road through the canyon, slide to the left to allow the infantry to pass, and do all of this under fire. Torbert, who was located further to the north with Averell and Merritt's cavalry divisions, was also directed to cross Opequon Creek, drive through the Confederates at Stevenson's Depot with his two cavalry divisions, then turn south to sweep up the Valley Pike.

Torbert reported that for the cavalry the Third Battle of Winchester began when Wilson's division moved (at 3:00 A.M.) on the Berryville and Winchester Pike in the direction of Winchester, in advance of the infantry. Merritt moved out on the right to cross Opequon Creek at Seivers and Locke's fords and Averell was ordered to cross Opequon Creek and move on the Winchester and Martinsburg Pike, in the direction of Winchester.

Wilson galloped up the canyon, scattering Confederate pickets. Then his division dismounted to hold against a determined counterattack by Ramseur's infantry division. Maj. Gen. Horatio G. Wright, commanding VI Corps (disregarding instructions calling for speed), had brought his baggage train with him; this compelled XIX Corps to wait until the road was clear before it could move through the canyon, which was not completed until after 10:00 A.M.

In response to Ramseur's call for help, Early had rushed from Stephenson's Depot to Winchester and by 10:00 A.M. he had three of his four infantry divisions in line across the Berryville Pike from Red Bud Run to Abraham's Creek. Early's other infantry division, with the bulk of his cavalry, remained at Stephenson's Depot with orders to fall back upon his main line if pressed.

Sheridan's intricate plan had been wrecked by a number of factors. These included:

1. The traffic jam caused by Wright's VI Corps baggage train, which held up XIX Corps.
2. Early's prompt reaction to the attack.
3. Sheridan's decision to funnel 20,000 men through a single, narrow, canyon.

Sheridan thereupon hastily cobbled together an assault column from the troops that were finally, slowly, moving through the canyon, aligning a single division at a time on either side of the Berryville Pike. His attack kicked off at noon.

The problem now was that Sheridan's new attack plan called for VI Corps to be guided by the Berryville Pike. Sheridan did not realize that 600 yards from the mouth of the canyon the pike turned south, which carried VI Corps away from XIX Corps and created a gap that Early soon noticed and exploited. Early's attack thus caused XIX Corps to break and flee into some woods.

Sheridan refused to panic and the two batteries of artillery that he had taken the precaution to place in a standby position gave him just enough time to summon David Russell's VI Corps division from where it had been placed in reserve to plug the gap. Russell was killed, but not before sending Emory Upton and his brigade into the woods, where XIX Corps had fled. It suddenly broke from concealment, shattered the Confederate flank, and halted the Confederate counterattack. There was then a lull as Sheridan waited for word from Torbert.

Merritt's crossing, Torbert noted in his official campaign report, was opposed by Confederate infantry, but his division drove them about a mile and a half back to a secondary position, where they succeeded in holding Merritt in check for some time, being posted behind stone walls and hastily erected fieldworks. Meanwhile, Torbert reported, Averell was steadily driving the Confederate cavalry before him in the direction of Winchester and proceeded to get into the rear of the Confederate infantry who were opposing Merritt, causing the Confederate troops to abandon their position and fall back. With the obstruction posed by the Confederate infantry removed, Merritt moved forward rapidly with his division and joined Averell in the vicinity of Stephenson's Depot.

At mid-afternoon, after receiving no word from Torbert, Sheridan shifted Crook's Army of West Virginia/VIII Corps troops from his left flank to his right flank. By this move Sheridan abandoned any hope of bottling up the Confederates inside Winchester. Sheridan's orders to Crook (as noted in his official report) called upon him "to act as a turning column, to find the left of the enemy's line, strike it on the flank and rear, [and] break it up." (Crook, supported by at least one eyewitness—after his friendship with Sheridan had cooled following the war— claimed that Sheridan had merely said "to look out for our right," thus giving Crook a claim to take credit for the flanking maneuver. If Crook was correct, what Sheridan was doing was allowing him to act upon his own initiative as the situation developed, thus demonstrating the fact that only those commanders who failed to act upon their own initiative were ever blackballed by Sheridan.)

Crook threw one of his two small divisions forward into the woods occupied by the routed XIX Corps on the Union right. The other division Crook took across Red Bud Run, beyond the Confederate left. Then the two divisions attacked simultaneously, hitting Gordon's Confederate infantry division in front and on the flank, forcing it back. Upon Crook's success on the right, Sheridan had his center and left advance.

At that moment Torbert's cavalry (Merritt and Averell's divisions) arrived. By this time the Confederate line was bent into the shape of an inverted "L" on the plateau east of Winchester.

Both of the cavalry divisions with him, Torbert reported, were quickly reformed to advance upon Winchester, with Averell on the right of the Valley Pike and Merritt on the left of the pike. According to Torbert his two divisions were now about four miles from Winchester and began advancing at a rapid pace. Near Winchester, Torbert and his two cavalry divisions came upon the left flank of Early's army, which was hotly engaged with Sheridan's infantry. Torbert's troopers immediately charged, at first slowly, then faster and faster moving down the pike as they approached Early's line. The sudden massed charge of Torbert's two cavalry divisions on Early's flank, unchecked by any Confederate cavalry, caused Early's infantry to break, completely buckling Early's line and driving his entire army through Winchester. Only darkness stopped the pursuit.

The pursuit was resumed at first light on September 20, with Averell moving on the Back Road to Cedar Creek; Merritt on the Valley Pike to Cedar Creek; and Wilson, through Stephensburg and Cedarville, on the Front Royal Pike, to confront Williams C. Wickham's Confederate cavalry division that was tasked with holding open Early's line of retreat through the New Market Gap. The pursuit ended when it was found that the Confederates had forted up in the massive natural fortress that was Fisher's Hill.

Sheridan, still seeking the total annihilation of Early's army, was presented with a plan by Crook for using a turning movement to force Early off of Fisher's Hill; if at the same time Torbert and part of his cavalry could swing around Early's army, through the Luray Valley, and close New Market Gap, Sheridan would have Early exactly where he wanted him. With Early caught between Torbert's anvil and the hammer formed by Sheridan's infantry (specifically VI Corps and XIX Corps) the entire Confederate Valley District Army could possibly be destroyed.

Torbert, taking Merritt and two of his brigades, headed off to join Wilson at Front Royal, leaving Devin's brigade from the First Cavalry Division and Averell's cavalry division with Sheridan. Torbert started off for the Luray Valley and Sheridan had every expectation of success.

11

Failure at Milford

Before Torbert — with Custer's and Lowell's brigades of Merritt's First Cavalry Division — joined Wilson's Third Cavalry Division at Front Royal on September 21, Wilson had had himself a busy 24 hours.

Sheridan — having learned that Williams C. Wickham's Confederate cavalry division was on the other side of Massanutten Ridge at Front Royal — had sent Wilson to drive them out. Wilson therefore had first driven Wickham's cavalry across the North Fork of the Shenandoah River. Then, at daybreak September 21, Wilson made his follow-up attack early in the morning, while under cover of a dense fog.

Because of the fog, Wilson had been afraid that the individual units within his division would lose touch with each other. Therefore, when he ordered his bugler to sound the charge he also ordered that it be picked up and repeated by all of the buglers in his division, all 250 of them. When the moment came, the high imperious notes of 250 bugles echoed up and down the Blue Ridge and some who witnessed it said it sounded more like 10,000 buglers than a mere 250. Under the sound of the bugles came the muted sound of rolling thunder from the hooves of the horses of Wilson's troopers as they charged. Wickham and his division could not stand against them and they were driven back to Gooney Run.

When Torbert and Merritt arrived Wilson was still stalled there, about six miles south of Front Royal. When Wickham learned that Wilson had been joined by Torbert, who had brought with him Merritt and two of his three brigades of cavalry, he ordered a withdraw under cover of night, moving south to Milford, about 12 miles from Luray, while Torbert's united force camped north of Gooney Run.

All of the bridges over Gooney Run had been destroyed, precluding a frontal attack along Wickham's presumed position.[1] In addition, at this point the Luray Valley narrowed so as to seem to preclude a flanking movement. Torbert — not yet realizing that Wickham was already leaving the area using the darkness to hide his movements — decided to attempt a flanking maneuver anyway. At midnight Torbert sent Custer and his Michigan Cavalry Brigade from Front Royal. Custer followed the South Fork of the Shenandoah River to McCoy's Ford. He crossed the river and by a roundabout route placed himself and his brigade in what was thought to be Wickham's rear. If Wickham had not already retreated to Milford it is likely that Torbert's maneuver would have succeeded, and from there Torbert could have, upon eliminating Wickham, moved into a position blocking Early's retreat and accomplish what Sheridan had intended when he had first sent Torbert and his cavalry around Early's army.

At the same time, Wilson had been instructed by Torbert to take the two brigades of his division, positioned north of Gooney Run, and attack the Confederates from across the stream when Custer appeared on their right flank and rear. Custer arrived on schedule, but when Wilson moved out to make the attack it was found that Wickham and his division had already decamped during the night.

Torbert pursued Wickham with his entire force and Wickham's cavalry division was found at 7:00 A.M. September 22, 1864, in a position behind Overall's Run at Milford. Wickham's troopers had been constructing fieldworks all along their position since they had arrived from Gooney's Run. Soon they had made it even more formidable than the position they had occupied at Gooney's Run. The Confederate cavalry was posted, dismounted, on a bluff above the stream, giving them the advantage of holding the high ground. Their left flank was anchored upon the South Fork of the Shenandoah River, while their right flank was anchored upon a spur of the Blue Ridge Mountains. Thus both of Wickham's flanks were protected and neither would be easy to turn. Of Wickham's two brigades, one was positioned along the edge of the river, while the other was placed between Milford and the mountain, with Wickham's horse artillery occupying a knoll to the rear.

The Confederate position presented a problem, which Torbert was totally unable to solve. However, it leaves one wondering what Merritt, Custer or Lowell might have been able to do on their own, without Torbert.

However, it was Wilson's division that made first contact with Wickham's strong position. Upon making contact, Wilson brought forward his own horse artillery, thus opening up the fight, what there was of it, with an exchange of artillery fire. Soon Wilson's dismounted skirmishers were adding their carbine fire to the artillery fire. Because Torbert was reluctant to make a full-scale assault on what appeared to be such a strong position the skirmishing continued for several hours. Late in the afternoon, Torbert attempted a feint toward the Confederate dismounted cavalry brigade occupying the ground between Milford and the mountain spur, while at the same time attempting to outflank on the right the brigade that was posted along the river.

Confederate Col. Thomas Munford (who due to Army of Northern Virginia politics would never be promoted to the rank of brigadier general, which he showed he so richly deserved here, and in a dozen other battles and situations) commanded the brigade along the river. He was also directing Wickham's entire division at this time, since Wickham had left the area to confer with Early. Munford countered Torbert's movement by sending a squadron to support the 2nd Virginia Cavalry Regiment that was covering the flank. Munford then attempted a ruse using three buglers. The buglers were posted, with enough space between them for a full regiment. At a given signal they blew the charge. Coupled with the musketry and carbine fire they were receiving from the reinforced 2nd Virginia, Torbert's overly tentative move to turn the flank was itself turned back.

For some reason, whatever aggressiveness and initiative Torbert possessed deserted him with an abrupt suddenness. He thereupon disengaged and retired northward down the Luray Valley. In his official report, Torbert attempted to explain his actions: "Not knowing that the army had made an attack at Fisher's Hill, and thinking that the sacrifice would be too great to attack without that knowledge, I concluded to withdraw to a point opposite McCoy's Ferry."

All in all this was a rather lame excuse. Torbert certainly knew that his Luray Valley expedition was intended to support an attack on Fisher's Hill. In addition, by this time Torbert should have known Sheridan well enough not to be in any doubt whether or not Sheridan would actually attack Fisher's Hill.

Sheridan was disappointed, at the very least. His rage at Torbert's failure, compounded when Averell failed to pursue Early's beaten army, was so great that somebody's head was going to have to roll. Since Averell was handy and Torbert was not, the head that rolled (this time) was Averell's.

Torbert's own head was safe, now that Sheridan's rage had been appeased. But still, Sheridan could never see any justification for Torbert's performance, or lack of it. He never understood just what had happened, and it appears he brooded about it. Torbert was going to have to watch his step in the future.

In his official report on the Shenandoah Valley Campaign Sheridan stated, "Had General Torbert driven this defile and reached New Market, I have no doubt but that we would have captured the entire rebel army." Twenty-four years after the incident, when his memoirs were published in 1888, just prior to his own death, he still didn't understand what had happened and said so, loudly.

One must take care when using memoirs or even official reports as a source. In memoirs, such as Sheridan's, there can be a gap of many years between the event itself and the retelling of that event. Such a gap can produce "inaccuracies." In official reports (as well as memoirs) sometimes, in an effort to appear to be more on top of things than the author actually was at the time, there can be "exaggerations." Sheridan in his memoirs and official reports sometimes allowed such "inaccuracies" and "exaggerations" to escape. In addition, Sheridan could also be two-faced by slanting what he was writing for his particular audience, whether it was Grant (in the case of his dispatches and official reports) or the general public (where his memoirs were concerned). In addition, he tended to forget to mention or glossed over the embarrassing parts. But, in this case it appears that he can be taken at his word, as stated in his memoirs:

> Our success was very great, yet I anticipated results still more pregnant. Indeed, I had hopes of capturing the whole of Early's army before it reached New Market, and with this object in view, during the maneuvers of the 21st [September 21, 1864] I had sent Torbert up the Luray Valley with Wilson's division and two of Merritt's brigades, in the expectation that he would drive Wickham out of the Luray Pass by Early's right and by crossing the Massanutten Mountains near New Market, gain his rear. Torbert started in good season, and after some slight skirmishing at Gooney Run, got as far as Milford, but failed to dislodge Wickham. In fact he made little or no attempt to force Wickham from his position, and with only a feeble effort withdrew. I heard nothing at all from Torbert during the 22nd [September 22, 1864], and supposing that everything was progressing favorably.
>
> I was astonished and chagrined to learn on the morning of the 23rd [September 23, 1864], at Woodstock, to receive the intelligence that he [Torbert] had fallen back to Front Royal and the Buckton Ford. My disappointment was extreme, but there was now no help for the situation save to renew and emphasize Torbert's orders, and this was done at once, notwithstanding that I thought the delay had so much diminished the chances of his getting in the rear of Early as to make such a result a very remote possibility, unless, indeed far greater zeal was displayed than had been in the first attempt to penetrate the Luray Valley.
>
> The Battle of Fisher's Hill was, in a measure, a part of the Battle of Opequon Creek [Third Battle of Winchester]; that is to say, it was an incident in the pursuit resulting from that action. In many ways, however, it was much more satisfactory, and particularly so because the plan arranged on the evening of the 20th [September 20,1864] was carried out to the very letter by Generals Wright, Crook, and Emory, not only in all of their preliminary maneuvers but also during the fight itself. The only drawback was with the cavalry, and to this day I have been unable to account satisfactorily for Torbert's failure. No doubt Wickham's position near Milford was a strong one, but Torbert ought to have made a fight. Had he been defeated in this, his withdraw rather then to await the results of Fisher's Hill would have been justified, but it does not appear that he made any serious effort to dislodge the Confederate cavalry; his impotent attempt not only chagrined me very much, but occasioned much unfavorable comment throughout the army.

Sheridan was not the only one who could not understand what had happened. Col. James H. Kidd, commander of Custer's 6th Michigan Cavalry Regiment, and the man who would shortly succeed Custer in command of the Michigan Cavalry Brigade, was one of those for whom Torbert's actions were incomprehensible. He was probably one of the people who were voicing unfavorable comments over Torbert's action, or lack of it, within the army.[2]

According to Kidd:

> On the 22nd [of September], Torbert was sent to Milford in the Luray Valley, taking Wilson's and Merritt's divisions. His orders were to break through one of the passes in the Massanutten Mountains and come out in the rear of Early's army, where Crook's flanking maneuver on the

other side would have driven him off of Fisher's Hill. Crook's attack was completely successful and Early was "whirling up the valley" again. Torbert made a fiasco of it.

He allowed Wickham, with at most two small brigades, to hold him at bay and without making any fight of it. I remember very well how the Michigan Brigade lay in a safe position at the rear of the line listening to the firing and was not ordered in at all. If Custer or Merritt had been in command it would have been different.

Torbert resumed his retreat on the morning of September 23 when he pulled out of his camp at McCoy's Ford. Wilson's division, on Torbert's orders, crossed the South Fork of the Shenandoah River at the ford, proceeding to Buckton's Ford on the North Fork of the Shenandoah River. With his baggage, ambulance, and supply train in front, Torbert moved back to Front Royal with Custer's Michigan Brigade and Lowell's Reserve Brigade of Merritt's division. Lowell's Reserve Brigade was immediately behind the baggage, ambulance, and supply train. Custer's Michigan Brigade was in the rearguard position following the Luray Road.

As Torbert approached Front Royal, a force of guerrillas from John S. Mosby's 43rd Virginia Battalion of Partisan Rangers attacked the baggage, ambulance, and supply train. Due to a hasty and faulty reconnaissance they missed the fact that two whole brigades of Union cavalry were following the wagons. The commander of the wagon guard was killed (either during the skirmish or after he surrendered and was robbed) and at least six of the guerrillas were taken prisoner.

Torbert, either to impress Sheridan with his ruthlessness or seeking some sort of a consolation prize to appease Sheridan's wrath, questioned at least two of the prisoners personally, demanding to know where Mosby's hideout was. (At this particular time Mosby was recovering from a gunshot wound, which probably explains the faulty Confederate reconnaissance.) The two men refused and were hanged, almost certainly on Torbert's orders. Two other prisoners were taken to a vacant lot behind the Methodist Church and were shot, apparently by some kind of firing squad, again probably under Torbert's orders. The other two prisoners were also shot, in two more widely separated locations and apparently not in any organized fashion, suggesting that those particular shootings may have been more of a case of not taking prisoners rather than of shooting already surrendered prisoners.

Kidd also noted that Sheridan had not yet given up on his grand design. Sheridan tried one more time to trap Early's army and bring the campaign to a triumphal conclusion, to go, in effect, beyond his twin victories at Winchester and Fisher's Hill. Success, of a sort, came when Torbert, due to Sheridan's pushing, finally did on September 24 what he probably should have done on September 22.

"Sheridan ordered Torbert to try again," Kidd recalled. "Custer, followed by Lowell, was sent to the front and in the forenoon of September 24, Wickham's troops were scattered in flight and the way opened for Torbert to carry out his instructions. Even then the march was leisurely and the two divisions arrived in New Market on September 25, only to find it was too late. Early had escaped again."

Once again, what might have been is brought to mind. Merritt, Custer, or Lowell would have pressed the advantage. The pace would have been forced and there would have been no leisurely advance. There would have been no second disappointment and no second escape for Early and his Valley District Army.

While Torbert was having his adventures in the Luray Valley, Sheridan and his main body had caught up with Early at Rude's Hill after they had cleared Mount Jackson and Sheridan had fired Averell. Sheridan probed the Confederate position with artillery, sending Thomas Devin and his cavalry brigade along the river to turn the Confederate right. Col. William Powell (who had replaced Averell) was sent west toward Timberville to envelop the Confederate left flank. Sheridan then sent forward infantry skirmishers to make contact with the Confederates on Rude's Hill.

Rude's Hill gave Early and his army an unobstructed view of the Union positions and they could see exactly what the Union troops were doing. Early's baggage train had already departed and he ordered his infantry and artillery to follow it. Half of the brigades in each of Early's divisions withdrew first, falling back about a mile up the turnpike and then redeploying. The remaining brigades released their hold upon Rude's Hill, moved through the new line and redeployed another two miles further back. Using this method, Early leapfrogged his army as it retreated; each new line providing cover for the troops that were on the move. Early's army retreated in this way through New Market before taking up a complete battle line formation at Tenth Legion Church, with Sheridan dogging their steps every foot of the way.

One witness noted that the entire procedure was one of the most magnificent sights of the entire war.[3] Sheridan's troops and scouts from the tops of the hills overlooking the Valley could see Early's troops stretched in their battle lines across the Valley floor as they moved away from their pursuers. Placed before the actual lines of battle were clouds of Confederate skirmishers seeking to delay the Union advance as the Confederate army leapfrogged its way to safety. The Confederate skirmishers were constantly under attack by Devin and Powell's cavalry. Behind the Union cavalry came Union infantry skirmishers. Whenever the cavalry's advance was checked, the Union infantry skirmishers reinforced them as the Confederate troops kept moving back.

By 5:00 P.M. on September 24, Sheridan halted his pursuit for the night just south of New Market. Just before the halt Sheridan made one final attempt to entice Early's infantry into making an attack, but Early wasn't biting and Sheridan knew he had run out of time and couldn't force an engagement before dark. Sheridan was not about to risk a night battle since it would have been practically impossible to control it.

In order for Early to extricate his army, Wickham's cavalry had to keep the New Market Gap open. This they did during the fighting with Torbert on September 24, mostly due to Torbert's excessive caution on that day. By nightfall, Wickham had managed to disengage his cavalry division (after having been finally driven from New Market Gap by Torbert) and had moved south, camping for the night along the South Fork of the Shenandoah River. Torbert's troopers, on the other hand, camped at the foot of New Market Gap.

That night Early's infantry and artillery were on the move again. They halted at midnight, slept for a few hours, and by daybreak were on the move by way of Port Republic. By sunset on September 25, Early's army was encamped at Brown's Gap of the Blue Ridge Mountains, while Lomax and his cavalry division were picketing the South Fork at Port Republic. Wickham and his cavalry division rejoined Early's army during the night.

Ironically, Early's army had been saved through the efforts of Brig. Gen. Williams C. Wickham's cavalry division. It was ironic because Early distrusted his cavalry arm and did not expect much from it. Sheridan, on the other hand, was one of the few Union generals (especially army commanders) who understood the potential of his cavalry and how best to use it. Sheridan used his mounted arm as a striking force in much the same way 20th and 21st century military commanders would use armored columns of tanks and truck or armored personnel carrier-mounted infantry in blitzkrieg operations in World War II and the First Gulf War's Operation Desert Storm and the Second Gulf War's Operation Iraqi Freedom. But in this instance Sheridan was let down by his cavalry, or rather by the commander of that cavalry, while Early would be succored by his cavalry, although they would receive very little thanks and even less credit for it.

12

Hesitation at Tom's Brook

Sheridan had not forgiven Torbert for his missteps in the Luray Valley. Just 13 days later—during what became known as The Burning—came an incident that once again showcased Torbert's inadequacies, particularly his lack of aggressiveness and his apparent need to be closely supervised. Where Averell became confused when he was under close supervision, Torbert failed—in many instances—to react properly without it.

Once Sheridan ended the pursuit of Early's army on September 25, 1864, the Shenandoah Valley Campaign entered into a new phase. For Ulysses S. Grant, the campaign had always had two components: First, to defeat and if possible destroy Jubal Early's Confederate Valley District Army; second, the practical destruction of the Shenandoah Valley, for Grant clearly understood that he could not attain victory in Virginia without its reduction.

According to his initial orders from Grant, Sheridan would, "in pushing up the Shenandoah Valley, as it is expected you will have to go, first or last, it is desirable that nothing should be left to invite the enemy to return.... Take all provisions, forage, and stock wanted for the use of your command ... such as cannot be consumed, destroy." Grant did not want the Valley's fertile soil and its mills to continue to feed the soldiers and animals of Lee's army and he did not want its tanneries providing leather for shoes and harness, or its horses to continue providing remounts for Lee's cavalry or to be available to pull his wagons and artillery. Sheridan had originally replied with a joke: That any crows flying over the Shenandoah Valley would have to carry their own rations, for they would find nothing to eat there.

Sheridan had been rather inhibited for the first seven weeks of his campaign, since he had taken command of the Middle Military Division on August 7, because Early and his Valley District Army had successfully barred the way and kept Sheridan away from the larders of the Upper Shenandoah Valley. Now Sheridan was able to carry out his boast to Grant. What had been sporadic before now became a daily occurrence from September 26 to October 5 while Sheridan's army lingered in the Harrisonburg–Port Republic–Staunton area.

During this period there were a few changes in the dramatis personae. Since there was a little lull in the fighting, Sheridan got caught up on his paperwork and named George A. Custer to take command of the Second Cavalry Division, Department of West Virginia, officially succeeding Averell. Before Custer could manage to join his new command, however, Brig. Gen. James H. Wilson, commander of the Third Cavalry Division, Cavalry Corps, Army of the Potomac, was ordered to join Sherman and thereupon form a new cavalry command. Sheridan didn't wait for the telegraph wires to cool down before relieving Custer of command of the Second Cavalry Division, Department of West Virginia (which was left still under the command of Col. William H. Powell), and then ordering Custer to assume command of the Third Cavalry Division, Cavalry Corps, Army of the Potomac. Command of Custer's own Michigan Cavalry Brigade (as previously noted) descended upon Col. James H. Kidd, commander of the 6th Michigan Cavalry Regiment.

In addition, there were a few changes on the Confederate side as well. Brig. Gen. Thomas L. Rosser (who happened to be Custer's close friend and West Point roommate) and his Laurel Brigade joined Wickham's Cavalry Division on October 5. Almost immediately Rosser assumed command of the division (to the great chagrin of Munford, who did not have a high opinion of the ersatz Texan, Rosser having been born in Virginia and having grown up in Texas) when Wickham resigned his commission to take the seat he had recently been elected to in the Confederate Congress.

Also on October 5, Sheridan issued orders to his army for a full-scale retrograde movement down the Valley. Early's army having been, more or less, disposed of for the time being as a factor within the Shenandoah Valley, it was time to get on with Grant's work. As Sheridan moved down the valley he intended to leave only ashes in his wake.

From October 6 through October 8, 1864, Sheridan's army (and particularly his cavalry) methodically blasted, burned, and devastated nearly everything within the Valley between the Alleghenies and the Blue Ridge. The economic loss was devastating, one expert estimating it at $20 million based upon the value of depreciated Confederate currency in 1864. Early's army could do nothing except follow in the wake of the destruction left by Sheridan's soldiers, desperately seeking some way to avenge the devastation, if not to put a stop to it.

However, Early did direct his cavalry, and Rosser in particular, "to pursue the enemy, harass him, and to ascertain his purposes." Rosser's division directly followed Sheridan's army along the Back Road, while Lomax and his division made for the Valley Pike. Rosser directed his attention to Custer's division, while Lomax used his division to keep Merritt busy.

Rosser's cavalry (much of it — particularly in the Laurel Brigade — having been recruited from the Shenandoah Valley area) was enraged at the destruction and Custer simply happened to be in their way since he commanded Sheridan's rear guard. Immediately when the destruction began Rosser pounced upon Custer's trailing regiment, the 1st Vermont Cavalry. It held off two attacks before it was driven into Custer's trailing brigade.

Custer wanted to turn around and smack Rosser down, but Torbert would not hear of it. The reason may not have been a lack of aggressiveness, as Custer and others believed following Torbert's performance during the Luray Valley Expedition. Since, on the other hand, Torbert could have been simply following what he believed to be Sheridan's intentions, if not his direct orders. After all, Sheridan had ordered the army to withdraw, not fight, and Torbert was not about to, on his own initiative, go against what he perceived to be Sheridan's orders. (In this case, he failed to understand that Sheridan wanted his subordinates to use their initiative to build upon whatever orders they were given, since Sheridan well understood that situations could change without warning and that his subordinates, due to the state of battlefield communications, or the lack of them, during the American Civil War might not have the time to contact headquarters, ask for, and to receive new or specific orders to meet the changing situation.)

Torbert also did not inform Sheridan about what was going on and ask for a change, if not a clarification, to his previous orders, something that Merritt would certainly have done. Custer, if left to his own devices, would have most likely smacked Rosser down first and then talked to Sheridan about it.

For three days, Rosser's jabs and attacks against Custer's division continued. The 18th Pennsylvania Cavalry Regiment (which replaced the exhausted 1st Vermont Cavalry Regiment) was worn down to a frazzle trying to block Rosser's repeated jabs. Finally, the sound of gunfire from the rear of his column grew so intense that Sheridan decided to find out what the heck was going on. Custer has been described at being so angry at Torbert's apparent lack of aggressiveness that he was practically in tears when Sheridan succeeded in finally catching up with him. Earlier in the day, Rosser had snapped up a wagon filled with runaway slaves and a blacksmith's forge with a broken wheel, which had fallen behind. Then to top it all off, one of Custer's aides blew these two incidents so far out of proportion that he managed to give Sheridan the mistaken impression that Rosser had somehow been able to capture an entire wagon train and a battery of artillery and that Torbert could not be persuaded to do anything about it.

Once again Sheridan lost his temper with Torbert. He cursed his way into a towering rage and then went off in search of his chief of cavalry. Torbert, completely and totally unaware of the storm that was about to break over his head, was at his headquarters with his staff and was just about to finish devouring a turkey dinner when Sheridan arrived. He stormed into the room just as the last of the bones were being picked clean. Bursting through the dining room door, Sheridan must have been quite a sight that night.[1]

Sheridan's short, livid figure, with his dark eyes blazing, was accompanied by the ringing castanets of his spurs as he stomped his way to Torbert's place at the head of the table. Then once he got there, the fragile dam holding his temper in check broke and he began thundering his wrath — the sound of his voice, in his rage, according to some of the witnesses present, being enough all by itself to make the china rattle and the silverware jump: "Well, I'll be damned! If you ain't sitting here stuffing yourselves, general, staff, and all, while the Rebels are riding into our camp! Having a party, while Rosser is carrying off your guns! Get on your nice clothes and clean shirts! Torbert, mount quicker than hell will scorch a feather! I want you to get out there in the morning and whip that Rebel cavalry, or get whipped yourself!"

It was, in effect, the same order that Averell had been given when he failed, in Sheridan's perception, to properly pursue the fleeing enemy in the immediate aftermath of the Battle of Fisher's Hill. Torbert, not wanting his head to be rolling alongside that of Averell's, got moving. The result on October 9, 1864, was one of Custer's most complete and satisfying victories at the Battle of Tom's Brook.

Sheridan halted his infantry so he could watch the battle as it took place from Three Top Mountain. As Sheridan recalled in his memoirs, when he decided that Rosser was to be chastised, Merritt and his division was encamped at the foot of Three Top, which was just north of and overlooked Tom's Brook. Custer's division was located some six miles further north and west, near Tumbling Run. During the night Custer had been ordered to retrace his steps before daylight by the Back Road, which was parallel to and about three miles from the Valley Pike, and attack the enemy at Tom's Brook Crossing. Merritt's instructions were to assail the Confederate cavalry of Lomax upon the Valley Pike in concert with Custer's attack.

At about 7:00 A.M. on October 9, 1864, Custer's division of two brigades encountered Rosser's division, which had three. It was almost perfect cavalry terrain, with very little in the way of obstacles. Rosser, who outnumbered Custer by about 1,000 men, was waiting on the south bank of Tom's Brook, having taken a strong position on a steep ridge overlooking the stream. Custer knew what had to be done. First he had to tie down Rosser, without hobbling his own efforts; then he had to probe for a weak spot, locate it, and then go for broke.[2]

Once his division had deployed, Custer galloped far out in front of his line, stopping where every man on both sides could see him. (Custer, who by this time had adopted a more regular uniform, had decided that this was a special event and was dressed in all the sartorial splendor of his original nonregulation black velveteen uniform.) With a swift, sweeping motion he raised his right hand to his broad-brimmed hat and swept it down to his knee in an extravagant salute, bowing gracefully in the saddle to his friend, and opponent. Custer was also taking advantage of this piece of military theatre since it allowed him to get far out in front of his division and look for some advantage. When he had determined exactly where Rosser was most vulnerable, he clamped his hat back on his head, raced back to his division and charged!

Sheridan in his memoirs noted that while the sound of the resulting artillery duel was reverberating through the Valley, Merritt moved briskly to the front and fell upon Lomax where his division held the Valley Pike. Merritt then extended his right, quickly made contact with Custer, and the two divisions moved forward together, under Torbert's direction. Sheridan wrote:

> The engagement soon became general across the Valley, both sides fighting mainly mounted. For about two hours the contending lines struggled with each other along Tom's Brook, the charges and counter-charges at many points being plainly visible from the summit of Round Top (actually Three Top Hill), where I had my headquarters for the time.
> The open country permitting a sabre fight, both sides seemed bent on using the arm. In the center, the Confederates maintained their position with much stubbornness, and for a time seemed to have recovered their former spirit, but at last they began to give way on both flanks, and as these receded, Merritt and Custer went at the wavering ranks in a charge along the whole front. The result was a general smash-up of the entire Confederate line, retreat quickly degenerating into a rout the like of which was never before seen. For 26 miles this wild stampede kept up, with our troopers close to the enemy's heels.... Some of Rosser's troopers fled to the mountains by way of Columbia Furnace, and some by way of the Valley Pike, apparently not discovering that the chase had been discontinued.

Torbert had taken advantage of the rivalry between Merritt and Custer and had provoked them into competing for the battle honors, thus getting the best possible performance out his two chief subordinates. "There could hardly have been a more victorious rout," Torbert wrote in his official report. "The cavalry totally covered themselves with glory and added to their long list of victories." This event in addition had caused General Early to remark to General Rosser the next time he saw him that he had not previously known that "the laurel was a running vine."

The Battle of Tom's Brook demonstrated, as nothing else did, the Confederate cavalry's descent from the glorious days in 1862, when under Stuart they could ride over, around, or through their opposition. Now, they were more and more powerless to stop the horsemen in blue. Still, the Confederates in the Valley District Army had a lot of fight left in them, however much it may have appeared that they had been whipped beyond redemption. It was now the turn of Sheridan's Army of the Shenandoah to become overconfident, having been given the completely erroneous impression that Early's army was "thoroughly and permanently broken, dispirited, and disposed of."

Unfortunately, Sheridan himself shared this opinion. He believed that the Shenandoah Valley Campaign had been concluded and that most of the units of his army could be better used "somewhere else." Thus he ordered the army to continue its retrograde movement and prepared to begin detaching portions of his army, in particular preparing for dispatching VI Corps back to the trenches at Petersburg. Sheridan differed markedly from other American Civil War generals, Union or Confederate. He did not call constantly for more men. He was even willing to have his own independent command broken up when circumstances seemed to no longer appear to justify its continued existence.

However, Grant had other ideas. Through Halleck in Washington, Grant told Sheridan that he had better retain XIX Corps, for the time being, although he left the return of VI Corps and the return of at least one of his cavalry divisions to Sheridan's own discretion. In reply, Sheridan now decided to retain VI Corps, at least for the time being.

Sheridan and Grant continued to debate over what to do next. Grant wanted an operation to be directed against the Virginia Central Railroad and the James River Canal. But Sheridan did not agree and Grant failed to make a direct order that this was to be done. Although Grant failed to issue a direct order he kept on prodding Sheridan, who finally mounted an expedition using only Powell's cavalry division. This became the pattern when Sheridan did not want to do something that Grant wanted him to do. Sheridan would order a half measure just to get Grant off his back. The result was an impasse that effectively succeeded in stopping Sheridan in his tracks, something that Early had utterly failed to do.

Then Edwin M. Stanton, Lincoln's secretary of war, decided to put his two cents worth in. He suggested that there be a conference to decide the next move. Sheridan hesitated, but finally decided to go to Washington on October 15 — although he was worried about Early, who had been too quiet too long — until his worries were eased by several reconnaissance probes. Thus, this sequence of events had brought Sheridan's army into an encampment on October 14 located between Cedar Creek and Middletown. This was intended only to be a convenient stopping place until a final decision upon the future course of the army could be reached.

There still remained the question of what, if anything, should be done about Torbert. By now Torbert had failed Sheridan twice, once in the Luray Valley and once just prior to Tom's Brook. Rumor had it that Sheridan was grooming Col. Charles R. Lowell, commander of the Reserve Cavalry Brigade in the First Cavalry Division, for the job as chief of cavalry, but that seems unlikely since Wesley Merritt was the most obvious candidate to succeed Torbert, if Sheridan was to finally decide that Torbert had to go.

Then the God of War intervened just two weeks after the Battle of Tom's Brook. On October 19, 1864, Sheridan would have quite a bit more to keep his mind occupied with than brooding over the fate of his chief of cavalry.

Early was coming.

13

The Battle of Cedar Creek

The camps of Sheridan's army were sprawled across a series of ridges that were located between Cedar Creek and the village of Middletown. The terrain had governed the dispositions of Sheridan's army, with the infantry and artillery being placed en echelon running five miles east and west. In addition, Torbert and the First and Third Cavalry divisions patrolled somewhat more even ground on the far right that extended towards the Back Road.

The VI Corps was on the right, between Torbert's cavalry and Meadow Brook, a tributary of Cedar Creek, occupying what were described as a "mass of hillocks and hollows." It was believed that if there were a Confederate attack it would be directed at the right flank. However, if there was an attack upon the left, it would be hard for Maj. Gen. Horatio G. Wright, VI Corps commander, and in Sheridan's absence the commander of the army, to shift troops to the left due to a deep ravine that had been carved out by Meadow Brook.

On the other side of this ravine was positioned XIX Corps, which occupied some high ground that rose above Cedar Creek for about 150 feet. Some fieldworks had been constructed and the bivouac sites covered the ground behind them that sloped toward the Meadow Brook ravine. As positioned, XIX Corps could shatter any frontal attack, which first had to cross Cedar Creek and then climb the high ground to reach them.

The Army of West Virginia/VIII Corps, under Crook, came next, occupying ground to the east of the Valley Pike on the extreme left flank. Positioned with them was a provisional division under the command of Col. Howard Kitching that had recently joined Sheridan's army as reinforcements. The reliability of the division in combat, and of its commander, was not considered very high. Because this position was considered naturally strong, no defensive fieldworks were constructed.

Kitching and Rutherford B. Hayes' divisions were placed on a barren ridge, 400 yards from the Valley Pike and due east of XIX Corps. Crook's other division, under Col. Joseph Thoburn, occupied a knoll that was described as a sort of bastion half a mile south of Hayes and Kitching and a mile south by southeast of XIX Corps. All in all it was considered a good place to rest and obtain water, but it soon proved to be a bad place in which to fight.

Sheridan left for his conference on the evening of October 15, taking with him Merritt's cavalry division. It was intended that Merritt, joined with Powell, would make another raid against the Virginia Central Railroad. The next morning, a courier from Wright arrived from where Sheridan had stopped for the night, with an intercepted message that Longstreet was about to reinforce Early. Sheridan didn't believe it—and as a matter of fact the message was false (being designed to prevent the transfer of Union troops from the Valley to Petersburg)—but still Sheridan decided to drop the cavalry raid for the time being and ordered Merritt to return to Cedar Creek. Sheridan himself figured to be back at his encampment by October 18, at the latest.

The primary factor that intervened to upset Sheridan's calculations was Old Jubilee. Jubal

Early was not quite yet convinced that his army was beaten. He did not accept Sheridan's view that the victories at Winchester, Fisher's Hill and now Tom's Brook, along with the destruction within the valley, meant that the campaign was over. As Early saw it he had two options. "I was now compelled," as he stated it in his memoirs, "to move back for want of provisions or forage, or attack the enemy in his position with the hope of driving him from it, and I determined to attack." The campaign was not going to be over until Jubal Early said it was over.

Early also received a lengthy dispatch from Lee that was dated October 12. Lee noted that he had weakened himself to send reinforcements (Kershaw's infantry division) to Early and that this had been done with the expectation of a victory that would allow Early to return the troops, if not rejoin Lee himself. Lee further discussed the recent setbacks, for which he went out of his way to say that he did not blame Early. Lee also offered suggestions regarding possible solutions to the problems of morale, discipline, and the cavalry.

It was clear that Lee wanted a victory to compensate for the sacrifices he had made on Early's behalf. Furthermore, if Sheridan sent any of his troops to Grant, Lee advised Early to move against Sheridan and crush him. As Lee saw it the key to success was for Early to use his entire army in a coordinated assault. In addition, Lee thought that Early was not nearly as outnumbered as Early maintained. (Unfortunately, in this instance, Lee was completely wrong.) Lee concluded that an attack upon Sheridan could succeed if Early relied on his judgment, ability, and the cooperation of his officers and men.

As far as Early was concerned, Lee's message cinched it. He decided to gamble everything on one final smashing attack. On October 17, Early summoned his senior infantry division commander, Maj. Gen. John B. Gordon, along with Brig. Gen. Clement A. Evans (one of Gordon's brigade commanders) and Maj. Jedediah Hotchkiss, who had been Stonewall Jackson's mapmaker. Early asked them to climb to the top of the Three Sisters at Fisher's Hill, which overlooked the Union encampment at Cedar Creek, and see if an attack could be made. Early himself was not physically up for the climb so he was depending on the judgment of these three officers.

They made their ascent that afternoon. Hotchkiss drew up a map of Sheridan's encampment that they could use to report their findings to Early. Gordon and Hotchkiss concurred on a plan, discussing their findings on the way down.

Early currently had available the three divisions of Stonewall Jackson's old II Corps that he had brought with him to the Shenandoah Valley. In addition, there was one small infantry division (Brig. Gen. Gabriel Wharton's) that was permanently attached to the Valley District. Finally, Kershaw's Division of Longstreet's I Corps had been sent to him by Lee as reinforcements. There were also Rosser and Lomax's cavalry divisions and Imboden's cavalry brigade, which like Wharton's division, was permanently assigned to the Valley District.

Early in the morning of October 18, 1864, two very different plans were presented to Early for the projected assault upon Sheridan's encampment at Cedar Creek. Brig. Gen. John Pegram, who was the acting commander of Ramseur's Division (Ramseur having taken over the division of the late Robert E. Rodes), proposed that an attack be made upon Sheridan's right flank, which was the obvious target for an assault. Hotchkiss then outlined Gordon's scheme to attack Sheridan's left, referring constantly to the map he had drawn. Early deferred his decision to a full council of war.

What Gordon proposed was a night march by II Corps (consisting of his own, Ramseur's and Pegram's infantry divisions) around the exposed left flank of Sheridan's army, to be followed by a concentrated assault by Early's entire army. The man who had to be convinced, however, was not Early, but rather Pegram. He wanted to know just exactly how Gordon proposed to take an entire corps, march it between the sheer northern face of Massanutten Mountain and the North Fork of the Shenandoah River that flowed at its base, and do this under the collective nose of Sheridan's entire army. His objections had merit since Sheridan evidently thought that it was impossible. (If Sheridan thought such a movement to be impossible, than Gordon thought it might very well work and supply the surprise that the whole scheme needed to be successful.) Gordon responded that a way would be found and that he would accept full and complete responsibility for any failure. Eventually the council of war unanimously endorsed Gordon's proposal.

The rest of the plan fell quickly into place. While Gordon led II Corps over the river and along the mountain, Kershaw would take his division, advance to Bowman's Mill, where Cedar Creek could be forded, and attack Thoburn's division of Crook's Army of West Virginia/VIII Corps. Wharton was to take his division and the artillery, follow the Valley Pike to Hupp's Hill, and cross the stream after Gordon and Kershow attacked, pressing his attack down the pike towards Middletown. Rosser and his cavalry division, crossing at Mineback Ford, would initiate the battle by engaging Torbert's Union cavalry. Col. William H. Payne's brigade of Rosser's Division would precede II Corps. His job was to capture any Union pickets and to charge down upon Belle Grove plantation, Sheridan's headquarters, and capture Sheridan. (The Confederates did not know that he was not present.)

Rosser, however, had wanted to follow the infantry attack with a charge by his cavalry division up the Valley Pike, thus adding to the shock of the assault and increasing the momentum of any breakthrough; however, his suggestion had been overruled by Early. The proposal had merit for its concentration of applied force and its appropriate use of cavalry. Early rejected it because he felt that Rosser's cavalry division would be better used to keep the Union cavalry from interfering with the assault.

Early's other cavalry division, under Lomax, was miles away from Cedar Creek to the southeast at Front Royal, where it was keeping Powell's Second Cavalry Division, Department of West Virginia, busy. Neither unit was to see any action during the coming battle at Cedar Creek. Also positioned elsewhere was Imboden's cavalry brigade, which was also not utilized in the coming battle.

What Early had approved was a stunning infantry attack. But then, with his cavalry, Early screwed up. He was misusing his cavalry, which he had never completely understood or trusted. It was dangerously divided and as a whole was awkwardly placed. All that really was needed with Powell was to keep an eye on him, and this could have been done utilizing Mosby's Rangers or Imboden's brigade instead of an entire division that could have been better placed elsewhere. In addition, the objectives (as far as Rosser's division was concerned) were tentative, uncoordinated, and unrealistic.

All units were to be in position ready to attack by 4:30 A.M., October 19, 1864.

Sheridan, after boarding a train at Rectortown, arrived in Washington at about 8:00 A.M. on October 17. He had breakfast at Willard's Hotel before going to the War Department to meet with Stanton and Halleck. During the conference, Sheridan's views prevailed. It was decided that the bulk of his army would rejoin Grant at Petersburg, while engineers laid out a defensive position east of the Blue Ridge in the neighborhood of Manassas Gap.

With the conference concluded, Sheridan and his party boarded a westbound Baltimore & Ohio train shortly after noon headed towards Martinsburg. They spent the night at the supply depot. Sheridan, with an escort of 300 cavalry, then rode the next morning [October 18] to Winchester. Since there was nothing urgent that required his immediate return Sheridan decided to stay the night at Winchester and return to Cedar Creek on October 19.

While Sheridan was away the troops he had left behind at Cedar Creek mostly rested and did various camp chores. Crook had dispatched a brigade to the top of nearby Hupp's Hill on a reconnaissance expedition that found nothing. He decided to repeat the exercise the following day, October 19, with General Wright's permission. Sheridan, by telegraph, was informed of Crook's intention.

At 8:00 p.m. October 18, Gordon led II Corps as it moved out from Fisher's Hill. It crossed the North Fork of the Shenandoah River, two miles south of Strasbourg. It passed through some open fields until it came upon Massanutten Mountain. Then they turned north, following Gordon's route, having to march single file due to its narrowness. When the troops reached the end of the mountain they turned east, marching to the lane running down to Bowman's Ford. It helped that there was a heavy fog, which blanketed and totally concealed Gordon's movements.

In a degree of coordination that was astounding, at about 4:30 a.m. October 19, Rosser nodded to Payne, who spurred his horse forward, while Early gave the order to advance to Kershaw. Rosser's dismounted troopers attacked Custer's sleeping camp, Payne's little brigade took out the pickets and then spurred towards Belle Grove plantation, and Kershaw ordered his sharpshooters to take out Thoburn's sentinels at the Cedar Creek ford below Strasbourg. The battle had begun.

The Michigan Cavalry Brigade, under Col. James H. Kidd, reacted quickly to the noise of Rosser's attack. In minutes Custer's entire division was mounted, while Merritt sent Kidd to support the videttes and dispatched an order to Lowell, whose brigade had been on its way on a reconnaissance mission. It was ordered to halt at the picket line and await developments. Custer and Merritt both believed that the attack upon their camps was nothing more than a feint and they eagerly awaited orders.

Seven miles to the south, Payne's brigade was galloping across the creek, while behind them came II Corps. Powell remained at Front Royal, for Wright had failed to "close up Powell" as Sheridan had directed before he left. Powell did have some videttes out in the direction of Cedar Creek but when the attack began they naturally retired in the direction of Powell's command. Thus no warning was given to Crook's Army of West Virginia/VIII Corps. Gordon's Confederate troops moved to the northeast as fast as they could, moving a mile to the east of Thoburn's position, while angling toward the unprotected edge of Hayes' camp.

The pickets targeted by Kershaw's sharpshooters were badly posted and negligent so that the sharpshooters simply rose up and ran them down without actually firing a shot. Kershaw's Division pushed across the ford, deploying, in the fog, under Thoburn's position from a marching column into a line of battle, without skirmishers. Kershaw intended to give the enemy no warning and hit them with his main line.

Early recalled that Kershaw began his attack exactly at 5:00 a.m., en echelon by brigades from the right. Col. Thoburn was killed in the opening moments of the attack and his division was overrun by Kershaw, losing its organization with Thoburn's death and offering very little opposition, as they were immediately routed and sent running from the field.

Early saw off Wharton's advance then made for Hupp's Hill, arriving at the same time as his artillery. The sounds of battle in the meantime had completely roused the Union camps and Hayes was forming his command and Kitching's provisional division. His battle line, with Kitching to the left, was parallel to the Valley Pike, facing south and east, while Generals Crook, Wright, and Emory arrived. Due to the fog, nothing could be seen of the Confederates, although they could hear musketry to the front and both flanks, and the Rebel yell.

The attack by Gordon and II Corps, when it came, did not come from the southwest (where Kershaw had smashed Thoburn) where it was expected and everything was ready, but from the east and into Hayes's left flank. The Confederates came in, not shooting but howling the Rebel yell, driving in Hayes' skirmishers, saving their musketry for Hayes' main line. However, long before they closed upon Hayes' position the soldiers in his main line cut and ran.

When Hayes and Kitching's line collapsed, Generals Wright and Emory moved into the gap between what had been Hayes and Kitching's camps and the fieldworks built by XIX Corps, when the only remnant of Thoburn's division arrived. Someone was needed to buy a little time and they were elected. The remnant was ordered to charge, and they did, with Wright leading the charge. Wright was slightly wounded, the charge was forced back, and they withdrew to where XIX Corps was now forming.

The Army of West Virginia/VIII Corps had simply melted away, until, at Belle Grove, Crook and Hayes managed to cobble a formation together. Next was XIX Corps.

From Hupp's Hill, Early's artillery was hammering away at its lines; Wharton's Division was across Cedar Creek and was moving to its left. The men couldn't see much of anything due to the fog as the sounds of disaster swelled from the left and rear. Emory's XIX Corps had formidable fieldworks and more time to prepare. They also had time to take stock of their fears. The gap between Emory and Crook's camps, which had been filled by one XIX Corps brigade, had now become the Union army's left flank. That brigade was facing attack by Kershaw's Division from the right and all of Gordon's II Corps forces from the left.

It appeared to Wright that the Union army was going to have to abandon its fieldworks and make a fighting retreat to a new position further north. (Wright was so occupied that he failed to give Torbert and his two divisions of cavalry any orders whatsoever.) Therefore, XIX Corps had to hold; otherwise, panic could run through the entire army and lead to its complete annihilation. The XIX Corps brigade on the far left was driven from its position, it rallied, and the survivors were ordered to retreat northward along the Valley Pike.

It was a confusing situation as Kershaw's Division slammed into XIX Corps from the left and Ramseur's Division came onto the high ground in the Union rear. While the attack was under way at XIX Corps headquarters an attempt was made to save its baggage and supply train. Finally the order was given for XIX Corps to abandon its fieldworks. As XIX Corps retreated, it passed in front of Belle Grove and what was left of Crook's command, which had been reduced to the size of a single, tiny brigade.

While most of XIX Corps filed to the rear past Belle Grove, Crook's remnant advanced and held off Kershaw and Wharton for half an hour, which gave the baggage and supply trains time to escape. To Crook's right, a brigade of XIX Corps was conducting a similar holding action while another brigade somewhat to his left and rear did the same.

Torbert, who had been at Belle Grove since the beginning of the attack, now rode to Merritt and Custer's camps, finding his First and Third Cavalry divisions formed and ready to resist Rosser. However, Rosser seemed content to hold his position while firing on the Michigan and Reserve brigades of Merritt's division. The Union cavalry, however, was being held out of the battle by a simple lack of orders and most certainly not by Rosser. (This was where Wright, upon whom command of the army had devolved upon Sheridan's absence, had his biggest failure. He seemed to have completely forgotten that he had any cavalry and that it might be used to retrieve the disaster that was overtaking the rest of the Army of the Shenandoah by moving it from the right flank to the left flank, leaving a small covering force to keep Rosser honest, where it might have held off the attacking Confederates long enough to keep XIX Corps from collapsing. Eventually this was done, but only after the main Confederate assault had eventually more or less petered out.)

The VI Corps, which had been in reserve well away from the point of impact of Early's assault, had plenty of time to prepare before it was committed to the battle. The officers and men of VI Corps kept their heads. Wright had ordered Brig. Gen. James B. Ricketts, in temporary command of VI Corps, to move to the left and try to get in front of the attack. Despite the fog and confusion, these orders were promptly obeyed, although when the leading VI Corps brigade had arrived at a field just west of Belle Grove it was broken up and forced back by the fugitives from the Army of West Virginia/VIII Corps and XIX Corps.

The VI Corps troops succeeded in stopping Kershaw, giving the Union troops a breather. With remarkable speed the corps was to scrape together a more or less contiguous line extending for a mile and a half to the west and about half a mile south of Middletown.

Gordon, however, was satisfied with the progress of the assault so far. The Confederate infantry had driven all but VI Corps and Torbert's cavalry from the field. Gordon now kept his troops moving, supported by Kershaw. There was, however, going to have to be a pause for reorganization and reconcentration before the attack could be continued and VI Corps could be driven from the field with the rest of Sheridan's army. But Gordon was not ready to stop, and continued forcing VI Corps back.

By 8:00 A.M. the last of the fog was being burnt away by the sun, which had risen two hours earlier.

Gordon and Kershaw had flawlessly executed Gordon's battle plan, but now Early called a halt, convinced that the battle was won and that what was left of the Union army would withdraw from the field and therefore, except for the clean up, there was little left for the Confederates to do. Gordon realized that a pause was needed, but not a complete halt. VI Corps still remained to be smashed. Thus ensued what later became known as the fatal lull. Although fighting continued to some degree, the Confederate attacks were half-hearted, piecemeal, and uncoordinated.

All this time Torbert's cavalry was kept waiting until, at 9:00 A.M., orders were finally received for the two divisions to move to the left and secure the Valley Pike. Torbert was opposed to the move as long as Rosser's cavalry remained to threaten the Union right, and left three of Custer's regiments to keep an eye on Rosser. However, inexplicably Rosser did nothing, which was both against his orders and his nature.

The cavalry moved left, unflinchingly, into the fire of Early's artillery. When Early spotted the move he fully passed from the offensive to the defensive, which allowed the battered Union infantry a chance to reassemble on VI Corps. Although Wright had managed to hold the army together, he did not inspire, he did not encourage, and he did not reassure. But help was on the way.

When Sheridan got up early on the morning of October 19 in Winchester he could hear the ominous sound of artillery fire coming from the direction of Cedar Creek. At first he believed that this was from artillery supporting fire for the proposed reconnaissance in force to Hupp's Hill. Sheridan was in no hurry when he left the house he was staying at between 8:30 and 9:00 A.M. He mounted his favorite horse, Rienzi, and started on his way back to Cedar Creek.

By the time they reached the outskirts of Winchester, however, the artillery fire could be heard with an increasing roar. At Mill Creek, about a half mile outside of Winchester, their escort, the 300 men of the 17th Pennsylvania Cavalry Regiment, joined Sheridan and his party. They had just topped a rise, a short distance from Mill Creek, when the first hint of the disaster at Cedar Creek—a stalled jumble of wagons—could be seen. Sheridan ordered one of his aides to ride ahead and find out what was going on. The aide soon learned that there had been an attack on the encampment at Cedar Creek and that the army Sheridan had left behind had been defeated. The aide immediately rode back to Sheridan with this information. This news was confirmed when another officer who had been at Cedar Creek arrived.

Sheridan reacted at once. He, a few aides, and a reduced escort would ride for Cedar Creek. An aide, some engineer officers, and the remainder of the escort would stay and form a roadblock to stem the flood of fugitives. Sheridan then spurred up the road riding hard for Cedar Creek, rallying his troops as he found them along the road, sending them back to Cedar Creek and then riding on, and soon beginning to outdistance his escort. It was not long until the news spread throughout the entire army that Little Phil was coming.

By about 11:00 A.M. he had arrived at the battlefield and assessed the situation. All in all, the condition of the army was not that bad. It was dispersed but was in good order. Immediately Sheridan, between 11:00 A.M. and noon—building on what Wright had already accomplished—completed the reorganization and redeployment of the army for a counterattack.

(Wright, however, apparently never considered the possibility of a counterattack, being primarily concerned with saving the army.) While Sheridan was thus occupied the Confederates failed to renew their assault.

At about midday it was suggested that Sheridan ride along the new Union line to show the troops that he was on the scene. The result of such a ride had not been seen since George B. McClellan appeared before the army retreating to Washington from its defeat at the Second Battle of Manassas/Bull Run in 1862. Sheridan's army, upon seeing him, was struck by a renewed spirit as the men seemed to realize that with Sheridan back everything would be made right again, as Sheridan demonstrated the hold he had on the imagination of the soldiers of his army. They immediately began breaking out into wild cheering. (It surpassed the moment when Grant himself had been cheered by one corps of the Army of the Potomac when it realized that they were advancing, not retreating, after the Battle of The Wilderness, and Grant just happened to pass by. The difference lay in the fact that just one corps had cheered Grant; here Sheridan was being cheered by the entire army.)

Just to the south were the victors of the morning's battle. Early intended to pursue what he still thought of as the defeated Union army, but only when everything was ready. Conditions on the field precluded anything happening on the Confederate side before 11:00 or 11:30 A.M. As it was, nothing happened until 1:00 P.M., when there was an abortive advance by Kershaw, Ramseur and Evans, leading Gordon's own division. The thrust lacked vigor and by then it had little or no chance of success.

What happened during this assault is uncertain. Confederate accounts hardly make any mention of it. Early, in his memoirs, noted that only skirmishers were engaged and that Gordon did not press the assault. Union accounts tell of a blazing struggle, although one Union account noted that the sortie was repulsed with only three or four volleys and that the Confederate troops lacked the dash they had shown just a few hours earlier in their original attack.

The assault, which was more like a spectacular reconnaissance-in-force, was quickly repulsed. The Union line was now too strong for a frontal attack. The Union troops had superiority in numbers, a compact front, and the protection of light fieldworks. With the repulse and partial retirement of Gordon's force there was another lull, except for some probes by Union cavalry on the flanks, until about 4:00 P.M.

Apparently Early believed that he had won a great victory, dismissing the very idea of a Union counterattack, and was content with the morning's work as being more than sufficient. But he did not fully pull back Ramseur, Kershaw, and Evans to the positions they had held before 1:00 P.M.

At 4:00 P.M. Sheridan launched his counter-stroke. It was an assault that Sheridan had been planning ever since he had arrived on the battlefield, and now everything was ready. His redeployment of Custer's Third Cavalry Division from the left flank to the right had only been an initial step. When Gordon had advanced his reconnaissance-in-force at 1:00 P.M. and had been repulsed, the result had been to give Sheridan the initiative. The three hour delay was caused by a mistaken report that Confederate infantry were coming to reinforce Early. Apparently Lomax's cavalry had been mistaken for Longstreet's infantry.

A probe by Merritt's First Cavalry Division provided some prisoners who verified that only Kershaw's division of Longstreet's corps was present. Shortly after Merritt relayed this information to Sheridan, it was confirmed by Powell's cavalry that Longstreet was not in the area at either Newtown or Winchester, thus removing the only obstacle to Sheridan ordering the assault.

Just before 4:00 P.M. 200 buglers positioned all along Sheridan's line blew the charge and the troops stepped out from the woods that had been obscuring their line. The XIX Corps was on the right, VI Corps in the center, and what was left of the Army of West Virginia/VIII Corps was on the left. The XIX Corps was to turn the left flank of Gordon's advanced position; VI Corps supported by Crook's remnant was to hammer the Confederate front.

Unknowingly, XIX Corps poured straight into a gap between two brigades of Gordon's division. Although caught for a time in Confederate enfilading fire, they had soon grabbed the Confederate high ground. But the advance stalled until Custer and his cavalry division arrived at about 4:30 P.M. His appearance was the signal for one XIX Corps division to charge perpendicularly down the Confederate line, smashing unit after unit like a row of dominoes going down as the Confederates began to break apart and stampede in panic.

However, not everyone ran and there were isolated pockets of resistance that strove desperately to stem the tide of the Union advance. But they could not stand long. Once the Confederate army was shattered and the Union infantry advanced in pursuit, they were simply engulfed.

Early's men fled for the natural fortress of Fisher's Hill. That and darkness saved what was left of the army. During the final assault Union Col. Charles R. Lowell and Confederate Maj. Gen. Stephen Dodson Ramseur were both mortally wounded. Ironically, shortly after Lowell's death his commission as a brigadier general arrived at Sheridan's headquarters from the War Department.

And that was just about the end of Sheridan's Shenandoah Valley Campaign of 1864. Soon Lee reclaimed II Corps, Kershaw's Division, as well as — after the Gordonsville Raid in December — the cavalry division of Lunsford Lomax. Eventually the winter forced the temporary disbandment of Rosser's cavalry division. His men were told to go home to their families, obtain remounts and wait for a call to reassemble. That call came on February 27, 1865, when Sheridan left his winter camp. Rosser could do nothing about Sheridan and eventually moved his division to Petersburg to join Lee, arriving just in time for Five Forks and eventually Appomattox. Early remained in command of the Valley District but he had only the troops of Wharton's infantry division and Imboden's cavalry brigade. Almost immediately Grant reclaimed VI Corps. One of Crook's divisions went with it, while the other went into winter quarters at Cumberland, Maryland. Early and his remnant went into winter quarters around Staunton, while Sheridan, with XIX Corps and with Merritt's, Powell's and Custer's cavalry divisions, did so at Winchester.

14

Flunking the Final Exam at Gordonsville

Although he had gone into winter quarters, Sheridan, in response to Grant's constant nagging about the Virginia Central Railroad and despite the rigors of the weather, planned one final raid.

Ever since the failed raid that had resulted in the Battle of Trevelian Station, Grant had carried a fixation upon the Virginia Central Railroad. He was constantly bombarding Sheridan with suggestions that, when the Shenandoah Valley Campaign was over, he wanted Sheridan to move against and destroy the railroad and then go join Sherman, who was about to take Savannah as a "Christmas present" for Abraham Lincoln and who was by this time preparing to move up through the Carolinas.

Grant's thinking was probably inspired by the success of Col. Benjamin H. Grierson's raid during Grant's Vicksburg Campaign in the spring and summer of 1863. In a 17-day romp across Mississippi and Louisiana, Grierson's 1,700 troopers tied up thousands of Confederate infantry and diverted attention from Grant's final successful advance upon Vicksburg, in which Gant crossed the Mississippi River, marched on the Confederate relief forces gathering at Jackson, Mississippi, and then swung around to attack Vicksburg from the only direction it could be successfully assaulted, the east. All of this led to the siege and the surrender of the city, along with Lt. Gen. John Pemberton's entire army.

One of the primary reasons why the raid had been successful, however, lay in the fact that General Joseph E. Johnston, the Confederate Western Theatre of Operations commander charged with directing both Bragg's Army of Tennessee and Pemberton's Army of Mississippi, had earlier stripped Pemberton of all his cavalry so that he had only infantry with which to chase Grierson.

It is not known what Sheridan really expected to accomplish in this raid. Sheridan took pains to inform Grant that the weather was so bad that he was not hopeful for much success from the raid. The Shenandoah Valley region was undergoing its worst winter in decades. Like previous raids aimed at the Virginia Central Railroad, maybe all that Sheridan wanted to accomplish with this raid was to stop Grant's incessant nagging, since Sheridan did not want to move against the railroad, and then maybe head off to join Sherman.

What he wanted to do was to return to the Union siege lines at Petersburg and to be in on the kill when Lee was finally brought to bay. Eventually, Sheridan would get what he wanted and in his insistence, which many contemporaries (and some modern historians) believed either bordered upon insubordination or had actually crossed that particular line. Thus he became one of the chief architects of the final surrender of Lee's Army of Northern Virginia at Appomattox Court House.

On December 19, 1864, Sheridan reluctantly sent Torbert out with the entire Cavalry Corps.

Torbert, with Merritt's First Cavalry Division, Cavalry Corps, Army of the Potomac, and Powell's Second Cavalry Division, Department of West Virginia, crossed the Blue Ridge Mountains through Chester Gap at Front Royal. The plan called for them to strike the Virginia Central Railroad at Gordonsville and advance to Charlottesville and Lynchburg. Custer's Third Cavalry Division, Cavalry Corps, Army of the Potomac, was to move independently up the Shenandoah Valley to Staunton and join Torbert, Merritt, and Powell at Lynchburg. Custer was to act as a decoy; hopefully by threatening Staunton, he could draw Confederate troops away from Trobert's main body.

From the start, the raid was an abysmal failure due to both the weather and Confederate resistance. The Confederates had been keeping Torbert and Custer's columns under observation and Early had quickly ordered Lomax to Gordonsville to stop Torbert. Custer had — despite the weather conditions — moved fast and had arrived at Lacey's Springs by the evening of December 20, where he bivouacked for the night, sending out strong videttes from five of his nine regiments. He thereupon instructed his brigade commanders to wake their men at 4:00 A.M. and for them to be in the saddle by 6:30 A.M.

Early himself was in Staunton when he received word of Custer's movement from the signal station on Shenandoah Peak. Early gathered all of the infantry of Gabriel Wharton's division who could still walk and had Rosser gather all the cavalrymen from his division who could still ride. Then they moved north to head off Custer, through bitter cold and alternating rain and hail.

Rosser, whose promotion to major general had been confirmed on November 24, had by now recovered from whatever lethargy had stricken him at Cedar Creek. On the night of December 20, while Wharton struggled toward Harrisonburg, Rosser found Custer's camp at Lacey's Springs, nine miles to the north. Rosser had only 600 men with him — even with Wharton he would still be outnumbered two-to-one — when he decided that the only way to stop Custer was by a night attack. He began stealing up on Custer's command by way of the Back Road.

Conditions that night were awful. By the time Rosser's men got into position, Custer's men were struggling out from under six inches of new snow and were trying to obtain a warm breakfast. Custer's camp was so large that Rosser knew he would never be able to surprise the entire camp. Instead, he decided to single out the house where Custer had established his headquarters near the bivouac of Custer's Second Brigade. Then he simply gathered his men and swept down upon Custer like an avalanche.

Rosser hit Custer's Second Brigade on the right flank and rear at about 5:30 A.M. December 21. Custer was still in bed when the attack came and one column of Rosser's cavalry headed straight for his headquarters. At the first shot, Custer was out of bed and dressing as he rushed to a window to see what was going on. Taking out a Confederate officer's coat and hat belonging to Rosser that he had captured at Tom's Brook, he quickly put them on and walked out of the house (without bothering to pull on a pair of boots) through Rosser's troopers, who thought he was one of their own officers. Then Custer jumped on the first horse he came to, stripped off Rosser's coat and led a countercharge in his shirtsleeves and stocking feet, driving off Rosser's cavalry from his encampment. Custer lost 22 dead and 47 prisoners, while Rosser left 50 casualties behind him. Custer seemed to be somewhat unnerved by the entire experience. He was apparently flustered a bit by Rosser's attack and his own close shave. In addition, the miserable weather may have had as much or more to do with the decision he then made as the sudden attack of Rosser's cavalry. Declaring that he had made an ample diversion for Torbert, Custer abandoned his mission and retreated to Winchester. In his report, he stated that he had retreated not because he was afraid of further attacks from Rosser but "if it was decided to return, the sooner my return was accomplished, the better it would be for my command." Perhaps the 230 men he had suffering from frostbite had something to do with it.

Sheridan wrote in his memoirs that as soon as Custer's retreat was assured, Wharton's infantry division was sent to Charlottesville to check Torbert. However, Lomax had already done this with the assistance of supporting infantry, which had been sent up from Richmond.

Torbert's portion of the raid got under way when he left Winchester on December 19 on his way to Gordonsville. Torbert set out with 5,000 men and no artillery (to get bogged down and impede his march). On this first day he marched 22 miles by way of Front Royal, crossed both branches of the Shenandoah River and spent the night at Chester Gap. On December 20, with freezing rain falling nearly the whole day, Torbert marched another 29 miles heading in the direction of Criglersville. In his official report Torbert noted that it hailed and sleeted all night long.

Torbert first met Confederate resistance the next day at Madison Court House during a hail and snowstorm that lasted the entire day. The First Cavalry Division, under Wesley Merritt, collided with one of Lomax's cavalry brigades at Madison Court House, driving them from the town with slight loss. Col. William Powell's Second Cavalry Division, Department of West Virginia, camped on the Robertson River near Criglersville.

The march was resumed on December 22 and met Lomax's cavalry division at Liberty Mills on the Rapidan River. The Confederate defenders had burned the bridge, which had delayed Torbert's advance for a full day until he had organized and dispatched flanking columns to both the right and the left. The flanking columns were not in position until dusk and Lomax was driven back although the fighting mostly occurred after dark. Torbert noted that both the day and the night were intensely cold. The fighting was resumed the next day and Torbert succeeded in taking two Confederate cannon.

The Confederate cavalry under Lomax had then fallen back upon Gordonsville, making a stand within two and a half miles of Torbert's target. Lomax stopped retreating at the top of the gap in Southwestern Mountain and then Lomax fortified the narrow pass. Torbert attacked with half his force while attempting another flanking movement with the rest of his troops.

Then two brigades of infantry arrived by rail from Richmond to reinforce Lomax. Thus, Torbert had found more opposition at Gordonsville than he cared for. His men were cold, wet, and, like Custer's, frostbitten. It was not long before Torbert reached the conclusion that "it was useless to make a further attempt to break the Virginia Central Railroad." Torbert then ordered a return to Winchester and withdrew without harming the railroad, and five days later his two exhausted divisions straggled back into Winchester, thus earning his third and final big black mark in Sheridan's personal ledger. Torbert, in the performance of his task, Sheridan noted, succeeded only in capturing the two pieces of artillery at Liberty Mills on the Rapidan River. In return for those two guns Torbert had lost 102 casualties and 258 horses.

"The country through which we passed," Torbert wrote in his report, "was thoroughly cleaned of stock and forage. The command was obliged to live on the country for six days. Altogether it was an extremely hard trip on both men and horses on account of the intense cold and bad weather. For six days out of ten it either rained, hailed, or snowed, and sometimes all three."

By December 27, Torbert and Custer were both back in their winter camps near Winchester recovering from the experience and this completed Union operations for what remained of the winter.

Sheridan could forgive Custer for his failure, noting in his memoirs only that "Custer did not accomplish all that was expected of him," but he had had enough of Torbert and placed the full blame for the failure of the raid at Torbert's doorstep. Perhaps Sheridan gave Custer the benefit of the doubt that due to the weather he may have made a correct decision; after all, there was a reason why American Civil War armies generally went into winter quarters and remained there almost totally inactive until the arrival of spring.

After the abortive Gordonsville Raid, Torbert again suffered from an abscess to the spine, the same ailment that had waylaid him just as the Overland Campaign had begun the previous May. Since things were quiet, he requested a medical leave. On January 10, 1865, Torbert left on his medical leave. He had first requested 20 days and had then extended it to more than six weeks, with his return to Winchester being scheduled for February 28.

Generally, Sheridan was a man of direct action, but this time he showed that he could also be devious as well. Apparently he decided immediately after the Gordonsville Raid that Torbert had to go. But, he decided to do it if possible without the controversy that had followed on his relief of Averell.

Sheridan, without telling Torbert of his plans to leave his winter camp a month early (at the end of February, rather than March), approved Torbert's medical leave and its extension (forbidding Torbert's staff to tell him of Sheridan's plans to begin the campaigning season a month early) and then left to rejoin Grant at Petersburg on February 27 with the First and Third Cavalry Divisions, now under Merritt's command as chief of cavalry, with Brig. Gen. Thomas Devin taking command of the First Cavalry Division. While en route Sheridan had Custer smash the last remnant of Early's Valley District Army at Waynesboro on March 2, 1865.

On his march to rejoin Grant, Sheridan finally took care of the James River Canal and the Virginia Central Railroad along with the Richmond, Fredericksburg & Petersburg Railroad. He took Charlottesville, destroying the canal locks, and as he moved toward Grant he took out both railroad bridges and track.

Sheridan, as soon as he reached Grant — after a march that took him about three weeks, was designated by Grant as commander of the Army of the Shenandoah serving with the Army of the Potomac, making Sheridan in effect an autonomous strike force commander.

Torbert, when he returned to Winchester on February 28, found that Sheridan was gone, with the two cavalry divisions that had originally been borrowed from the Army of the Potomac and that he, Torbert, was now in command of whatever was left of the military units remaining in the Middle Military Division and of the division itself. This left Torbert without any officially valid reasons for complaint. After all, Sheridan had not fired him, officially, and had even given him what could be seen as a promotion.

What Sheridan had done would have been perfectly obvious to any business executive or any chief executive officer of a major corporation. He had taken a subordinate whose output had disappointed him on at least three separate occasions and rather than firing him outright he had kicked him upstairs where he could do no more harm.

Torbert was a brave and generally competent officer, and if provided with the proper supervision could even be highly effective, as demonstrated by the brevets, or honorary promotions, he had won in both the regular and volunteer services. He had received a brevet for his actions at the Third Battle of Winchester and had been named to the rank of brevet brigadier general in the regular army for Cedar Creek. He was also brevetted a major general of regulars for the war.

However, he was one of the best examples of the Peter Principle in action during the American Civil War. As a brigade and division commander he turned in solid, acceptable performances; but on the corps level, when he had to act independently or autonomously with little or no supervision, he was prone to failure and that was why Sheridan in the end decided to get rid of him.[1]

Torbert was mustered out of the U.S. Volunteers on January 15, 1866.

After the war Torbert wanted to remain in the army, but he was only a captain in the regular army. His only hope for promotion lay in impressing officials in Washington, D.C., with his record. Despite his efforts, and those of his friends, there was no promotion and in the end he remained in the army only until October 31, 1866, when he resigned. From 1869 to 1878, during the Grant and Hayes administrations, Torbert held minor diplomatic positions in Central

America, Cuba, and France. After that he was a businessman in Mexico. On August 29, 1880, he drowned on a steamer that was wrecked during a hurricane off Cape Canaveral, Florida.

Few people are lucky enough to die in a way that tends to validate their entire life, but Torbert was one of them.[2] Due to the courage that he had shown during the shipwreck and his solicitation for others (especially the young boy who Torbert insisted on being saved) Torbert became something of a national hero, even more so than he had ever been during the American Civil War, and was therefore given a hero's funeral.

The people of Milford, Delaware, where he made his home, declared that they were "justly proud of him, proud of him in life, and proud of him in death."

Part III

Gouverneur Kemble Warren

The Man Who Suffered from Combat Fatigue

Major General of Volunteers Gouverneur Kemble Warren, who was The Man Who Suffered from Combat Fatigue. His relationship with Ulysses S. Grant soured not because one of them was right and the other was wrong but because both of them were right (Library of Congress).

15

The Master Engineer, Cartographer and Teacher

Gouverneur K. Warren and Philip H. Sheridan should have gotten along like a house on fire, since Warren had demonstrated in 1862 and 1863 that he had the spark that Sheridan was generally looking for in his subordinates. But by 1865, especially after the Bristoe Station, Mine Run, and Overland Campaigns, that spark was practically gone. Although it would flare up one more time at Five Forks, Sheridan would not recognize it.

Warren was talented, a born leader, the general who, although he commanded no troops, was the "Savior of Gettysburg" but who could not save his own career in an army whose high command eventually found what was described as his "arrogance and insolence" to be intolerable.[1]

Warren seemed to overflow with excited suggestions about everything from how a march should be properly conducted to how a battle could be won. He seldom hesitated to make his views known to everyone within earshot, including his superiors. Although charged with nervous energy he was thorough and methodical, as only a man trained as an engineer can be, who exercised much deliberation before putting plans—his own or those of others—into execution. Eventually, this particular character trait would cause him a great deal of grief.

Less than two years following his triumph at Little Round Top during the Battle of Gettysburg, Warren had the dubious distinction of becoming the highest ranking commander in the history of the Army of the Potomac to be summarily relieved for alleged deficiencies in his leadership. (There were plenty of other high ranking generals in the Army of the Potomac who definitely showed deficiencies in leadership, but, while eventually they may have been gotten rid of, they were not summarily relieved.) What happened to him at Five Forks was a disgrace from which he never really recovered and he spent the next 17 years struggling for vindication. He died three months before the decision of a court of inquiry exonerated him from the most serious "imputations" against him.

Warren was born on January 8, 1830, in Cold Spring, New York, the fourth of 12 children. He entered the United States Military Academy at West Point, New York, at the age of 16 in 1846, graduated second in his class in 1850, and was assigned to the U.S. Army Corps of Topographical Engineers. A gifted engineer and mapmaker, after his graduation and until 1853 Warren served on several important survey expeditions. From 1853 to 1855 he assisted in a study to determine the best possible transcontinental railroad route, examining reports of all explorations west of the Mississippi dating back to Lewis and Clark. As part of this analysis, Warren began work on the first comprehensive map of the trans–Mississippi United States. He also studied flood control on the Mississippi River. He proved himself to be a truly talented cartographer (mapmaker) and he enjoyed the wandering existence of a U.S. Army topographical engineer.

His ability as a mapmaker would be crucial after the war, when his maps and his testimony were principally responsible for the exoneration of Maj. Gen. Fitz John Porter, who in 1863 had been court-martialed and dismissed from the Union army for supposedly sabotaging the efforts of General John Pope at the Second Battle of Manassas/Bull Run. In point of fact, Pope pretty much sabotaged himself.

In 1855, Warren served as the chief topographical engineering officer in Brig. Gen. William Harney's expedition against the Sioux in southern Nebraska Territory (now the states of Nebraska and South Dakota). During this assignment he had to travel 300 miles of unknown territory from Fort Pierce (now Pierre, South Dakota) to Fort Kearney, near the Platte River. On this journey he displayed courage and determination. In addition, Warren sympathized deeply with the casualties suffered on both sides. His basic unwillingness to throw away the lives of fighting men (most especially those under his command) for little or no return was something that would remain with him for the rest of his military career. It would also be a factor in his removal from command as he clashed first with George G. Meade and then with Ulysses S. Grant.

In 1856 he commanded a successful survey mission in northern Nebraska Territory and along the Missouri River and up the Yellowstone River (in what are now the states of North Dakota and Montana). In 1857 he led a survey of the Niobara River and the Sioux-occupied Black Hills. These expeditions were integral both to the Pacific Railroad report and to the building of military roads within the Nebraska Territory.

Warren spent the following year in Washington, D.C., completing several official reports and completing his map of the United States from the Mississippi River to the Pacific Ocean, which accompanied then U.S. Secretary of War Jefferson Davis's final report to Congress on the results of the transcontinental railroad route investigation. Warren then spent 1859–1861 as an assistant mathematics professor at West Point. Some of his students included prominent Civil War generals, among them the future boy generals Wesley Merritt, George A. Custer, H. Judson Kilpatrick, and Ranald S. Mackenzie for the Union, as well as Confederates Stephen Dodson Ramseur, Thomas L. Rosser, Joseph Wheeler, and George Washington Custis Lee, the youngest son of Confederate General Robert E. Lee.

In May of 1861, seeking advancement, Warren was granted a leave of absence from West Point and joined the U.S. Volunteers, accepting the lieutenant colonelcy of the 5th New York (Zouaves) Infantry Regiment on May 14, 1861. By the end of the month Warren and his regiment were stationed outside of Fortress Monroe, Virginia, seeing action at the Battle of Big Bethel Church on June 10, 1861, well before the First Battle of Manassas/Bull Run.

In May of that year Confederate Col. John Magruder had been placed in command of operations on the Lower Peninsula. In particular he was to hold a line from the James to the York rivers and thus prevent Union troops at Fortress Monroe from advancing up the peninsula. On June 6 he sent then Col. Daniel H. Hill and his North Carolina regiment to an advanced position at Big Bethel on the Hampton Road, about 13 miles below Yorktown. While there, three companies of Virginians, two troops of cavalry, and a battalion of howitzers reinforced Hill. Hill took up position behind a bend in a branch of the Back River, building a small enclosed earthwork covering a bridge in his front and all approaches to it. He was protected on the left by dense woods while a small ravine and the bend in the river protected his right. On June 8, Magruder arrived and took command in person.

Maj. Gen. Benjamin Butler, the political lawyer in command at Fortress Monroe, saw Confederate outposts such as Big Bethel as a nuisance and he decided to get rid of it. To accomplish this mission Butler decided to send one column on the road from Hampton to Newport News and another column on the road from New Market Bridge. The columns were to rendezvous about a mile and a half south of Little Bethel and make a surprise attack upon Magruder and Hill's outpost. They were also to destroy the smaller Confederate outpost at Little Bethel while they were at it.

The first column consisted of Warren's 5th New York (Zouaves) Infantry Regiment (under its colonel, Abram Duryea), which was supported by the 3rd New York Infantry Regiment and two howitzers. The second column was composed of elements from the 1st Vermont Infantry Regiment and the 4th Massachusetts Infantry Regiment, supported by the 7th New York Infantry Regiment, along with a section of artillery (two field guns). To avoid confusion when they met at the rendezvous, the second column was to wear white armbands and both sides were to shout the password: "Boston." No one seemed to realize that the troops might not be able to see white armbands in the dark or early dawn and that someone might just start shooting before anyone got close enough to shout "Boston!"

The first column moved out at 1:00 A.M. June 10 and all went well until they reached the fork in the road where they were to meet the second column, when the 7th New York opened fire on the 3rd New York. Two men were killed and nine were wounded and any chance of surprise was lost. Brig. Gen. Ebenezer W. Pierce, in command of the expedition, decided to proceed but sent for reinforcements and the 1st New York Infantry Regiment and the 2nd New York Infantry Regiment were immediately dispatched.

Arriving at Little Bethel he found that the Confederates had abandoned their outpost there (and had fallen back upon Big Bethel), so Pierce burned the Little Bethel outpost before advancing on Big Bethel, forming a line of battle when they were within 800 yards of Magruder and Hill's troops. Hill, taking advantage of the Union delay, had quickly deployed his men.

The 5th New York and the elements from the 1st Vermont and 4th Massachusetts advanced against the Confederate left but were prevented by a creek from making any serious assaults. However, they threatened to take the ford below the bridge and overwhelm the small detachment defending it, which Magruder reinforced and which then threw back the attack. The 3rd New York, with 150 men of the 5th New York as skirmishers, attacked on the right. As the 3rd New York moved out, however, one of its companies was separated from the rest of the regiment by a thickly hedged ditch, although it continued to march forward in line with the remainder of the regiment. Hill thereupon directed a company to move out of the woods. It stopped the advance of the Zouave skirmishers, and the Confederates thought that it was this action that stopped the advance of the 3rd New York, which in turn won them the battle.

In actuality what was going on was that the commander of 3rd New York thought that his detached company was a Confederate force that was in the process of outflanking him. Therefore, the 3rd New York withdrew and that ended any chance of the Union forces winning the fight.

Having been repulsed on the right, Pierce gave the left another try. A column consisting of the elements from the 1st Vermont and 4th Massachusetts crossed the creek and appeared at the angle of the Confederate left, apparently thinking they would find the Confederate fieldworks open at that point. They weren't. The officer commanding the attack was killed and the assault sputtered out. When the 1st New York and the 2nd New York arrived at 11:00 A.M., Pierce considered renewing the attack, but received an order from Butler to withdraw.

The primary result of the battle was to raise Southern morale while chilling Northern ardor and it also brought calls for Butler's removal. In addition, it gained for Magruder a promotion to brigadier general, and that, as they say, was that.

Warren served in this battle with coolness and efficiency under fire. This helped him win the colonelcy of his regiment some three months later. He had won the respect and admiration of his troops by his obvious concern for their welfare and for his courage under fire. If there was one thing that soldiers of both sides demanded of their officers it was courage under fire. The most respected officers were those who led from the front, when necessary, not those who habitually commanded from the rear. It was not long before Warren's superiors had marked him as a man who appeared to be destined for great things.

Warren spent the remainder of the year drilling his regiment and assisting in the construction of the defenses of Baltimore, Maryland, and Washington, D.C. The defenses of Baltimore would never be tested but those at Washington would be at least probed during Jubal Early's great raid, in the summer of 1864. On September 11, 1861, Warren was promoted to full colonel, U.S. Volunteers, and was given full command of the 5th New York.

Shortly afterwards, in November, Maj. Gen. George B. McClellan, who had been named commander of the Army of the Potomac, had taken over from Bvt. Lt. Gen. Winfield Scott the position as general-in-chief. McClellan (or Little Mac, as he became known to his soldiers and admirers) would prove to be one handy-dandy little organizer, creating the Army of the Potomac, then stamping it indelibly with his personal style of command. In many ways he was also one of the most brilliant strategists ever produced by the U.S. Army. However, as a tactician he severely lacked a major requirement — a killer's instinct. Another problem was his unwillingness to risk everything and go for broke. As Robert E. Lee once put it, a good commander must love the army, but a great one must be willing to risk the death of the thing he loves. McClellan could not, and never was, able to take that ultimate risk.

President Lincoln had trouble with McClellan because he never seemed to be ready to attack the enemy, and he refused to inform Lincoln of his plans. Therefore, Lincoln issued on February 22, 1862, General War Order No. 1 that called for a general movement of Union land and sea forces against the Southern Confederacy. What Lincoln expected to happen was that McClellan would take his army against Joseph E. Johnston's army in Northern Virginia. Instead, McClellan proposed to make an end run at Richmond, taking his army by sea from Washington, D.C., and landing it at Fortress Monroe, at the lower Chesapeake Bay peninsula, and advancing on Richmond from the south. Reluctantly, Lincoln accepted the proposal. Lincoln was reluctant because he feared leaving Washington uncovered to a possible Confederate thrust. Lee would masterfully use this fear to deny McClellan the reinforcements he felt were vital for his success.

In April 1862, McClellan landed his army (including Warren and his 5th New York [Zouaves] Regiment at Fortress Monroe) and launched what became known as the Peninsula Campaign. McClellan soon demonstrated that while he could develop masterful plans he never considered what might possibly happen if something went wrong; there was never a Plan B and he was incapable of improvising. Philip Sheridan, on the other hand, would eventually prove himself to be a master at battlefield improvisation.

During the campaign, Warren led his regiment at the Siege of Yorktown, where, in a bit of military theatre provided by Magruder, who was still in command of the Confederates on the peninsula, McClellan was fooled into failing to press an enemy whom he outnumbered by a factor of ten to one, allowing Johnston to bring his entire army from Northern Virginia to the defense of Richmond. On May 18, 1861, Warren was named commander of the Third Brigade, Second Division, V Corps, Army of the Potomac. Warren would command this brigade until February 5, 1863.

McClellan finally began his advance and arrived within four miles of Richmond by the end of May. McClellan, being McClellan, then dug in, passing the initiative to the Confederates and allowing himself to be attacked by Johnston on May 31, during the Battle of Seven Pines/Fair Oaks. Johnston decided to take advantage of the fact that the Chickahominy River bisected McClellan's army and that heavy rains on May 30 had washed away many of the bridges that connected the two wings of the Army of the Potomac. The attack was mismanaged by the inexperienced Confederate army high command and General Edwin Sumner managed to get his II Corps across what bridges remained. McClellan held his position and did not make any counterattacks, while immediately calling for reinforcements.

These reinforcements were denied because Lincoln was worried about the vulnerability of Washington. Stonewall Jackson's 1862 Shenandoah Valley Campaign—which was the brainchild of one Robert E. Lee, who was then serving as the military advisor to Confederate President Jefferson Davis—reinforced Lincoln in that worry. Jackson kept at least three Union forces busy (the troops of Irvin McDowell, I Corps; John C. Fremont, later reorganized as XI Corps, and Nathaniel Banks, later reorganized as XII Corps), each Union force being generally bigger than his own and demonstrating how the use of terrain and mobility could offset a lack of numbers. Lincoln therefore decided to keep Irvin McDowell and his I Corps, which had been earmarked as McClellan's reinforcements in the vicinity of Washington, at one point using it to help chase Jackson.

The Battle of Seven Pines/Fair Oaks had one primary result, however—a change in command of the Army of Northern Virginia. Joseph E. Johnston had been severely wounded during the battle, taking months to recover, and Davis (following the breakdown of Johnston's second in command) named his erstwhile military advisor, Lee, to take command.

Between June 12 and June 16, Lee had his cavalry commander, James Ewell Brown (J.E.B.) Stuart, take his horsemen and ride completely around McClellan's entire army. The ride was spectacular and was right up Stuart's alley. It also provided Lee with valuable intelligence, which had been its real objective, since it revealed that the right flank of McClellan's army north of the Chickahominy River was still "in the air" (that is, that it was unprotected by any natural or man-made obstructions), and that nothing much had been done by McClellan to improve the situation that had existed before the Battle of Seven Pines/Fair Oaks and that had led directly to it.

The end result was that Lee pulled Jackson out of the Shenandoah Valley to reinforce him at Richmond. Lee wanted Jackson to lead the offensive he planned to launch. This became the Seven Days', which was aimed at destroying McClellan's army and winning the war. Lee, although he saved Richmond, was not fully successful, since he failed to destroy McClellan's army, and the war continued.

The battle began on June 25 with attacks directed against Fitz John Porter and his V Corps, which was separated from McClellan and the rest of the Army of the Potomac by the Chickahominy River and which featured a battle just about every day for the next seven days. Unfortunately, Jackson was late at Beaver Dam Creek, near Mechanicsburg. McClellan ordered Porter to withdraw to Gains Mill, where Warren was slightly wounded during the renewed fighting on June 27, 1862.

Although the Union army was not beaten, McClellan was, and his only thought was to protect his retreat as he "changed his base" to Harrison Landing on the James River. This turned a tactical defeat into a strategic victory since it accomplished Lee's first objective to disrupt any possibility of a siege of Richmond. At Gains Mill, Jackson was late once again. Finally, a breakthrough was achieved in the center of Porter's line, which collapsed. The arrival of fresh Union troops allowed Porter to prevent a rout and withdraw his battered corps. During this time, Magruder again dazzled McClellan's troops on the other side of the Chickahominy; McClellan took no action.

As McClellan pulled his army back, Lee sought to attack it on the flank while it was on the march. Although Lee quickly put together a plan, poor staff work, bad maps, natural obstacles of the terrain, timid commanders, stout resistance from McClellan's troops, and Jackson's continued unexplainable slowness thwarted it. (Jackson may have been suffering from both illness and exhaustion brought on by his exertions in the Shenandoah Valley and his march to join Lee at Richmond.)

Lee made his first attempt on June 29 at Savage's Station; he tried again the next day at Glendale and then one last time on July 1, 1862, at Malvern Hill. Union artillery at Malvern Hill totally dominated all of the approaches to the position of McClellan's army and Lee erroneously believed that the retreat of the previous week had shown that the Army of the Potomac had become demoralized. While McClellan himself was definitely demoralized, his army was not.

When Lee launched his assault the Union artillery totally dominated the battlefield, disrupting Confederate artillery support and smashing the Confederate assault with only a few Union infantry units actually being involved in the battle at all. Warren's brigade happened to be one of them; it repulsed a Confederate division and it was engaged in skirmishing the next day at Harrison Landing.

McClellan might have counterattacked; in fact, many of his officers, including Porter, who was a protégé of McClellan's, urged him to do so. Many military historians believe that if McClellan had counterattacked at any time during the Seven Days' he might well have been successful; after all, he outnumbered Lee by about 120,000 to 85,000. But McClellan had convinced himself throughout the campaign that he was outnumbered, a conclusion aided and abetted by his chief of intelligence, Alan Pinkerton, who did a better job of catching Confederate agents (which was not much of a leap from his prewar occupation as a private detective) than at supplying McClellan with information. Pinkerton was soon reduced to going with the flow and telling McClellan exactly what he wanted to hear.

Instead of counterattacking, McClellan retreated to Harrison Landing and began regrouping with the idea of starting over again. But Lincoln had had enough and ordered the army removed to Washington, under McClellan's supervision, and it was sent off piecemeal to reinforce John Pope, who was given an army formed from the units that Jackson had humiliated in the Shenandoah Valley (XI Corps and XII Corps) before leaving the Valley to join Lee for the Seven Days'.

While this was going on, Lee, recognizing the weaknesses in the Army of Northern Virginia during the Seven Days', reorganized it. Before the Seven Days', the Army of Northern Virginia had never fought together as a unit. Jackson's troops and several other brigades did not join the army until just before the Seven Days' and Lee had not had enough time to put together an effective command structure.

He proceeded to remedy these defects by transferring various division commanders whom the fighting revealed to be too timid, sending most of them West, to the detriment of the Confederate war effort in that especially vital theatre, since it was there that the Union won the war while it could only lose it in the East. Next, due to difficulties in communicating adequately with eight or nine individual division commanders, Lee grouped his divisions into two unofficial corps. One was placed under Longstreet, while the other was placed under Jackson. In addition, Jackson soon recovered from whatever had been his problems during the Seven Days' and never again let Lee down.

The first major result of the Seven Days' occurred when Lincoln brought Henry Halleck east and replaced McClellan with him as general-in-chief to coordinate a new offensive making use of John Pope's army north of Richmond and McClellan's troops on the peninsula. While McClellan sulked, Halleck decided that the best thing to do was to unite the two armies, bringing the Army of the Potomac back to Washington and forwarding its units to Pope. Lee, however, had other ideas.

16

Showing the Spark at Second Manassas/Bull Run

President Lincoln created John Pope's Army of Virginia on June 26, 1862, due to the failures and command complications in the Shenandoah Valley. Pope's mission called for his army to accomplish the following:

1. Protect Washington, D.C.
2. Guarantee the safety of the Shenandoah Valley for the Union.
3. Threaten Lee's railroad communications in order to draw off troops from Richmond and thus make McClellan's task before Richmond easier.

However, when McClellan did nothing, Halleck, Lincoln's new general-in-chief, decided by the end of July it would better to unite these two armies.

While Lincoln and Halleck were reaching this decision, Pope was moving against the important Virginia Central Railroad nexus at Gordonsville, northwest of Richmond. To protect Gordonsville, Lee dispatched Stonewall Jackson and some 12,000 troops on July 13. When McClellan did nothing at Harrison Landing, Lee dispatched A.P. Hill and his 13,000-man Light Division to reinforce Jackson on July 27. In turn, Lincoln was persuaded to reinforce Pope by the strength of Jackson's reputation. As Lee realized that McClellan's army was being withdrawn from the Peninsula he began moving his troops by rail to Gordonsville.

In order to reach and reinforce Pope, the Army of the Potomac (II Corps, III Corps, V Corps and VI Corps) would first have to move by water down the James River, along Chesapeake Bay, up the Potomac River to Washington, and then march to join Pope in northern Virginia. While the Union troops had to go around the barn, Lee had a straight shot to Gordonsville from Richmond by using the Virginia Central Railroad. Meanwhile, McClellan's opposition to the movement and his subordinates' distaste for Pope was not helpful.

Jackson got the ball rolling when he moved against Pope's two advance divisions, under Nathaniel Banks, at Cedar Mountain, 20 miles south of Lee's concentration point at Gordonsville. Expecting imminent reinforcements, Banks attacked on August 9, 1862. The surprise attack threw back Jackson's troops and even routed the elite Stonewall Brigade. A.P. Hill and his division counterattacked, causing Banks to fall back for several miles.

Within the next two days the rest of Pope's army arrived and Jackson fell back to Gordonsville. The result of this confrontation was the confirmation that operations would be transferred from the Peninsula to the Rappahannock. For the next 10 days Lee sparred with Pope, both of them having about 55,000 men (Lee having left just two brigades behind at the Peninsula to keep an eye on McClellan).

To gain information and to wreck a railroad bridge at Rappahannock Station, Lee sent Stuart's cavalry into the rear of Pope's army. Stuart found Pope on August 17, northwest of Clark's Mountain, preparing to march. Stuart raided Pope's headquarters, capturing many papers and Pope's dispatch book. From these Lee learned that massive reinforcements from McClellan's army were on the way to join Pope. With the arrival of only the first of these Pope would outnumber Lee by about 85,000 to 55,000. Lee knew he had to move fast.

He sought to isolate a portion of Pope's army, while Pope sought to hold his position until reinforcements from McClellan's army on the Peninsula reached him; once he outnumbered Lee he could then conduct an offensive. Since Lee wanted to prevent this from happening he divided his army and sent Jackson's corps on a flank march to cut Pope's rail communications in his rear. Lee's action defied military conventions about never dividing your army in the face of the enemy, especially if outnumbered.

Lee was gambling, giving Pope the opportunity to smash first one part of his army (Jackson) and then turn upon the other (Lee and Longstreet). But Lee believed that the Confederacy simply could not win by following military conventions and he was prepared to flaunt them. At this time, however, Lee did not intend to give battle. It was only after Pope lost his grasp upon the situation that Lee actually attacked, and it was Jackson who made it all possible.

Pope detected Jackson's march on August 25, which was headed northwest along the Rappahannock River. He thereupon jumped to the conclusion that Jackson was heading for the Shenandoah Valley. But Pope's weak cavalry failed to detect Jackson's turn eastward. That turn allowed Jackson to march unopposed to Pope's huge supply depot at Manassas Junction, 25 miles in Pope's rear and to seize it, sack it, and destroy what his soldiers could not consume outright or otherwise carry off. To do this Jackson's corps covered more than 50 miles in just two days, once again earning it the title of Jackson's Foot Cavalry (which it had originally won during Jackson's Shenandoah Valley Campaign). Pope, on his part, saw Jackson's raid as an opportunity to "bag" Jackson before Lee and Longstreet could interfere.

The only problem in doing this lay in finding Jackson, who had seemingly vanished into thin air. Pope's cavalry reported Jackson to be in several locations. This caused Pope to march and countermarch his troops. By this time Pope had under his command XI Corps and XII Corps of his own Army of Virginia, I Corps (under McDowell from the Washington, D.C., area), V Corps (from the Army of the Potomac under Porter, who had recently called Pope an ass), along with a portion of IX Corps (drawn from the North Carolina coast), which were all marching to join him. McClellan was holding another two corps of the Army of the Potomac at Alexandria, Virginia. While these troops could have marched to join Pope, they would not participate in the coming battle. The remaining troops of the Army of the Potomac were still on the way from the Peninsula and also would not have any effect upon the coming confrontation between the forces of Lee and Pope.

Meanwhile, Jackson had gone to ground on wooded Stoney Ridge, which was only a couple of miles west of the previous year's Manassas/Bull Run battlefield. Lee and Longstreet, unknown to Pope, were only a few miles away after having marched through an unguarded gap in the Bull Run Mountains. Stuart and his cavalry were busy maintaining communications between Lee and Jackson, so that Jackson knew that Lee would be joining him sometime on the morning of August 29.

On August 28, however, one of Pope's divisions managed to stumble upon Jackson's position at Groveton and there was a fierce firefight at dusk. (It was during this fight that Richard Ewell—then one of Jackson's division commanders—was wounded, losing a leg. It would be over nine months before Ewell would return to the Army of Northern Virginia.) Having finally found Jackson, Pope concentrated his troops to confront Jackson during the night and morning of August 28–29. Pope believed that Jackson was preparing to retreat towards Longstreet (when in actuality Longstreet was moving to join Jackson), therefore, Pope conducted a number of piecemeal assaults, which almost broke Jackson's line several times, but Jackson's troops hung on and threw all of the Union assaults back.

Not engaged yet were the 30,000 Union troops in I Corps and V Corps (including Warren's brigade) and a portion of IX Corps, which were marching to join Pope. McDowell, the senior general of the reinforcements, maneuvered rather ineffectively that entire day. It was only after dark that a few of his regiments managed to skirmish with Jackson.

Porter, when he arrived with his corps on August 29, received orders from Pope to attack immediately. However, Porter was unfamiliar with everything from the battlefield (not having been involved in the First Battle of Manassas/Bull Run), to the generals he was supposed to be operating and coordinating his movements with. Therefore, he took his time following those orders. He used his time to reconnoiter and he discovered that Longstreet had moved in on Jackson's right flank; when Porter reported this to Pope, Pope refused to believe him.

No matter what Pope believed, Porter, on August 30, was convinced that Longstreet's entire corps was in his front—and by noon it actually was. Therefore, Porter, with 10,000 men, did nothing. Refusing to believe that Longstreet had arrived, Pope ordered Porter to attack Jackson's right flank that afternoon. Porter was unable to comply because Longstreet connected with Jackson's flank. In addition, Porter disdained Pope and resented taking orders from him; against his better judgment he eventually made three assaults upon Jackson, as ordered. All three of the attacks failed and, as the third attack was ebbing, Longstreet counterattacked, which crumpled Pope's left flank, leading to the general collapse of Pope's army. (For not immediately following Pope's orders Porter was court-martialed beginning in November 1862. Porter was convicted in 1863 and cashiered from the army. Porter never ceased seeking a new trial or a court of inquiry and finally got one in 1878-1879. Testimony by Confederate officers and Confederate records demonstrated that Longstreet had indeed been in Porter's front and therefore Porter could not have obeyed Pope's orders.[1] Whatever Pope's response, Porter failed to do much of anything, which many have considered to have been in and of itself worthy of at least some adverse consequences.)

When Longstreet got his 30,000 men in position on Jackson's right during the afternoon of August 29, Lee asked (but did not order) him to attack. Longstreet demurred, preferring to receive an attack rather than making one. Thus Longstreet on the one hand, and McDowell and Porter on the other proceeded to neutralize each other.[2]

During the night, Jackson pulled back a few of his brigades from advanced positions to readjust his line. Pope assumed that this realignment was in reality a retreat; therefore Pope immediately telegraphed Washington saying he had won a "victory" and was prepared to "pursue" the "defeated" Confederates. The "pursuit" became an assault that almost broke Jackson's line and Jackson was forced to call upon Longstreet for reinforcements. Longstreet had a better idea. He used his artillery to enfilade Pope's attacking troops while on Lee's insistence launching an assault of his own with his five divisions of infantry, hitting Pope's troops like a sledgehammer. Right in the path of that massive assault was Warren and his brigade.

According to Warren's official report, dated September 6, 1862, at that time Warren's brigade consisted just of his own 5th New York Infantry and the 10th New York Infantry, an aggregate of only about 1,000 men. Porter was in the process of making an assault upon Jackson's position, and Brig. Gen. Daniel Butterfield's brigade was about to move out and attack. When a battery was left uncovered by Union troops moving forward to the assault, Warren on his own responsibility moved his brigade to cover it and Porter's own left flank, which also had been left uncovered. In his report, Warren wrote that his intention was to make all the show of force that he could. He then sent a courier to notify Porter of his actions and his intentions.

Porter received the message and sent one back to Warren, ordering him to hold on and sending him a number of mounted orderlies to keep Porter informed about what was happening on the flank Warren was covering. Warren later wrote:

> As soon as General Butterfield's brigade advanced up the hill [towards the Confederate position], there was a great commotion among the rebel forces, and the whole side of the hill and the edges of the woods swarmed with men before unseen. The effect was not unlike flushing a covey of quails. The enemy fell back to the line of the railroad, and took shelter on the railroad cut and behind the embankment and lined the edges of the woods beyond. Butterfield's advance beyond the brow of the hill was impossible and taking his position his troops opened fire on the enemy in front, who from his sheltered position returned it vigorously, while at the same time a battery, somewhere in the prolongation of the line, opened up a most destructive enfilading fire with spherical case-shot.
>
> It became evident to me that without heavy reinforcements General Butterfield's troops must fall back or be slaughtered, the only assistance he received being from Hazlett's battery which I was supporting, and Weed's. After making a desperate and hopeless fight General Butterfield's troops fell back, and the enemy immediately formed and advanced. Hazlett's battery now did good execution on them, and forced one column, that advanced beyond the point of the wood to fall back into it. Unwilling to retire from the position I held, which involved the withdrawal of this efficient battery and the exposure of the flanks of our retreating forces, I held on, hoping that fresh troops would be thrown forward to meet the enemy, now advancing in the open fields well knowing, however, that my position was one from which I could not retreat in the face of a superior force.
>
> Reynolds' division on my left, probably aware of the superior force of the enemy gathering in his front, fell back. The enemy advanced with rapidity upon my position, with the evident intention of capturing Hazlett's battery. The 10th New York was compelled to fall back, scarcely arriving at the position held by the 5th New York before the enemy, and in such a manner as to almost completely prevent the 5th from firing upon them. While I was endeavoring to clear them from the front, the enemy opened fire from the woods on the rear and left flank of the 5th with the most fearful effect. I then gave the order to face about and march down the hill, so as to bring the enemy all on our front, but in the roar of musketry I could only be heard for a short distance. Capt. Boyd, near me, repeated the command but his men only partially obeyed it. They were unwilling to make a backward movement. He was wounded while trying to execute it. Adjutant Sovereign carried the order along the line to Capt. Winslow, commanding the regiment and to the other captains, but was killed in the act....
>
> Before the colors and the remnant of the regiment could be extricated 298 men of the 5th and 133 of the 10th were killed or wounded.

Pope's troops fell back to Henry House Hill, where they made a stand that halted Longstreet's juggernaut.

There had been no Union panic and that night Pope decided to retreat, beginning an orderly withdrawal the next day. Lee, hoping to strike at Pope's rear, sent Jackson on another sweep. The time the Union troops were prepared and on September 1 a vicious rear guard action against Jackson was fought by two of Pope's divisions at Chantilly Mansion, just 20 miles from Washington. (It was here that Philip Kearney, one of the Union division commanders, was killed.) Afterwards the Union troops fell back to Washington.

Army morale plunged. Although the troops had fought well, they knew that they had been mismanaged and they blamed McDowell and Pope. McDowell and Pope blamed McClellan and Porter for lack of cooperation and refusal to obey orders, respectively.

Pope was sent to Minnesota to put down an Indian uprising, while the Army of Virginia was merged with the Army of the Potomac and McClellan was put back in charge temporarily because there was no one else to reorganize and repair the physical and morale damage to the Army of the Potomac, which still had faith in McClellan although Lincoln had long ago lost his.

Court-martial charges were filed against Porter two weeks after the battle. He was not tried immediately due to the Maryland Campaign and the Battle of Antietam/Sharpsburg. When McClellan was relieved, so was Porter. He was tried before a court packed with enemies of

McClellan. Partly Porter was a stand-in for McClellan, who could not be tried because of his popularity with the army. Porter, on the other hand, was just one general among many. The politicians had decided that someone had to take the blame for what happened at Second Manassas/Bull Run and Porter was selected. Pope from the very beginning insisted that the "unsoldierly and dangerous conduct" of the generals from McClellan's Army of the Potomac had caused his defeat, singling out Porter in particular.[3]

An objective person reading the transcript of the court-martial would be hard put imagining that Porter would be found guilty.[4] All of the prosecution's main points against Porter were excellently and easily refuted by the defense. For instance, cross-examination of Porter's chief accuser, Pope, clearly demonstrated that Pope's knowledge of the location of his own troops, not to mention those of his Confederate opponents, was so clearly erroneous that it was obvious Pope had no idea of what the actual tactical situation had been. Another major witness against Pope, Irvin McDowell, was so transparently selective in his memory as to make it abundantly clear that he was intent on saving his own hide rather than seeing that any kind of justice was actually done.

The composition of the court itself makes it clear from the beginning that it was fixed for the sole purpose of convicting Porter. The president of the court was Maj. Gen. David Hunter, a mediocrity at best and a military incompetent at worst. The members included Maj. Gen. Ethan Allen Hitchcock, a fainthearted warrior and believer in the occult who admitted in his diary that he was cowed by Secretary of War Edwin M. Stanton; Silas Casey, a general who was not partial to McClellan and his disciples; Napoleon Bonaparte Buford, a general whom Stanton had hoped would replace McClellan and who was suborned by Secretary of the Treasury Salmon P. Chase with promises of promotion and an army posting for his son; Rufus King and James B. Ricketts, who should have been disqualified for conflicts of interest, King at one point even testifying in the trial against Porter; Benjamin M. Prentiss and James P. Slough, both considered to be "friendly" towards Porter; and the final member, James Garfield, a protégé of Chase who tended to play prosecutor from the bench. The composition was also improper because the normal number of court-martial board members was 13 instead of nine. This meant that only a majority of five instead of seven would be needed to convict Porter.

Robert E. Lee stated after the war that if Porter had attacked as ordered "I suppose we should have cut him to pieces." But, at the same time, Porter discovered hardly anything about the force in front of him, except that it was there.[5] At the moment he sighted the dust of Longstreet's approach, Porter had stopped short, deployed his own troops to await whatever was coming, and that was all. He did not develop the Confederate position and he did not probe aggressively to discover their strength. Finally, he did not immediately report to Pope what he had encountered. When the next morning he reported to Pope that Longstreet was present he could not provide any evidence or concrete details and it was for this reason that Pope flatly refused to believe him.

In addition, McClellan had inflated Porter's reputation to such an extent that it was believed that with all of his supposed skill his failures at the Second Battle of Manassas/Bull Run could only be explained as deliberate. Lee's opinion about Porter's qualities as a general are interesting, as he said after the war that "Porter was not a strong man, would do well enough with somebody to tell him [what to do], but [was] rather timid under responsibility."

It took the judges just three and a half hours to reach a verdict. After President Lincoln reviewed it according to procedure, it was released to the public. The guilty verdict was a complete and total surprise. Lincoln's own turn of mind can be glimpsed in his reaction when an officer offered the opinion that McClellan had sought only a stalemate in the Battle of Antietam/Sharpsburg so that a conservative, negotiated peace which preserved slavery could be reached. As soon as Lincoln heard about the incident he had the offending officer dismissed from the army. Therefore, Lincoln might have considered a guilty verdict against Porter as proper in order to provide the officer corps of the Army of the Potomac with "an example and a warning." But Porter may have been lucky. At least one defeated British admiral during the Anglo-French Wars of the 18th century, and defeated generals during the French Revolution, had been shot "in order to encourage the others."

There would always be, before and after the trial, two extreme poles around which opinions gathered. George Templeton Strong believed that Porter belonged at the bottom of the American military pantheon, just above Benedict Arnold. The other pole held the opinion that Porter was simply a gallant soldier who had suffered a "very great injustice," as Ulysses S. Grant came to eventually believe.

After the war, when Warren was not pressing his own case for a court of inquiry, he joined those who were seeking justice for Fitz John Porter. One of these was a former regimental and brigade commander whose regiment joined V Corps after the Second Battle of Manassas/Bull Run, one Joshua Lawrence Chamberlain, formerly lieutenant colonel and then colonel of the 20th Maine Infantry Regiment. In *The Celebrated Case of Fitz John Porter* Otto Eisenschiml told the story of one of Chamberlain's efforts, the cumulative effect of which may explain Grant's eventual change of mind regarding Porter's case.

Chamberlain, after the war, while governor of Maine, attended a meeting of V Corps veterans, at which a resolution had been passed requesting that Porter's case be reopened, and Chamberlain, as a friend and political ally of Grant's (who was now president) was asked to present the resolution at the White House. Grant invited his caller to breakfast, but when he learned of the reason of the visit he said, "The friends of General Porter are making a mistake when pressing for a rehearing. I have been through the case carefully seven or eight times. They had better leave it alone. It will be worse for him if it is reopened."

However, like water wearing away a stone, Chamberlain's efforts apparently bore fruit, for both Rutherford B. Hayes, who ordered the court of inquiry, and Grant changed their minds. Hayes, like Grant, was originally of the opinion a professional soldier's obedience to orders and the proper conduct before an enemy were two of the essential rules of war making.[6] In addition, Hayes had been a regimental officer in 1862 and noted, "I was an eye-witness to the terrible inertia that was exhibited by those officers about me when Pope took command."

But Hayes came around and eventually appointed the Schofield Board, consisting of John M. Scholfield, Alfred H. Terry, and George W. Getty, in 1878 to provide a review of the case. It was this board that exonerated Porter, although corrective action based on the findings of this board was blocked.

In the December 1882 issue of the *North American Review*, Grant wrote an article titled "An Undeserved Stigma." In this article Grant decided to go before the public and do penance. "I feel," he wrote, "a double interest in this case, because when as General of the Army, when I might have been instrumental in having justice done to General Porter, and later as President, I labored under the firm conviction that he was guilty. Having become better informed, I at once gave, as I have continued to give, every earnest effort to impress the minds of my countrymen with the justice of this case, and to secure from our government the restitution due to General Fitz John Porter."

Grant in his article analyzed the Second Battle of Manassas/Bull Run and showed that in his opinion Porter had acted with good judgment throughout. He questioned whether there had been a similar engagement during the entire war where generals did not exercise their discretion, as Porter had done, "and with far less justification." Grant noted that Porter had engaged Longstreet's attention with little risk to himself, thereby doing more for Pope's relief than if he had gone directly to his assistance. All in all, Porter had, in Grant's new and reconsidered opinion, deserved nothing but praise for his soldierly conduct. Grant even made a specific suggestion about how the wrong to Porter could be undone in the most direct manner: "General Porter should be declared by Congress to have been convicted on mistaken testimony, and, therefore, to have never been out of the army. This would make him a major general of volunteers until his muster out, after which he should be continued as a colonel of infantry and brevet brigadier general of the U.S. Army."

Grant's article provided a first-class sensation. That Grant had begun to waver and had finally changed his opinion about the Porter case had not been generally known until the publication of his article. Grant had therefore been considered one of Porter's most convinced foes. Now that he had publicly announced that he had indeed changed his mind, many people were immediately and lastingly influenced by his courageous action.

Ever since Porter's conviction there had been a political fight going on seeking to reverse it. When President Hayes ordered that there be a court of inquiry to look into the case, Warren, who had steadfastly stood by his former commander, testified at the court of inquiry, where he demolished much of the prosecution's case in the court-martial that had convicted Porter in 1863. He demonstrated, for instance, that the maps used in the 1863 court-martial that purported to show the positions of the Union and Confederate armies were simply wrong.

In 1879 the court of inquiry announced its conclusions as follows: "In our opinion, justice requires such action as may be necessary to annul and set aside the findings and sentence of the court-martial in the case of Maj. Gen. Fitz John Porter and restore him to the position that sentence deprived him." But it was not to be, just yet.

James Garfield, who had sat on the original Porter court-martial board and was now a prominent member of Congress, blocked any action upon the court of inquiry's report. After Garfield became president nothing more was done until Congress took up the case and in 1884 approved a bill providing a redress of grievances for Porter. The bill was promptly vetoed by Garfield's successor as president, Chester A. Arthur.

Congress eventually passed a new bill in 1886, calling for the court of inquiry's findings to be enacted. In July of that year President Grover Cleveland, the first Democrat to be elected president since the American Civil War, signed the bill and on August 5, 1886, Porter was reappointed a colonel of infantry to rank from May 14, 1861. Two days later Porter, on his own request, was placed on the retired list.[7]

Warren, however, had won praise for the strategic holding maneuver that had cost him half of his brigade. His under-strength brigade was held in reserve with the rest of V Corps during the Battle of Antietam/Sharpsburg on September 17, 1862, which saw in its aftermath the final firing of George B. McClellan. Nine days later, on September 26, 1862, Warren was promoted to the rank of brigadier general, U.S. Volunteers. At the Battle of Fredericksburg on December 13, 1862, Warren's brigade was again held in reserve and did not see action.

Warren left combat command for a time when Joseph Hooker took command of the Army of the Potomac after Fredericksburg and asked Warren to join his staff on February 2, 1863, as the army's chief topographical engineer. As a member of Hooker's staff, Warren served mostly as an advisor.

On March 3, 1863, Warren was named chief engineer of the Army of the Potomac when the Corps of Topographical Engineers was merged with the Corps of Engineers. Then it was Hooker's turn to dash himself upon the rock that was Robert E. Lee and the Army of Northern Virginia.

17

The Hero at Chancellorsville and Gettysburg

During the Battle of Chancellorsville the commander of the Army of the Potomac, Maj. Gen. Joseph Hooker, apparently lost his nerve at the first collision of his troops with those of Robert E. Lee's Army of Northern Virginia as they moved through what was known as the Wilderness. It was here that Gouverneur K. Warren was offered a second chance to bring victory to the Army of the Potomac.

The summer before, he had lost half of his brigade in a strategic holding action at the Second Battle of Manassas/Bull Run, trying to stem the tide of James Longstreet's irresistible onslaught. Now he would try, and fail, to stiffen Hooker's backbone so that he could regain his nerve and go on to win the Battle of Chancellorsville.

It happened on May 1, 1863, midway between Chancellorsville and Tabernacle Church. Hooker, who outnumbered Lee two to one, had already divided his army, half of which was in the rear of Lee's army. Lee had scrambled a single division, that of Richard H. Anderson, to buy him enough time to wriggle out of Hooker's trap.

Hooker had Maj. Gen. Henry W. Slocum, and his XII Corps, supported by Maj. Gen. Oliver Otis Howard and his XI Corps, advancing on the right. Maj. Gen. George G. Meade and his V Corps were on the left, supported by Maj. Gen. Darius Couch and his II Corps, with Maj. Gen. Daniel Sickles and his III Corps in reserve. Slocum and Meade believed that they would soon be out of the woods and converging on each other for the final blow against Lee's army.

Their paths had diverged and Slocum and Meade were soon out of touch with each other. In addition, Meade and his V Corps and Couch and his II Corps had also become separated. The leading V Corps division had penetrated the Wilderness by about two miles and was on a long slope—whose crest was in open country on the other side of the Wilderness—when it collided with Confederate skirmishers. Upon driving them back, they came upon Anderson's division, which threatened the Union division's flanks, and the Union troops withdrew. Then II Corps arrived and its leading division advanced to stabilize the situation, but a courier from Hooker suddenly and inexplicably ordered both divisions to be withdrawn at once.

Couch considered disobeying the order, an action that was urged upon him by Warren, who happened to be accompanying Couch to observe the advance and was horrified at what seemed to be happening. Hooker had everything he wanted in the palm of his hand. All he needed to do was to close his fingers and his army would be out of the Wilderness, where Hooker wanted it to be, in position to fall upon the rear of Lee's badly outnumbered army, which Maj. Gen. John Sedgwick was holding in place with I Corps and VI Corps. But now Hooker was refusing to do just that.

Warren immediately volunteered to return to Hooker's headquarters to get the order rescinded so that the advance could be resumed. While Warren hurried back to Hooker's headquarters to help Hooker find his nerve and rescind the order, Couch decided that he would obey it. Just as Couch disengaged both divisions, another courier arrived, calling on him to "hold until 5 P.M." Apparently Warren, just a shade too late, had persuaded Hooker to reconsider. Couch was so disgusted that he told the courier, "Tell General Hooker he is too late, the enemy are already on my right and rear. I am in full retreat." After the battle Couch was so disgusted with this performance that he would ask to be relieved and sought an immediate transfer, for he refused to serve any longer under Hooker's command.

Slocum, on Couch's right, had been engaged by Anderson's Division and was also obeying Hooker's order to retire. Meade was even more outraged than Couch to receive Hooker's orders to retire, for most of his V Corps had encountered nothing and he was within reach of Bank's Ford, the capture of which would shorten the lines of communication between the two separated wings of Hooker's army.

Although Hooker outnumbered Lee and had even outmaneuvered him, Hooker now allowed Lee to out-menace him. It would not be long before Lee and Jackson would send Hooker scurrying back to Washington and Lincoln would have to find a new general, his sixth, who could defeat the Confederates in the East. About two months later Warren would have his third chance, and this time he would earn immortal fame as the "Savior of Little Round Top."

The Army of the Potomac and the Army of Northern Virginia, after the Union troops had once again pulled back across the Rappahannock River where they could cover Washington, spent the rest of the month of May licking their wounds and preparing for the next round.

Lee in particular used the time to his advantage to totally reorganize his army. It is not clear if he intended to go ahead with the reorganization before Stonewall Jackson's death or not, but afterwards it became imperative, because Jackson was not replaceable.

First, he promoted Jackson's senior division commander, Richard Ewell, from major general to lieutenant general when he finally returned to the army after being wounded at Groveton during the Second Manassas/Bull Run Campaign, losing a leg. Ewell had also in the interim gained a wife. It would remain to be seen if he had retained the fire and dash that had marked his career in the Confederate army before Second Manassas/Bull Run. Ewell was given Jackson's command, now designated II Corps, Longstreet retained his command, I Corps, and Lee set about the creation of a brand new III Corps. He detached Maj. Gen. A.P. Hill and his Light Division from what had been Jackson's corps. This six-brigade division would be the nucleus of the new corps and Hill, now a lieutenant general, would be in charge. Two brand new infantry brigades had joined the army and were assigned to III Corps. Hill wanting to keep his old Light Division intact, as much as possible, detached two veteran brigades and joined them with the two new brigades to form a new division that was given to Henry Heth, a favorite of Lee's, to command. Hill's senior brigadier, Dorsey Pender, was promoted to major general and was given the Light Division. Finally, Richard H. Anderson's Division from I Corps was transferred to the new III Corps.

Stuart's cavalry was not ignored in this reorganization. He received two more brigades, which raised the number of brigades in his division from four to six. The artillery was also reorganized, with the artillery reserve being disbanded and the various artillery battalions being distributed among the three corps. Brig. Gen. William Pendleton, Lee's official chief of artillery, lost his command of the reserve artillery and became just another member of Lee's staff. Lee, in addition, was planning his second invasion of the North.

President Davis wanted to do something to relieve the pressure being placed by Ulysses S. Grant upon Vicksburg and by Benjamin Butler upon Port Hudson. These were the last two

Southern strongholds upon the Mississippi River. As long as they held out the South was not broken in two pieces by the great river. One proposal was to send Lee and at least a portion of his army West to join Braxton Bragg's Army of Tennessee and John Pemberton's Army of Mississippi and turn the tide. Lee, however, wanted nothing whatsoever to do with this proposal and proposed instead an invasion of the North, specifically Pennsylvania, during which the Army of the Potomac was to be destroyed, north of its namesake river. Lee believed that if he could accomplish this, he could win the war.

Reluctantly, Davis went along, although he hedged his bets, refusing to go for broke, as Lee wanted. He retained two brigades from Pickett's Division and another two-brigade division that officially belonged to Longstreet's I Corps to garrison Richmond. Although no threat to North Carolina, Southwest Virginia, or East Tennessee materialized during the Gettysburg campaign, he refused to call upon the four additional divisions scattered there or for Maj. Gen. D.H. Hill, commanding in North Carolina, to join Lee. Although Longstreet was not consulted when Lee reorganized the Army of Northern Virginia, it had been D.H. Hill, not A.P. Hill, whom Longstreet felt should have been given the new III Corps. By June 3 most of the Army of Northern Virginia was on the march, leaving A.P. Hill and his corps to hold Fredericksburg and keep an eye on Hooker's army.

Meanwhile, back at the Army of the Potomac, which had returned to the north side of the Rappahannock River, it had begun to sink in that while the army had been humiliated by the result of the Chancellorsville Campaign it had not been particularly badly hurt by the battle.

Aside from cavalry commanders George Stoneman and W.W. Averell, whom he sacked with some justification, Hooker also blamed his loss on Sedgwick and Howard, with a good deal less justification, especially in the case of Sedgwick. Lincoln and Halleck, however, for the time being seemed to retain at least some confidence in Hooker, because he was not immediately relieved, only given priority orders to protect both Harper's Ferry and Washington itself. Hooker, however, realized that something was up and sent his cavalry, now under Alfred Pleasonton, with infantry support, to find out just what.

Stuart and his cavalry had orders to begin moving west on June 10. Just before that, he concentrated his entire division for two grand reviews. It was just after the second review that Pleasonton burst his bubble at the First Battle of Brandy Station. Hooker was delighted with the performance of his cavalry, which not only held its own against Stuart's entire command but also accomplished its reconnaissance mission and informed Hooker that there were large concentrations of Confederate infantry around Culpepper and that Stuart was preparing to ride west.

Now certain that Lee was moving into the Shenandoah Valley, Hooker moved his army towards Manassas after A.P. Hill left Fredericksburg to join Lee. Lee was indeed using the Shenandoah Valley to move his army. Ewell smashed a Union force at Winchester (in what was the Second Battle of Winchester) and all of the other small Union garrisons in the area were ordered to concentrate on the Maryland Heights above Harper's Ferry.

Stuart's cavalry, which was screening Lee's infantry, fought additional battles with Pleasonton's cavalry at Aldie, Middleburg, and Upperville. Then Stuart got the bright idea of taking three of his best brigades and riding around the Army of the Potomac. Although his orders did not specifically prohibit such an action, Lee for the next crucial week had no idea where Stuart and at least half of his cavalry were or what it was doing. Stuart would not rejoin the army at Gettysburg until late on July 2, where the Battle of Gettysburg had already been raging for two whole days. (Lee, however, seemed to have forgotten that he had four other brigades of cavalry available and made no particular use of them.)

Hooker in the meantime had become fed up due to the twin millstones of Harper's Ferry and Washington restricting his actions. He was also upset because he had been refused reinforcements and Lincoln and Halleck kept rejecting his offensive proposals. Finally he tendered his resignation, which was promptly accepted, and the commander of V Corps, George G. Meade, who was also a friend of Warren, was ordered to take command on the night of June 27, 1863. Within 96 hours the battle of Gettysburg would begin.

The Battle of Gettysburg had begun as a meeting engagement on July 1, 1863, when Henry Heth's Confederate infantry division, looking for shoes, collided with Brig. Gen. John Buford's Union cavalry division. Both sides fed in additional troops but the Confederates (as Nathan Bedford Forrest would have put it) got there first with the most and won a tactical victory, driving the Union I Corps and XI Corps to the high ground on the other side of the town. Meade accepted the judgment of Buford, Maj. Gen. John F. Reynolds (the commander of I Corps, who was killed early in the fighting) and Maj. Gen. Winfield Scott Hancock (the new commander of II Corps)—whom Meade had sent to take over on the field after Reynolds' death until Meade could get there—that Gettysburg was the place to fight the battle.

On the second day of the battle, July 2, 1863, Lee intended to attack both flanks of Meade's army, sending Ewell to strike at Culp's Hill on the Union right and Longstreet to smash the Union left. While Longstreet was maneuvering to get into position to strike his blow, Daniel Sickles, still commanding III Corps, was not happy, since he did not like where Meade had positioned him. Sickles was holding Meade's left flank along where Cemetery Ridge petered out before the heights of Little Round Top and Big Round Top. He could see that there was slightly higher ground than what he was occupying along Cemetery Ridge—to his front in the Peach Orchard—and if attacked he did not want to let the Confederates have it.

This had happened at the Battle of Chancellorsville, where he was ordered to give up some high ground his troops held at Hazel Grove. Once his troops had left the Confederates took possession of Hazel Grove, emplaced their artillery there, and were able to shell Sickles and his III Corps with impunity. Sickles did not want that to happen again, so without seeking the permission of Meade, whom he neither liked nor respected anyway, he advanced his corps to occupy that high ground in the Peach Orchard. A side effect of his advance was to completely uncover Little Round Top, which was occupied only by a Signal Corps station.

In the course of the fighting when Longstreet made his delayed attack William Oates and his 15th Alabama Infantry Regiment were ordered to clear the heavily wooded Big Round Top of Union sharpshooters. Troops of the 1st and 2nd U.S. Sharpshooters, belonging to III Corps, positioned on Big Round Top were proving to be very irritating to the attacking Confederates.

While doing that, Oates was ordered to advance along the spur between Big Round Top and Little Round Top and to attack Little Round Top, which prior to the battle had been cleared of trees. If the Confederates could take and hold Little Round Top and place artillery there they could succeed in turning the Union flank and force Meade out of his position. Then the Confederates could seize his supply and baggage wagons and smash the entire Army of the Potomac in the open, particularly since V Corps was only beginning to arrive and VI Corps would not arrive at all until later that afternoon.

Oates, being the senior officer present, soon collected four other regiments, two more from Alabama and two from Texas, to assist and led the five regiments over to Little Round Top; however, just as they reached the crest of the hill Union soldiers appeared from out of nowhere, meeting them with a volley and driving them back down the hill to regroup.

That there were defenders on Little Round Top to meet Oates and his five regiments of attackers was due to the vigilance and perceptions of one man, Gouverneur Kemble Warren. Even though he was a brigadier general, as chief engineer of the Army of the Potomac Warren was still a staff officer with no direct command authority over troops at all.

"Just before the action," Warren wrote in his official report just after the battle, "General

Meade sent me to the left to examine the conditions of affairs and I continued to Little Round Top." What he found there disturbed him greatly. As an engineer Warren could see at a glance how vital holding Little Round Top was to the Army of the Potomac, which was fighting for its life. There were no soldiers, no artillery, defending Little Round Top. The only thing there was the signal station that the officer in command, knowing that the Confederates were coming, was preparing to evacuate.

Warren wrote in his report:

> I saw that this was the key to the whole position. Our troops in the woods in front of it could not see the ground in front of them; therefore, the enemy would come upon them before they would be aware.
> The woods west of the Emmitsburg Road furnished a concealed place for the enemy to form, so I requested a battery just in front of Little Round Top to fire a shot into those woods. The sound of the shot whistling through the air reached the enemy's troops causing them to glance up in that direction. This motion revealed to me the glistening gun barrels and bayonets of the enemy battle line, already formed and far outflanking our troops; his line of advance to Little Round Top was unopposed. This discovery was intensely thrilling and appalling.

Warren quickly ordered the signal corps party to remain and keep wagging their flags to make it look like the summit of Little Round Top was occupied. (Oates knew that it was not occupied since he could plainly see the summit of Little Round Top from Big Round Top before he made his attempt to take Little Round Top.) Warren then sent his aide to notify Meade of the danger to the entire Union left flank and to tell him that troops were needed there in a hurry. The aide reached Meade, who used him to pass the word to Maj. Gen. George Sykes of V Corps ordering him to send troops to Little Round Top. Sykes in turn attempted to pass the word on to the commander of his leading division, who could not be found; however, Col. Strong Vincent intercepted the messenger and on his own authority led his brigade to the summit of Little Round Top. Vincent and his brigade arrived at the summit of Little Round Top just 15 minutes before Oates did and had deployed his brigade just in time to stop Oates' first rush.

Vincent placed the 20th Maine Infantry, commanded by Joshua Lawrence Chamberlain, on the left of the line and extended it to the right with the 83rd Pennsylvania, 44th New York and 16th Michigan. They had arrived none too soon. The 4th Alabama and the 4th and 5th Texas struck at Vincent's right while the 14th and 15th Alabama engaged his left. Chamberlain's 20th Maine, being hit on the left and front, refused their line at a 90-degree angle. (One company had been detached further to the left, and had been joined by some of the sharpshooters Oates had chased from Big Round Top, whereupon they were cut off and ignored thereafter by the Confederates.) Taking what cover they could, Vincent's men unleashed a devastating first volley and then threw back attack after attack. Vincent climbed atop a large boulder near his right flank brandishing only a riding crop, since he had left his sword with his horse on the other side of the hill, as he shouted encouragement to his men.

Not knowing for sure if his message had reached Meade, or whether Meade had reacted properly, Warren went looking for more troops himself. He came upon Hazlett's Battery, which he had supported and covered in his stand at the Second Battle of Manassas/Bull Run. Warren persuaded Hazlett to take his guns to Little Round Top and helped Hazlett manhandle a two-gun section from the battery to the top of Little Round Top. That being done, Warren went looking for infantry to support the guns.

What he found was his old brigade, now under the command of Brig. Gen. Stephen H. Weed, marching west on the road leading out to the Peach Orchard. They had been ordered to help succor Sickles and his III Corps, which were being hammered to pieces by Longstreet. Weed's rear regiment — the 140th New York Infantry — was under the command of Col. Patrick O'Rorke (who had been one of Warren's students at West Point) when it was intercepted by Warren and sent to Little Round Top. O'Rorke protested that his men were under orders to join Sickles.

"Never mind that, Paddy," Warren had replied, not wasting time to find Weed. "Bring them up on the double-quick, and don't stop for aligning. I'll take the responsibility."

O'Rorke did as he was directed and Weed, when he found out what was going on, turned the rest of the brigade around and followed O'Rorke to Little Round Top, double-timing it as best they could up the steep, boulder clogged incline and over the crest to find the struggle raging furiously below them on the steep and rocky southwest face of the hill.

While Warren was gone, Vincent's brigade faced a crisis. The 48th Alabama, which had taken part in the by now successful attack on Devil's Den at the foot of Little Round Top, moved forward to join the attack on Vincent's right, and the 16th Michigan, which bore the brunt of the renewed Confederate assault, began to give way. Col. Vincent ran to the threatened point, brandishing his riding crop, and yelling, "Don't give an inch!" It was then that a Confederate bullet slammed into Vincent's groin and he went down in agony.

This was the closest the Confederates ever got to taking Little Round Top. Their chances for outright victory were snatched away with the arrival of O'Rorke and the 140th New York. Not bothering to deploy and arriving in a column of fours, with O'Rorke at their head, the 140th barreled right into the action. Moments after his regiment arrived, O'Rorke was also shot down, but his arrival had secured the crest of Little Round Top. Suddenly there were eight Union infantry regiments and two field guns holding the high ground with only seven Confederate infantry regiments trying valiantly to take it from them.

On the far left, the 20th Maine of Vincent's brigade, under Col. Joshua Lawrence Chamberlain, faced off against Oates' own 15th Alabama. In the fighting to see who would retain possession of Little Round Top, Vincent, O'Rorke, Weed, and Hazlett were all killed. Casualties on both sides were heavy and Oates received orders to hold the place at all hazards; however, he did not receive any reinforcements. Without reinforcements, Oates could see that the struggle could only end in defeat.

Finally, he ordered a withdrawal, and just as the word was being passed, Chamberlain and the 20th Maine, having run out of ammunition, launched a bayonet attack. (The attack was supported by fire from the sharpshooters and the company that had been cut off, who, because the Confederates had completely ignored them, still had ammunition.) "When the signal was given we ran like a herd of wild cattle," Oates would later admit.

Near the base of the hill they rallied, being joined by the troops of the other Confederate regiments. On the lower western slopes of Little Round Top the survivors began collecting rocks of all shapes and sizes, constructing barricades to fight behind, and all the while soldiers of both sides kept up a hot fire. "Both sides were whipped," a Texas private explained afterwards, "and all were mad about it."

Warren had acted completely on his own to save Little Round Top and the battle itself.[8] Hancock had done the same to prevent other breakthroughs, first at the lower end and then at the center of Cemetery Ridge (completely sacrificing the 1st Minnesota Infantry Regiment at one point); but practically no one — Oates the exception and lacking the authority to make it count — had acted with corresponding initiative on the Confederate side.

There was, as always, no lack of Confederate bravery, and the army's combat skill had been demonstrated amply by the fact that, despite its role as the attacker and being outnumbered, it had inflicted even more casualties than it had suffered; yet these qualities could not make up for the crippling lack of direction from above and the equally disadvantageous lack of initiative from just below the top.

The next day, July 3, 1863, Lee tried again, this time striking at the center of Meade's line with Pickett's Charge while at the same time trying to turn the Union right with his cavalry.

The effort was a complete, total, and dismal failure. The two armies spent Independence Day, July 4, glaring at each other, and then when Meade failed to use VI Corps, the only body of relatively fresh troops on either side, for a counterattack, Lee picked up and headed for home, with Meade eventually following him, somewhat dilatorily.

For his actions at Little Round Top, Warren received the Congressional Medal of Honor. He was also promoted to the rank of major general, U.S. Volunteers, which was backdated to May 3, 1863, possibly in recognition of his attempt to help Hooker regain his nerve.

18

A Strong Performance at Bristoe Station

After the Battle of Gettysburg, Meade and his Army of the Potomac had followed Lee and his Army of Northern Virginia back into Virginia from Pennsylvania. President Lincoln was not happy when Meade simply sat down along the Upper Rappahannock River and waited for Lee to make the next move. Although Meade believed that taking the offensive would be risky, he still offered to do so if Lincoln's government so desired.

For the three months following the Battle of Gettysburg the two armies remained at arm's length from each other as they recovered from the titanic struggle they had left behind in Pennsylvania. Since Hancock had been severely wounded at the decisive moment during Pickett's Charge at Gettysburg he had been sent home to recuperate and Warren, on August 16, 1863, took temporary command of II Corps. Both Richmond and Washington took advantage of the lull to send reinforcements to East Tennessee as the Union Army of the Cumberland and the Confederate Army of Tennessee fought over who would control the vital town of Chattanooga, Tennessee, the jumping off place for any Union offensive against Atlanta, Georgia, which was second in importance only to Richmond itself. As it happened, Richmond moved first, sending two divisions of Longstreet's I Corps, and Longstreet himself, along with other troops under newly promoted Lt. Gen. D.H. Hill west to reinforce General Braxton Bragg's Army of Tennessee.

When Washington learned what was going on it sent XI Corps and XII Corps, with Joseph Hooker in command, from the Army of the Potomac. They did not arrive in time to affect the Battle of Chickamauga (Longstreet and D.H. Hill did), but they did arrive in time to have an effect on the Battles for Chattanooga, assaulting and taking Lookout Mountain in the Battle Above the Clouds. They never returned to the Army of the Potomac and were eventually amalgamated into XX Corps, which adopted the five-pointed star badge of XII Corps. Lee, however, eventually got Longstreet and his two divisions back.

By October, Meade's remaining 80,000 troops in the Army of the Potomac had been deployed from Culpepper to the Rapidan. Lee, with 46,000 troops, was camped at Orange Court House. When Lee learned that Hooker had taken XI Corps and XII Corps west he decided that he would "initiate a move on General Meade to keep him from detaching further reinforcements west to either Rosecrans or Grant." In addition, Lee saw an opportunity to evict Meade from Virginia entirely, for the winter.

Meade's main force was located in a strong position on high ground north of Culpepper. Therefore, Lee decided that he would try to turn Meade's right flank and strike his main body as he retreated. To facilitate this move Fitzhugh Lee and his cavalry division were directed to remain upon the Rapidan River to guard the rear, while Stuart took Wade Hampton's cavalry division to screen the movements of Ewell's II Corps and A.P. Hill's III Corps. (Stuart's cavalry division having been in the interim reorganized into a corps of two divisions).

It all began when Lee's veterans crossed the Rapidan River on October 9, 1863. However, Lee was unable to maintain the vital element of surprise when his movements were observed by a Union Signal Corps observation post.

When Lee began his offensive, Meade had already considered and abandoned the idea of attacking Lee. On being informed about Lee's movements, Meade told the War Department that he was uncertain whether Lee was retreating or maybe making a flank movement. Buford's Union cavalry division was therefore dispatched with orders to follow Lee if he retreated, while Hugh Judson Kilpatrick's cavalry division was posted to watch for any movement from Madison Court House.

Stuart did his job on October 10 when he drove in Kilpatrick's division, thereby clearing the way for Lee to advance to Culpepper, which was reached the next day. On October 11, in the morning, Stuart pressed Pleasonton's Cavalry Corps, which formed Meade's rear guard to Brandy Station. There Buford, who had been chased from the Rapidan by Fitzhugh Lee, joined Kilpatrick. After a melee with Kilpatrick, Stuart and Wade Hampton's division joined Fitzhugh Lee and they drove the Union cavalry to a position on the Fleetwood Heights, just north of Brandy Station in the Second Battle of Brandy Station.

During the cavalry fight, Lee made fresh plans calling for Hill's corps to sweep wide to the northwest to Sperryville and then back to Amissville, Waterloo and Warrenton. Meanwhile, Ewell's corps would follow the direct route through Jefferson and Sulphur Springs to unite with Hill at Warrenton. From there, Lee sought to cut behind Meade, somewhere along the vital Orange & Alexandria Railroad.

On October 12, Hill's corps started its wide, encircling march. As a matter of fact, it was a very nice fall day, the weather being cool and the roads dry. Hill by nightfall reached Amissville. At the same time, Ewell's corps—with Lee accompanying him and Stuart's cavalry screening the advance moved toward Jefferson, which was being defended by three regiments from David M. Gregg's cavalry division — dismounted behind a stone wall that enclosed a churchyard. Stuart drove off this opposition with little trouble while two of Ewell's infantry divisions (those of Rodes and Johnson) crossed the river and went into bivouac for the night.

Meade, by the next day, October 13, was uncertain where exactly Lee was and just what his intentions might be. He thought that Ewell and Hill were still at Culpepper so he ordered a show of force at that point. The II Corps, V Corps, and VI Corps from Meade's army, along with Buford's cavalry division, were ordered to recross the Rappahannock River and advance along the Orange & Alexandria Railroad.

While doing so, Buford, at about 2:00 P.M., collided with the 5th Virginia Cavalry Regiment, under Thomas L. Rosser (then still a colonel), which had been left to guard Brandy Station by Stuart. Rosser slowly retreated to a point about a mile and a half from Culpepper, where some South Carolina cavalry joined him and a brisk Confederate gunfire discouraged Buford's advance. During the night, Rosser built a large number of campfires to make it appear that he had received reinforcements. Having recovered Brandy Station, Buford's troopers buried the dead from the earlier cavalry fight and provided treatment to the wounded.

That night, Meade learned that Lee had crossed the river in force and he immediately ordered his five dispersed infantry corps to move to Warrenton Junction, now! When he deduced that it was Lee's plan for Hill's corps and Ewell's corps to converge on Warrenton, Meade abandoned any thought of making an attack of his own, and instead retired to the heights of Centreville. His II Corps and III Corps were ordered to fall back through Auburn and Greenwich, while I Corps, V Corps, and VI Corps were ordered to retire along the railroad. This turned what became known as the Virginia Campaign of 1863 into a race for Bristoe Station. The odds of who the winner would be were just about even. Lee had moved first. Meade was closer.

On October 13, Lee ordered Stuart to make a reconnaissance towards Catlett's Station. While doing so, Stuart learned that a large Union force occupied Warrenton Junction, five miles to the southeast. Continuing his reconnaissance, Stuart next discovered that Meade was retreating towards Manassas and Centreville, and he immediately sent a courier to Lee to inform him that he now had an opportunity to attack Meade while he was in motion during the approaching night. However, a portion of Stuart's cavalry had just been evicted from Auburn by Meade's III Corps.

Stuart, learning by this move of Meade's III Corps that he was now boxed in between Union troops moving along the railroad and by Meade's III Corps passing through Auburn, decided to head to Auburn, skirmishing on the move with various III Corps pickets, and deciding not to attempt a breakout during the darkness. Then, just east of Auburn, Stuart found a small cleared valley rimmed by trees that hid the grassy interior of the valley from the view of Union troops that were moving southeast by a road only 150 yards away. Stuart moved into the hidden valley and dispatched couriers to Lee.

The Union troops advancing along the road happened to be from III Corps, which were being screened by Kilpatrick's cavalry division, and they were moving on Greenwich. Stuart, deciding that the Union troops were too strong, had rejected the idea of making an attack upon them, and he and his command, except for their own pickets, then went to bed.

Warren's II Corps had bivouacked for the night at Auburn and Warren informed Meade that he was concerned that Confederate cavalry might tell Lee about the strung-out position of Meade's army. Meade thereupon instructed Warren to turn east from Auburn, move to Catlett's Station, and then follow the railroad to Centreville, rather than remain upon the original route north through Greenwich. Warren, being completely unaware of Stuart's presence in that hidden valley, faced one infantry division and three batteries of artillery in the direction from which he thought that Lee might attack—west toward Warrenton.

By morning, fog and mist enveloped the Auburn area, each commander, Union and Confederate, being intent upon extricating his troops from a precarious position. Suddenly, from the direction of Warrenton, came the sound of musketry. Stuart took this to be a full-scale attack by Lee's main force and rained a storm of canister and shells upon the division Warren had posted (facing toward Warrenton), which at that time was having breakfast. The Union infantry division was quickly rallied and then changed front to meet this attack from Stuart's unexpected position. When an attack by Ewell from Warrenton failed to materialize, the Union division marched on Stuart in his hidden valley. Stuart was able to withdraw his horse artillery and managed to extricate his command and head off towards Warrenton.

Warren, like Stuart, thought that he was surrounded, but quickly realized that the Confederates were escaping, not attacking. Warren ordered that the dead be buried and the wounded be recovered, and set his corps to marching towards Catlett's Station. While Warren was bringing up the rear of Meade's army, Ewell's troops, screened by the rest of Stuart's cavalry, took the road to Greenwich via Auburn.

Meanwhile, Hill's corps of Lee's army had been hurrying since 5:00 A.M. north along the Warrenton-Alexandria Turnpike. Hill, upon receiving reports that Union troops were heading from Greenwich towards Buckland (just three miles away), ordered one of his divisions (under Maj. Gen. Richard H. Anderson) to attack. The Union force turned out to be cavalry retreating from Fitzhugh Lee. Therefore, Anderson moved off to the right and rejoined Hill at Greenwich. The Union troops were racing to Bristoe Station, just eight miles due east, and Hill followed.

Hill rode ahead to assess the situation and when he arrived at the high ground overlooking Bristoe Station, Broad Run, and the plains to the north, he saw swarms of Union troops. He assumed these troops were from III Corps and he ordered Heth to hurry forward with the leading brigades of his division.

The troops that Hill had seen were actually from V Corps. They had been moved through Bristoe Station after III Corps, which meant that the only troops actually south of Bristoe Station were Warren's II Corps. It was V Corps there waiting for Warren and II Corps to follow Meade's order to get out of the way from any attack from Lee.

Warren's II Corps was moving towards Bristoe Station with Gregg's cavalry division on the flanks. V Corps had reached Bristoe Station by mid-afternoon, upon which Warren's leading II Corps troops engaged Heth's skirmishers. Warren's leading division commander placed an artillery battery on a hill north of Broad Run and sent his leading brigade across to link up with V Corps.

Next Warren arrived with a second division from II Corps. Being familiar with the terrain, Warren deployed his two divisions behind a railroad embankment, which formed a shield two to ten feet high facing Hill's oncoming Confederate troops. The division that arrived with Warren was ordered to form to the left. The other division was ordered to pull its brigades back to the west bank of Broad Run and take position on the extreme right of Warren's Line. The battery was left, unsupported, on its hill north of Broad Run where it could enfilade any attacking Confederates.

Hill, unaware of Warren's presence behind the railroad embankment, kept urging Heth to rush his troops into line so that an attack could begin before the Union troops could escape. While waiting for some of Heth's troops to change into old uniforms for the attack, to preserve newly issued fresh uniforms, Hill ordered a battery of artillery forward to disperse scattered knots of V Corps troops, who were ignorant of any Confederate presence as they clustered around their campfires sipping coffee.

Hill ordered Heth to cross Broad Run, advance, and attack the enemy. Spotting some Union skirmishers from II Corps, west of the railroad, Hill ordered Heth to suspend his advance while Anderson, whose division had arrived to the right and rear of Heth's advance, was ordered to send forward a battery and quickstep two brigades to guard the flanks of Heth's attacking soldiers.

A reconnaissance by Hill or Stuart before actually making an attack just might have been in order, but Hill was too impatient. (His impatience with Jackson's slowness during the first two of the Seven Days' back in 1862 had helped screw up that offensive.) Stuart, while covering Ewell's flank, had gone off course and failed to arrive at Bristoe Station until after dark.

During this interval, Warren's skirmishers opened fire upon Heth's flank, which revealed that Warren's line extended behind the railroad as far as the Confederates could see. This information was given to Hill, who nevertheless ordered the advance to resume, as he felt that Anderson could take care of any threat from this quarter.

When Heth's attacking brigades approached Warren's position, the Confederate losses were soon appalling. Ordered to charge to avoid exposure from the murderous enfilading fire of the battery on the hill north of Broad Run, the Confederates surged forward, losing soldiers at every step, and got to within 50 yards of the embankment, whereupon another Union battery opened fire with canister and shrapnel. This withering fire forced Heth to withdraw and form a new line 400 yards to the rear.

Hill re-formed his men, but no new attack was ordered. Hill had lost for Lee 1,900 men with his impetuous attack. Union losses numbered only about 550. That night Warren and his II Corps followed V Corps and resumed the march to Centreville, while Hill assumed full responsibility for the fiasco and thus ended the Virginia Campaign of 1863.

19

Moral Courage at Mine Run

Now it was Meade's turn to contemplate an offensive, the result of which was the Mine Run Campaign of November 1863. This would be the very last time that Meade would confront Lee alone, before the advent of Ulysses S. Grant from out of the West to assume complete and total control of the Union's military effort. Oddly, there were no pitched battles, since a decision by Gouverneur Warren would cause everything to stop just short of a blood bath.

Back in October, Lee had turned on Meade, who, in response had moved back to Centreville. Centreville had been the place the Union forces had retreated to following their defeats at the First and Second Battles of Manassas/Bull Run in 1861 and 1862. Now that it was 1863 it appeared that falling back on Centreville for the Army of the Potomac had become an annual event. By this time the Army of the Potomac had about 96,000 men, while the Army of Northern Virginia had about 56,000. Meade, however, thought that the numbers were just about even and was therefore reluctant to go after Lee. Lincoln and Secretary of War Edwin M. Stanton were well aware of Meade's defensive posture, which deeply concerned them both. They were so concerned that at their direction General-in-Chief Henry W. Halleck wired Meade as follows: "If Lee has turned his back on you, he has seriously exposed himself to your blows, unless his army can move two miles to your one. Fight him, before he again draws you to such a distance from your base as to expose your communications."

Meade replied, "It is impossible to move this army until I know something definite about the position of the enemy.... Whatever route he has taken, it is too late for me to overtake him."

Halleck in turn commented sharply, "Lee is unquestionably bullying you. If you cannot ascertain his movements, I certainly cannot. If you pursue and fight him, I think you can find out where he is."

Meade, who was not known as "Old Snapping Turtle" for nothing, snapped back: "If you have any orders to give me, I am prepared to receive and obey them, but I must insist on being spared the infliction of truisms in the guise of opinions as you have recently honored me with, particularly as they were not asked for.... If my course does not meet with your approval, I desire to be relieved of command."

This exchange of messages marked the beginning of what became known as the Mine Run Campaign. Meade got the ball rolling on October 18 when he moved his entire army a few miles to the Bristoe-Gainesville Line. But Lee was pulling back beyond Warrenton Junction, leaving Stuart and his cavalry to chase Kilpatrick's cavalry division east along the pike in what became known as the "Buckland Races" (to the complete and utter disgust of one of Kilpatrick's brigade commanders, George A. Custer). The Confederates also destroyed the railroad as they went.

On October 20, Meade reported reaching Warrenton but that Lee had recrossed the river, leaving a bridgehead at Rappahannock Bridge. Meade reported it would take at least 10 days to rebuild the railroad that Stuart's cavalry had wrecked and that it would take most of the army to repair it as far as Culpepper.

"Under the circumstances," Meade wired to Halleck, "I do not see the practicality of an advance on this line to Gordonsville. It seems to me, therefore, that the campaign is virtually over for the season, and that it would be better to withdraw [the army] to a position in front of Washington and detach from it such portions as may be required to operate elsewhere."

In response, Halleck ordered Meade to come to Washington and confer with the president. Once Meade was there, Lincoln apparently told him that he was expected to take the offensive. In a message to Meade on October 24, Halleck confirmed the order: "The President desires that you prepare to attack Lee's army...."

Meade now had a definite order to attack, and with the railroad running again as far as Warrenton Junction supplies would be no problem. At this point Meade had several options:

1. He could attempt a turning movement to the west. However, this would stretch and greatly expose Meade's line of communications; in the advent of rain and snow the road net in the Amissville-Sperryville area would become mostly impossible to use due to the mud.

2. A straight-out frontal attack against Lee's lines seemed impractical. Meade and his corps commanders were simply unwilling (after their experience at Fredericksburg) to throw away lives wholesale in frontal assaults that gained nothing in particular.

3. Meade's preferred option was a swift movement to the southeast, to the heights above Fredericksburg, where he told Halleck he could place himself on Lee's flank and rear.

However, Lincoln and Halleck refused to sanction this option since it would require a change of base, and supplies would then have to be received by water at Aquia Landing and then go by rail to Falmouth. Meade was authorized by Lincoln and Halleck to make any "tactical" move he desired, while they disapproved any "strategic" change of base under the existing circumstances. It appears that the primary reason for this directive was that the Confederates were tearing up the railroad line between Aquia Landing and Falmouth, carrying away the rails and other hardware.

In compliance with Lincoln's orders, Meade notified Halleck on November 2 that he had decided to force a crossing of the Rappahannock River in preparation for a deeper penetration into Confederate territory. On November 7, Maj. Gen. John Sedgwick and his VI Corps launched an assault on Lee's bridgehead, smashing it, while inflicting about 2,000 casualties, mostly prisoners, upon the Confederates, while at the same time Maj. Gen. William French and his III Corps forced a crossing at Kelly's Ford.

Lee then withdrew from his temporary line between Culpepper and Brandy Station. Due to circumstances beyond Meade's control, Lee managed to avoid contact with Union forces as he pulled his army back. Heavy fog delayed John Sedgwick and his VI Corps as it crossed over Rappahannock Bridge, since it could not be determined if Lee still held the hills south of the river. French's III Corps came within striking distance of Lee on November 8. Neither French nor his leading divisional commander, however, was willing to strike at Lee on his own initiative. By the time Meade had concentrated his army, Lee had crossed the Rapidan, occupying an old trench line along the river.

The railroad, meanwhile, had been repaired by the Union as far as Brandy Station, where a siding and a depot were built. The rail line was functioning by November 19, and Meade was ready to resume his advance. He, however, hesitated to attack Lee's position along the Rapidan. Since Meade had been forbidden to make a wide turning movement via Fredericksburg, he now decided to make a narrower one aimed at enveloping, or turning, Lee's right (or eastern) flank. If the Army of the Potomac could move quickly enough, Meade figured, he could cross the lower fords of the Rapidan River and swing in behind Mine Run and then attack, catching Lee with only a portion of his army far enough east to meet the assault.

Meade issued orders for his planned movement on the night of November 23. Under these orders Warren's II Corps was to march at daylight, November 24, cross the river at Germanna Ford, and move via the German Plank Road and Orange Turnpike west to Locust Grove (also know as Robertson's or Robinson's Tavern). General George Sykes and V Corps, followed by General John Newton and I Corps would march via Culpepper and the Orange Plank Road to Parker's Store, and from there they were to move west, abreast of Warren and II Corps.

The main effort was to be conducted by Sedgwick's VI Corps and French's III Corps. They were to cross at Jacob's Ford, four miles to the right of Lee's lines, and then join Warren and II Corps at Locust Grove. Meade's plan called for a simultaneous river crossing of three columns, which were to march in unison westwards toward Lee's rear. Each column was to be preceded by cavalry with a cavalry division on each flank, and Custer's Michigan Cavalry Brigade would remain near Morton's and Raccoon fords.

There had been some rain, but by the time Meade issued his orders on November 23 the weather had been clear long enough to insure that the roads were dry. However, after midnight November 23–24 another heavy rain fell, causing Meade to delay the advance until November 26. There was a final meeting of Meade's corps commanders, which Warren forgot to attend. During this meeting they were given the latest intelligence, topographical information, and their particular role in the offensive.

Meade's plan was sound, although it did not take into account all of Lee's possible options. For instance, it made no allowance for the possibility that Lee might withdraw along the Orange & Alexandria Railroad in order to confront Meade in a new position. Meade's plan also did not allow for the possibility that Lee might seek to envelop Meade.

But, in any event, Meade was safe enough from those possibilities since Lee planned no such moves. In fact, Lee proposed to do what Meade wanted him to do, move out of his fortified lines and fight Meade in an area that was not fortified. Lee knew, from reports of Stuart's cavalry, that Meade was up to something. What Lee expected Meade to do was to head for Fredericksburg or Richmond, Lee not knowing that he had been forbidden from making such wide movements. Therefore, to meet either of these contingencies Lee selected a position perpendicular to the Rapidan River, which he intended to use as a base for attacking Meade. Jubal Early, acting commander of Ewell's corps, was on the right of the line as it faced north. Early was thus nearest Meade's army and the most probable avenues of its approach. Lee instructed Early to be ready to move out at short notice and attack Meade as soon as Stuart's cavalry located his troops, once they had crossed the river. Hill's Corps was ordered to march using the Plank Road and form on Early's southern flank, as Lee's army swung around to face east.

The primary weak link in Meade's plan was the lack of an engineering component, which was odd since Meade was, and always had been, at heart an engineer. The entire operation that he proposed, up to and including the river crossings, was an engineering project. Meade himself told Washington that the success of his offensive depended on a rapid march to the river and an unimpeded and swift crossing over that river by all three of his columns. Therefore, to ensure this, there should have been a timely and thorough reconnaissance of the roads and provisions for the work of pioneers (combat engineers), along with an accurate appraisal of the equipment and time required to construct any bridges that might be needed. The area Meade's three columns would be moving through was wooded, the roads were obscured, and there were forks where the heads of each column could take a wrong turn. Finally, the stream banks were steep and due to recent rains the water level in those streams would be high.

Although Meade did issue orders for a road reconnaissance, neither Meade nor any other senior officer (with the possible exception of Warren) personally rode over the route or checked the crossing sites. A few junior officers did reconnoiter. They reported that portions of the routes to the river were bad and that they needed much work by the pioneers. However, nothing much was done about it, although Sykes, whose V Corps had marched halfway to the river before being recalled on November 24, had reported that the streams themselves were swollen and that the roads were difficult.

When the movement did begin, Brig. Gen. Henry Prince, who commanded French's leading III Corps division, deserved much of the blame for what went wrong. French had specifically instructed Prince, in writing, to provide himself with a competent guide. Yet at 4:00 A.M. on the day that the march was to begin, Prince told Meade's headquarters that he had no guide and did not know how to get to the river. He was sent a civilian scout as a guide, who took 14 hours to get to Prince, two hours too late to do Prince any good.

Sykes and Warren's columns moved out on time, although Meade's orders issued at 4:30 A.M. did not get to them until 6:00 A.M. French's column was an hour or more late in starting due to Prince and more than two hours late in reaching the river due to rough road conditions near Mountain Run. Another problem was that Meade's headquarters baggage train blocked the road for half an hour or so. The baggage train was hauling the tons of tents, cots, chairs, and other camp equipment that Union commanders (except for Sherman) had a tendency to refuse to move without.

Sykes and V Corps reached Culpepper Ford by 10:30 A.M. and were across the river by noon. Warren and II Corps arrived at Germanna Ford by 9:30 A.M., where he was joined by Meade at 11:00 A.M. There they waited until they received word that French's III Corps had reached Jacob's Ford. At 2:00 P.M. they were told that, while French had reached the ford, he was in trouble. Due to the high water, engineers were just one pontoon short of having enough to bridge the river. Furious at the delay, Meade ordered the artillery to make a detour so that it could cross by way of Germanna Ford, which took it all night. III Corps was able to begin crossing at 4:00 P.M., but Prince, upon moving into the woods, immediately proceeded to get lost.

Thus Meade had lost a full day. Rather than having II Corps and III Corps at Locust Grove ready to launch an attack the following day, with the rest of the army within supporting distance, none of the Army of the Potomac had advanced more than four miles beyond the river and some units had not even crossed it yet.

Meanwhile, Lee was convinced that Meade was on the move. First, a spy had informed him on November 24 that Meade's I Corps had been issued eight days' rations and had been given marching orders. Second, he was also informed on November 24, and it was confirmed on November 25, that Union cavalry was moving to the southeast. Third, Lee kept his eye on the newspapers in Washington. (It was next to impossible to keep a military secret during the American Civil War. No one had any idea about how to maintain security. If the newspapers weren't breaching what security there was to print army movements then just about everybody and his uncle was running some kind of a secret service.)

Union movements on November 26 were shielded by fog, but when it lifted the Confederate signal station on Clark's Mountain discovered Union forces moving through Stevensburg towards Germanna Ford. Observers near Morton's Ford who could see Culpepper also could see Union troops moving towards the lower fords of the Rapidan River. At 8:00 A.M. Confederate cavalry videttes at Ely's Ford saw Union troops crossing the river and then moving in the direction of Chancellorsville. Confederate cavalry also reported capturing wagons belonging to I Corps and V Corps of Meade's army. All of this information tended to strengthen Lee's belief that Meade, after crossing the Rapidan River, was going to advance through the Wilderness at Spotsylvania, moving towards the Richmond, Fredericksburg & Petersburg Railroad.

Therefore, in accordance with what he believed that Meade was doing, Lee, on the night of November 26, decided to withdraw his forces from his positions on the Upper Rapidan River, march eastward, and strike Meade while his army was on the move. During the day, Lee had told Early to be ready to move Ewell's corps along the Old Orange Turnpike, to the vicinity of Locust Grove. Lee then put Hill on the alert to move his corps down the Plank Road.

Lee also made some precautionary moves; he had Early, who was nearest the hinge of Meade's slowly turning army, to send elements of John B. Gordon's brigade to the crossroads south of Zoar Church to guard the roads in the area against Union cavalry thrusts along the pike. Early alerted Ewell's corps to move after dark south of Bartlett's Mill, along the ridge west of Mine Run.

On the night of November 26–27, Early's troops left their camps and fieldworks along the Rapidan River and took up positions along the ridge, west of Mine Run. By 4:00 A.M., when Lee arrived, they were building fieldworks on their new position. Lee then told Early to move the corps towards Locust Grove. At 8:00 A.M. Early's own division started westward, followed half an hour later by Rodes' Division, which would march parallel on the Zoar Church–Locust Grove Road. Edward Johnson's division, echeloned still further to the rear, since there was a presumed threat to the left, moved out on the Raccoon Ford–Bartlett's Mill–Locust Grove Road.

If Early's first two divisions had moved as little as 15 minutes earlier they would have arrived at the Locust Grove ridge before Union troops arrived. Warren's II Corps ran into the advance elements of Gordon's Georgia brigade between 11:00 and 11:30 A.M. 100 yards west of the Locust Grove crossroads, which showed that the advance of II Corps was much too slow, since its leading division had marched only five miles since 8:00 A.M. and Gordon had advanced only three and a half miles. The leading Union brigade attacked promptly and drove Gordon's skirmishers west at least 500 yards; the rest of Warren's leading division quickly deployed on the high ground at Locust Grove.

For the remainder of the day on November 27 there was constant skirmishing along Warren's front, but there was no pitched battle. The Confederate division commanders, in the absence of Early, hesitated to attack, and when Early did arrive he decided that the terrain offered few possibilities for a successful attack. According to Early his troops occupied a "low and very unfavorable" position. This position was dominated by Union artillery on the high ground at Locust Grove and was hemmed in on both flanks by rough terrain and thick underbrush. Therefore, Early decided to remain where he was and to wait for Johnson's Division while he extended his lines to the north.

On the Union side, by the time Warren had deployed two of his divisions, Meade had ridden forward to Warren's vicinity. Warren reported to Meade that he was ready to attack; however, he had no contact with the other two Union columns that were supposed to be to his left and/or right.

"We will wait for them," Meade decided.

To the south, Sykes and his V Corps had only a seven-mile march on the Plank Road to New Hope Church, which he had been ordered to reach. He should have arrived there by about 11:00 A.M., at which time Warren was deploying II Corps at Locust Grove. However, Sykes did not arrive at New Hope Church until 4:00 P.M., much too late to join Warren in an attack.

He had met Gregg's cavalry division at Parker's Store. At that point the cavalry took the lead in the advance, making slow progress. It has been speculated that part of the reason for the slow progress was due to Sykes' quite proper concern about his lateral communications with Warren at Locust Grove. At 12:15 P.M. Sykes had sent a message to Meade's chief of staff noting that Gregg's cavalry had been skirmishing with the enemy for some time and that therefore his progress had been slow. Finally, late in the afternoon, Gregg's cavalry division drove in the Confederate skirmishers, who were dismounted cavalry, uncovering a division of infantry.

While Sykes was delayed, Meade's I Corps moved up into a position on Warren's left flank. Sykes and V Corps remained, by Meade's order, at New Hope Church. As the day dragged on dilatory skirmishing on Warren's front continued, while Meade wondered where the heck French and his III Corps were.

In fact, French should have arrived before Sykes, since he had only a four-mile march from his bivouac to where he was supposed to join Warren at Locust Grove. French should have begun early enough to have completed the relatively short march before a Confederate force, which he knew was moving down the Raccoon Ford Road, could interfere. French would have been justified in relieving Prince for moving too slowly, or he could have replaced Prince's division as the leading division with David Birney and his division; he did neither.

Prince, still in the lead of III Corps, at 7:00 A.M. on November 27 had moved about a mile south from his bivouac to a fork in the road. Not being sure which way to go, he sent couriers and a troop of cavalry down each fork and then waited for the next two hours for their report. This one particular delay would prove to be fatal to the current operation and to Meade's entire Mine Run Campaign. It was eventually discovered that French's III Corps could have moved down either fork in the road and would have reached Locust Grove at about the same time that Warren's II Corps did. When French arrived at the road junction the entire situation degenerated into a Keystone Kops comedy routine.

What French should have done was to move up and order Prince to proceed. He did not! Instead, he sent an aide to find out what was going on. The aide reported that Prince was uncertain about which fork to take and that he wanted instructions from French. After the aide had left, riding back down the column to French, Prince was informed that the left-hand fork was passable; he sent the information back to French, noting that he, Prince, preferred the left-hand fork. French, on the other hand, preferred the right-hand fork and they discussed this at length, sending the aide riding back and forth with their queries and responses.

While this farce was going on, the troop of cavalry Prince had sent off on the right-hand fork collided with the baggage train and rear guard of Johnson's Division of Early's corps, which led to the minor Battle of Payne's Farm between French's III Corps and Johnson's Division. The Keystone Kops comedy routine was not quite over yet. When the firing began and Prince was bringing up another brigade, French ordered him to cease operations. Prince obediently stopped what he was doing and waited for further orders while the Confederates kept on shooting. Prince thereupon rode back to French, who ordered him to go ahead with his entire division and if he needed support he was to call on General Joseph B. Carr's division. (By now it was 11:00 A.M. and French was receiving frantic orders from Meade telling him to force his way through to Locust Grove and join Warren.)

When Johnson attempted to flank Prince's division, Prince called on Carr for assistance, who, continuing the Keystone Kops comedy routine, refused to move unless and until he received direct orders from French to do so. To top it all off, French sent orders to Prince prohibiting Prince from moving forward until Carr had arrived.

Although Johnson had no idea what was happening on the Union side of the encounter he nonetheless took advantage of these lulls—which continued for the next two or three hours—to seize the initiative, drive in the Union skirmish line and get within 30 yards of Prince's two batteries of artillery. The artillery fire from the batteries managed to repel the attack. Johnson thereupon withdrew to the south while Carr got into position and was hit in turn by Johnson. Carr did not have any artillery with him and managed to withstand two attacks. Birney's division detoured around Carr's left and rear, relieving Carr's troops, who were nearly out of ammunition. The fighting ended at dark.

By holding off French's entire III Corps, Johnson had in turn neutralized Sedgwick's VI Corps, which was jammed up on the road behind III Corps. This in turn gave A.P. Hill enough time to bring up his corps and enabled Confederate engineers to extend Lee's Mine Run fieldworks to the south.

During the night, Meade received intelligence reports that seemed to indicate Confederate troops were concentrating on the turnpike and the Raccoon Ford Road. Thus when Warren asked permission to attack at daybreak, Meade gave it. At 3:00 A.M. Meade moved Sedgwick's VI Corps to cover Warren's right flank and Newton's I Corps was advanced a short distance to Warren's left. French and his III Corps were placed in reserve. At 5:30 A.M. November 28, Meade established his headquarters at Robertson's Tavern. Soon he learned that his advancing troops had found the enemy's positions to be empty.

Lee did not arrive on the scene at New Hope Church until late in the afternoon of November 27. At that time Lee was still inclined to believe that the Union troops at Locust Grove and New Hope Church were only Meade's rear guard and that the bulk of Meade's army was moving on Fredericksburg and the Fredericksburg, Richmond & Petersburg Railroad. It did not take long before reports from both Stuart and Early caused Lee to realize he was facing Meade's entire army and he immediately gave orders to withdraw west of Mine Run, where the terrain was more conducive to defense and where trenches had already been staked out by his engineers. He immediately moved all of his infantry to the high ground west of rain-swollen Mine Run. Lee's troops thereupon worked the rest of the night and into the next day building fieldworks.

At daylight, November 28, Union skirmishers followed the Confederates down the long slope to Mine Run, where they stopped. There was no battle. Instead, Meade ordered his corps commanders to reconnoiter and report back on the feasibility of making an assault. When they had completed their reconnoitering they were all appalled at what they were up against.

At a council of war on the evening of November 28, Warren proposed that his II Corps be sent on a flank march directed against Lee's right. In addition to being Warren's friend, Meade at this time had great confidence in Warren due to his performance at Gettysburg and Bristoe Station. What Warren said he wanted to do was "to make a demonstration in the enemy's right, to threaten it, and endeavor to discover a more favorable position to assault, and finally, if this could not be done, to move around as if to get in his rear, with the intention to make him abandon his present front." For this purpose Meade, with a division of VI Corps and about 300 cavalry, reinforced Warren.

Such a turning movement would have been a better idea on November 27, while I Corps and VI Corps were still on the Plank Road. This would have allowed Meade to make a powerful attack on Lee's flank early on November 28. Instead it was daylight, November 29, before Warren could make his move. By 10:30 A.M. Warren had reached the Union cavalry outposts, where he observed what appeared to be newly dug trenches behind the Confederate skirmishers. Warren thereupon spent the next two hours deploying two brigades and an artillery battery. What he thought were entrenchments turned out to be an unfinished railroad embankment.

Lee was able to shift troops to his right to confront Warren without weakening his center as Meade set the stage for a double-envelopment in a grand assault the following morning. Two divisions from III Corps, which occupied the space between Warren and the original Union line, were sent to strengthen Warren, who Meade intended to make the main effort. On the opposite flank Sedgwick with V Corps and VI Corps moved two miles to the right to be in a position to attack Lee's left. The battle was to begin with an artillery bombardment at 8:00 A.M. November 30, with the infantry to begin their assault at 9:00 A.M.

During the night the rain had ceased and there was a severe frost. Warren's men could hear muffled orders, the sounds of axes and spades, and the rumble of artillery moving up. At dawn, the Union troops under Warren's command could see new fieldworks had been built on the crest of the long hill in front of them. Warren personally reconnoitered the new Confederate works. He estimated that it would take at least eight minutes for his troops to reach the new works, exposed to Confederate infantry and artillery fire every inch of the way. Warren then made the most fateful and morally courageous decision of his entire life.

"The works cannot be taken," Warren said. "I would sooner sacrifice my commission ... than ... my men." A II Corps staff officer was sent off to inform Meade of Warren's decision, who immediately called off Sedgwick's attack. Meade was stunned and for a time was furious, riding off to see Warren, and the two of them exchanged hard words when Meade found him.

But after taking a closer look, Meade was forced to concur with Warren's decision and the attack was canceled. Although Meade had accepted Warren's decision, he was still furiously disappointed and the friendship between the two generals was never quite the same afterwards. Eventually their entire relationship would crumble completely.

Lee, on the other hand, prayed that Meade would launch an attack. When November 30 came and went without one, Lee planned a turning movement of his own. But, when he was ready to move at dawn on December 2, Meade was gone and the Mine Run Campaign was over.

20

The Long Hard Grind of the Overland Campaign

After the failure of the Mine Run Campaign, Meade finally put the Army of the Potomac into winter quarters. With the arrival of spring and the advent of the 1864 campaigning season, Grant was called East to assume the direction of the Union's entire military effort.

In the meantime Meade had decided upon a complete reorganization of the Army of the Potomac: I Corps and III Corps were eliminated, their troops being amalgamated with II Corps, V Corps, VI Corps, which were all retained. Although Meade claimed that the reorganization was being made for greater efficiency, part of the motive could have been his desire to get rid of some of the generals who had failed him during the Mine Run Campaign (the names of French, Prince and Carr come to mind), and in order to minimize any controversy he did not relieve them outright, but instead eliminated their commands out from under them.

This did not include Warren, however, despite his deteriorating relationship with Meade. When Hancock returned and resumed command of II Corps on March 24, 1864, Warren was given permanent command of V Corps, replacing George Sykes, in time for Lt. Gen. Grant's long Overland Campaign.[1] Originally Grant valued Warren very highly. "I had not learned the special qualification of the various corps commanders," Grant stated in his memoirs. "At that time my judgment was that Warren was the man I would suggest to succeed Meade should anything happen to that gallant soldier to take him from the field. As I have said before, Warren was a gallant soldier, an able man; and he was besides thoroughly imbued of the solemnity and importance of the duty he had to perform." Thus Sykes was out, without any fuss, muss, controversy, or even much notice, and Warren was in.

Grant himself totally dominated the war and the Army of the Potomac from then on. It was his vision, his understanding of the need for a truly coordinated effort that changed the entire nature of Union strategy. Simultaneous pressure, Grant realized, would eventually lead to a breech in the Confederate perimeter.

Grant took personal charge of the most prominent and politically sensitive theatre of war, that of Virginia. He was the general-in-chief in overall command of all of the Union armies in the field, but it was also understood from the beginning that he would personally direct the Army of the Potomac through its titular commander, Meade. Thus Meade had become an intermediary between Grant and the army. This soon proved to be something of an embarrassing situation, but it was also perhaps the best compromise to the command question.

Other minor Union forces within the Shenandoah Valley and along the James River were to assist. It took the combined efforts of Franz Siegle, David Hunter, and Benjamin Butler in command of these forces, along with those of Lee, to ruin Grant's plan for Virginia, and Grant was left to confront Lee alone. Siegle was stopped at New Market and Butler allowed himself to be bottled up at Bermuda Hundred, while Hunter would not be able to accomplish much of anything except for burning down the Virginia Military Institute. Lee, having neutralized the strategic distractions within the Shenandoah Valley and along the James River, was free to maneuver and to foil Grant's flanking movements. Lee would first fight, and then would slip ahead of Grant and dig in and again Grant faced the choice of fighting or retreating.

Each time his choice was to fight.

Grant began his Overland Campaign on April 27, 1864, when General Ambrose E. Burnside and his IX Corps (which returned to the Army of the Potomac from its exile in the West) left Annapolis to occupy Mead's old position between Bull Run and the Rappahannock River. Shortly after midnight on May 3–4, the Grand Army of the Potomac moved out of its positions north of the Rapidan River.

Warren and V Corps were in the lead on the right, marching on Germanna Ford, nine or 10 miles below Lee's left. Warren was preceded by the Third Cavalry Division, under James H. Wilson, and followed by John Sedgwick's VI Corps. Winfield Scott Hancock's II Corps was moving by another road, further east, to Ely's Ford, six miles below Germanna Ford. Preceding II Corps was David M. Gregg's Second Cavalry Division followed by the artillery. Alfred T.A. Torbert's First Cavalry Division was left north of the Rapidan River. Its job was to picket the river, prevent the enemy from crossing, and protect the army's rear. The cavalry seized the fords by daylight, and before 6:00 A.M. pontoon bridges had been laid for the crossing of the infantry and the artillery.

Burnside and IX Corps were left behind at Warrenton, guarding the railroad from Bull Run forward and maintaining control of it in case the crossings of the Rapidan were delayed. Once Burnside was informed that the crossings had been made, he was to advance. The notification was sent to him a little after 1:00 P.M.

Generally the country through which Grant's troops were moving was heavily wooded. Lee's headquarters was at Orange Court House and from there to Fredericksburg he had the Orange Court House Plank Road and the Orange Turnpike, good roads for that part of Virginia, Grant noted in his memoirs, upon which to move his army. They both ran nearly parallel to the Wilderness. Grant hoped to move through the Wilderness before Lee knew that he was coming.

On discovering that the Army of the Potomac was moving, Lee directed his corps commanders—James Longstreet, Richard Ewell, and A.P. Hill—to move to the right and attack. Hill was to move on the Orange Court House Plank Road, followed by Longstreet, who was at Gordonsville, 20 or more miles away. Ewell, who was nearby, was to take the Orange Turnpike. He arrived four miles east of Mine Run, where he bivouacked for the night.

Grant's orders, through Meade, called for Warren's V Corps to make an early advance on May 5. Warren was to move on Parker's Store, and Wilson's Third Cavalry Division, then at the store, was to move on Craig's Meeting House. Sedgwick's VI Corps was to follow Warren, closing on his right. The Army of the Potomac was facing west at this point, although the advance was actually to the south. Hancock's II Corps was to move southwest to join Warren on his left, with Hancock's left to reach Sandy Grove Church.

Warren discovered the enemy at 6:00 A.M., before reaching Parker's Store. He immediately sent word back that he had located the Confederates. He was ordered to halt and prepare to meet the Confederates and then attack. Sedgwick sent one division, under Horatio G. Wright, by any road he could find, to join Warren on his right. Sedgwick then sent a second division, under George W. Getty, which was ordered to move quickly by Warren's rear and get on Warren's left. This was the quickest way to reinforce Warren, according to Grant's memoirs, who was confronting Confederate troops on both the Orange Court House Plank Road and the Orange Turnpike.

While this was going on Meade moved his headquarters to Wilderness Tavern, four miles south of the river. Grant remained behind to hasten Burnside's crossing and to put him into position. At this time Burnside was not directly under Meade's command and in fact was senior to Meade. Grant, in his memoirs, noted that upon being informed of the proximity of Lee's army he told Meade, and, without waiting to see Burnside, forwarded his headquarters to join Meade.

Warren had not yet reached Parker's Store, where he was to stop, when he found the Confederates. Since neither side had any positional advantage, Warren was ordered to attack as soon as possible. Hancock at 9:00 A.M. was ordered to support Getty. Hancock arrived at Getty's position at around noon well ahead of his II Corps troops, and Getty was ordered to hold until relieved. At the same time, Warren began his attack, achieving favorable but not decisive results. Getty was isolated from Warren and his situation was precarious, and Wilson's cavalry, further south, was cut off. Hancock's II Corps began to arrive at 2:00 P.M. They were immediately ordered to join Getty and attack. Heavy timber and narrow roads kept Hancock from promptly getting into position. At 4:00 P.M. Hancock was again ordered to attack, with Getty also being ordered to attack whether Hancock was ready or not.

Hancock sent in two divisions and, later on, two brigades to support Getty. Another division and a brigade were sent to reinforce Hancock and Getty. The woods were so dense, there being no road, that these troops did not reach the area of conflict until nightfall and were therefore forced to bivouac where they were without getting into position.

That afternoon Sheridan sent Gregg's Second Cavalry Division to Todd's Tavern searching for Wilson's Third Cavalry Division. Gregg found Wilson engaged with a superior force of Confederate cavalry under Thomas L. Rosser, with infantry support, and Wilson was being forced to fall back. Together Gregg and Wilson drove the Confederates back beyond Corbin's Bridge. Hancock and Hill's troops continued fighting against each other until nightfall put a stop to the stalemated combat.

The next day, May 6, Grant knew that Longstreet and 12,000 men were on their way to join Hill, on Hill's right, near Brock Road. Grant thought that these reinforcements might reach Hill during the night and Grant was anxious that the Confederates might attack the next morning. Therefore, he ordered Hancock to attack at 4:30 A.M. Meade wanted a delay until 6:00 A.M. and Grant modified the order for the attack to begin at 5:00 A.M.

Hancock by this time had with him half of the Army of the Potomac. James Wadsworth's division was in position perpendicular to Hill's Confederate troops and he was to the right of Hancock. Wadsworth was ordered to attack Hill's left at the same time Hancock was to make his attack at 5:00 A.M.

Burnside, with two IX Corps divisions, was ordered to move in between Hancock and Wadsworth and attack as soon as he was in position. Sedgwick and Warren were also ordered to attack to keep as much as possible of Lee's army as busy as possible in order to prevent Lee from reinforcing Hill. If Burnside succeeded in breaking through the Confederate center he was to swing around to the left and envelop the Confederate right. Hancock was informed of all of these proposed movements.

Lee, possibly anxious to hold any attack on his right before Longstreet arrived, managed to launch an attack of his own before Grant did, even though Grant had set 5:00 A.M. as the starting time for his attacks. According to Grant, in his memoirs, his purpose was evident, but he failed.

Hancock was ready to attack on time, but upon learning that Longstreet was moving part of his corps by way of the Cartharpin Road and threatening his left flank, Hancock sent Francis Barlow's division with all the artillery to cover the approaches where Longstreet was expected. Once this was done, Hancock attacked as ordered. After an hour of desperate fighting the Confederates began to break up.

Grant believed that if Hancock and his troops had known about the Confederate confusion and panic, it would have been taken advantage of quickly enough to prevent Lee from making a stand outside of the Richmond defenses. John Gibbon, on Hancock's left, was ordered to attack, but did not accomplish much.

In the morning of May 6, Sheridan was to join Hancock on his left and attack in order to prevent Confederate cavalry from trying to get on Grant's left and rear. Sheridan found them at the intersection of the Brock and Furnace Roads and at Todd's Tavern, driving them back at both places. Sheridan was attacked later and managed to repulse it. Hearing the firing between Sheridan and Stuart, Hancock, thinking that the Confederates were advancing by Brock Road, reinforced his position guarding the entrance to Brock Road, which in turn weakened his attack column.

Hancock followed Hill's retreating troops for a mile or more. That afternoon Longstreet arrived, which caused Hill to counterattack. Hill's attacking troops, due to the thick woods, were able to approach within 100 yards of Hancock's position undetected, and it was through their attack that the Confederates swept away Hancock's advanced brigade. Hill and Longstreet hit General Mott's division — following up the advantage they had gained — making it fall back in great confusion. Hancock held his position for a time but fell back to his starting point.

On the Confederate side, Longstreet was severely wounded, which caused Lee to take personal command on his right. When he was not able to rally his troops in order to resume the attack upon Hancock, Lee withdrew to re-form his troops. Hancock then dispatched a brigade to clear his front, which encountered a Confederate brigade that withdrew without any fighting.

At 4:15 P.M. Lee attacked on Grant's left, causing portions of Gershom Mott and David B. Birney's divisions to give way and retire in disorder. The Confederates, under Richard H. Anderson, advanced, pushing through Grant's line and achieving a temporary success until a brigade from Gibbon's division drove them back.

During the fighting many of the wounded from both sides lay where it was impossible to reach them. Bursting shells set the woods on fire and many of these wounded men were burned or suffocated to death. The fire spread to Grant's fieldworks, much of which had been built of wood and which also caught fire in some places. Since the battle was still raging, Grant's troops fought through the fire as long as possible.

Lee had his own troubles. His troops were in confusion and he had failed to restore order; therefore, he withdrew. Grant was forced to suspend a further attack by Hancock because he had exhausted his ammunition and had not had time to replenish it. Meanwhile, Burnside, Sedgwick and Warren kept up their attacks throughout the day, preventing Lee from reinforcing his right.

Some of Sedgwick's troops on Grant's right had been sent to reinforce Hancock on the left. This had left Grant's right in danger of being turned, which would have allowed Lee to cut Grant off from his base of supply. Sedgwick refused his right and dug in, but late in the afternoon Early's division of Ewell's corps got in among Sedgwick's right, creating considerable confusion before Sedgwick managed to restore his lines a little further to the rear.

During the night Lee withdrew to his own fieldworks, ending the Battle of the Wilderness.

It was during this battle that the heavy duty of command and its attendant problems began to affect Warren's personality. For a long time he had driven himself relentlessly, ignoring relatively light battle wounds and illness, while finding it difficult to bear the mounting casualties suffered by his men, first in II Corps and now in V Corps. These and other factors combined to fuel his temper and caused him to vent his wrath on those around him, including his superiors. Men around him began to endorse the opinion that these fits of passion were symptoms of madness. In reality, they were symptoms of combat fatigue.

Warren was well aware of his irritability and irascibility, but seemed unable to control his temper. As a result he alienated many of his friends, including Meade, who also had a towering temper. In addition, Warren made no attempt to ingratiate himself with his superiors. However, he still managed to retain the affection of the common soldiers under his command (and later they would become his most vociferous supporters and defenders) because he never treated them with disregard.

The next day, May 7, Grant was informed that Butler and his Army of the James had taken City Point on May 5. (City Point would eventually become Grant's primary supply depot and headquarters when he moved to the James River and began the Siege of Petersburg.) Grant thereupon gave orders for the Army of the Potomac to move by its left flank, setting up what would become the Battle of Spotsylvania. Grant made this move because he feared that the Confederates would attack Butler before he could arrive. In addition, he also wanted to get between Lee's army and Richmond, if possible. If that proved not to be possible Grant at least wanted to draw Lee into battle upon an open field, without fieldworks.

Also on May 7, Sheridan collided with Confederate cavalry at Todd's Tavern, routing them and opening the way for the advance that Grant had determined upon. After dark, Warren's V Corps withdrew from his position, followed by Sedgwick's VI Corps. Grant and his staff, with a cavalry escort, preceded them, with Meade and his staff joining Grant.[2]

However, Lee beat the Union troops to Spotsylvania. Grant had ordered his baggage and supply trains east of the roads to be used by the troops for their movement. Lee thought that this meant that Grant was moving on Petersburg and ordered Longstreet's corps, now under the temporary command of Anderson, to move on the morning of May 8 upon Spotsylvania. Because the Wilderness was still burning, Anderson was unable to go into bivouac for the night, and, therefore, he began his march on Spotsylvania early.

Anderson, upon his arrival, had his troops dig in and was now located across Warren's front. Warren, supposing that these troops were the Confederate troops Merritt and his cavalry had engaged earlier, attacked and was repulsed. Warren re-formed his troops and attacked again with the whole of V Corps, gaining a position immediately in Anderson's front, where he dug in.

Grant, by this time, had established his headquarters at Piney Branch Church, and he wanted to crush Anderson before Lee and the rest of the Army of Northern Virginia could come to his support. Sedgwick, who was at Piney Branch Church, was ordered to support Warren. Hancock, at Todd's Tavern, was notified of the fighting at Spotsylvania and was directed to prepare to move there. Burnside, who was with the baggage and supply trains on Grant's extreme left, received the same orders. Sedgwick was slow in moving up to join Warren at Spotsylvania, so night had fallen before their combined forces were ready to attack. Sedgwick did not get into the engagement and Warren attacked piecemeal, one division at a time, which failed.

Meanwhile, Lee ordered Hill's corps—now under Early's temporary command—to move by the same road that Grant had used. This showed that early on the morning of May 8 Lee thought the Army of the Potomac was still on its way to Fredericksburg. Therefore, he reported to Richmond that he held Spotsylvania and that he was on Grant's flank.

One of Warren's fits of temper was directed against Sheridan. On May 8, while on the way to Spotsylvania, V Corps found its path clogged by two divisions of Sheridan's cavalry. Warren, bound by a rigid timetable, was rankled and complained to Meade. Sheridan and Meade argued about the incident and Sheridan may have started carrying a grudge against Warren. (A few weeks later, Sheridan was further enraged when Warren complained that during a recent operation Sheridan's cavalry had failed in its responsibility to guard the flanks of V Corps. At the same time, Warren also ran afoul of Grant. As the Overland Campaign wore on Grant became increasingly disenchanted with Warren's free-thinking. He was greatly annoyed when Warren questioned orders and sometimes suggested what he believed to be more viable ones. Grant was also inclined to think that Warren's abrasiveness prevented him from maintaining a proper relationship with his subordinates. In addition, Warren's slowness and deliberation gave him much trouble.)

The offshoot of Sheridan and Meade's argument came that same day when Grant directed Sheridan to pass around Lee's left and attack his cavalry. Sheridan was also told to cut two railroads — one running west to Gordonsville, Charlottesville and Lynchburg, and the other to Richmond — then move onto the James River and draw supplies from Butler's Army of the James. Thus Sheridan moved past the rear of Lee's Army of Northern Virginia.

Sheridan had two main objectives: first, annoy Lee by cutting his supply lines and telegraphic communications, and second, draw the Confederate cavalry, under Stuart, after him and thereby better protect the Army of the Potomac's flanks, rear, and communications. In addition, Sheridan's absence from the army would save the baggage and supply trains from drawing his supplies from Fredericksburg, which was now Grant's base. Sheridan began his raid on May 9 and returned 16 days later. The result was the destruction of the railroad and Confederate supplies at Ashland along with the defeat and death of Stuart at Yellow Tavern on May 11.

Meanwhile, back at Spotsylvania by noon on May 9, Lee occupied a semicircle facing north, northwest, and northeast, around Spotsylvania. Anderson was on the left, Ewell was on the center, and Early was on the right. Warren's V Corps was positioned on Grant's right, covering the roads that converged on Spotsylvania. Sedgwick's VI Corps was to Warren's left, and Burnside's IX Corps was on the extreme left. Hancock's II Corps was back at Todd's Tavern. When it became known that Early had left Hancock's front, Hancock was ordered to move up on Warren's right. He was placed on a hill overlooking the Po River. Hancock was then ordered to cross the Po, and get on the Confederate right flank, which was held by Anderson.

The position taken by Hancock's II Corps forced Lee to reinforce his left during the night. On the morning of May 10, when Hancock renewed his effort, he was met by some of Early's troops, who had been sent from Lee's extreme right during the night. Hancock thereupon succeeded in having only one brigade cross the Po.

Later that morning, Hancock reconnoitered with a view to forcing a crossing, if an advantage could be gained. Lee's troops were strongly dug in on high ground overlooking the Po River, commanding its bridge with artillery. Anderson's left rested upon the Po River, where it turned south; therefore, should Hancock cross the Po — although it would place him on the same side of the stream as the rest of the Army of the Potomac — he would be further isolated since he would have to cross the river twice in the face of Lee's army in order to unite his II Corps with the rest of the Union army. For these reasons Hancock abandoned any idea of crossing the Po River.

Since Lee had weakened the other parts of his line to obstruct Hancock, Grant decided to take advantage of it. Accordingly, Warren and Maj. Gen. Horatio G. Wright were issued orders for an attack on the afternoon of May 10. (Wright had succeeded to the command of VI Corps due to the death of Sedgwick, the victim of a Confederate sharpshooter.) Hancock was to be in command.

Between the Union and Confederate lines, where Warren was to attack, was a ravine grown up with large trees and underbrush, making it almost impenetrable, with the slopes on both sides also being covered with a heavy growth of timber. By noon Warren had launched reconnaissance probes along his front twice, first with one division and then with two, and being repulsed both times. But Warren had gained enough information to cause him to recommend an assault.

Wright also reconnoitered his front and gained an advanced position. He then organized a storming force of 12 regiments under the command of Col. Emory Upton, 121st New York

Infantry Regiment. The assault was ordered at about 4:00 P.M. with Warren's V Corps, Wright's VI Corps and Mott's division of Hancock's II Corps. The battlefield was so heavily wooded, Grant wrote in his memoirs, that little of it could be seen to determine the progress of the assault.

Warren was repulsed with heavy losses. There was success on the left, where Upton had made his attack, but the advantage was lost due to Mott's feeble efforts. Upton smashed forward and crossed the Confederate fieldworks, then, turning to both the right and the left, captured several guns and hundreds of prisoners. Mott was ordered up to assist Upton and exploit the breakthrough, but failed utterly. So much time was lost that Upton was ordered to withdraw; his troops were so adverse to giving up the advantage they had gained that Grant withdrew the order and, in order to relieve them, commanded a renewal of the assault instead. Hancock, who had gone with Birney's division to assist Barlow, had returned and his II Corps was joined with Warren's V Corps and Wright's VI Corps in this last assault. Many of the men participating in this assault got up to, and over, the Confederate fieldworks, but were unable to hold them and were withdrawn under cover of night.

Burnside's IX Corps, on the left, had gotten to within a few hundred yards of Spotsylvania Court House, turning Lee's right. However, he was not aware, and neither was Grant, of the importance of his success, which he had gained with little fighting and almost no loss. Burnside was now separated widely from Wright. That night he was ordered to join on to Wright's flank. That caused him to fall back a mile and the advantage he had gained was lost. Grant blamed himself for this mistake since he had failed to attach a staff officer to Burnside with the responsibility to keep Grant apprised of Burnside's position.

On May 11 there was no fighting and no action, except by Mott, who made a reconnaissance to see if there was a weak spot in Lee's line. Grant was informed at this time that Butler's Army of the James cavalry, under General A.V. Kautz, had cut the railroad south of Petersburg, separating Beauregard from Richmond and defeating D.H. Hill. News also arrived from Sheridan that he had destroyed 10 miles of railroad, the telegraph between Lee and Richmond, one and a half million rations, and most of Lee's medical stores.

Mott's May 11 reconnaissance had revealed a salient in Lee's lines upon the right center. Grant decided that an assault should be made at this point. Hancock was ordered to move II Corps, by the rear of Warren's V Corps and Wright's VI Corps, under cover of night to Wright's left, and from there form for an assault at 4:00 A.M. May 12. Due to darkness, heavy rain, and road problems, Hancock did not reach his jumping off point until after midnight, taking most of the rest of the night to get into position. Burnside, meanwhile, had been ordered to attack at the same time on the left of the salient. Warren and Wright were told to be prepared to join the assault if advisable. Hancock put Barlow in a double column on his left and Birney on his right; Mott followed Birney and Gibbon was in reserve.

That morning fog delayed the assault by half an hour.

The ground Hancock had to cover to reach the Confederate lines was ascending and heavily wooded to within 200–300 yards of Hancock's objective, while Birney had to cross a marsh. They pushed ahead quickly and with a rush went up and over the Confederate fieldworks. Barlow and Birney entered them almost simultaneously, where desperate hand-to-hand fighting broke out. At 6:00 A.M. Warren's V Corps was ordered to support Hancock. Burnside on the left advanced east of the salient. One of his divisions also managed to get over the Confederate fieldworks but was forced back.

Lee counterattacked Hancock furiously, forcing Hancock to fall back to the fieldworks he had captured. As Hancock held there, Wright was ordered to reinforce him, arriving by 6:00 P.M. At 8:00 P.M. Warren was ordered up again, but he was so slow in making his dispositions that by 11:00 P.M. Meade informed Grant, "Warren seems reluctant to assault."

"If Warren fails to attack promptly," Grant responded, "send [A.A] Humphreys [then Meade's chief of staff] to command his corps and relieve him."

Meanwhile, Burnside on the left kept Lee from reinforcing his center from that flank. Lee massed his troops heavily from his left flank onto the broken point of his line. He made at least five major assaults without dislodging Hancock's II Corps. It was 3:00 A.M. on May 13 before the fighting ended. During the night Lee took up a position in the rear of his former one and by morning was strongly dug in again. Thus ended the Battle of Spotsylvania. Both armies spent most of the next week glaring at each other like a pair of dogs after a dogfight.

When Grant learned of Franz Siegle's defeat at New Market, where he had been assigned to keep the Confederates busy in the Shenandoah Valley, and of Benjamin Butler's Army of the James being neutralized at Bermuda Hundred as it attempted to move up the Peninsula against Richmond, he decided upon a new movement on the left flank towards Richmond that commenced on the night of May 19 and resulted in the Battle of North Anna.

On May 23, Hancock's II Corps came to the wooden bridge spanning the North Anna River west of where it was crossed by the Fredericksburg Road. It was nearly night when Hancock arrived, finding the bridge well guarded. Deploying two brigades, Hancock quickly took the bridge, but due to nightfall he did not cross it until the next morning.

Lee's entire army was south of the North Anna River, with Grant's lines covering his front with six miles, covered by one division, separating the two wings of Grant's forces. To get from one wing to the other the river would have to be crossed — twice. Lee could reinforce any part of his lines from all parts of them with only a short march, or he could concentrate the whole of his army wherever he might choose in order to make an assault.

Grant was determined to draw Lee out of his present position, since the Army of the Potomac could do nothing where it was unless Lee attacked, and to make one more effort to get between Lee and Richmond. Grant did not expect to succeed, but he did expect to hold Lee far enough to the left to enable him to reach the James River. In addition, Sheridan and his cavalry rejoined Grant.

It was delicate moving the right wing of the Army of the Potomac from the south bank of the North Anna River in the presence of Lee's army. Wilson's Third Cavalry Division was brought from the left and moved south to Little River. Once there, he maneuvered to give Lee the impression there was going to be an attack upon his left. Then under cover of darkness Grant withdrew to the north side of the river, Lee being completely deceived by Wilson.

Sheridan moved on the afternoon of May 26, sending Gregg's Second Cavalry Division and Torbert's First Cavalry Division to Taylor and Littlepage's fords towards Hanover. Sheridan was followed by a division from VI Corps. On the morning of May 27 the crossing was effected, securing a position south of the Pamunkey River and leading to the Battle of Haw's Shop.

Hanover was about 20 miles from Richmond and two roads connected them. The shortest and most direct road crossed the Chickahominy River at Meadow Bridge, near the Virginia Central Railroad. The other road went by New and Old Cold Harbor. There was a third road a few miles out from Hanover by way of Mechanicsville to Richmond. New Cold Harbor was important because it covered the roads back to White House (where Lee drew his supplies) and the roads southeast that Grant's troops would have to use to get to the James River below the defenses of Richmond.

Sheridan advanced to near Old Cold Harbor on May 31, but dismounted Confederate cavalry in prepared fieldworks occupied it. After a hard fight Sheridan captured the place, and the Confederates, knowing its importance, returned in such force to retake it that Sheridan had decided to evacuate it and had already commenced doing so when he received orders from Grant, through Meade, to hold at all costs until reinforcements arrived. Sheridan turned to face his attackers and prepared his defenses, but night came on before the Confederates could make any assault.

Early in the previous evening Wright's VI Corps was told to march directly to Cold Harbor, passing by the rear of the army. They were supposed to arrive by daylight or before. But the night was dark, the distance was long, and it was 9:00 A.M. June 1 before Wright arrived. Before Wright's arrival Sheridan had to repulse two Confederate assaults.

By 6:00 P.M. Wright and General William F. Smith's XVIII Corps, which had been borrowed from the stalled Army of the James, were ready to make an assault. The ground was clear for several hundred yards and then it was wooded. Wright charged across the open space. From there he entered the woods and captured the first Confederate line of rifle pits, taking 700 to 800 prisoners. The Confederates counterattacked Wright three times but were thrown back each time. During the night there were frequent additional attacks but they all failed to dislodge the Union troops. This was the first assault upon Cold Harbor.

During the night, Hancock's II Corps was ordered to move in at Wright's left. Grant intended to attack again on the morning of June 2. The night was so dark, the heat and dust were so excessive, the road network was so intricate and hard to keep straight that Hancock's column did not arrive until 6:00 A.M. and it was not in position for the attack until 7:30 A.M. Preparations were made for an afternoon attack, but it did not take place until the next morning. While Warren and Burnside were adjusting their positions the Confederates made several attacks that were thrown back; however, there was no adequate follow up to these minor successes.

This fact so annoyed Grant that he instructed Meade to inform his corps commanders "that they needed to seize all such opportunities when they occurred, and not to wait for orders, all of our maneuvering being made for the very purpose of getting the enemy out of his cover."

It was about this time that Col. Theodore Lyman, one of Meade's aides, attempted to deliver a message to Warren, who could not be found. "This was Warren's great way," Lyman recalled, "to go about, looking thus after details and making ingenious plans; but, it kept him away from generalities, and made it hard to find him, so that he finally came to trouble as much by this, as anything else."

Lee moved his left up during the night to make his lines correspond with Grant's. Lee's lines now extended from Totopotomy to New Cold Harbor. Grant's lines extended from Bethesda Church by Old Cold Harbor to the Chickahominy River, with a cavalry division guarding his right. Grant ordered an assault for June 3 to be made by Hancock's II Corps, Wright's VI Corps, and Smith's XVIII Corps. Warren's V Corps and Burnside's IX Corps were to support it by threatening Lee's left. They were also to attack if Lee should support more threatened points by moving troops from his left, or if any favorable opportunities should develop.

Each of the corps commanders was told to select points where they would make their attacks, with everything to begin at 4:30 A.M. Hancock sent Barlow and Gibbon forward at the proper time, with Gibbon in reserve. Barlow pushed through thickets and swamps under heavy musketry and artillery fire, carrying a Confederate position outside their main line where the road made a deep cut through a bank providing good shelter for troops. When no assistance was provided, Barlow dug in and held his place. Gibbon found the ground over which he had to move cut up with deep ravines and a morass that was difficult to cross. His men struggled on until they got to the parapet that covered the Confederate troops, whereupon they dug in and held on.

Wright's VI Corps captured the outer Confederate rifle pits, but accomplished nothing more. Smith's XVIII Corps also took the rifle pits in their front. The ground Smith's troops had to cover was the most exposed, as it was an open plain, and was exposed to both direct and cross fire from Confederate positions.

It was all over by 7:30 A.M. and the only real tangible result were the 7,000 corpses and wounded men dressed in Union blue that now lay between the Union and Confederate lines, thus ending the second assault and the Battle of Cold Harbor.

Grant accepted the responsibility for the blunder and noted in his memoirs:

> I always regretted that the last assault at Cold Harbor was ever made.... At Cold Harbor no advantage whatever was gained to compensate for the heavy loss we sustained. Indeed the advantages, over those of relative loss, were on the Confederate side. Before that, the Army of Northern Virginia seemed to have acquired a wholesome regard for the courage, endurance, and soldierly qualities of the Army of the Potomac. They no longer wanted to fight them "one Confederate to five Yanks." Indeed, they seemed to have given up any idea of gaining any advantage of their antagonist in the open field. They had come too much to prefer breastworks to revive their hopes temporarily; but it was of short duration. The effect upon the Army of the Potomac was the reverse. When we reached the James River, however, all effects of the Battle of Cold Harbor seemed to have disappeared.

Maybe, but the effects upon one of his corps commanders remained and lay there just underneath the surface in his mind and soul and festered.

As the Overland Campaign wore on Warren, for his part, showed increasing signs of what would in World War I be known as shell shock and in World War II as combat fatigue, and which is today known as post-traumatic stress disorder (PTSD). Warren became more and more despondent about the mounting death toll while under Grant's command; in one of the more common symptoms of combat fatigue, or PTSD, his anger repeatedly kept on breaking out in bursts of passion. At one point he even cried out to Meade: "For 30 days now it has been one funeral possession past me; and it is too much! Today I saw a man burying a comrade, and, within half an hour, he himself was brought in and buried beside him. The men need some rest!"

When Grant heard about this outburst the chances are that his doubts about Warren, particularly concerning his stability, were greatly increased. The relationship between Grant and Warren was reaching a crisis stage. Grant knew that he could afford to absorb losses much better than Lee could, that in effect he could win a war of attrition. However, Warren realized that the Army of the Potomac was being bled white by these losses and that eventually, when the time came for the final push, the army would have nothing left to push with.

The real problem and tragedy lay in the fact that they were both right.

By this time Lee was so close to Richmond, and the swamps of the Chickahominy River that had so plagued McClellan during the Peninsula Campaign were such a great obstacle, that Grant decided that in his next move by the left flank the Army of the Potomac would move south of the James River.

This was a hazardous move for a number of reasons:

1. The Chickahominy River had to be crossed.
2. All of the bridges east of Lee's position had been destroyed.
3. The Confederates had a shorter distance and better roads upon which to travel.
4. There was more than 50 miles between the Army of the Potomac and the Army of the James, with both the Chickahominy and James rivers to be crossed.
5. The Army of the Potomac had to get out of a position that was only a few hundred yards away from Lee's army at its widest point.

Lee — if he did not choose to follow Grant — might, with his shorter distance to travel and with his advantage of the bridges over the Chickahominy and James rivers, move against the Army of the James (which, because Grant had borrowed XVIII Corps, consisted at the moment of only X Corps and a small division of cavalry) before Grant and the Army of the Potomac could come to Butler's relief. He might also spare enough troops to move against David Hunter, who had replaced Siegle and who was approaching Lynchburg, living off the country as he moved and with no more ammunition than he could carry.

In the end Grant felt that the move had to be made and he hoped that Lee would not spot the dangers which worried Grant. But Grant took all of the precautions that he could to guard against all of the dangers that he could see. Grant's ultimate target would be Petersburg. Since almost all of the railroads that connected Richmond with the rest of the Confederacy passed through Petersburg, the loss of that railroad hub would force the abandonment of the Confederate capital.

Sheridan, with two of his cavalry divisions, was sent on a raid in part to divert Lee's attention from the move to the James River. Unfortunately Sheridan would be turned back at the Battle of Trevilian Station, and the only objective that he actually accomplished was that of diverting Lee's attention from Grant's move upon the James River.

Instead of seeking to block Grant's move to the James River, Lee sent much of his cavalry to successfully confront Sheridan at Trevilian Station, and Early (now officially in command of Ewell's Confederate II Corps) was sent to the Shenandoah Valley to oppose Hunter.

The Army of the Potomac managed to reach the James River — without encountering any of the dangers that had worried Grant — on June 14. Grant took a steamer to Bermuda Hundred to confer with Butler and to direct a movement against Petersburg, while the Army of the Potomac crossed the James River. Smith's XVIII Corps was sent back from Cold Harbor by way of White House, then on steamers to City Point, to be returned to Butler as part of Grant's move against Petersburg. Butler sent 6,000 reinforcements to Smith, including his cavalry division under Kautz, and Smith then headed out on the road to Petersburg.

To reach the Confederate defenses around Petersburg, Smith had to move about six miles. The Confederate advanced line of fieldworks was only two miles outside of Petersburg. Smith was to advance under cover of darkness as close to the Confederate fieldworks as possible and attack at daylight. What wasn't known at the time was that Petersburg was defended by only about 2,500 Confederate troops that could have been easily overwhelmed. Smith began his advance but encountered a Confederate force between City Point and the Petersburg defenses. Although Smith successfully attacked there was so much delay that it was daylight before his troops could move any further and he was unable to close with the defenses of Petersburg under cover of night.

Grant informed Butler that Hancock's II Corps was to cross the James River and advance on Petersburg to support Smith, and then Grant returned to the Army of the Potomac and informed Meade about the instructions he had given Butler. Grant then ordered Meade to have Hancock's II Corps cross the river under cover of darkness, push forward to Petersburg in the morning, halting at a designated point until he heard from Smith and placing himself under Smith's direction.

Smith arrived at Petersburg early in the forenoon on June 15 and spent the day, until 7:00 P.M. reconnoitering what appeared to be almost totally empty fieldworks. Smith attacked, taking a portion of the works by 9:00 P.M. Smith was both surprised and suspicious about the ease of his success. In addition, he believed a rumor that Lee had already crossed the James River and was on his way to Petersburg. When Hancock's II Corps arrived, Hancock told Smith he had two divisions, fresh and ready to move out at Smith's direction. Smith's reply to the surprised Hancock was that no one was going anywhere. Instead, Smith ordered his and Hancock's troops to dig in and simply defend what they had already captured.

However, for more than five hours after Smith had captured those trenches, Lee did not believe that Grant had moved his entire army despite Beauregard's pleas for help while shifting troops from Bermuda Hundred. At one point Beauregard had just 14,000 men facing 80,000 Union troops. The troops that followed Smith and Hancock were so exhausted by their march and all of the previous fighting they had endured that they too did nothing.

When Lee finally realized what was happening he rushed his army to the threatened area.

Four days later a Union assault ordered by Grant fizzled. Meade was so angry about Warren's performance, or lack of it, during this assault that he wrote a letter complaining about it to General Grant's chief of staff, John Rawlins, suggesting that Warren should perhaps be relieved. However, no such action was taken. Five days after Smith had taken Petersburg's outer works, Grant placed the town under siege. In this instance, Warren had been proved right, for when it came time to press the button for a final maximum effort by the soldiers of the Army of the Potomac, which had been bled white as a result of the Overland Campaign, nothing happened.

The Army of the Potomac was then given the responsibility for the investment of Petersburg, while the Army of the James held Bermuda Hundred and all of the ground north of the James River. After investigating what had happened, Grant relieved Smith of his command and sent him to New York "awaiting orders," orders that never came.

Lee had been drawn into the situation he feared most, a protracted siege in front of the Confederate capital at Richmond. Before he reached that predicament Lee had observed to Lt. Gen. Jubal Early, "We must destroy this army of Grant's before he gets to the James River. If he gets there it will become a siege and then it will be a mere question of time." Grant had gotten there; and now, as Lee had said, it was only a question of time. That did not mean that Lee was not going to try to distract Grant from the siege. Early, who had been originally detached to the Shenandoah Valley with Jackson's old corps (which now became the solid core of Early's Valley District Army), was let loose to invade the North and raid Washington.

Following Early's raid, Grant responded by turning Sheridan loose in what was now the Middle Military Division with the Army of the Shenandoah. Sheridan's orders were to destroy Early's army and so devastate the Shenandoah Valley that it would no longer be a Confederate asset.

The Siege of Petersburg continued although an attempt was made by the Union forces to break through the defenses of Petersburg at the Battle of the Crater on July 30, 1864. Warren's V Corps was one of those units scheduled to participate in the assault, which was to follow the explosion of a huge mine placed in a 750-foot tunnel under the Petersburg defenders. The assault, however, by IX Corps was badly bungled, due in part to interference by Meade. (This resulted in Burnside being replaced as IX Corps commander by General John G. Parke.)

Warren was accused of failure to contain the Confederate troops opposite him, which allowed Confederate Maj. Gen. William Mahone to send in his division to smash the attack by IX Corps. Warren was able to show conclusively that he could not make an assault because IX Corps remained between his V Corps and the breach until after the Confederates had recovered from the explosion. In August and December, Warren earned distinction with his independent commands against the Weldon Railroad, a vital supply line to Petersburg. However, by this time Grant had changed his opinion of Warren. Grant wrote in his memoirs:

> Warren's difficulty was twofold: when he received an order to do anything, it would at once occur to his mind how all the balance of the army should be engaged as to properly co-operate with *him* [emphasis added]. His ideas were generally good, but he would forget that the person giving him his orders had thought of others at the time he had of him. In like manner, when he did get ready to execute an order, after giving most intelligent instructions to his division commanders, he would go in with one division, holding the others in reserve, until he could superintend their movement in person also, forgetting that division commanders could execute an order without his presence. His difficulty was constitutional and beyond his control. He was an officer of superior ability, quick perceptions, and personal courage to accomplish anything that could be done with a small command.

In the meantime, Sheridan had ended resistance in the Shenandoah Valley and had returned Wright's VI Corps to Grant. On February 27, Sheridan left his winter quarters at Winchester with the First and Third Cavalry divisions, smashed Early's last remnant at Waynesboro, and then marched to rejoin Grant. On his arrival, Grant made Sheridan co-equal with Meade, and Wesley Merritt was confirmed as the new commander of the Cavalry Corps.

21

On the Road to Five Forks

As the spring of 1865 began, Grant assumed that Lee would attempt to evacuate his entrenched positions at Petersburg and march quickly to combine his Army of Northern Virginia with what was left of the Army of Tennessee under Gen. Joseph E. Johnston in North Carolina, who was facing Sherman. He was right.

On March 26, General Lee informed Confederate President Jefferson Davis that Richmond and Petersburg were doomed; Lee said that it was necessary to prepare at once for a retreat away from the James River (evacuating Richmond and Petersburg), join forces with Johnston and continue the fight elsewhere. Lee told Davis that Grant's Army of the Potomac and Army of the James "seriously threatens our position and diminishes our ability to maintain our present line."

The writing was on the wall for the Confederacy[1]; except for the line to Richmond, it controlled only one railroad leading outside of Petersburg, the Southside Railroad, which ran west to the Tennessee state line. About 50 miles out, the Southside Railroad crossed the Richmond and Danville Railroad at Burkeville. The Richmond and Danville Railroad was the only lifeline remaining between Richmond and what was left of the Confederacy. Any supplies to Richmond or Lee's Army of Northern Virginia had to come by way of these railroads. The only good route for a retreat from Richmond to North Carolina to join Johnston was to follow the Southside Railroad to Burkeville and then turn south. If Union troops seized control of the Southside Railroad then Lee could neither stay in Petersburg nor retreat directly to North Carolina. His only option would be moving westward hoping to eventually slip south and keeping his army together while doing so. Therefore, the Southside Railroad had to be held at all costs!

That same day Sheridan arrived at the lines of the Army of the Potomac and the Army of the James where they had Petersburg under siege. On March 27 and 28, Grant withdrew three infantry divisions and its cavalry division from the Army of the James, leaving two infantry divisions and some cavalry units in the Union lines north of the James River. (In the interval since the beginning of the Siege of Petersburg, Butler had been relieved of command of the Army of the James, by Maj. Gen. Edward O.C. Ord, which had also been reorganized. XVIII Corps had consisted of two divisions of white troops and one of colored troops, while X Corps had consisted of one division of white troops and one of colored troops. The white troops were concentrated in the new XXIV Corps and the colored troops in the new XXV Corps. In addition, Brig. Gen. Ranald S. Mackenzie had replaced Kautz in command of the cavalry.)

The three Army of the James infantry divisions then replaced II Corps and V Corps in their trenches around Petersburg. Mackenzie's cavalry was detached with orders to guard the baggage and supply trains of the Army of the Potomac.

Now under General Andrew A. Humphreys (Hancock having suffered a relapse from his Gettysburg wound), II Corps, and Warren's V Corps, when relieved by the divisions from the Army of the James, were marched five miles west until they were beyond the Confederate right flank. From there they were to press north towards the Confederate lines. They were not to attack, however; the objective of their move was to flank the Confederates, forcing them to come out of their trenches to protect their rear and the Southside Railroad. Grant also intended to use them to assure the success of Sheridan's cavalry.

Sheridan's cavalry was to swing below and beyond Dinwiddie Court House, then north to the vital crossroads at Five Forks, working behind the Confederate lines. Once they arrived at Dinwiddie Court House, Grant's original instructions called for Sheridan to raid the nearby Southside Railroad and then either march to join Sherman in North Carolina or return to Petersburg.

Five Forks was strategically important because it was where the road from Dinwiddie Court House to the Southside Railroad crossed the east-west road that led to Lee's right flank and rear. If the Union held this crossroads then the Army of Northern Virginia could not remain in Petersburg.

Lee learned about Grant's movements on March 29. Pickett's Division had already been pulled out of Longstreet's corps to assist in an attack upon the Union's Fort Stedman, which was part of Grant's siege works against Petersburg. The division had not arrived in time and did not participate in that attack and was therefore available for Lee's countermove. Pickett was sent to bolster General Richard H. Anderson's provisional corps on the Confederate right.

In addition, Maj. Gen. Fitzhugh Lee and his cavalry division were summoned from the Confederate left. Fitzhugh Lee was to take his own cavalry division and those of W.H.F. (Rooney) Lee and Thomas L. Rosser to oppose Sheridan's cavalry. Since Fitzhugh Lee would be directing all three cavalry divisions, Col. Thomas Munford would take over tactical command of his division. (Wade Hampton, Lee's official chief of cavalry, had been wounded and while recuperating at his home in South Carolina had been stranded by Sherman's march through the Carolinas and had taken command of a scratch cavalry force that was now operating with Johnston in opposition to Sherman.)

Lee then had Anderson dispatch Bushrod Johnson's infantry division to determine the identity and strength of the Union infantry (Warren's V Corps and Humphreys' II Corps) advancing from the south. Warren's lead brigade (that of Brig. Gen. Joshua Lawrence Chamberlain) was approaching a sawmill on the Quaker Road when it encountered Johnson's Confederate division. His orders were to push up the Quaker Road to develop the enemy's position. The Confederates had destroyed the bridge over Gravelly Run Creek there and were placed behind defenses on the north bank of the creek, intending to check any advance. Chamberlain was supported in his attack by another brigade, which came under his direction, with a third in reserve.

Chamberlain's plan was to ford the stream above the destroyed bridge and strike the Confederate right flank obliquely under cover of supporting musketry. Chamberlain's brigade crossed Gravelly Run and advanced about a mile before the Confederates were reinforced and made a stand, with Chamberlain pressing them back; they reached the edge of a thick wood where they gathered behind some fieldworks and, with a withering volley, broke Chamberlain's brigade into small groups that were forced to make a slow retreat.

The Confederates counterattacked but were thrown back into the woods with heavy losses. Having cleared the field, Chamberlain re-formed his lines and made a second assault, making a straight dash up the Quaker Road. During the attack, Chamberlain and his horse were both lightly wounded; despite his own wound Chamberlain continued to lead the attack. He was both reinforced and had artillery support, and he succeeded in forcing the Confederate troops out of the woods and their fieldworks, allowing V Corps to advance up the road near the junction of the Boydton Plank and the White Oak roads. For this action on the Quaker Road, Chamberlain received a brevet to the rank of major general of volunteers.

The fight at Quaker Road caused Grant either to sense an opportunity or to come to a decision that he had been debating. Grant told Sheridan that he could forget both the railroad and marching to join Sherman; instead he ordered Sheridan to stay close to the infantry. He also informed Sheridan that in the morning (March 30) he was to push against the Confederates and get on Lee's right rear.

On the morning of March 30 heavy rain that had been falling since the previous day continued, as Humphreys' II Corps and Warren's V Corps edged closer to the Confederate trenches, despite the rain that made any movement difficult. In addition, Warren was being confounded by contradictory marching orders; therefore, he suggested that his V Corps put a force across the White Oak Road and thus isolate Pickett's troops from the Confederate right. Meanwhile, Sheridan sent Merritt with Thomas Devin's First Cavalry Division north from Dinwiddie Court House to Five Forks, directly upon Lee's probable escape route. Halfway there Merritt and Devin collided with Fitzhugh Lee's Confederate cavalry.

At noon Grant sent word to Sheridan calling off the entire operation due to the weather. Sheridan thereupon rode to Grant's headquarters to persuade Grant to continue the operation. Sheridan told Grant that the Confederate cavalry could be knocked out of the way at any time and if Lee were to send infantry to help them he would only be bringing about his own doom. When asked what he would do about providing forage for his horses Sheridan replied, "Forage? I'll get all the forage I want. I'll haul it out if I have to set every man in the command to corduroying the roads, and corduroy every mile of them from the railroad to Dinwiddie. I tell you I'm ready to strike out tomorrow and go to smashing things."

Under Sheridan's urging Grant decided the operation would continue, bad roads or not, and that there would be no stopping until there was a final showdown. Upon his return Sheridan kept George A. Custer's Third Cavalry Division working at repairing the impassable roads so forage and provisions could be brought up. He kept George Crook and his Second Cavalry Division at Dinwiddie Court House (David M. Gregg having resigned his commission and being succeeded by Crook) and ordered Merritt with Devin's division to develop the position and strength of the Confederate cavalry he had collided with. Merritt succeeded in driving Fitzhugh Lee's cavalry back to Five Forks, finding Pickett's Confederate infantry dug in there. Merritt fell back and reported to Sheridan that the Confederates definitely intended to hold Five Forks.

That evening Sheridan notified Grant of the presence of Pickett's infantry and Grant acknowledged that Sheridan needed infantry of his own to force Pickett out of his position. Sheridan immediately asked for Wright's VI Corps because he had worked well with Wright before in the Shenandoah Valley, but the corps was too far away. Grant suggested instead that Sheridan utilize either Humphreys' II Corps or Warren's V Corps, with V Corps being better positioned at the time to move to Five Forks. The question of which infantry to use remained unresolved. However, Warren's proposal to move V Corps across the White Oak Road received approval from General Meade, the titular commander of the Army of the Potomac.

On the morning of March 31, the rain finally stopped and Merritt sent Devin's First Cavalry Division back north to locate the Confederates. Crook's Second Cavalry Division remained to defend Dinwiddie Court House. Custer's Third Cavalry Division remained behind escorting Sheridan's baggage and supply train.

Early that morning, V Corps had advanced north beyond the Boydton Plank Road towards the main Confederate position at the junction of the White Oak and the Claiborne roads. Warren dispatched an infantry division (under R.B. Ayres) to see how strongly the White Oak Road was defended and the division marched into a Confederate flanking force dispatched by Anderson. A second division (under S.W. Crawford) was on the right rear of Ayres in echelon with him. Charles Griffin and his division, including Chamberlain's brigade, were to the rear.

In addition, Nelson A. Miles and his II Corps division had extended its lines to the left of the Boydton Plank Road and was to connect with Griffin's division. Chamberlain's brigade was to be on the extreme left of Griffin's position; another of Griffin's brigades that had been placed under Chamberlain's orders was positioned on Chamberlain's left, with his line bent back 90 degrees along a country lane leading from the Boydton Plank Road to the Claiborne Road. Some artillery was also placed in Chamberlain's lines to strengthen the flank. It was understood that Grant wanted V Corps at this time to gain possession of the White Oak Road in its front. Griffin's division was to guard the extreme left flank of V Corps and II Corps and to be ready to assist in case of trouble as the Union troops moved against the Confederates to their front upon the White Oak Road.

Ayres advanced without skirmishers and the Confederates made a counterattack that was both swift and sudden, enveloping the entire front of Ayres' division and overwhelming his leading troops and demoralizing his supporting troops. The only thing that could be done was to fall back, and when one of Ayres' brigade commanders was killed the entire force panicked and the retreat became a rout. These troops came back upon Crawford's division, which was also routed, breaking through Griffin's right, where they were rallied and re-formed and the pursuing Confederates were checked by sharp musketry from Griffin's troops.

Chamberlain was then ordered by Warren and Griffin to attack. He drove the Confederates back as they made stand after stand. At the same time, Miles and his II Corps division had flanked one Confederate brigade and had driven it back to its starting point. This caused the Confederates opposing Chamberlain to retreat to a formidable position on the crest of a ravine. With support from other units Chamberlain, after a short pause, renewed the attack and drove the Confederates into their fieldworks along the Claiborne Road.

At noon, Sheridan discovered that, beside Confederate cavalry on the road to Five Forks, a large force of Pickett's infantry was moving around Sheridan's left to attack Dinwiddie Court House. Two of Crook's brigades were sent to meet this threat from the west.

By 2:00 P.M. the Confederate flanking force had hit Crook hard, driving one brigade from Crook's division and two brigades from Devin's division nearly a mile east, almost to the Dinwiddie Road. Pickett then wheeled his infantry and marched south to Dinwiddie Court House. At the same time, Rosser and Rooney Lee's cavalry divisions attacked from the west and drove two of Sheridan's brigades south.

Concurrently Warren counterattacked on the White Oak Road with Chamberlain's brigade, which restored the line. The assault then surged ahead to the White Oak Road. Warren, upon hearing the musketry from the direction of Dinwiddie Court House, figured that Sheridan might need some assistance and dispatched a brigade to help. Sheridan had ordered a reconcentration at Dinwiddie Court House and had called Custer up, who formed a defensive line on the last high ground north of Dinwiddie Court House. Before darkness fell, ending the fighting, Custer withstood two assaults and then counterattacked.

Contradictory orders after night fell rained down on Warren. First he was told to withdraw from the day's advance and send a brigade to Sheridan — which he had already done. The streams were running high, due to the heavy rain that had fallen since March 29, and the bridge over Gravelly Run was out. Orders from Grant, Meade, and Sheridan suggested other routes, then demanded that a full division be sent to Sheridan. Despite the confusion, Warren (as well as Sheridan) realized that Pickett was vulnerable.

At 8:40 P.M. Warren sent a dispatch to Meade suggesting moving all of V Corps west to attack the Confederates on one side while Sheridan attacked on the other. An hour later Meade relayed the idea to Grant, suggesting that one V Corps division be sent directly to Sheridan and the other two divisions be sent to the Confederate rear by way of a parallel road. Grant approved and sent a message to Sheridan telling him to expect Warren by midnight.

Sheridan was in a dangerously exposed position, holding Dinwiddie Court House with Pickett just outside of musket range, in that Pickett had more men on hand than Sheridan did and they were well beyond the left of Sheridan's main line. But Sheridan also realized that Pickett was in an even more exposed position and could be isolated and cut off. If handled properly, none of Pickett's troops would make it back to Lee's lines. Sheridan immediately asked for VI Corps to provide the infantry he needed to smash Pickett. However, it would have taken at least two days, and possibly more, for VI Corps to get to him. Warren and V Corps were no more than six miles away. Since Warren had much more infantry than Pickett had and Sheridan had more cavalry available than Fitzhugh Lee, between the two of them they could destroy Pickett's entire force and Lee was so short of manpower that such a result would be the beginning of the end. Sheridan, on being informed that Warren would reach him by midnight, made plans to renew the battle the next morning upon the expected arrival of Warren and his V Corps.

In his memoirs Sheridan noted that, because he had repeatedly requested that VI Corps and not V Corps be sent to him it was alleged that he was prejudiced against General Warren. Sheridan claimed that not to be so: "As we had never been thrown much together, I knew little of him. I had no personal objection to him and certainly could have none to his corps." Sheridan, however, in his memoirs neglected to mention the fact that he and Warren had tangled at least twice during the Overland Campaign. However, Sheridan might not have minded it very much since one of these tangles had resulted in Sheridan's raid on Richmond, the Battle of Yellow Tavern (where Sheridan triumphed), and the death of J.E.B. Stuart.

But, it was not until almost 11:00 P.M. that Grant's approval was relayed back, through Meade, to Warren at his bivouac.

The night of March 31–April 1 was a foul night for a forced march.[2] It was very dark and although the rain had stopped the roads were covered in a deep mud; in addition, all of the creeks had overflowed their banks. And then there was Gravelly Run, where the bridge was out, which flowed across the principal road Warren's troops had to use. Finally, there was confusion about maps and place names, and some of Warren's troops were still in close contact with the Confederates back on the White Oak Road. Yet Warren immediately set to work, although there was no way in God's green — or at least God's soggy brown — earth that he was going to meet the midnight deadline.

22

Broken Hero at the Fatal Victory of Five Forks

Things began happening on April 1 (April Fool's Day) even before daylight. By 2:00 A.M. (well after Sheridan had been told to expect Warren) the Boydton Plank Road Bridge over Gravelly Run was finally repaired and one of Warren's divisions was placed on the road. Confusion between Warren and Meade, however, continued. At 3:40 A.M. Mackenzie's cavalry division was ordered to join Sheridan and hit the road. At 6:00 A.M., by which time Sheridan had expected Warren to be in position to attack the Confederates at Dinwiddie Court House, Warren's other two divisions set out to join Sheridan.

By the time daylight arrived, Pickett, realizing how exposed he was at Dinwiddie Court House, ordered a retreat, closely followed by Merritt's First and Third Cavalry divisions. Crook's Second Cavalry Division remained behind, charged with maintaining Sheridan's link to the rest of Grant's forces and protecting his baggage and supply trains. Sheridan, afraid that Pickett would get away, sent urgent orders to Warren to get into position and to attack at once. The division that started moving at 2:00 A.M. did not begin to arrive at Dinwiddie Court House until 7:00 A.M., by which time Pickett was gone and Sheridan was furious.

Pickett stopped his retreat at Five Forks, although there are some reports that he wanted to pull back to the other side of Hatcher's Run, where he would not be as badly exposed and would be in what he thought was a better position from which to protect the Southside Railroad. Lee, however, is supposed to have telegraphed orders to Pickett to stand and fight at Five Forks.[1]

Chamberlain's brigade was the first V Corps unit to reach Sheridan and was met personally by Sheridan:

"I report to you general, with the head of Griffin's division," Chamberlain later recalled saying, to which Sheridan responded sternly.

"Why did you not come before? Where is Warren?"

"He is in the rear of the column, sir."

"That is where I expected to find him. What is he doing there?"

"General, we're withdrawing from the White Oak Road, where we fought all day. General Warren is bringing off his last division, expecting an attack."

Chamberlain never doubted that the reason for Warren's relief later that day was due to Sheridan's irritation with Warren's apparent slowness in reaching him. But, as Chamberlain noted, Warren had been working and fighting the whole previous day to hold the advanced left flank of Grant's then chosen position, and was harassed all night with conflicting and stultifying orders while held between two threatening forces. On Warren's left there was nothing to prevent Pickett from striking V Corps a crushing blow, having disengaged from Sheridan. On the right there was Lee in person, with all the troops he could gather, ready, for all Warren knew or could have known at that time, to deliver a mortal strike.

When Warren left the White Oak Road to join Sheridan he did so under the very eyes of Lee himself; Warren's rear division was facing by the rear rank, ready for a not improbable attack. Warren himself was the last Union soldier to leave the White Oak Road.

Merritt, in the meantime, had reported that Pickett had returned to his position at Five Forks and Sheridan immediately devised an attack plan. Pickett's fieldworks ran about a mile or so along the White Oak Road, facing south. At the eastern end, for flank protection, the line of fieldworks made a 90-degree turn to the north for a few hundred yards. Pickett placed his five brigades of infantry within those fieldworks with Munford's cavalry on the left and two of Rooney Lee's cavalry brigades on the right. Rooney Lee's third brigade was placed on the far left to keep open the link between Pickett's troops and the rest of Lee's army. Rosser and his cavalry was a mile or two to the rear, resting their worn out horses and guarding Pickett's baggage and supply wagons.

While Pickett seemed content with his position, Sheridan realized at once that Pickett was actually in about as much danger as he had been at Dinwiddie Court House. There was a wide gap, of about three miles, between his force and the rest of Lee's army that was covered only by the tiny brigade of two equally tiny North Carolina cavalry regiments that had been drawn from Rooney Lee's cavalry division.

At some point during this period, Grant sent a special courier to Sheridan bearing the message that if Sheridan desired to do so he had the authority to relieve Warren. Grant eventually, in his memoirs, explained why he had given Sheridan this authority:

> I was so much dissatisfied with Warren's dilatory movements ... and in his failure to reach Sheridan in time, that I was very much afraid that in the last moment he [Warren] would fail Sheridan. He [Warren] was a man of fine intelligence, great earnestness, quick perception, and could make his dispositions as quickly as any officer, under difficulties where he was forced to act. But I had before discovered a defect which was beyond his control that was very prejudicial to his usefulness in emergencies like the one just before us. He could see every danger at a glance, before he had encountered it. He would not only make preparations to meet the danger, which might occur, but he would inform his commanding officer what others should do while he was executing his move.
>
> I had sent a staff officer to General Sheridan to call his attention to these defects, and to say that as much as I liked General Warren, now was not a time when we could let our personal feelings for anyone stand in the way of success; and if his removal was necessary to success, not to hesitate. It was upon that authorization that Sheridan removed Warren. I was very sorry that it was done, and regretted still more that I had not long before taken the occasion to assign him to another field of duty.

Chamberlain believed that he knew what had caused Grant to give Sheridan blanket authority to relieve Warren.[2] Two hours after Chamberlain, at the head of V Corps, reported to Sheridan, an officer on the artillery staff had the occasion to seek the location of V Corps. He went to where Warren had set up his headquarters the previous night. Warren, leaving at daybreak to join Sheridan at Dinwiddie Court House, had not removed his headquarters material; but in consideration of his staff who had been on duty all night he had allowed his chief of staff and a few others to stay and take a little rest before assuming the duties of the coming day. It was at about 9:00 A.M. when the artillery officer reached Warren's old headquarters and roused Warren's chief of staff to ask where V Corps was. The chief of staff in sleep-dazed simplicity said that when he had gone to bed V Corps had been halted to build a bridge at Gravelly Run on the Boydton Plank Road.

No time was lost reporting this to Grant's headquarters, without making any further inquiries as to the whereabouts of V Corps, which by then had been for three hours with Sheridan on the Five Forks Road. That was when Grant sent word to Sheridan that "if he had any reason to be dissatisfied with General Warren," or as it was thence put, "if in his opinion the interests of the service gave occasion for it ... he [Sheridan] might relieve him [Warren] from command of his corps."

Meanwhile, after almost six hours on the road, Mackenzie and his cavalry division arrived at Dinwiddie Court House at 9:00 A.M., and he was ordered to rest his men while Sheridan waited for the rest of V Corps and Warren to arrive.

Sheridan and Warren finally met at 1:00 P.M. and discussed Sheridan's plan. Sheridan decided to push on and attack Pickett at Five Forks. First, he dismounted Custer and Devin's cavalry divisions under Merritt and ordered them to hold the attention of Pickett's center and right flank, while Warren's V Corps was to attack where Pickett had bent his line back along the White Oak Road to guard his otherwise exposed left flank. As Warren made his movement, his right flank and rear were to be screened by Mackenzie's cavalry division, after they first cleared out any Confederate pickets, thus entirely cutting off Pickett's troops from communication with Lee's right flank, which rested at the junction of the Claiborne and the White Oak Roads.

There was a delay as Warren's troops reached their jump-off positions. In his Five Forks report Warren wrote,

> During the formation of my troops I used all the exertions possible to hasten their arrival, and everything was so prepared for them that they marched at once to their assigned position without a halt. General Sheridan expressed the apprehension to me that the cavalry, which continued to fire on the enemy, would use up their ammunition before my troops would be ready. I informed him that they would not all be in position until 4 P.M., but that I was ready to move at once, with whatever was at hand if he directed, and let the rest follow, but he did not. His impatience was no greater than I felt myself, and which I strove to repress and prevent any exhibition of, as it would tend to impair confidence in the proposed operations.

Later it was said that as usual Warren made extensive preparations, causing the delay that also raised concerns that Lee might dispatch reinforcements to Pickett that could disrupt the assault. According to Chamberlain and Warren much of the delay was due to the formation and placement of the three V Corps divisions that Sheridan desired Warren to utilize. There was also an extensive reconnaissance made of Pickett's position that took time. At the same time, Mackenzie was ordered to move by a crossroad to the White Oak Swamp Road, to a point three miles to the right of Five Forks, and to take possession of the White Oak Road.

Although Sheridan, in his memoirs, noted that he became more and more concerned, worried, and irritated as time went on without Warren being ready to make his assault, Warren himself remained quite calm — which Sheridan mistook for apathy — as he continued his preparations. When Sheridan urged him to get a move on he noted, "Warren did not seem to me to be at all solicitous; his manner exhibited decided apathy, and he remarked with indifference that 'Bobby Lee was always getting people in trouble.' With unconcern such as this, it is no wonder that nearly three hours was consumed in marching his corps ... to Gravelly Run Church [the jumping off point for the attack] though the distance was but two miles."

In Warren's opinion, as stated in his official reports, one reason for the apparent delay (as previously noted) was due to Sheridan's failure to allow for the necessary time for Warren to put his troops into the precise formation that Sheridan had directed that he utilize.

At about this time Pickett and Fitzhugh Lee were given invitations to attend a shad-bake being given by Rosser from his position, a couple of miles to the rear. Rosser had utilized his time, while resting his horses and guarding Pickett's baggage and supply trains, in catching the fish who were running in the nearby streams, to supplement his rations; as usual Lee's entire army was on reduced rations.

Between 1:30 and 2:00 P.M. Mackenzie found, attacked, and dispersed Roberts' Brigade, detached from Rooney Lee's cavalry division, which formed the sole link between Pickett's troops and the rest of Lee's army. Just before Mackenzie's division dispersed this brigade General Lee visited it himself. He rode up with one or two staff officers and noted the condition of the brigade's front, since the prospect of a cavalry fight at that moment seemed unusually good. After doing this Lee slowly rode away in the direction of Burgess' Mill and his headquarters. Less than 10 minutes later Mackenzie attacked.

By 2:00 P.M., when Mackenzie was launching his attack upon Roberts, Pickett and Fitzhugh Lee decided to accept Rosser's invitation. It is believed that Pickett did so for three reasons:

1. By that time Sheridan had shown no intention of attacking and so Pickett believed there would be no attack that day.
2. Pickett believed that he could successfully withstand an assault by any number of Union cavalry.
3. That if infantry were to be sent against him reinforcements from Lee would come to his aid.

Why Pickett felt so secure is an open question. It has been speculated that he simply did not recognize the seriousness of his position, simply taking it for granted that Lee would somehow extricate his command from any possible tight spot.

Just as Fitzhugh Lee was leaving, Col. Munford, who reported that Mackenzie had just severed their communications with Anderson, accosted him. When Munford told his commanding officer that Roberts' Brigade had been scattered and that their communications with the rest of the Army of Northern Virginia had been severed, Fitzhugh Lee simply replied: "Well, Munford, I wish you would go over in person at once and see what this means. If necessary draw up your division and let me hear from you."

Fitzhugh Lee then rode off with Pickett, who was not told about Munford's information. Rooney Lee, on the far right, was not informed about the shad-bake, or that Pickett and Fitzhugh Lee had left the field, which made Rooney Lee the senior officer present. The shad-bake lasted some two or three hours and may have included some alcoholic libations. When Sheridan did begin his attack, an "acoustic shadow" masked the sound of the battle, which was only about a mile and a half away from where the three generals were enjoying their shad-bake.

By 4:15 P.M. Warren's V Corps had just completed forming its attack columns in full view of the Confederate left. Munford, in the meantime, had ridden off to the left in accordance with Fitzhugh Lee's informal instructions. When he got to the far end of the Confederate line he saw Union cavalry on the White Oak Road and was told they were from Mackenzie's division. In a field near the White Oak Road Munford saw Union infantry, who by their Maltese crosses he identified as being part of V Corps. Munford immediately sent a courier to report the impending attack to Pickett and Fitzhugh Lee and ordered his division up. This courier, and others later dispatched, did not find the two wayward Confederate generals until it was too late.

Shortly thereafter the attack was launched. Relying on intelligence supplied by Sheridan from the earlier reconnaissance, Warren intended to send all three of his divisions against an open point in Pickett's east-west line where it made the 90-degree angle north. However, Sheridan's information was faulty as to just where the line turned north. The resulting attack misfired when two of Warren's divisions (under Crawford and Griffin) marched three-quarters of a mile too far to the east and failed to strike the angle in Pickett's line. His third division, under Ayres, corrected its course and made its thrust further to the left, leaving it exposed to a withering fire from the Confederates that caused the division to waver. As a result, instead of crushing Pickett's left, the attack was only nudging it a little.

In his official report, Warren wrote he did not realize what had happened until they arrived at the White Oak Road, where they met Mackenzie's cavalry that had arrived just before them. Warren, in the meantime, had established his headquarters in a large field where he could keep an eye on all three of his divisions. Only when he did not hear from General Griffin or General Crawford did Warren leave his headquarters to investigate the situation.

This allowed Sheridan to have his cake and eat it, too, concerning his "imputations" about Warren's conduct during the course of the battle. First he could accuse Warren of failing to inspire confidence in the troops that broke when not under a severe fire (Ayres) and for not being where Sheridan expected to find him when he wanted to find him.

Chamberlain was the first person to realize what was happening. Chamberlain, although his orders were to follow Crawford, had managed to move towards the left until his brigade had gotten past Crawford's left rear, when a sudden burst of musketry indicated that Ayres had found the Confederate position. Chamberlain halted his advance and rode ahead until he reached some high clear ground, at the southeastern corner of what was known as Sydnor Field. (It was in this field that Chamberlain saw Warren's headquarters flag, although he did not see Warren.) Upon the opposite edge of the field Chamberlain could see skirmishing along Crawford's front. To the south, along broken stubby ground, Chamberlain could see Ayres' division engaged in a confused whirl. Chamberlain judged the distance between Ayres and Crawford at about 600 yards. This gap caused him to realize that something was wrong.

Chamberlain was out of touch with both Griffin and Warren and could see that Ayres was fighting alone, and that "was not in the program." Therefore, he took it upon himself to move his brigade to the left instead of the right, where, according to his orders, he was to move. Chamberlain pulled his brigade out of the woods by the left flank and told the next brigade of Griffin's division to follow him and sent a courier to the commander of Griffin's third brigade, telling him what he was doing, as he pushed his brigade across a muddy stream and up a ravine toward Ayres. Halfway up the ravine, Chamberlain met Griffin, who did not stop but simply waved Chamberlain on to follow up the head of the ravine and to attack up Chamberlain's right, along the bank of the ravine, where, hidden by brush and scrub, the Confederates had a line (the angle that had been the target of the attack) perpendicular to their main one on the White Oak Road. The Confederates were commencing a slanting fire in Ayres' direction.

At the head of the ravine Chamberlain's brigade went into line of battle, scrambling up the rough, brambly slope. The moment Chamberlain's men showed their heads they were at close quarters, firing a volley, then coming on with a rush, while making a series of right half-wheels by battalion to meet the Confederate fire, and all the while gaining to the left, which stopped the cross fire upon Ayres.

Sheridan came upon Chamberlain and his brigade just as he was hitting the Confederate line. "By God, that's what I want to see," Sheridan yelled to Chamberlain, "general officers at the front." Sheridan then asked Chamberlain where Warren and the rest of V Corps were. Chamberlain told Sheridan he had seen Warren's flag at the big field to the north and, seeing that Ayres was in trouble and by Griffin's order, he had come to help him. Sheridan interrupted his explanation and told Chamberlain to take charge of the infantry in the immediate vicinity and to press his attack. Then he and his staff rode off looking for Warren and the rest of the missing infantry.

Chamberlain's actions, orders from Sheridan, and Warren's personal actions turned the other brigades of Griffin's division. Sheridan was all over the field, not staying in any one place for very long. When the line of Ayres and Griffin's divisions was as he wanted it, Sheridan then led both of the divisions over the Confederate fieldworks, breaking up the Confederate flank.

At the same time, Sheridan related in his memoirs, Devin's cavalry division, which had been assaulting the Confederate front, went over the Confederates works in company with Ayres; hardly halting to re-form, the intermingled infantry and dismounted cavalry swept down the fieldworks, pushing into and beyond Five Forks, which eventually resulted in the capturing of thousands of prisoners. The right of Custer's cavalry division (one brigade) gained a foothold on the Confederate works simultaneously and in cooperation with Devin's division, but on the far left Custer (with his other two brigades) had a severe fight with two brigades of Rooney Lee's cavalry division and part of Pickett's infantry. This resistance collapsed once the other Union troops got in behind the Confederate fieldworks just before dark. Custer, with some infantry support, then drove the last of the Confederate cavalry westward on the White Oak Road. At the same time, Custer advanced his left until it met the right of V Corps (Crawford's division), trapping in the pocket nearly 5,000 Confederate troops who had no recourse but to surrender. Meanwhile, Warren had gone off after Crawford, found him in the Confederate rear, wheeled the division and attacked with it southward, cutting off Pickett's line of retreat.

Sometime after 5:00 P.M. two couriers found Pickett and Fitzhugh Lee and gave them the news that Union troops were advancing upon the White Oak Road. The two couriers were immediately dispatched back to Five Forks, when Mackenzie's cavalry suddenly appeared and captured one of them. Seeing this, Pickett then rode for Five Forks, being covered by some of Munford's cavalry and arriving there just as his entire force was collapsing.

Pickett managed to organize a rear guard that was smashed in an attack led personally by Warren. That done, Warren sent his chief of staff to Sheridan with the news. When Warren's chief of staff found Sheridan he announced that Warren was in Pickett's rear, cutting off his retreat, and had many prisoners. Sheridan was in a rage—V Corps had been late in arriving at Dinwiddie Court House, it had been late getting into position at Five Forks, and, when it finally attacked, two-thirds of it had gone wandering off away from the battle; and then to top it all off its commander, Warren, had been nowhere to be found.

Sheridan's response was totally unexpected:

"By God, sir, tell General Warren he wasn't in the fight!"

Warren's chief of staff was thunderstruck.

"Must I tell General Warren that, sir?"

"Tell him that, sir!"

"I would not like to take a verbal message like that to General Warren, may I take it down in writing?"

"Take it down, sir; tell him, by God, he was not at the front."

This was done. Soon afterwards Sheridan came upon Griffin and without preface or index, told the astonished general, "I put you in command of the Fifth Corps."

When Sheridan sought out Warren—and could not find him—that was the last straw. Warren had left his command post to personally halt and re-form the attack. Sheridan, for his part, was incensed that Warren had not remained at a spot where he could be easily reached.

By 6:45 P.M. the last Confederate resistance had collapsed (with a final attack led personally by Warren, who by this time had received Sheridan's message that he had not been in the fight and who may have been seeking to throw that charge in Sheridan's face by being killed upon the field—at least this was what Chamberlain believed) and by 7:00 P.M. Sheridan, dissatisfied with Warren's performance and acting under the unrequested authority provided him by Grant, officially removed Warren from command of V Corps. Grant and Sheridan both felt that Warren was overcautious in committing his troops offensively, and when Warren was delayed by conflicting orders in reinforcing Sheridan at Five Forks, Sheridan used this and other perceived failures as his justification in relieving Warren from his command.

At the end of the battle, when Warren was given the official order relieving him of his command, Warren approached Sheridan and asked him to reconsider the order. Sheridan's response was, "Reconsider. Hell! I don't reconsider my decisions. Obey the order!"

With a bowed head and without another word, Warren did so.

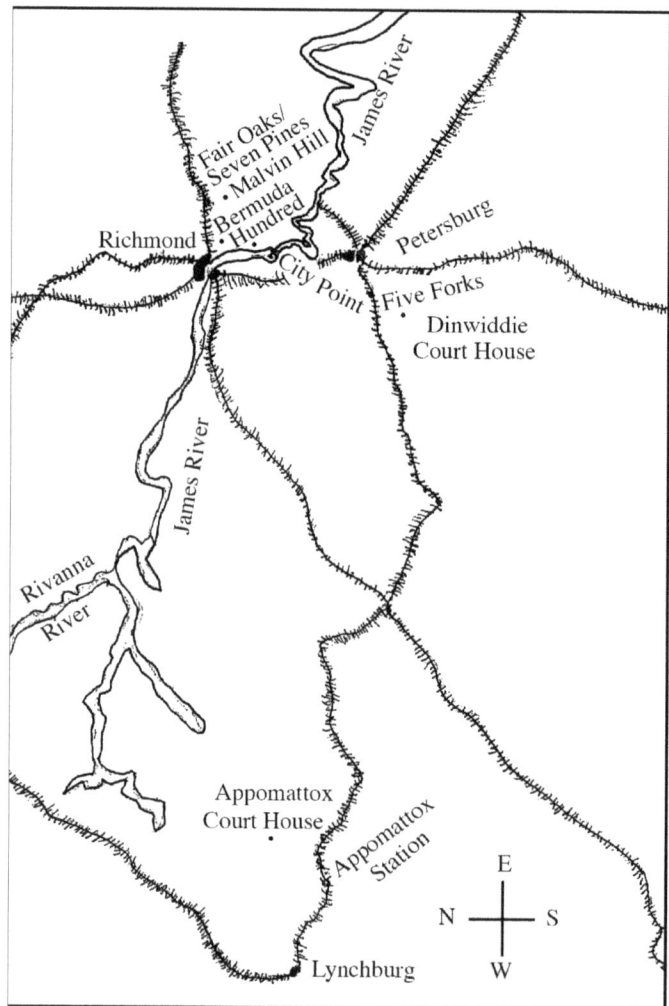

Central Virginia and the area around Richmond, VA, are depicted above. This map in particular depicts U.S. Grant's movement to the James River and upon Petersburg, in addition to the climactic Appomattox Campaign, which resulted in the final surrender of the Army of Northern Virginia and the end of the war (Library of Congress).

Afterwards, in his memoirs, Sheridan said he did not want to use Grant's authority to relieve Warren but did so because he feared that Warren simply was not the man to make the swift attack that he wanted. It seems clear, however, that Sheridan would have relieved just about any corps commander since none of them would have moved fast enough to suit him. In addition, that reasoning would be valid if Sheridan had relieved Warren before the attack was made, not afterwards when the battle had been won due in great part to Warren's exertions to redirect the assaults made by Griffin and Crawford's divisions when they went astray due in large part to faulty information provided by Sheridan in the first place.

After his removal from command of V Corps, Warren was given command first of the defenses of the Petersburg and the Southside Railroad and then of the District of Vicksburg, Department of Mississippi, and later the entire department (May 14, 1865, to June 25, 1865). He tendered the resignation of his volunteer commission on May 19, 1865, although he remained in the regular army as a major of engineers (as of June 25, 1864).

23

The Court of Inquiry

From the very first, Warren sought an official court of inquiry into his removal at Five Forks, insisting that he had done everything humanly possible to ensure victory on that battlefield. Over the next 14 years he tried repeatedly to get an official hearing on the charges (or imputations) against him. Due to the tumultuous events that occurred in the weeks following the Battle of Five Forks (on April 1, 1865), including the surrender of Lee's Army of Northern Virginia on April 9 (Palm Sunday) and Lincoln's assassination just five days later on April 14 (Good Friday), little attention was given to Warren's request.

Sheridan issued two official reports on the Battle of Five Forks. The first, dated April 2, 1865, was relatively short and made no mention at all of Warren's relief or of Sheridan's reasons for taking the action that he did. In the second report, dated May 16, 1865, however, Sheridan wrote as follows: "Had General Warren moved according to the expectations of the lieutenant general [Sheridan having been informed by Grant that Warren should arrive by midnight March 31–April 1], there appears to have been but little chance for the escape of the enemy's infantry from in front of Dinwiddie Court House."

Sheridan in his report went on to say that at 2:00 P.M. he had given orders for V Corps to get into position for its attack but when he rode to the jump-off point to observe the attack he had found V Corps "coming up very slowly; I was exceedingly anxious to attack at once, for the sun was getting low and we had to fight or go back. It was no place to entrench and it would have been shameful to have gone back with no results to compensate for the brave men who had fallen during the day. In this connection I will say that General Warren did not exert himself to get up his corps as rapidly as he might have done, and his manner gave me the impression that he wished for the sun to go down before dispositions of the attack could be completed."

Sheridan then stated in his report that he had ordered the assault to begin. "During this attack I again became dissatisfied with General Warren," Sheridan wrote in his report. "During the engagement a portion of his line gave way when not exposed to a heavy fire, and simply from want of confidence on the part of the troops, which General Warren did not exert himself to inspire. I therefore relieved him from command of the Fifth Corps, authority for this action having been sent to me before the battle, unsolicited."

It should be remembered that—as Sheridan's official report indicates—the original impetus for the removal of Warren came not from Sheridan but from Grant, who used Sheridan to do the dirty work. Generally speaking, Grant and Sheridan's accusations (or imputations as the court of inquiry eventually put it) against Warren included:

1. Warren should have moved forward with all three of his divisions against the White Oak Road, instead of just one on March 31. Because he didn't, they and one other division were driven back at the Battle of the White Oak Road until the third stopped the attack.

2. Warren failed to move his corps fast enough to suit Grant on the night of March 31–April 1, thereby allowing Pickett's command to fall back from its exposed position at Dinwiddie Court House to its previously prepared defensive position at Five Forks.
3. Warren did not get V Corps moving fast enough on April 1, acting as if, in Sheridan's words, "waiting for the sun to go down" and thus seeking to prevent a battle from being fought.
4. When one of the attacking V Corps divisions (Ayres) began to give way under heavy fire during the battle, Warren failed to inspire the confidence needed to rally his troops.

During those years after the war, Warren prepared official maps and reports of his campaigns during the American Civil War and spent 1866–1867 conducting surveys of the Mississippi River system. Throughout the 1870s he was engaged in extensive bridge-building and harbor improvement projects. These included surveying the construction of a canal at Washington, D.C., superintending improvements on the Upper Mississippi River, and surveying the Gettysburg Battlefield Park. In 1869–1870 he oversaw construction of the Rock Island Railroad Bridge over the Mississippi. Over the next 12 years he worked on river and harbor projects along the Atlantic coast and the Great Lakes, though in failing health. On March 4, 1879, he was promoted to the rank of lieutenant colonel of engineers.

In all of these years one of Warren's staunchest supporters (as he was of Fitz John Porter's quest for exoneration) was Joshua Lawrence Chamberlain, although he remained closely affiliated with Grant. When Grant ran for president in 1868, Chamberlain endorsed Grant, spoke out in favor of Grant's candidacy, campaigned on Grant's behalf, and celebrated when Grant won. But Chamberlain had both direct and indirect disagreement with Grant over his old general's complete and total endorsement of Warren's dismissal by Sheridan.[1] Eventually relations between Chamberlain and Grant became so strained that Chamberlain would express a considered amount of surprise at receiving an invitation to attend Grant's funeral.

Sheridan, supported by Grant, had humiliated Warren by summarily relieving him for not being aggressive enough during the Battle of Five Forks. Veterans of the Army of the Potomac considered what had happened to Warren to be both high-handed and absolutely unnecessary.[2] Warren had been popular with his troops and had a stellar record as one of the heroes of Gettysburg. Many V Corps veterans, on the other hand, saw Sheridan as an abrasive interloper. Chamberlain, by this time governor of Maine, threw his loyalty and wholehearted support to Warren and thus did not support Sheridan in the controversy that grew and expanded as time went on.

At the time, the controversy and clamor among V Corps veterans calling for Warren's service to be recognized and Sheridan's action to be condemned aroused considerable political comment and involved the reputations of Grant, Meade, and Sheridan, as well as those of Warren's brigade and division commanders, including Chamberlain.

There was more at stake than the simple question of whether or not Sheridan had been justified in relieving Warren. The controversy over Warren's removal had become a political football and battleground. Those who rallied to Warren's defense were seen as calling into question Sheridan's judgment on a number of issues unrelated to Five Forks, the most important of which was Sheridan's defense of Radical Republican Reconstruction policies.

However, Warren never ceased in his efforts to obtain an investigation into his removal from command of V Corps at Five Forks. But not until the close of the Grant administration and well into the administration of Rutherford B. Hayes was his request for a court of inquiry granted. Finally, in December of 1879, President Hayes ordered a court of inquiry.

The members of the court of inquiry were Bvt. Maj. Gen. C.C. Augur and Bvt. Maj. Gen. John Newton, with Lt. Col. Louis L. Langdon acting as recorder. This court of inquiry took testimony from all of the surviving participants, Union and Confederate, along with the owner of the land where the battle took place, the transcript of the proceedings consisted of over 1,700 pages. One of the witnesses called was Chamberlain, who was well known as a committed Warren loyalist, which led to an uncomfortable moment when Chamberlain began his testimony on the same day that Sheridan completed his.[3]

Chamberlain testified that Warren had never purposely circumvented or ignored an order, and he impressed the court with his firm belief that Warren had been the victim of battlefield confusion and conflicting orders — by which Chamberlain meant that orders issued by Grant, Meade, and Sheridan were mutually confusing, conflicting, and ambiguous. Chamberlain maintained that the main problem was that there were simply too many chiefs, with Sheridan, commander of the Army of the Shenandoah, serving with the Army of the Potomac; Meade, commander of the Army of the Potomac; Ord, commander of the Army of the James, all of whom were subordinate to Grant, who was in the field. This, Chamberlain believed, was the root cause of any delay there might have been in Warren reaching Sheridan on the morning of April 1, 1865.

This command confusion began when Grant decided to make his headquarters in the field with the Army of the Potomac, while at the same time retaining Meade as the titular commander. At least one staff officer noted that this mixed command structure did not produce the best results that either Grant or Mead, acting on their own, was capable of producing. Even Grant was eventually forced to admit that the arrangement, although perhaps the best compromise available, had been something of a mistake.

Most likely Grant had retained Meade for the simple reason there was no one else on hand that could have done a better job. Meade on his part had tried to make the arrangement work, but the pressure of combat, in addition to differences in character and point of view, doomed the relationship and drove a wedge between Grant and Meade. Further blurring the command situation was Grant's action in making Sheridan what amounted to be an autonomous strike force commander and Meade's co-equal.

Within the space of two hours, Chamberlain related, Warren received orders involving movements for his entire corps in four different directions. These arrived in rapid succession as follows:

1. To dig in where he was (on the White Oak Road) and be ready for a fight in the morning. This was from Grant.
2. To fall back with his entire corps from the White Oak Road to the Boydton Plank Road and send a division by this road to relieve Sheridan. This was from Grant.
3. Griffin's division was to be pushed down the Boydton Plank Road, but the rest of the corps — Ayres and Crawford's divisions — were to go across the fields to the Crump Road and attack the enemy in the rear, who was opposing Sheridan. This was from Meade.
4. It required a movement in the opposite direction from that indicated in the previous order — which was already being at least partly executed, since Ayres had already started. Meade's advice was to send these troops by the Quaker Road (a 10 mile detour) and give up the rear attack.
5. To these may be added the actual final movement, which was that Ayres went down the Boydton Plank Road while Griffin and Crawford went by the "dirt" road across country to the Crump Road as indicated in Meade's previous orders.

Another problem, according to Chamberlain, lay in there being a double and possibly mutually exclusive objective for the entire operation. One objective was Sheridan's independent operations to cut Confederate communications, the other the turning of Lee's right and the breaking up of his army by the Union infantry. Furthermore, Grant and Meade were too far away from what was happening, so that on March 31 it was impossible for them to have a complete mutual understanding at the minute when orders were to be put into effect. Nor were they familiar with the local situation — such as the condition of the ground and bridges— or with the existing state of things at important junctions owing to rapid and unforeseen changes.

Chamberlain later wrote extensively about the controversy in his memoir, *The Passing of the Armies*. The book had its origins in Chamberlain's desire to write a history of V Corps, but he was unable to begin the project before another V Corps veteran wrote a history of the corps that was published in 1896. Chamberlain, encouraged by the success of a number of magazine articles he had written, wrote his book while he was in his eighties, nearly 50 years after the events he was writing about, and it must be admitted that it holds Warren's actions in the best possible light while at the same time casting Sheridan's in the worst.

The Warren court of inquiry finally convened in January of 1880 and closed in July of 1882 to consider a verdict. The verdict was announced on November 22, 1882, and the findings of the court were as follows:

1. Regarding the imputation in Grant's report on his operations that "On the morning of the 31st [March 31, 1865] General Warren reported favorably to getting possession of the White Oak Road, and was directed to do so. To accomplish this he moved with one division instead of his whole corps, which was attacked by the enemy in superior force and driven back on the second division before it had time to form, and in turn forced back upon the third division; when the enemy was checked. A division of the Second Corps was immediately sent to his support, the enemy was driven back with heavy losses and possession of the White Oak Road gained,"

The court of inquiry's opinion stated:

> There seems to be no evidence that General Warren on the morning of March 31, or at any other time, reported favorably as to getting possession of the White Oak Road.... General Warren's report ... that he had given orders to drive the enemy's pickets off the White Oak Road and develop what force of the enemy held it, cannot be fairly construed as being able to take possession of it.
>
> With regard to that portion of the imputation contained in the statement that General Warren was ordered to take possession of the White Oak Road ... the evidence before the court shows that this order was not relayed to General Warren until the fighting that resulted from this attempted reconnaissance had begun.
>
> It is in evidence by Ayres and Crawford's testimony that General Warren had in his advance two divisions, though this evidence does not clearly show how long before the attack of the enemy upon Ayres that the division of Crawford reached him.
>
> Griffin's division was held in reserve along the branch of Gravelly Run nearest to and northwest from the Boydton Plank Road, and it may have been so held to carry out the intentions of the ... dispatch from Meade's headquarters...."
>
> [This dispatch cited by the court of inquiry reported firing along the front of II Corps and that Meade desired Warren to be ready to send his reserve forces to support II Corps.]
>
> The court is further of the opinion that, considering the Fifth Corps constituted the extreme left wing of the armies operating against Richmond and that the corps was in a delicate position and liable to be attacked at any moment, of which liability General Warren had been repeatedly warned, he should have been with his advanced divisions, guiding and directing them, and that he should have started earlier to the front than he did and not have waited at the telegraph office to keep in communications with General Meade's headquarters, unless he had direct orders that morning to do so, which, however, does not appear in the evidence.

2. Regarding the imputation in Sheridan's May 16, 1865, official report of the Battle of Five

23—The Court of Inquiry

Forks and the resulting Appomattox Campaign that "had General Warren moved according to the expectations of the lieutenant general, there would appear to have been but little chance for the escape of the enemy infantry in front of Dinwiddie Court House,"

The court's opinion stated:

> It is supposed that "the expectations of the lieutenant general" referred to in the imputation are those expressed in his dispatch to General Sheridan of 10:45 P.M. of March 31, 1865....
>
> If this supposition is correct, the court is of the opinion, considering the condition of the roads and the surrounding country over part of which the troops had to march, the darkness of the night, the distance to be traveled, and the time the order for the march reached General Warren, 10:50 P.M., that it was not practical for the Fifth Corps to have reached General Sheridan by 12 o'clock on the night of March 31....
>
> It appears from the dispatches and General Warren's testimony that neither Generals Meade, Sheridan, nor Warren expressed an intention of having this column attack before daylight.
>
> The court is further of the opinion that General Warren should have started with two divisions, as directed by General Meade's dispatch, as early after its receipt at 10:50 P.M. as he could be assured of the prospect of Ayres' departure down the Boydton Plank Road, and should have advanced down the Crump Road as far as directed in that dispatch, or as far as practicable or necessary to fulfill Meade's intention; whereas the evidence shows that he did not start until between five and six o'clock in the morning of the 1st of April and did not reach J. Boisseau's [Sheridan's position] with the head of the column until seven o'clock in the morning.
>
> The dispatches show that Generals Meade and Warren anticipated a withdrawal during the night of the enemy's forces fronting General Sheridan, which was rendered highly probable by the known position in their rear of a portion of the Fifth Corps (Bartlett's brigade) at G. Boisseau's, and the event justifies the anticipation.

3. Regarding the imputation in Sheridan's May 16, 1865, official report that "General Warren did not exert himself to get his corps up as rapidly as he might have done, and his manner gave the impression that he wished the sun to go down before dispositions for the attack could be completed,"

The court stated as follows:

> The court was of the opinion that there was no unnecessary delay in this march of the Fifth Corps, and that General Warren took the usual methods of a corps commander to prevent delay.
>
> The question of General Warren's manner appears to be too intangible and the evidence on it too contradictory for the court to decide, separate from the context, that he appeared to wish "for the sun to go down before dispositions for the attack could be completed;" but his actions, as shown by the evidence, do not appear to have corresponded with such a wish, if he ever entertained it.

4. Regarding the final imputation in Sheridan's report of May 16, 1865, that "During this attack I again became dissatisfied with General Warren. During the engagement portions of his line gave way when not exposed to a heavy fire, and simply from want of confidence on the part of his troops, which General Warren did not exert himself to inspire,"

The court stated as follows:

> General Warren's attention seems to have been drawn, almost immediately after Ayres received the flank fire from the "return" and his consequent change of front, to the probability of Crawford with Griffin diverging too much from and being separated from Ayres, and by continuous exertions of himself and staff substantially remedied matters; and the court thinks that this was for him the essential point to be attended to, which also exacted his whole efforts to accomplish.

General William T. Sherman, as general-in-chief of the army, had the final word, and his review of the findings and recommendations of the court of inquiry and his own opinion are as follows:

> Headquarters of the Army,
> Washington, D.C., July 15, 1882

The opinion of the court of inquiry in various branches of the case of Gouverneur K. Warren, lieutenant colonel of engineers, brevet major general, United States Army, and the elaborate review of the same by Judge Advocate General Swaim, having been submitted to me for consideration, I have to state that my official action is in no sense necessary to give strengths to the conclusions reached or effect to whatever Executive action is eventually called for.

The court of inquiry was ordered by President Hayes, on the urgent and repeated request of General Warren, and although General Warren could not have been tried by a general court-martial because of the prohibition as to time in the 103rd Article of War, yet the power and right of the President of the United States to order an inquiry into "the nature of any transactions of, or accusations or imputations against, any officer" is clearly given by the 115th Article of War, without limitations as to time and circumstance, and it is for the President of the United States alone to make such application of the results of this inquiry as his judgment may approve. To aid him in this I venture to condense a few points in this most elaborate record.

In the month of March, 1865, Abraham Lincoln was President of the United States, and constitutional Commander-in-Chief of the Army and Navy. The United States were engaged in a war involving the existence of the government, and had vast armies in the field, one of which — the Army of the Potomac — under the immediate command of Maj. Gen. Meade, was operating south of the James River, near Petersburg, against the enemy's capital, and against his chief army, commanded by General Lee.

The Army of the Potomac was organized into corps, divisions, and brigades. The corps commanders were always appointed by the President, whilst the division and brigade commanders were usually designated by the commanding general. On the 31st of March 1865, General G.K. Warren commanded the Fifth Corps, comprised of three divisions — Griffin, Ayres, and Crawford — on the extreme left of the Army of the Potomac.

At that date there were other armies operating against that same enemy, viz, the Army of the James and a corps of cavalry under General Sheridan. Lt. Gen. Grant commanded all of the Armies of the United States, but was personally present with the Army of the Potomac. He possessed the absolute confidence of the President, and was vested with every power necessary to success. About that date he had sent General Sheridan to feel for and attack the extreme right flank of the enemy's line at or near Five Forks, he General Sheridan, on March 30, encountered a force too large to overcome with cavalry alone and called for reinforcement. This was promptly ordered by Lt. Gen. Grant through General Meade, who ordered the nearest corps — Fifth, General Warren — which corps was ordered to report to General Sheridan at or near Dinwiddie by daylight of April 1, and be subject to his orders. The court of inquiry does not state that the President had deputed to General Grant his undoubted authority to appoint and remove corps commanders, but this is inferred and unquestioned. Yet it is clearly found that General Grant had deputed to General Sheridan the right to remove General Warren and give the command of the Fifth Corps, as he saw fit, to General Griffin, of the division commanders.

The court found that the Fifth Corps did not reach General Sheridan as early on the 1st of April, as he had reason to expect, or as it might have done.

On that 1st day of April, under the immediate command of General Sheridan, was fought the Battle of Five Forks — one of infinite importance. The history of it is given in great detail in the proceedings of this court, and the findings are that the tactical handling of the Fifth Corps by General Warren was unskillful, and that though the general result was a success and victory, yet the victory resulted in spite of the misdirection of two of the three divisions of the Fifth Corps, for which the corps commander was held responsible.

General Sheridan, then using the authority, vested in him, relieved General Warren of his command, and devolved it on the next in rank, General Griffin. He had full authority for doing so; was sustained at the time by his immediate superior, Lt. Gen. Grant, and his action was never questioned by the then President Lincoln, or his immediate successor, Johnson. There the matter ought to have ended.

But General Warren appealed to the successive Presidents for a court of inquiry, but did not succeed until 1881 [actually 1879], when by President Hayes he was granted the opportunity for a full hearing before an impartial court of inquiry, whose proceedings contain a complete history of these important events, and whose findings confirm substantially what was officially reported on the dates of occurrences.

It would be an unsafe and dangerous rule to hold the commander of an army in battle to a technical adherence to any rule of conduct for managing his command. He is responsible for **results** (emphasis added), and holds the lives and reputations of every officer and soldier under his orders as subordinate to the general end—victory. The most important events are usually compressed into an hour, a minute, and he cannot stop to analyze his reasons. He must act on the impulse, the conviction, of the instant, and should be sustained in his conclusions, if not manifestly unjust. The power to command men and to give vehement impulse to their joint action is something which cannot be defined by words, but it is plain and manifest in battles, and whoever commands an army in chief must choose his subordinates by reason of qualities which alone can be tested in actual conflict.

No one has questioned the patriotism, integrity, and great intelligence of General Warren. These are attested by a long record of most excellent service, but in the clash of arms at and near Five Forks, March 31 and April 1, 1865, his personal activity fell short of the standard fixed by General Sheridan, on whom alone rested the great responsibility for that and succeeding days.

My conclusion is that General Sheridan was perfectly justified in his action in this case, and he must be fully and entirely sustained if the United States expects great victories by her armies in the future.

All the other branches settled by this court belong to the domain of history rather than military inquiry.

W.T. Sherman
General

Chamberlain had his own opinion about the court's findings and Sherman's review of the case. These included:

1. There was an unfavorable judgment of Warren's manner of handling a corps; an uncomfortable sense of certain intellectual peculiarities of his; a dislike of his self-centered manner and habit generally; and his rather injudicious way of expressing his opinion on tender topics.
2. There was a variety of antagonisms toward Warren stored up in Sheridan's mind, and the tension of a heated moment brought the catastrophe.
3. Chamberlain maintained that while there was no doubt that Sheridan had a right to remove Warren, but was it right? The simple transfer of a corps commander is not a disgrace, nor necessarily an injury, Chamberlain noted, and Warren had no vested right to command V Corps. Chamberlain was convinced that it was the time, place, and manner of this removal, the implications involved in it, and the vague reasons given for it, which made the grievance for Warren. For such reasons as given for this affected Warren's honor, and therefore he persistently sought a court of inquiry, Chamberlain noted.
4. Thus, it was Chamberlain's opinion that such a court provided the opportunity for the facts, motives, and feelings affecting the case to be brought out and placed in the public record. The court found little to censure in the conduct of Warren as commander of V Corps at Five Forks. The court sustained Sheridan in his right, but Warren felt that the revelation of the facts (during the court of inquiry) was of the nature of a vindication, Chamberlain maintained.

Despite Sherman's review, Chamberlain continued to maintain that essentially the court exonerated Warren of all the major accusations made against him related to the Battle of Five Forks. The court ruled that while he might have been slow in arriving at Five Forks, his efforts had greatly contributed to the crushing victory. In addition, there were hints at criticism concerning the manner of Warren's removal.

However, Warren would never know that his name had finally been cleared. He died on August 8, 1882, of "acute liver failure" related to diabetes, believing to the last that he had been

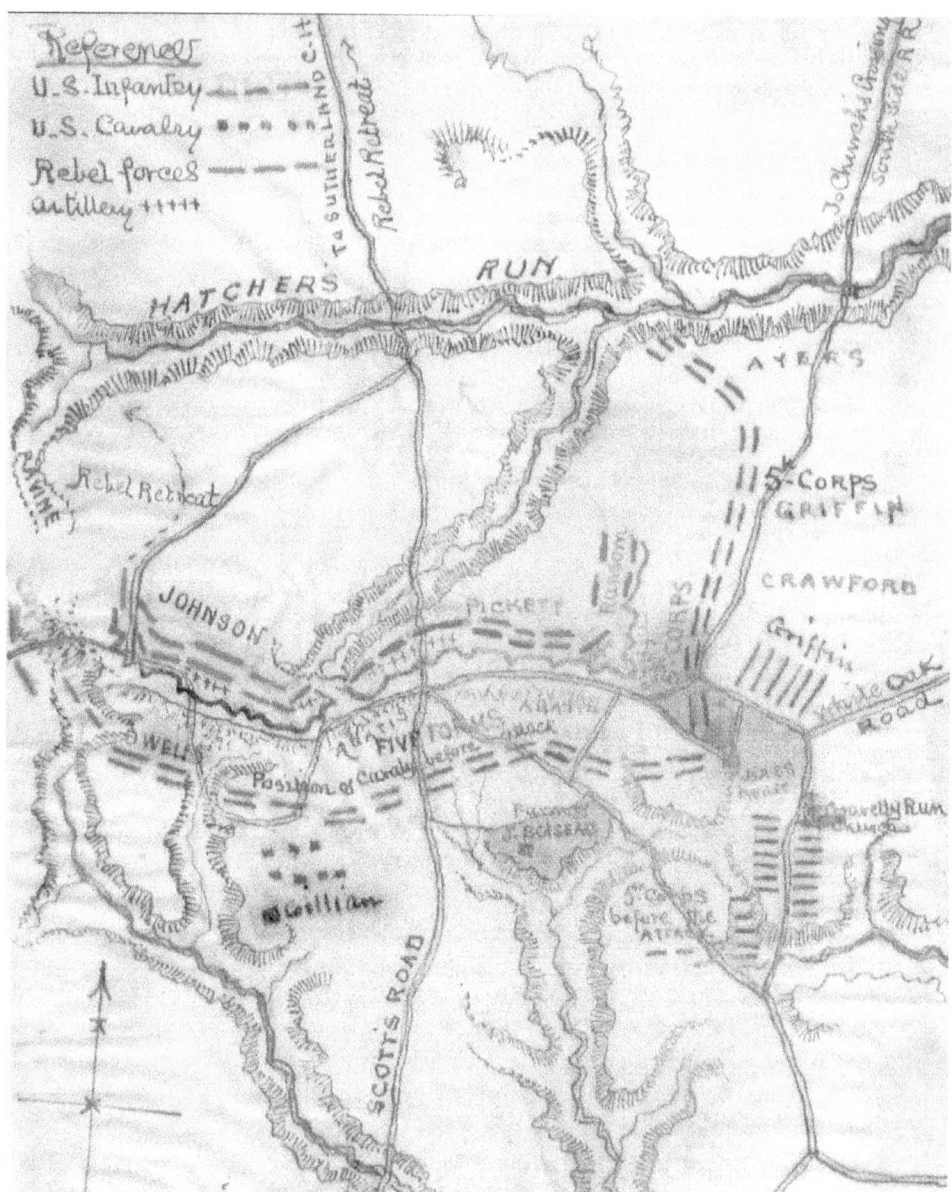

The Battle of Five Forks, Virginia, fought March 31 through April 1, 1865, was the Confederacy's Waterloo, resulting in the fall of Petersburg, the evacuation of Richmond, and eventually in the final collapse and surrender of the Army of Northern Virginia on April 9, 1865, at Appomattox Courthouse. This map does include an error in that the units of Ayres and Crawford's divisions are mislabeled, as it depicts the situation as it was planned and not as it actually happened (Library of Congress).

wronged and humiliated by the army. He also died believing that his life held no honor or significance and that his military accomplishments in effect counted for nothing.

He, therefore, left instructions that he was not to be buried in his uniform — not in his uniform as a brevet major general or in his uniform as a lieutenant colonel of engineers — and in addition that there were to be no patriotic emblems at the funeral. Thus, bitterly, died the victim of what may have been one of the greatest injustices of the American Civil War.

Part IV

Ranald Slidell Mackenzie

The Man Who Proved the Rule

Brigadier General of Volunteers Ranald Slidell Mackenzie, who was the Man Who Proved The Rule. He most clearly demonstrated what Sheridan was looking for in a subordinate commander, yet in the end he was probably the most tragic figure of all (Library of Congress).

24

The Most Promising Young Officer in the Army

At one time he was among the most celebrated soldiers of the United States Army; Ulysses S. Grant himself called him the most promising young officer in the army. During the Indian Wars, which followed the American Civil War, he became Philip H. Sheridan's most reliable troubleshooter, yet today he is almost entirely unknown.

Born on July 27, 1840, he died on January 14, 1889, at the age of 48 and was buried at West Point, practically forgotten. He had two younger brothers, Alexander Slidell Mackenzie, Jr., and Morris Robinson Slidell Mackenzie, and a younger sister, Harriet Slidell Mackenzie. His brothers both joined the navy. Alexander was killed in 1867 when he led a landing party on Formosa to rescue some missionaries, and Morris would eventually attain the rank of rear admiral. Their brother's name was Ranald Slidell Mackenzie; and if one should wish to know the man — most especially in this case — one should know the father. Sometimes the measure of a man can be found in his family, in his parents. In the case of Ranald Slidell Mackenzie it is necessary to first take a look at his father, Alexander Slidell Mackenzie, Sr.

Mackenzie Sr. was a naval officer, the brother of a U.S. Senator, John Slidell, who, as one of two Confederate commissioners to Britain and France, was involved in the "*Trent* Affair." As Alexander Slidell he entered the U.S. Navy as a midshipman in 1815, at about the age of 12. He assumed the surname of Mackenzie, after a maternal uncle, in 1837. He was a contemporary of Henry Wadsworth Longfellow, he was a personal friend of Washington Irving, and he was the author of a number of books, biographies of American naval heroes, including *Life of John Paul Jones, Life of Commodore O.H. Perry,* and *Life of Commodore Stephen Decatur.*

The elder Mackenzie was also something of a visionary. He sought to completely change and reform the way recruits were trained to man the navy's ships and young men were educated to become officers in the U.S. Navy. Allied with Matthew C. Perry, the younger brother of Oliver Hazard Perry, who also happened to be his brother-in-law and a senior captain who would command the main U.S. naval squadron during the Mexican War, their efforts — in a completely unintended way — helped lead to the creation of the U.S. Naval Academy at Annapolis, Maryland.

Originally, recruitment and training of seamen and officers for the U.S. Navy was a haphazard affair. The enlisted crews of naval warships would be recruited for each voyage, not for a set term of years, and they were certainly not subjected to any form of standardized training. Usually there was no training at all before they stepped aboard their first ship, and what training they got was strictly "on the job." It really wasn't much better for officers.

The boys — and they were boys (the youngest on record was David G. Farragut, who entered the navy as a midshipman at the tender age of 10 and retired with the rank of vice admiral some 60 or so years later) — were given a warrant from the secretary of the navy to be midshipmen, or apprentice officers. They were actually placed within the line of command and then (like the seamen) they were taught to be naval officers by being, in effect, naval officers.

How much real education each midshipman actually received depended on the captain and the officers of the ships to which he was assigned. Mostly they did manage to learn mathematics and navigation. After a time they were given an examination and those who passed became passed midshipmen to be placed upon the lieutenant's list when the next vacancy occurred. There was no limit to how many times a midshipman could take the test and if they failed to pass this examination they stayed as midshipmen until they finally did pass or left the navy.

The more progressive naval officers, like Perry and Mackenzie, realized that something better was needed. One stopgap was the creation of special naval prep schools ashore that prepared midshipmen for their examination. Perry and Mackenzie, however, wanted to try an entirely different approach.

They wanted, in effect, to have a floating naval prep school, which would not be just for student officers. They saw it as a training ground for seamen, too. The bulk of the crew would be enlisted, not for a single voyage but for a term of years. Their first voyage would be aboard the school ship as a training voyage under the direction of handpicked, experienced seamen. When they returned from that voyage they would be transferred to other naval ships, while a new crop of recruits joined the school ship for its next voyage. For the midshipmen the officers would be specially selected with an eye for the best teachers and the voyage would be used to get them ready for their lieutenant's examination.

The plan was to train young recruits and midshipmen in the way of the navy while limiting their exposure (at their most impressionable age and level of experience) to what were considered to be the crude lower classes that heretofore had comprised the bulk of the enlisted personnel that actually, outside of the officers, formed the crews of the navy's warships.

In 1842, Perry and Mackenzie were given a chance to try out their theories. They had built, from the keel up, their school ship, the U.S.S. *Somers*. But, they had made a fatal mistake. They built their ship much too small. The *Somers* was a small sailing warship referred to as either a gun brig or a brig of war. They would have done much better to have purchased or hired a clipper ship or converted one of the navy's sailing frigates like the U.S.S. *Constitution*.

Mackenzie, who in his temperament was a fiery man and an extremely strict disciplinarian, was the obvious choice to be given command of the new school ship. Her first voyage, a trip to Africa and back, was begun on September 13, 1842. The ship was dreadfully overcrowded and conditions were far from ideal.

On the trip back to the United States, Mackenzie and his officers uncovered what they believed to be a plot to seize the ship, murder Mackenzie and his officers, and turn pirate. It is not now known whether or not there was an actual plot or if the whole thing was due to misinterpreted youthful exuberance. Mackenzie decided to take immediate and direct action, arresting all of the plotters he could identify.

Because the *Somers* had been built too small there was no brig, no place to put the prisoners, so they were chained on her open deck, completely exposed to the elements. Due to growing discontentment among the crew because of this treatment of the supposed mutineers, Mackenzie and his officers held a summary court-martial in which the three supposed ringleaders were tried for the crime of mutiny and found guilty. They were thereupon immediately hanged from the ship's yardarm. Thus ended the first, and only, recorded case of mutiny aboard a United States warship.

When the *Somers* returned to New York, that was when the fecal matter hit the rotary impeller, so to speak, for one of the three ringleaders that Mackenzie hanged happened to be one Philip Spencer, the son of President John Tyler's secretary of war. Spencer had been something of a wild young man whose antics greatly concerned his father, John C. Spencer, who had been convinced by Thomas Gilmer, Tyler's secretary of the navy, that a voyage on the *Somers* as a midshipman under Mackenzie's command would make a man out of his son.

The event caused a furor, to say the very least. It also caused a feud between two of Tyler's cabinet members—Spencer and Gilmer—that only ended when Gilmer was killed when a cannon aboard the U.S.S. *Princeton* (the navy's first screw propeller driven warship) burst during the firing of a salute on a demonstration cruise up and down the Potomac River. (President Tyler, who had gone below to be with his fiancé, who had become ill, was not harmed, although her father was among those killed in the accident. John Ericcson, the inventor of the screw propeller, who designed the ship, was made the scapegoat for the disaster, while Cmdr. Robert F. Stockton, who had designed and built the defective cannon, escaped any blame.)

In an effort to put the "*Sommers* Affair" to rest, a hasty court of inquiry was called that decided no action needed to be taken. But the controversy refused to die. Finally, Mackenzie requested that there be a court-martial to clear his name and to forestall possible criminal and civil action in civilian courts. The not guilty verdict that Mackenzie received turned out to be a negative judgment and not the positive affirmation of his actions that Mackenzie sought. Too many people thought that the trial had been a navy whitewash. Officially, as far as the navy was concerned, Mackenzie had been acquitted and exonerated and that was that.

Unofficially, however, it was a different story. Due to the notoriety and the scandal Mackenzie was placed on half-pay and was left awaiting orders, since the navy had no further use for his services, not then, not ever. His career as a United States naval officer was over and the elder Mackenzie more or less retired and became something of a gentleman farmer in Morristown, New Jersey. But he was convinced to the end of his days that he had been right and that the actions that he had taken aboard the *Somers* had been correct in every detail. (The other accused mutineers aboard the *Somers*, who had not been hanged by Mackenzie, were very quietly released from custody and discharged by the navy and faced no further inquiry into their conduct.)

Not long afterwards the various naval prep schools that had been unofficially established were brought together in a former and inactive coastal fortification to become the U.S. Naval Academy at Annapolis, Maryland, under the direction of Franklin Buchanan, who during the American Civil War would become the captain of the Confederate ironclad C.S.S. *Virginia* and when he was promoted to admiral would be the ranking officer in the Confederate States Navy.

The *Somers* would be lost in a hurricane off the coast of Mexico during the Mexican war. Her captain at the time was Raphael Semmes, who also became a Confederate naval officer. He captained the Confederate raider cruisers *Sumter* and *Alabama* and was promoted to the rank of rear admiral for his cruises aboard those two ships. Later he commanded the Confederate James River Defense Fleet and received a commission from Confederate President Jefferson Davis as a brigadier general of artillery when, during the final evacuation of Richmond, his ships were scuttled and his sailors and marines thus became soldiers. Buchanan and Semmes were the only two men to achieve the rank of admiral in the Confederate States Navy.

Alexander Slidell Mackenzie, Sr., died in September 1848 when he went for a horseback ride; when the horse came back alone a search was immediately initiated. Ranald was the one who found his father's body. Mackenzie Sr. had suffered a massive heart attack and died instantly.

Although he was completely exonerated at the naval court-martial the "*Somers* Affair" colored the remainder of the elder Mackenzie's life, and beyond. Since then the U.S. Navy has had several ships named Mackenzie, including at least one destroyer named *Alexander Mackenzie*. When asked, officials have maintained that these ships were all named in honor of Alexander Slidell Mackenzie, Jr., for his exploits during the American Civil War and for his death on Formosa, which says quite a bit about the navy's unofficial opinion concerning the life and career of Alexander Slidell Mackenzie, Sr.

Young Ranald apparently venerated his father's memory and became determined to emulate him and, if at all possible, to vindicate his father's memory. His chance to do both would come during the American Civil War. As the oldest of four children, and the eldest son, this reaction to his father's disgrace and death is not unusual, according to many mental health professionals.

His first years, until his father's retirement from the navy, were spent in Terrytown, New York, on the Hudson River, then the family moved to the farm at Morristown. He originally entered Williams College in 1859, and at the start of his junior year he transferred to the U.S. Military Academy at West Point.

Originally Mackenzie would have graduated from West Point in 1863, since the military academy had changed over from a four-year to a five-year curriculum during the 1850s. But the American Civil War broke out and, due to the emergency, it was decided to return to a four-year curriculum. That meant that in 1861 there were two graduating classes, the class that had been scheduled to graduate that year and the class that had been scheduled to graduate in 1862.

It was at West Point that Mackenzie first met a man who would have a great influence upon his life; that man was then 1st Lt. Gouverneur K. Warren, who at the time was serving as an instructor in mathematics. One cannot consider Warren's heroics at Gettysburg or his relief at the Battle of Five Forks without stumbling over Mackenzie; nor can one consider Mackenzie's American Civil War career without repeatedly stumbling over Warren. It's as if these two men, student and teacher, mentor and protégé, were joined at the hip.

On June 17, 1862, Mackenzie graduated from West Point first in his class and was immediately commissioned a second lieutenant in the U.S. Army Corps of Topographical Engineers. He was 5-feet-9, fine boned, of slight build, and clean shaven; except for a mustache he added later, he remained that way in an army known for the heavily bearded faces of its officers.

After graduation from West Point, class ranking determined a cadet's assignment to the various branches of the army, although they were allowed to state their preferences. (Although cadets could state their preferences this had very little influence upon their eventual branch of service postings.) Those with the highest class rankings were generally assigned to the topographical engineers and, in descending order, to the engineers, artillery, infantry, dragoons and mounted rifles, and at the very bottom by the 1860s the cavalry.

Mackenzie received his baptism of fire at the Second Battle of Manassas/Bull Run, where he was assigned as an assistant engineer to IX Corps and served on the staff of Brig. Gen. Jesse L. Reno. It was during the battle that Mackenzie received the first of six wounds during the American Civil War. Later, during the Indian Wars, he would be wounded for a seventh time. Until he left the engineers to take command of his own regiment two years later, Mackenzie would alternate between staff duty and serving with the Engineer Battalion, Army of the Potomac.

Mackenzie recovered from his wound in time to direct bridging operations during the Maryland Campaign, which led to the Battle of Antietam/Sharpsburg. During the Battle of Fredericksburg he served as Edwin V. Sumner's engineer officer, being promoted to first lieutenant on March 3, 1863. But, in February, Gouverneur K. Warren reentered his life and his career. Maj. Gen. Joseph Hooker was in command of the Army of the Potomac and he had named Warren to be his chief topographical engineer and later, when the Corps of Topographical Engineers merged with the Corps of Engineers, Warren became chief engineer of the Army of the Potomac. He immediately selected his former student, Mackenzie, to be his top aide. While serving as Warren's aide Mackenzie would earn brevets for the Battle of Chancellorsville and the Battle of Gettysburg.

It was at Gettysburg on July 2, 1863, that Mackenzie accompanied Warren when he went to assess the situation on the Union left flank at Little Round Top for General George G. Meade, who had replaced Hooker as commander of the Army of the Potomac just a few days previously.

24—The Most Promising Young Officer in the Army

When Warren discovered that that there were no Union troops at Little Round Top, which was one of the keys to the Union position at Gettysburg, and that Confederate troops were approaching, Warren immediately sent Mackenzie with a desperate dispatch to Meade describing the situation as he had found it and urgently requesting that troops be sent immediately to Little Round Top.

When Longstreet's massive assault on Sickles' III Corps and the left flank of the Army of the Potomac began, V Corps under General George Sykes, which was just arriving on the field, had been ordered to support III Corps. When Mackenzie reached General Meade with General Warren's message, Meade immediately recognized its importance. He dispatched Mackenzie to find Sykes and gave him orders directing Sykes to detach one of his brigades and send it immediately to Little Round Top. When Mackenzie presented Meade's order to Sykes, Mackenzie was directed to locate General James Barnes, commander of the leading V Corps division, and tell him that he was to have his leading brigade drop whatever it was doing and go immediately to Little Round Top. However, Mackenzie had trouble finding General Barnes.

Col. Strong Vincent was on horseback at the head of his brigade, stationed on the lower reaches of Cemetery Ridge, when Mackenzie came galloping by in search of Barnes, who was Vincent's divisional commander. When Mackenzie stopped and breathlessly inquired about the whereabouts of Barns, Vincent guessed instantly that the staff aide was carrying orders.

"What are your orders?" Vincent had demanded. "Give me your orders!"

"General Sykes told me to direct General Barnes to send one of his brigades to occupy that hill yonder," Mackenzie replied, pointing to the rocky elevation of Little Round Top. Vincent told Mackenzie to forget about finding Barnes.

"I will take the responsibility of taking my brigade there," Vincent said, and he did so.

In the fighting for control of Little Round Top, Vincent was mortally wounded, but Little Round Top was saved and Mackenzie won his brevet for Gettysburg. He also received a mild wound there while assisting Warren, Mackenzie's second wound of the war. On November 6, 1863, Mackenzie was promoted to captain, U.S. Engineers, and when Grant came East the following spring Mackenzie served with the Engineer Battalion, Army of the Potomac, during the Overland Campaign and in the early operations against Petersburg, when he was wounded once again.

And then Mackenzie received his big chance.

25

The Perpetual Punisher

It just so happened that the 2nd Connecticut Heavy Artillery Regiment was in need of a new colonel. The regiment, part of VI Corps, had lost its colonel when Elisha S. Kellogg was killed during the Battle of Cold Harbor. Although a volunteer, not a regular officer, Kellogg had been both a strict disciplinarian and popular with his men, and the regiment's lieutenant colonel had refused the promotion to colonel and command of the regiment.

This is where Warren stepped back once again into Mackenzie's life. Since the Battle of Gettysburg, Warren had been placed in temporary command of II Corps in place of the wounded Winfield Scott Hancock. Warren commanded II Corps during the abortive Bristoe Station and Mine Run operations. In March 1864, during Meade's reorganization of the Army of the Potomac, he had been named commander of V Corps, succeeding Sykes, since Hancock had returned to his II Cops command.

Warren suggested and supported his former aide to fill the vacant colonelcy of the 2nd Connecticut Heavy Artillery Regiment. After being appointed to fill the vacancy by the governor of Connecticut, Mackenzie assumed command of the regiment on June 10, 1864, just a month prior to his 24th birthday. Since his graduation from West Point two years previously, Mackenzie had fought in eight major battles and now he was to be tested in his first regimental command.

When he took command of the 2nd Connecticut Heavy Artillery Regiment, Mackenzie found his regiment to be dispirited and disorganized. The heavy losses at Cold Harbor and the death of its stern but loved colonel had left it barely effective as a combat unit. Mackenzie realized that it was up to him to fix the problems. He acted swiftly to restore discipline within the regiment.

The result was that the men in the regiment soon hated their new commanding officer. First Lt. Theodore Vaill, who eventually wrote the regimental history of the 2nd Connecticut Heavy Artillery Regiment, wrote that Mackenzie was a cruel martinet. (Perhaps seeking to emulate and vindicate his father, Mackenzie had chosen to adopt his father's methods.) Vaill wrote that Mackenzie's predecessor (Kellogg) "had chastised us with whips, but Mackenzie dealt in scorpions."

Mackenzie apparently made the decision to push his men to the limit, possibly as a distraction from their memories of Cold Harbor. Possibly he also wanted to distract them from the fact that he was only 23 years old. In addition, he may have set himself up as an object of his men's hatred in order to unify his command. Mackenzie developed a public persona of himself as a soldier who was more of a machine than a human being. There was no hint of this in his personality before he took command of the regiment, and behind the scenes he could show a different aspect of his personality than he showed to the men of his regiment, being relaxed, jovial, and even at times demonstrating that he actually was a human being, not an impersonal military machine.

In effect, Mackenzie may have been playing what became for him a lifelong role that was possibly in conflict with his true personality, which he apparently felt he could only let out in private or during the heat of battle. (His men would be astonished at the transformation that would occur upon their first battlefield together.) It might have been for this reason that Mackenzie swore off personal relationships such as marriage—because he believed that such involvements would interfere with and be at the detriment of his military career. (This is not unusual, for the rule of thumb in professional armies of the time was that lieutenants can't marry, captains may marry, majors should marry, and colonels must marry.) Thus it is not hard to come to the conclusion that he was more or less by choice a lonely and isolated man. Then, too, the conflict between the persona that he showed to the world and his own true self in the years to come may have had tragic personal consequences.

When he took command of the regiment, and thereafter, Mackenzie made no attempt whatsoever to be popular with the men in the ranks. Popularity, he believed, was no prerequisite for good leadership; nor did he believe that a leader's popularity led to a regiment becoming a good combat unit. "No enlisted man ever saw him laugh or smile, except in a fight," according to Vaill. It was enough that Mackenzie was respected (if not feared outright) and was obeyed by his men without question. Suddenly faced with a very young, aloof, strict and even harsh disciplinarian who had succeeded the stern but popular Kellogg, the men of the 2nd Connecticut Heavy Artillery Regiment did not react well. There were soon rumors that some soldiers in the regiment intended to shoot the "Perpetual Punisher," as they called Mackenzie, at the first opportunity.

On June 22, 1864, while his regiment was in the siege lines at Petersburg, Mackenzie was wounded once again, losing two fingers on his right hand, which would eventually lead to his being known among the Indians as "Bad Hand" or "Broken Hand" after the American Civil War. Mackenzie, not really giving himself much time to heal from this latest wound, insisted upon returning to his regiment only two weeks later, on July 10, 1864.

Mackenzie and his regiment went with VI Corps to the Shenandoah Valley when Philip H. Sheridan assumed command of the Middle Military Division on August 7, 1864, and spent the next month marching up and down the Shenandoah Valley. Since Mackenzie had taken command of the 2nd Connecticut Heavy Artillery Regiment it had not been in any major combat. Therefore the men had not been able to judge their commander under fire and the intention of some of his soldiers to murder him at the first opportunity had not been diminished. Both circumstances would come to a head on September 19, 1864, along the banks of Opequon Creek at the Third Battle of Winchester/Opequon Creek. It was here that Mackenzie would first come to the attention of Sheridan.

With the 1864 elections fast approaching, Lincoln desperately needed a victory in the east to stay in office. Farragut had won at Mobile Bay the previous month and Sherman had just taken Atlanta. But it was Sheridan who would give Lincoln what he most desperately needed, at Winchester, Fisher's Hill, and most especially and spectacularly at Cedar Creek.

An electoral defeat of Lincoln was the Southern Confederacy's final strategic hope. The Democratic Party had nominated George B. McClellan and had adopted a peace plank in its platform for the election. Lincoln himself believed that he would lose on November 8 (and that McClellan, who had rejected the peace plank, no matter what his personal preferences, would be forced by circumstances to acquiesce to negotiations that Lincoln believed could only lead to the permanent sundering of the Union), therefore he had been only partially boosted by the victories at Atlanta and Mobile Bay. What was vitally needed was a victory in the Eastern Theatre of Operations, particularly since Jubal Early had managed to offset the effects of those two victories when he had conducted the third invasion of the North, getting as far as Washington, D.C., and forcing Grant to divert troops from the Siege of Petersburg to save the capital.

During August, Sheridan had been constricted by fears of a possible defeat, and that had caused Early to underestimate Sheridan and become overconfident. Sheridan had marched from Harper's Ferry to Front Royal and had then retired to Halltown, maneuvering with dexterity, guarding himself where necessary to make a stand, parrying Early's threatened second raid upon Washington and Pennsylvania. And when Early was weakened by the return of Joseph Kershaw's division of James Longstreet's I Corps back to Lee's Army of Northern Virginia at the Siege of Petersburg, Sheridan promptly resumed the offensive.

Early had been using Winchester as his base since August 17, 1864. From there he could threaten both the vital Baltimore & Ohio Railroad and the Chesapeake & Ohio Canal, while at the same time posing a constant threat to Pennsylvania and Maryland. Then Early made the blunder of dispersing his Valley District Army, giving Sheridan a chance to destroy it piecemeal and bringing on the Third Battle of Winchester/Opequon Creek.

Under Sheridan's plan, Wesley Merritt and his First Cavalry Division was to force a crossing of Opequon Creek on the Charlestown Road and push on to hook up with William W. Averell's 2nd Cavalry Division, Department of West Virginia, coming south on the Martinsburg Pike where it joined the Charlestown Road at Stephenson's Depot. The two cavalry divisions under the direct command of Alfred T.A. Torbert, who was Sheridan's chief of cavalry, were to sweep down the Martinsburg Pike to hit Early's left flank. Although it took a little time, this part of the plan scored a bull's-eye.

At the same time, James H. Wilson's Third Cavalry Division was to clear the crossing of Opequon Creek at the Berryville Pike for the infantry. Horatio G. Wright's VI Corps, including Mackenzie's 2nd Connecticut Heavy Artillery Regiment, was to cross first, taking a position south of the Berryville Pike, and was to be followed by XIX Corps, to form north of the pike and outflank one of Early's separated divisions commanded by Stephen Dodson Ramseur. The Army of West Virginia/VIII Corps under George C. Crook was to be held temporarily in reserve east of the Opequon. The plan called for these troops to eventually cross the creek and take the Senseney Road to the Valley Pike, south of Winchester, cutting off Early's only escape route. This part of the plan would completely misfire and it would be up to Mackenzie and his regiment to save the day at a crucial moment.[1]

Wilson got the ball rolling just before daybreak on September 19, when he attacked and dispersed Confederate pickets and splashed across Opequon Creek heading into a long narrow gorge, or ravine, blocked at the extreme western end with small earthworks. One of his two brigades charged through the gorge and captured the earthworks. Then the leading elements of Wright's VI Corps filed through the gorge and deployed south of the Berryville Pike. Right on schedule VI Corps formed into its line of battle and right there was when things began to go wrong.

When XIX Corps tried to move through the gorge, its way was blocked by the supply, baggage and ammunition wagons of VI Corps. Fearing this very event Sheridan had ordered that the wagons were not to move into the gorge until XIX Corps had passed, but his order was disregarded. The key to Sheridan's entire battle plan had lain with VI Corps and XIX Corps being able to hit Ramseur and his division quickly and overwhelm him before he could be reinforced.

Early — as soon as he found out that Sheridan had crossed Opequon Creek — sent John Gordon's division to reinforce Ramseur. Early then rode out to see the situation for himself. Realizing instantly that a major offensive was under way he immediately ordered John Breckinridge and Robert Rodes to bring up their two infantry divisions to the scene of the action at once. (Rodes' Division would be immediately placed in the line while Breckinridge's Division would become Early's primary reserve.) The traffic jam within the gorge had given Early the time he needed to keep his army from being destroyed piecemeal.

Ramseur, under pressure from VI Corps, withdrew slowly and skillfully until about 10:00 A.M., when Gordon and Rodes arrived. The leading elements of XIX Corps were just leaving the gorge and starting to curl around Ramseur's left. Gordon, who arrived first, was placed on the extreme left to check this flanking movement. When Rodes arrived he was placed between Gordon and Ramseur and ordered to attack.

Rodes' attack began at 11:00 A.M., just as his troops were coming into line and were therefore off balance. In the meantime, a dangerous gap had opened between VI Corps and XIX Corps, just north of the pike. Rodes and Gordon saw the opportunity and attacked with vigor (even though Rodes was killed at the very beginning of the assault). Meanwhile, Ramseur succeeded in halting the VI Corps attack on the right. The VI Corps and XIX Corps divisions located at the junction of the two corps where the gap had developed were driven back in confusion, widening the gap and pushing in Sheridan's center.

Brig. Gen. David Russell's First Division, VI Corps, rushed forward from their reserve position, and, although Russell was killed, Brig. Gen. Emory Upton, commanding Russell's Second Brigade, marched his men towards the gap. Then, finding he was too late to plug it, he placed half his men, Mackenzie's 2nd Connecticut Heavy Artillery Regiment, at an angle to the Confederate line of advance, whereupon, like the veterans they were, they fixed bayonets and waited.

When the Confederate troops were within 200 yards and Upton ordered the charge, Mackenzie became transformed — from the stern, distant, almost inhuman military machine the 2nd Connecticut Heavy Artillery Regiment thought it knew and hated but had never before seen in combat — into the very ideal of an American Civil War combat commander. Vaill described Mackenzie as grinning broadly and waving his hat joyfully as he galloped through "a perfect hailstorm of Rebel lead and iron, with as much impunity as though he had been a ghost. The men hated him with the hate of hell, but they could not draw a bead on a man as brave as that."

During the fight, Mackenzie rode his horse along his regiment's front, his kepi held aloft on the point of his upraised sword so that every man could instantly know where he was, and braved a hail of Confederate fire, commanding his soldiers to hold fast, not just by his shouted orders but also by his own personal and undaunted courage and example, along with his sheer joy of combat.

And hold fast they did, in sheer awe, for it was obvious that Mackenzie should have been killed in that hail of Confederate fire. He was wounded and his horse was literally cut in two by an artillery shell. Sheridan himself ordered Mackenzie to go to the rear to receive medical attention, but he refused to do so and stayed with his men until the battle was over. Then, and only then, did he go to the rear to be treated for his injuries.

With the 2nd Connecticut in the lead, Upton's brigade pinched off the Confederate advance, took hundreds of prisoners and restored the Union line. After the battle, Upton took command of the division, succeeding Russell (who had been a close friend of Sheridan's), while Mackenzie took command of the brigade.

At noon Sheridan abandoned his original plan to send Crook's Army of West Virginia/VIII Corps to join Wilson's Third Cavalry Division and envelop Early's right. Instead he ordered it to cross Opequon Creek and come into line on the right flank of XIX Corps, opposite Early's left, with one of his two divisions extending north of Red Bud Run.

In the meantime, Merritt's First Cavalry Division had scattered Fitzhugh Lee's Confederate cavalry pickets, and Breckinridge's infantry division at Stephenson's Depot was ordered to drive the Union cavalry back. Although Breckinridge was dug in behind a railroad cut and poured in a heavy fire, Merritt's cavalry, in a series of mounted and dismounted charges, slowly pushed Breckinridge back. Not only that, Merritt's cavalry kept Breckinridge occupied for hours and left him unable to move to where the main battle was going on. Although Breckinridge had been ordered by Early to disengage and join him, it was noon before Breckinridge was able to comply and he did not join Early until about 2:00 P.M.

By that time the Union line was straightened out and was deployed all along the front as Early pulled back to a new defensive position placing two of Breckinridge's brigades on his right to support Ramseur and the other on his extreme left next to Gordon. The new Confederate line now took the shape of an inverted "L."

It was 4:00 P.M. before Crook got into position on the Union right, with one division hitting Gordon's left while the other crossed Red Bud Run and came down on Breckinridge's brigade from the north. At the same time, Torbert, in command of Merritt and Averell's cavalry divisions, launched a frightening, morale-shattering, old-fashioned cavalry charge along the Martinsburg Pike, with Merritt on the east side of the pike and Averell on the west. The charge came in on the left flank and rear of Breckinridge's brigade, driving the broken cavalry division of Maj. Gen. Fitzhugh Lee through the infantry lines. (It was here that Fitzhugh Lee was badly wounded, and he would not resume command of his division until after the conclusion of Sheridan's Shenandoah Valley Campaign of 1864.)

Merritt's cavalry division made at least three charges, caving in Early's left flank. Although Averell had practically no opposition on his front, his charge was broken and halted temporarily by horse artillery that had been placed on Fort Hill, just west and slightly north of Winchester.

In response, Early sent the other two brigades of Breckinridge's division from his right to his left, but, under pressure from Crook's Army of West Virginia/VIII Corps and the cavalry charge, his lines broke and Early's army was routed. John William DeForrest, a captain in XIX Corps, watched as Torbert's cavalry delivered the coup de grace.

"I saw," he wrote in a magazine article after the war, "a brigade of these gallant troopers in a long, straight line along the crest of the hill, rush upon Early's rear, and break up and sweep away his disorganized regiments as easily, to all appearance, as a billow tosses its light burden of sea-weed.... It was, I believe, the most effective cavalry charge that has been delivered during the war; and it was certainly one of the most spirit-stirring and magnificent spectacles conceivable."

Three days later Sheridan forced Early out of the natural fortress at Fisher's Hill where he had taken refuge. Here Mackenzie, his regiment, and now his brigade, once more distinguished themselves. He came to the attention of Sheridan once again at the Battle of Cedar Creek. Early and his Valley District Army attacked Sheridan's camp at Cedar Creek, in Sheridan's absence, and almost succeeded in driving Sheridan's Army of the Shenandoah from the field.

Sheridan returned, and although the army had already rallied, Sheridan was the man who determined that there would be a counterattack and who organized that counterattack. The army that had been badly whipped that morning attacked in the late afternoon and by evening had scattered Early's army once again. During the Battle of Cedar Creek, Mackenzie was once again wounded and had two horses shot out from under him.

Mackenzie's performance during all three battles certainly did get him noticed, by Sheridan and others. After Cedar Creek, in January 1865, he was promoted to the rank of brigadier general, U.S. Volunteers, to date from October 19, 1864, the day of the Battle of Cedar Creek. This backdating of a commission was usually done to underline exactly where and exactly why the promotion had been earned.

Since the battle of Cedar Creek had all but ended Sheridan's 1864 Shenandoah Valley Campaign, Mackenzie and his brigade returned to the Army of the Potomac's siege lines around Petersburg with Mackenzie being an especially marked man. Soon, however, VI Corps, to the horror of its commander, Horatio G. Wright, was about to lose Mackenzie forever.

26

Mackenzie at Five Forks

As the spring of 1865 and the new campaigning season approached, Grant, possibly acting upon the suggestion of Sheridan, asked Meade if he could spare Brig. Gen. Ranald Slidell Mackenzie. Grant was in the process of reorganizing the Army of the James. He had already replaced Benjamin Butler with Edward O.C. Ord and had reorganized and redesignated the troops within its X Corps and XVIII Corps as XXIV Corps and XXV Corps. In addition, Grant was not happy with its current cavalry division commander, Augustus V. Kautz, and wanted to replace him with Mackenzie.

When the commander of VI Corps, Horatio G. Wright, found out about Mackenzie's pending transfer he resisted it to no avail. "I can't replace him with so good an officer," Wright had protested, thereby clinching the deal in Grant's mind. If Mackenzie was so good that his current commanding officer would risk Grant's wrath in order to keep him, than maybe he was the perfect choice to command that division of cavalry.

By the time Mackenzie and his division had been called in for the kill, to join Sheridan at Five Forks, Grant had Godfrey Weitzel, with two divisions of the Army of the James, in front of Richmond; General Parke's IX Corps (Ambrose E. Burnside having been replaced following the fiasco at the Battle of the Crater), Wright's VI Corps, and three divisions of Ord's Army of the James to hold the siege lines in front of Petersburg ready to pounce on Lee's entrenchments; and G.K Warren's V Corps and A.A. Humphreys' II Corps prepared to move southwest across Hatcher's Run, menace Lee's right flank, and support any offensive move that Sheridan might make.

Lee, immediately realizing Grant's intentions, had concentrated two-thirds of his infantry and all of his cavalry on his right flank (leaving 11,000 men to hold 11 miles of trenches around Petersburg). At Longstreet's suggestion Lee had created an independent striking force under Maj. Gen. George Pickett consisting of three of his own four brigades and two brigades drawn from Bushrod Johnson's division and sent them to Five Forks on March 30 to join Lee's three cavalry divisions, which were under the direction of his nephew, Maj. Gen. Fitzhugh Lee.

However, one thing that Lee had not realized was the extent of the psychological damage that had been suffered by Pickett when his division had been almost totally destroyed more than a year and a half previously at the Battle of Gettysburg.[1]

Lee had chosen Pickett's Division, composed entirely of Virginians, to spearhead his climactic assault on the Union center up on Cemetery Ridge on July 3, 1863. Pickett bore little personal responsibility for the failure of that assault and for the losses suffered by his division. What he had done was to follow Lee's orders that sent his division forward against what was a virtually impregnable Union position. When his men faltered and broke, Pickett was haunted by what had happened for the rest of his life and it adversely affected his future performance as a general.

Pickett was convinced to the end of his days that the lives of the men in his division had been squandered when they were left without proper support. After the battle he wrote a scathing official report that was sharply critical of this lack of support. Lee refused to accept the report and instructed Pickett to destroy it. There is some question as to whether or not Pickett did so. His wife hinted as late as 1899, well after Pickett's own death, that the report had not been destroyed; however, she never produced it and it is considered to be one of the most important lost documents of the war.

In fact, Pickett blamed Lee for the destruction of his division. After the war Pickett and John S. Mosby met with Lee. After the meeting Pickett complained to Mosby, "That old man ... had my division massacred at Gettysburg." He would eventually mellow somewhat; when he was asked — well after the war — who was to blame for the Confederate loss at Gettysburg Pickett had scratched his head and instead of blaming Lee, Longstreet, Ewell, or anyone else, for that matter, had simply said, "Well, I always thought that the Yankees had something to do with it."

After Gettysburg the Confederate War Department persisted in giving Pickett new and important responsibilities and he failed each and every time to meet those responsibilities, with the sole exception being his actions to hold the city of Petersburg long enough to prevent it from falling like a ripe plum into Union hands, which had resulted in the Siege of Petersburg.

He first failed in an offensive designed to drive Union forces from their coastal enclaves in North Carolina. In the aftermath of this failure he executed 22 captured members of the 2nd North Carolina Infantry Regiment (U.S.) who had been former North Carolina home guardsmen and who had changed sides and were now wearing Union blue. After that, Pickett had been left in command of the Petersburg defenses. Although he had been officially relieved of the Petersburg command and was about to return to his division in Lee's army, Pickett had stayed on in Petersburg due to a delay in the arrival of P.G.T. Beauregard, who had been ordered to relieve him and had succeeded Pickett in command of the department that comprised southern Virginia and North Carolina.

For days Pickett had warned that Union troops were about to attack Petersburg. In fact, he had cried wolf so long and so often that Confederate officials in Richmond derided him. Pickett, when the attack came, rushed what troops he had to the crucial railroad junction near Petersburg; he scraped together mounted and armed civilian volunteers to form a makeshift cavalry screen and ran empty railroad trains in and out of the town to make it appear that reinforcements were on the way.

Finally, Pickett collapsed from nervous exhaustion, but his meager forces had held onto Petersburg. It wasn't pretty but out of sheer desperation Pickett had taken control and saved Petersburg. As soon as possible he left for Hanover Junction and resumed command of his division, which was part of Longstreet's I Corps, on June 19, 1864. Pickett's Division during the Siege of Petersburg served as Lee's central mobile reserve. Pickett was also Lee's senior division commander, although, until the emergency at Five Forks, he was not entrusted with anything remotely resembling an independent or autonomous command.

Mackenzie noted in his report of the Battle of Five Forks and of the Appomattox Campaign that followed it that his command's participation in the final operations of the Army of the Potomac began when his division left its camp near the New Market Road on March 28.

At this time his division's First Brigade consisted only of the 5th Pennsylvania Cavalry Regiment and G Troop, 20th Pennsylvania Cavalry Regiment. The rest of the 20th Pennsylvania Cavalry was retained, along with two divisions from the Army of the James, in its positions near Richmond. The other three divisions were being withdrawn to take the place of II Corps and V Corps that Grant was utilizing in his move against Lee's right that would result in the Battle of the Quaker Road on March 29, the Battle of the White Oak Road on March 31, the Battle of Dinwiddie Court House on March 31, and the Battle of Five Forks on April 1. The Second Brigade consisted of the 11th Pennsylvania Cavalry Regiment, 1st Maryland Cavalry Regiment, and a battalion of the 1st District of Columbia Cavalry Regiment (this regiment also formed the uniformed arm of Col. Lafayette C. Baker's National Detective Police, a sort of American Civil War precursor to both the FBI and the CIA). Altogether the effective strength of Mackenzie's division at this point was 54 officers and 1,629 enlisted men.

The march continued until early on the morning of March 29, when the division went into bivouac near Varina Station on the Norfolk & Petersburg Railroad. By 8:00 A.M. the division was moving again to the vicinity of Humphreys' Station, where the division went into camp. At the same time, Mackenzie received orders to force a crossing of the Rowanty River in the vicinity of Reams' Station the next day and to guard the baggage and supply trains of the Army of the Potomac that were assembled there.

Mackenzie's Division remained there until the early morning hours of April 1, when orders were received from Lt. Gen. Grant, through Maj. Gen. Ord (commander of the Army of the James), to proceed at once to Dinwiddie Court House and to report to General Sheridan. Mackenzie began his march at about 3:30 A.M., joining Sheridan at about 9:00 A.M. Mackenzie's old teacher and mentor—Maj. Gen. Gouverneur K. Warren—and his V Corps had also been ordered to reinforce Sheridan, who originally had only the three divisions of cavalry that formed the Cavalry Corps, Army of the Potomac, under the command of General Wesley Merritt, with him.

Sheridan's mission was to smash Confederate Maj. Gen. George Pickett's reinforced infantry division, which was supported by what was left of the Army of Northern Virginia's cavalry.

By this time Pickett had fought the Battle of Dinwiddie Court House against Sheridan's cavalry, actually winning a tactical victory, when he realized that V Corps was moving against him. He thereupon withdrew to his previously prepared and entrenched position at Five Forks where he believed that he could better protect the vulnerable Confederate right flank and the vital Southside Railroad, a decision that apparently did not make Lee happy. The reason for that belief, once again, are the orders Lee supposedly telegraphed to Pickett after he received Pickett's report on the Battle of Dinwiddie Court House and news of Pickett's decision to withdraw back into his previously prepared fortifications at Five Forks.[2]

"Hold Five Forks at all hazards," Lee's purported telegram said. "Protect the road to Ford's Depot and prevent Union forces from striking the Southside Railroad. Regret exceedingly your forced withdrawal, and the inability to hold the advantage you had gained."

After the war, Pickett maintained that he had asked for and expected to receive reinforcements. However, no existing documentation has ever been found showing that Pickett had requested reinforcements or that Lee had promised any reinforcements to Pickett. The telegram from Lee, if it existed at all, may have been interpreted by Pickett as an implicit promise of reinforcement. After the fiasco at Five Forks, Pickett blamed the disaster upon others, convinced that just like at Gettysburg he and his men had been left to the slaughter.

However, Pickett's own carelessness can be seen in his deployments. There was only one tiny 300-man cavalry brigade consisting of just two skeleton-sized North Carolina regiments placed to cover the three-mile gap between Pickett's position at Five Forks and the rest of Lee's Army of Northern Virginia. Then Pickett and Fitzhugh Lee went off on that famous shad-bake of Thomas L. Rosser's. It would have been better to have used Rosser's cavalry division, exhausted horses or not, to have maintained Pickett's communications with the rest of Lee's army and to have used Roberts' tiny cavalry brigade to guard Pickett's baggage and supply wagons.

Although Mackenzie did not know it at the time, this was to be Warren's last battle—for Sheridan would relieve him of command of V Corps just as the battle was ending—and over 15 years later Mackenzie would be called to testify at the court of inquiry that was convened by the order of President Rutherford B. Hayes (who during the war commanded one of the two divisions in George C. Crook's Army of West Virginia/VIII Corps) to investigate and determine the causes and the reasons for Warren's removal.

After his division arrived Mackenzie met with Sheridan (although he did not know that Sheridan was seething at what he considered to have been a missed opportunity when Warren's V Corps did not arrive in time to keep Pickett from slipping away from his exposed position at Dinwiddie Court House and back to Five Forks) at the side of the road, and receiving no immediate orders Mackenzie and his division spent the rest of the morning resting from their march, until Sheridan became concerned that Lee might send more troops that could take him in the flank as he moved against Pickett. Sheridan therefore ordered Mackenzie and his cavalry division to ride up from Dinwiddie Court House to Five Forks and then turn east on the White Oak Road.

Mackenzie wrote in his report that he was ordered to go by a crossroad to the White Oak Swamp Road, at a point about three miles to the right of Five Forks, and was told to take possession of the White Oak Road. In his court of inquiry testimony Mackenzie said that this order was brought by one of Sheridan's staff officers, who told Mackenzie that he was to hurry up his movement and that General Sheridan was anxious about Mackenzie acting promptly in getting hold of the intersection of those roads. This was done after a sharp skirmish, in which a squadron (two companies) of the 11th Pennsylvania Cavalry made a very successful charge, dislodging Roberts' dismounted Confederate cavalry brigade of Rooney Lee's cavalry division from defensive breastworks blocking the intersection. By doing so he cut Pickett off from the rest of Lee's army and set Pickett's entire force up for the catastrophe which followed. This act was probably what led to Mackenzie's being commissioned a brevet major general of volunteers—his new commission being backdated to March 31, 1865, the day before the Battle of Five Forks.

Sheridan now planned to use Devin and Custer's cavalry divisions—under Merritt—to hold Pickett and his Confederate infantry in their fieldworks, forming dismounted along their front while overlapping the Confederate right. Then, while Custer, on the left, threatened a flank attack with two mounted brigades, the full weight of V Corps was to be brought to bear at the angle on the Confederate left (which Sheridan saw as the key point in the entire Confederate line). Mackenzie's division, which had already broken Pickett's link with Lee, would screen the right flank and rear of Warren's V Corps infantry attack and block Pickett's line of retreat. In effect it was a left jab to be followed by a right cross. The battle, however, would not go exactly as Sheridan planned and, although the eventual victory would be as complete as anyone could have possibly wanted it to be, Warren would be relieved because of it.

After Roberts' tiny Confederate cavalry brigade had been dispersed, Mackenzie paused for a breather, picketing the road to the right between 2:00 and 4:00 P.M., as he testified during the Warren court of inquiry some 15 or 16 years later, until Sheridan, pushing the attack begun by Warren's V Corps at about 4:15 P.M., by courier ordered Mackenzie to swing around to the east in an attempt to hit Pickett's flank and rear. Mackenzie thereupon led his division (except for a battalion of the 5th Pennsylvania Cavalry that was left to picket the right flank) down the White Oak Road in the direction of Five Forks until he met Sheridan himself, who thereupon directed him to move on the right of the infantry, which caused him to deflect his division to the right and to increase its gait, or pace, of the advance.

In his Warren Court of Inquiry testimony Mackenzie stated that he recalled that Sheridan's orders were given in an exceedingly vigorous manner, which Mackenzie said showed him that Sheridan wished to impress upon him "the necessity of energetic action."

The First and Third Cavalry divisions under the command of Bvt. Maj. Gen. Wesley Merritt were to hold the attention of the Confederate center and right, while Warren's V Corps was to hit their left flank, with Mackenzie's cavalry screening Warren's right flank and rear. However, the attack was misdirected and only one of Warren's infantry divisions struck the enemy where it was supposed to do so. George C. Crook's Second Cavalry Division was to maintain Sheridan's connection with Grant in order to keep the Confederates from doing to Sheridan what Sheridan was about to do to Pickett. Mackenzie's men were slowed and scattered by the thick woods they were moving through and they were unable to reach Hatcher's Run, which had guarded the Confederate front until after Warren's V Corps had dislodged Pickett's infantry.

The 1st Maryland Cavalry, leading the advance, was just about to charge down the road when the infantry of V Corps made their appearance and instructions were received from General Sheridan to move up on their right flank. Thereupon Mackenzie diverted his division even more to the right so as not to interfere with the advance of the infantry. Mackenzie wrote in his report that his division moved rapidly on the right of this infantry, and soon reached the right and rear of Pickett's line at Five Forks, at which point Mackenzie wrote in his official report of the battle that the Confederates were giving way without much resistance.

However, during the Warren Court of Inquiry, Mackenzie testified that as his division moved further into the Confederate rear his troopers kept running into the Union infantry and had to deflect their course more and more upon the right until Mackenzie found himself on Hatcher's Run. Upon doing so he found a crossing that had been carried by some of his troopers and crossed Hatcher's Run. However, after doing so Mackenzie said he became convinced that he was now too far to the right. He also said he knew that the fighting was continuing because he could hear the sound of heavy musketry coming from the left.

For a moment, Mackenzie said, he was unsure about what was the best and safest course to pursue, and then he made up his mind that the best thing for him to do was to get closer to the sound of the musketry which was coming from the left, or south. Mackenzie then crossed back over Hatcher's Run and moved in such a direction as to be a little north of the musketry, a position that Mackenzie believed would be on the rear and flank of Pickett's position, from where the musketry was coming. So moving in that direction Mackenzie soon arrived at the Ford Road, "where I found that the matter had been settled — that we had won."

Pickett's entire command had abruptly disintegrated and only the cavalry managed to maintain its organization as it got away and rejoined Lee. By the time the final rearguard had been smashed in an assault led personally by Warren (who by this time realized Sheridan was about to relieve him), his own chief of staff reached him with Sheridan's written message that he, Warren, had not been in the fight. Warren therefore may have been seeking his own death upon the battlefield, something he was denied. Shortly thereafter a courier arrived from Sheridan officially relieving him of his command.

During this period Mackenzie's division captured a large number of prisoners and they were turned over to the infantry, while the division kept moving. A squadron of the 1st Maryland Cavalry led the advance and it and the 5th Pennsylvania Cavalry charged "handsomely" through the thick woods. By its action in reaching Hatcher's Run, Mackenzie's division had prevented the remnants of the infantry of Pickett's command from attempting to return to the Petersburg lines. It was estimated that the troops under Sheridan's command took 5,000 prisoners, 18 flags, 10 cannon, and enough rifled muskets to corduroy the road between Dinwiddie Court House and Five Forks, which was promptly done.

With this battle and in the Appomattox Campaign that immediately followed Sheridan showed how a powerful and well-indoctrinated cavalry force could be used as a flanking spearhead of precisely the type that the infantry had shown itself unable to provide, particularly as it failed to take Petersburg when that city was held only by a mere handful of troops. It would not have happened if Sheridan had not resisted Grant's habitual preference to send the cavalry off on an independent raid. Sheridan insisted that the cavalry should be kept with the Army of the Potomac and used for a truly decisive purpose by prolonging the army's left flank in order to force Lee to evacuate Petersburg and Richmond rather then making a sweep to tear up some railroad track and then march away from what Sheridan saw as the crucial theatre of battle in order to join Sherman for the purpose of simply trapping Lee between Grant and Sherman.

It is doubtful that Mackenzie and his men knew or really cared what Sheridan and their division had managed to accomplish at Five Forks. Once the fighting had ended Mackenzie's division bivouacked where it was on the battlefield and got some very well earned rest for what remained of the night.

After the battle, what remained of Pickett's Division, which mostly consisted of the brigade that had not gone to Five Forks, was simply consolidated with another division and Pickett himself was released or dismissed from the army at Lee's command. During the final retreat Lee noticed the presence of Pickett who, not having anywhere else to go, had remained with the army. This caused Lee to ask in angry bewilderment, "Why is that man still with the army?"

27

The Pursuit to Appomattox

Mackenzie's cavalry division was also instrumental in the final confrontation with Lee's army that occurred eight days later on April 9, 1865, at Appomattox Court House. On the day following the Battle of Five Forks, April 2, Mackenzie's cavalry division was moved to Gravelly Ford on Hatcher's Run and, after skirmishing with Confederate troops, strongly posted on the opposite bank, and he was ordered to proceed to Ford's Station. The division crossed Hatcher's Run and moved in the direction of the Namozine Road, and Mackenzie thereupon reported to Merritt before ordering his division into bivouac for the night.

Meanwhile, at daybreak on April 2, the II Corps division of Nelson A. Miles reported to Sheridan, who ordered Miles to take his division up the White Oak Road towards Petersburg and attack the enemy at the intersection with the Claiborne Road. Sheridan sent two V Corps divisions to back him up. Miles pushed the enemy beyond Hatcher's Run and followed the Confederates on the road to Sutherland's Depot, where A.A. Humphreys, II Corps commander, arrived and took back control of Miles and his division.

Sheridan thereupon took V Corps and returned to Five Forks, and then marched out on the Ford Road toward Hatcher's Run. He reached the Southside Railroad at Ford's Depot and then marched toward Sutherland's Depot, catching the Confederates opposing Miles, as he continued his advance, on the flank and rear. The Confederates retreated along the main road by the Appomattox River and there was a slight engagement involving some of Sheridan's cavalry and Crawford's division of V Corps at about nightfall.

That same day General Robert E. Lee faced a grave military dilemma. The previous day George Pickett's combined infantry and cavalry command, with some artillery support, had been shattered at Five Forks, on the extreme right of his army. Lee's army had been stretched for 35 miles, from Richmond to Five Forks, and Lee had often warned that sooner or later this line would break. On April 1, 1865, Grant was finally able to turn Lee's flank and on April 2 the line simply broke.

Godfrey Weitzel, XXV Corps commander, with two infantry divisions (one from XXIV Corps and one from his own XXV Corps) from the Army of the James and some cavalry from Mackenzie's division (primarily the 20th Pennsylvania Cavalry Regiment) had remained in the trench lines facing Richmond, where he was later joined by the 5th Massachusetts (Colored) Cavalry Regiment. On April 1, the day that the Battle of Five Forks had been fought, he was informed that, while one Confederate infantry division remained in the Confederate trenches facing his troops, the Confederate troops at Bermuda Hundred seemed to have been reduced.

At about 5:00 P.M. his chief signal officer informed Weitzel that great excitement could be seen in the streets of Richmond; later he was told by Grant of the great success that had been achieved at Five Forks and Weitzel began preparations for an assault upon Richmond. Grant returned to Weitzel the XXV Corps division that Ord had taken with him when his troops moved into the trench lines that had been occupied by II Corps and V Corps, which had been moved out to get around Lee's right, culminating in the Battle of Five Forks.

Grant, upon receiving word of what had happened at Five Forks, had ordered an all out assault all along the lines held by XXV Corps, VI Corps and IX Corps, to begin at about 1:30 A.M. April 2. In a matter of hours there was a hole punched into Lee's center and his left flank had been cut off. Lee learned of this latest catastrophe at 4:00 A.M. while in a conference with Lt. Gen. James Longstreet and Lt. Gen. A.P. Hill. Hill immediately rushed off to rally his soldiers and was killed.

By 10:30 A.M. Lee indicated he had bowed to the inevitable when the following message from him arrived at the War Department: "I see no prospect of doing more than to hold our position until night. I am not sure I can do that. I advise that all preparations be made for leaving Richmond tonight."

While President Davis was attending church services he received another message from Lee: "I think that it is absolutely necessary that we should abandon our position tonight. I have given all necessary orders on the subject to the troops, and the operation, although difficult, I hope will be performed successfully. I have directed General Stevens to send an officer to Your Excellency to explain the routes by which the troops will be moved to Amelia Court House, and furnish you with a guide and any assistance that you may require for yourself."

Upon receiving the message, Davis left the church without another word and headed to his office in the War Department. There remained only one option, evacuation of both Richmond and Petersburg and a retreat west to the Richmond & Danville Railroad where Lee could hope to find supplies, most especially food, at Amelia Court House, and then seek to join Joseph E. Johnston and his army in North Carolina. The evacuation began at 8:00 P.M.

As Lee's army began slipping away from Petersburg and the Confederate government abandoned Richmond, inside the city itself chaos reigned. The populace of Richmond, who had been confused but orderly when the evacuation began, became an unruly and dangerous mob, particularly once Lt. Gen. Richard Ewell's Richmond garrison began setting fire to all tobacco, cotton, and munitions warehouses as well as machine shops and government buildings to prevent their capture. The mob, by this time joined by stragglers and deserters (from the army) and prisoners (both civilian and military) abandoned by their guards, set more indiscriminate fires that were fanned by the wind and soon spread.

Plans for an evacuation of the city had been discussed for nearly a year, but nothing had been finalized, possibly because to do so had seemed to be too much like an attack of defeatism. The loss of the city, becoming all the more likely as time went on, was something that most people, in and out of the military and in and out of the government, had chosen to deny. Instead, the city's residents seemed to expect Lee to pull one more miracle out of his hat.[1]

Weitzel was informed at 3:00 A.M. on April 3 that fires had broken out in Richmond. At about the same time, he received intelligence through a prisoner that the Confederates were evacuating their works. A forward movement of his pickets confirmed this report and Weitzel had therefore ordered that his troops be awakened and prepared for action at dawn. At daylight Weitzel ordered that a reconnaissance be made toward Richmond. This reconnaissance got all the way to the capitol square within the city meeting hardly any resistance. Richmond had fallen.[2]

Weitzel immediately moved his troops into the city and put them to work at the task of fighting the fires that were still raging within the city to try to keep them from spreading. Weitzel was immediately named the military governor of the city and once the fires were under control set about restoring order.

That morning, April 3, Union forces awoke to find Lee and his army gone from Petersburg. Lee had escaped north of the Appomattox River and was concentrating his troops as they left Richmond and the Petersburg lines, proceeding to Amelia Court House. From there he planned to move to the southwest, first to Danville, Virginia, where President Davis was moving the government, then on to join Johnston and his army. Once Lee and Johnston had joined forces the plan was to hit Sherman and then swing north to meet Grant.

Mackenzie's cavalry division on April 3 moved to the Appomattox River at two points, the lower at Leonard's Mills and the other three miles higher up the stream — picking up about 300 prisoners and taking a battery of four field guns. The division, after reaching Leonard's Mills, retraced its steps to the Namozine Road and moved to the vicinity of Deep Creek. According to Sheridan's official report (dated May 16, 1865), V Corps had followed the cavalry in this pursuit, V Corps and Crook's Second Cavalry Division spent the night at Deep Creek on the Namozine Road.

On April 4 Mackenzie's division crossed Deep Creek and after a sharp skirmish reached a position about a mile from Amelia Court House and again bivouacked. During this time Mackenzie received a number of reports from many different sources that Lee's Army of Northern Virginia was at this time at or in the immediate vicinity of Amelia Court House; during the night Mackenzie received orders from General Sheridan to remain where he was with his division and to be watchful and demonstrate but not push the Confederates.

Also on April 4, Sheridan directed Crook to strike the Danville Railroad between Jetersville and Burk's Station and then move up toward Jetersville. The V Corps moved rapidly to that point and Sheridan himself arrived at Jetersville at about 5:00 P.M., learning at the same time that Lee had moved to Amelia Court House. Then V Corps was ordered to build fieldworks and hold Jetersville until the rest of the army arrived. Sheridan then forwarded everything he had learned to Meade and Grant.

Lee had indeed marched to Amelia Court House, but when he arrived he discovered that there had been a major blunder. He found that ammunition but no food had been shipped there. A frantic Lee immediately sent out foraging parties, but they returned with little or nothing and Union cavalry, like Mackenzie's division, was blocking the way south. This one day delay for foraging doomed Lee's army, for it gave Grant's pursuing troops time to catch up with him even as they ignored the masses of Confederate stragglers on the road.

On April 5, Mackenzie demonstrated toward the Confederates with one brigade that caused the Confederates to attack with a strong force of infantry, but without inflicting any real damage to Mackenzie's division. "I have reason to believe," Mackenzie wrote in his report, "that the enemy were considerably delayed in their movements by our skirmishing at Amelia Court House." During the skirmishing, Mackenzie noted, the Confederates themselves destroyed a large amount of ammunition and other ordnance property, including caissons and limbers.

While Mackenzie was engaged, Sheridan directed Crook to send one of his brigades to make a reconnaissance and this brigade ran into a Confederate wagon train, which was destroyed. During this fight the rest of Crook's division was dispatched to support the leading brigade when the Confederates attempted unsuccessfully to attack and cut it off with infantry. During the afternoon and evening, Humphreys' II Corps arrived at Jetersville and the Confederates demonstrated strongly in front of Jetersville against two brigades of Crook's cavalry division, although no serious attack was made upon them.

Lee, in the meantime, resumed his retreat and again turned west, this time seeking to reach the railroad at Lynchburg. His army began moving to Farmville to reach the railroad, which was still open from there to Lynchburg.

On April 6, Lee's rear guard was caught at Saylor's Creek, where it was destroyed by Sheridan's cavalry, principally Custer's Third Cavalry Division and Crook's Second Cavalry Division with infantry support; about a third of what remained of Lee's Army of Northern Virginia (Ewell's Richmond garrison and Richard H. Anderson's provisional corps) had been lost. At Farmville,

Lee's troops had just begun drawing rations when word arrived that the pursuing Union troops had crossed the Appomattox. (Lee's troops had crossed earlier to reach Farmville and had set afire the bridges they had used to make the crossing. However, the bridges were not fully destroyed and the Union army engineers quickly repaired them.) Sheridan sent a message to Grant, which was forwarded to President Lincoln: "If the thing is pressed I think Lee will surrender." Lincoln's response was, "Let the thing be pressed."

Lee's troops immediately resumed their march and escaped. Now they had to march another 25 miles to Appomattox Court House, where additional trains and supplies awaited them at nearby Appomattox Station. On the night of April 7, Lee received a communication from Grant seeking his surrender. But Lee declined, knowing he could still escape if his army won the footrace to Appomattox Court House.

At dusk on April 8, another message arrived from Grant offering generous terms. Lee replied, offering to discuss "the restoration of peace." But, since this answer smacked of politics, Grant would not consider it. Grant had previously been instructed that he should not talk to Lee, other than to discuss the capitulation of his army. In addition, he was instructed, "to press to the utmost your military advantage." However, by 9:00 P.M., when Lee sent his dispatch to Grant, artillery fire from Appomattox Station told him that he had most likely lost the race.

Mackenzie reported that on April 6, 7, and 8 his division moved by rapid marches through Jetersville, Burkeville, and Prince Edward Court House, with the advanced portion of the division reaching Appomattox Station. In addition, at Prince Edward Court House the division advanced units, the 1st District of Columbia Cavalry and a portion of the 11th Pennsylvania Cavalry, had a slight skirmish and took some 30 prisoners.

Mackenzie's division on the morning of April 9 was moved to the left of George C. Crook's Second Cavalry Division at a point about a mile and a half from Appomattox Court House and immediately on the road to Lynchburg. At this time Mackenzie was no longer "officially" reporting to General Sheridan, having been ordered on April 6 to report to General Ord, commanding the Army of the James, but since many miles usually separated Mackenzie's division from the other units of the Army of the James, Mackenzie generally continued to act under Sheridan's orders, and on this occasion at Sheridan's direction under the orders of General Crook.

By Crook's directions Mackenzie sent the 11th Pennsylvania Cavalry some distance to the left of the road to guard the left flank. Soon afterward, Mackenzie noted in his report, the Confederates attacked and he was ordered by Crook to withdraw slowly when it became necessary, as it would be, very soon. The Confederates, Mackenzie wrote, had for some time been moving a column of cavalry around his left and rear, while attacking with infantry in front. "There would have been no trouble repulsing the enemy from our immediate front," Mackenzie wrote in his report, "but the attack came so soon after our arrival that the connection which I had commenced establishing ... between my right and General Crook's left could not be made."

Mackenzie had dismounted the 5th Pennsylvania Cavalry, 1st District of Columbia Cavalry, and 1st Maryland Cavalry and formed them across the road. After a sharp exchange of fire they were being slowly withdrawn in accordance with the previous orders Mackenzie had received. The 5th Pennsylvania Cavalry had been directed to completely withdraw, move down the road, remount and return. However, Mackenzie noted, "some unauthorized person" had moved the regiment's horses such a long distance to the rear that the regiment was delayed in remounting. This same person had sent one field artillery piece, which had been supporting Mackenzie's line, down a road to the left as Mackenzie's division fell back, causing the gun to be captured.

At about this time the infantry of XXIV Corps arrived. Immediately after the arrival of XXIV Corps, Mackenzie was directed to move his division to Lynchburg to assist Brig. Gen. Henry E. Davies and his brigade of Crook's Second Cavalry Division, which was being strongly pressed by the Confederate cavalry that had earlier been circling around Mackenzie's left flank.

After some skirmishing and when Mackenzie was about to attack, news was received of the suspension of hostilities.

That morning Lee had found that the Union forces in his front were simply too strong to break through and he agreed to surrender his army. He also dismissed out of hand any suggestion, and there were several offered, that he simply disband and scatter his army to allow his soldiers to continue the war as guerrillas.

All four of the cavalry divisions from the Army of the Potomac and the Army of the James, those of Thomas C. Devin, George A. Custer, George C. Crook and Mackenzie, had cut off Lee's retreat. Grant in his report noted: "On the morning of the 9th [April 9, 1865] General Ord's command [XXIV Corps, Army of the James] and the Fifth Corps [Army of the Potomac] reached Appomattox Station just as the enemy was making a desperate effort to break through our cavalry. The infantry was at once thrown in. Soon after, a white flag was received [by Custer], requesting a suspension of hostilities pending negotiations for a surrender." After Lee and Grant met at Appomattox Court House and Lee had agreed to surrender his army, Mackenzie took custody of the surrendered Confederate property and afterward commanded the cavalry in the Department of Virginia.

But the war was not quite over yet. There remained other Confederate armies, such as Johnston's in North Carolina and Confederate forces in the Trans-Mississippi Department, mainly in Texas, under General Edmund Kirby Smith. Until they surrendered the war was not over.

In actuality Joseph E. Johnston surrendered his army twice. Although Sherman acted in what he perceived to be the spirit of Abraham Lincoln the new government of Andrew Johnson rejected the first surrender and Sherman had to try again. Johnston surrendered for the second time on receipt of the exact same terms that Grant had given Lee. It really was not over until General Edmund Kirby Smith finally surrendered the Confederate forces within his Trans-Mississippi Department in June 1865 at a ceremony held in New Orleans.

Some 20 years after the war ended, Grant, broke and dying, wrote his memoirs of the war and in those memoirs he was still highly impressed with Mackenzie's sheer ability:

> [Charles] Griffin, [Andrew A.] Humphries, and [Ranald S.] Mackenzie were good corps commanders [here Grant was mistaken, since Mackenzie only advanced as far as to command the Cavalry Division, Army of the James, before the war ended; Grant was possibly confused by Mackenzie's appointment as chief of cavalry, Department of Virginia], but came into that position so close to the end of the war as not to attract public attention. All three served as such in the last campaigns of the Armies of the Potomac and the James, which culminated at Appomattox Court House, on the 9th of April 1865. The sudden collapse of the rebellion monopolized attention to the exclusion of almost everything else. I regarded Mackenzie as the most promising young officer in the army. Graduating at West Point, as he did, during the second year of the war, he had won his way up to command of a corps [division] before its close. This he did upon his own merit and without influence.

28

The Most Tragic One of Them All

At the end of the American Civil War, Ranald S. Mackenzie had reverted to his permanent army rank of captain, U.S. Army Corps of Engineers, but he wasn't to remain at that rank long. He had impressed both Ulysses S. Grant, who was still general-in-chief of the army, and Philip H. Sheridan, who would eventually be placed in charge of all U.S. military forces on the western frontier.

In addition, even as the volunteer forces that had fought and won the war were being disbanded, the regular army was about to undergo an expansion. Prior to the war the U.S. Army had a strength of just 16,000 men, which had been just barely adequate to patrol the frontier and keep the Indians in check, although it may be questionable whether or not it really managed to even do that.

Besides its traditional duties on the frontier the army was now being tasked with enforcing Reconstruction in what had been the Southern Confederacy. Therefore, the new peacetime strength of the army was set at over 50,000 men. This strength level did not last, as more and more of the former Confederate states regained their own state governments and the army was much reduced in strength, finally being cut in half to an authorized strength of 25,000, and seldom even reaching that pitifully tiny authorized strength. (A move by Southern members of Congress to further reduce the army's strength to just 22,000 in order to make impractical any declaration of martial law in any of the former Confederate States to enforce civil rights legislation was itself narrowly averted by popular uproar over the defeat of Custer's 7th Cavalry at the Battle of the Little Big Horn.)

Mackenzie was mustered out of the U.S. Volunteers on January 15, 1866, and when the army was reorganized Mackenzie was immediately promoted to the rank of colonel and given command of the brand new 41st U.S. Infantry Regiment, a regiment of colored troops, in March 1867. At the age of 26, he had become the youngest colonel to be retained in the U.S. Army. He led the 41st and later the 24th U.S. Infantry (into which the 41st was soon merged) against marauding Indians, Mexican bandits, and white outlaws.

During and after the American Civil War, attacks by Indians, especially in Texas, reached unprecedented proportions. As a matter of fact the Indians actually succeeded in Texas in driving the frontier back over 150 miles. This was the first and only time that had happened during the entire westward expansion of the United States. (Red Cloud in 1868 did successfully defend Sioux territory against white inroads. It stopped expansion for the moment, but did not actually set the frontier back, and at the earliest opportunity western expansion into Sioux territory was continued.) North Texas was literally depopulated by the Southern Arapahoes and Southern Cheyenne; at the same time, the Kiowas, Comanches, Lipans, Kickapoo, and Apaches controlled West Texas, into New Mexico. In addition, U.S.-based Indians raided Mexico, while Mexican-based Indians raided Texas, New Mexico, and Arizona.

The Apaches were particularly notorious for using the international boundary to obtain sanctuary from pursuers, be they Mexicans or Americans, by moving back and forth over the border. The Kickapoos and Lipans followed the example set by the Apaches and also took advantage of the border. The Southwestern tribes (mostly the Southern Arapaho and Southern Cheyenne) used their reservations in the Indian Territory (now Oklahoma) as sanctuaries. The way it worked was that once on the reservation Federal law protected them from Texas authorities (i.e., the now resurgent Texas Rangers). In addition, the Comanches and Kiowas had secret hideouts throughout what was called the Llanco Estacado, or Staked Plain.

During the American Civil War the Union, or United States, had only token forces available to police the frontier and they did not operate in Texas, which was one of the Confederate States. Although the Confederacy did have military forces in Texas they were mostly concerned with keeping Union forces out and patrolling the border with Mexico to keep an eye on the French forces that were occupying that country while they attempted to make a colony, or at the very least a protectorate, out of it. There was little or nothing to spare for the Texas frontier.

Immediately after the war what troops were in Texas were mostly concerned with Reconstruction and not the frontier. Only one regiment, the 6th U.S. Cavalry, was actually placed on the Texas frontier and it was rather apathetic in its approach to the troubles caused by the Indians. (The 6th Cavalry would also fail spectacularly during the opening phases of the Nez Perce War in 1877.)

By 1870, when many of the former Confederate States had been fully readmitted to the federal union, Mackenzie had been reassigned from command of the 24th U.S. Infantry Regiment to command of the 4th U.S. Cavalry Regiment, and Mackenzie (when his 4th Cavalry replaced the 6th Cavalry) began developing a plan for dealing with the almost impossible situation in Texas.

Mackenzie was not your usual type of army Indian fighter. He fought Indians as an Indian would have fought them. He refused to waste time or exhaust his soldiers in useless pursuits. (Although he could, and did, conduct tenacious pursuits whenever he judged there was a chance of success.) Instead, he generally located the Indian hideouts and villages and fell upon them like a whirlwind, destroying everything—horse herds, personal belongings, weapons, food stores—and killing as many of the warriors and capturing as many of their women and children for use as hostages as Mackenzie and his soldiers could find and catch. His actions were responsible for the pacification of much of the Great Plains west of the Mississippi River, south of the Canadian border, and north of the Rio Grande.[1]

In 1871, with 600 troopers from his 4th Cavalry, he invaded the Staked Plain, the heart of Comancheria, for the first time. (Comancheria consisted of the home territories of the federated Southern Plains Indian tribes: the Kiowa, Comanche, Southern Cheyenne and Southern Arapaho.) The Indians scored first by driving off 70 of Mackenzie's horses. Mackenzie pursued and drove the Comanches into a canyon. While Mackenzie paused to align his troops to continue the battle, Quanah Parker, the crossblood chief of the Comanches, escaped with the bulk of his warriors. Mackenzie continued his pursuit until bad weather ended the skirmishing. Mackenzie himself considered this first campaign against the Indians of the Staked Plain to be a failure. However, he did succeed in exploring the then unknown Staked Plain, and the knowledge he had acquired helped subsequently to bring white settlement of the region, which eventually eliminated it as an Indian sanctuary. During the fighting Mackenzie was also hit by an arrow in the leg. It was his seventh, and last, battle wound.

Mackenzie, once winter was over, went back onto the offensive in 1872. In March he led his troopers out of Fort Concho, San Angelo, Texas, in pursuit of a band of Comanches, who headed west towards New Mexico. In an unprecedented example of military tenacity, Mackenzie followed them until, in the vicinity of Alamagordo, New Mexico, the exhausted Indians split up into individuals and small groups in a desperate effort to elude him, thus completely shattering their resistance as an organized band.

That September, Mackenzie struck at a Comanche village on McClellan Creek, a tributary of the North Fork of the Red River. His troopers killed about 20 Indians, captured another 130 (mostly women and children), and grabbed a horse herd of over 3,000 animals. His own losses were one killed and three wounded. The Comanches later counterattacked and recaptured the herd. After that, Mackenzie would order captured Indian horses to be killed immediately (except for those horses he commandeered as remounts for his troopers). Mackenzie and his 4th Cavalry were honored for their achievements by being commended in general orders issued by the War Department. (This was before there were Presidential Unit Citations.)

In 1873, General Sheridan and then President Ulysses S. Grant's secretary of war, William W. Belknap, visited Mackenzie at Fort Clark. They discussed with Mackenzie the shifting of his operations south and told him to move against the Lipans, Kickapoos, and Apaches who were rampaging into South Texas from their Mexican sanctuaries. When Mackenzie pointed out that the only way he could accomplish these suggestions would involve the violation of an international boundary (the U.S.-Mexico border) and that he could not violate it without written orders or other authorization, Sheridan roared: "Damn the orders; damn the authority! You are to go ahead on your own plan of action, and your authority and backing will be General Grant [by then President Grant] and myself. With us behind you in whatever you do to clean up the situation, you can rest assured of the fullest support. You must assume the risk! We will assume the final responsibility, should any result."

Once the visit was concluded, Mackenzie immediately embarked upon a training program for his 4th Cavalry. He told only his adjutant, 1st Lt. Robert Carter, about the proposed incursion into Mexico. The rest of the regiment believed that the special training was only for another hard campaign against the Comanches. Then, without warning, on May 17, he led his 4th Cavalry across the Rio Grande River, which marked the border with Mexico. His objective was the San Rodrigo River, which marked where the hostile Indians were known to have located their permanent encampments, or rancherias.

Mackenzie set a grueling pace, which was too much for even his pack mules, because he intended to strike the rancherias before sunup. However, his scouts lost their way and the rancherias were not sighted until well after daylight. Mackenzie immediately attacked, leading the charge personally. The Indians were taken by surprise and fled in all directions. When the attack ended, 19 Indians were known to have been killed, although others whose bodies were not recovered were also believed to have been killed (an early example of the body count). Among the captured were at least one Lipan chief, 65 horses (many with Texas brands), and 40 women and children. Mackenzie's own losses were exceedingly light: one killed and two wounded.

What he had just succeeded in doing was to demonstrate to the Apaches, Lipans, Kickapoos, and whatever other hostiles there may have been that there as no longer any sure, safe refuge to be found from the United States Army in Mexico. The Mexicans, however, were considerably upset (to say the least) by what they perceived to be an unprovoked invasion. Mexican regular army troops, ranchers, townsmen, brigands, and constabulary troops dropped whatever they might have been doing and joined together in the pursuit of Mackenzie and his 4th Cavalry.

Mackenzie, not seeking a clash with Mexican forces and wanting to avoid it if at all possible, immediately began a retreat for the Rio Grande and safety within United States territory. On its round-trip the 4th Cavalry moved 160 miles in 32 hours. Just 15 hours after destroying the hostile rancherias, Mackenzie and his men were back across the Rio Grande.

Immediately after Mackenzie's raid was concluded the Mexican government, as Sheridan and Mackenzie had fully expected it would do, made vehement protests against this incursion.

Sheridan, for his part, kept his word and Mackenzie was not subjected to any disciplinary action. But as a direct result of this raid the Indians' own raids from Mexico into the United States diminished, although they did not completely cease. In the years to come, Mackenzie would make several other raids into Mexican territory, which caused the hostiles to move their rancherias further away from the border, and ultimately large-scale Indian raids from Mexico into Texas ceased altogether, which had been the objective of the exercise in the first place. (It was Mackenzie's forays into Mexico that provided the background for the John Ford/John Wayne movie *Rio Grande;* as a matter of fact, Mackenzie's assumed military persona was so close to John Wayne's characterization of Col. Kirby York as to be almost identical).

In 1874, due in part to Mackenzie's incursions into Mexico, many of the Indians who had been based in Mexico moved north to the Staked Plain, joining the Indians who already made their homes there. In addition, they were joined by many Southern Cheyennes, Southern Arapahoes, Kiowas, and Comanches (who had left their reservations). All of these Indians were determined to bring to an end the indiscriminate slaughter by white hunters of the buffalo upon which the Indians were totally dependent for their way of life.

The resulting Red River Indian War (which also marked the total collapse of President Grant's Indian Peace Policy) began with an attack by the Indians upon the buffalo hunters' base at Adobe Walls and upon the newly reorganized Texas Rangers of the Frontier Battalion in the Lost Valley Fight. Other attacks by these Indians against the frontier settlements were marked by both great cruelty and great audacity. In response to these attacks Sheridan ordered five columns of troops to converge upon the Staked Plain.

The plan was to drive the Indians out and harry them, summer and winter, giving them no time to rest or hunt, burning their villages, capturing their horses, violating their last refuges until the warriors—cold and debilitated, encumbered by their women and children—broke and surrendered unconditionally.[2]

The five columns would include those of Col. Nelson A. Miles striking southward from Fort Dodge with elements of the 6th Cavalry and his own 5th Infantry. Maj. Williams Redwood Price was to stab westward with elements of the 8th Cavalry from Fort Bascom, New Mexico. Mackenzie and his 4th Cavalry would move out from Fort Concho, Texas. Col. George G. Buell would move northwestward from Fort Griffin with his 11th Cavalry. Finally, Lt. Col. John W. Davidson would strike westward from Fort Sill in the Indian Territory (Oklahoma) with his 10th Cavalry.

There was a battle at Anadarko in the Indian Territory and Miles would be outfought in the Battle of Red River, which was mostly noise. Although the Indians' material losses were considerable, they were not defeated. They were eventually able to disengage. Other Indians fleeing from the battle at Anadarko accidentally and unintentionally severed Miles' communications and supply lines. Eventually, Miles was forced to pull back by his supply problems. When he was finally resupplied during the winter of 1874-1875, Miles returned with a vengeance. His unrelenting winter campaign eventually forced the surrender of several hostile bands.

Mackenzie and his Texas column arrived at the Staked Plain in late summer. By this time the 4th Cavalry's previous combat experience under Mackenzie, combined with his harsh and raw discipline, had made them the army's premier Indian fighting command. On September 26-27, 1874, Mackenzie's column fought a bitter battle with the Southern Cheyennes. When the Cheyennes sought to draw him off, using a false trail, Mackenzie, remembering the lay of the land from previous operations (he had not graduated first in his class from West Point and then served as an engineer for two years during the American Civil War for nothing), surmised that the Indians were attempting to lead his column away from their villages, which he believed were located in the vicinity of the Palo Duro Canyon.

Mackenzie, to make the Indians believe that their deception was succeeding, allowed them to lead his column away from the canyon until dusk on September 27. When the Indians broke off, Mackenzie reversed direction under cover of darkness and as rapidly as possible marched his troopers to the canyon. By dawn he had arrived at the rim of the canyon, where he and his men were able to look directly down into a number of Indian villages (consisting of both the Southern Cheyennes he had been chasing and Comanches). Mackenzie first dismounted his men, and then, with each trooper leading his horse, he led them single file down a narrow, crooked trail to the floor of the canyon.

However, an Indian horse guard, who raised the alarm, spotted Mackenzie and his troopers, and the canyon immediately erupted with hostile Indians as if someone had just kicked over an anthill. Some of the hostiles took cover behind boulders and commenced opening fire on Mackenzie and his attacking soldiers, their primary hope being to force Mackenzie's troopers to either retreat or delay them long enough to permit the villages containing their women and children to escape. But Mackenzie and his troopers succeeded in descending to the canyon floor and deployed for an assault upon the villages. Once that happened many of the Indians fled, abandoning everything they owned. Mackenzie's assault was so rapid that most of the Indians managed to take only their personal weapons and a few horses with them.

Once the fighting had ended and Mackenzie controlled the canyon, he ordered everything that had been abandoned by the Indians to be destroyed. This included armaments, food supplies, clothing, saddlery, blankets, ammunition, and about 1,400 captured horses. Mackenzie's victory was so devastating and so complete that most of the Indians returned at once to their reservations.

Mackenzie had left them only two options, to voluntarily return to the reservation or to starve; thus at the Battle of Palo Duro Canyon he completely broke the resistance of the Comanches and their allies. All that remained were mopping up operations that were left to Miles during the winter.

In recognition of his victory, Mackenzie and the 4th Cavalry were reassigned and sent to Fort Sill, Indian Territory in 1875, where Mackenzie was given complete and total responsibility for the entire Indian Territory. Their mission was to police the reservations and to make sure that the Indians stayed there. It was here that Mackenzie came afoul of the overly ambitious Nelson A. Miles.

Miles met his match in Mackenzie when he attempted to get half of Mackenzie's 4th Cavalry transferred to his command so that he could share in Mackenzie's command of the Indian Territory. Where Miles had deliberately cultivated connections with influential individuals to support his ambition, Mackenzie's connections were through earned recognition. When Mackenzie realized what was going on he appealed directly to Sheridan, stopping Miles' attempt to muscle in upon his command in its tracks.[3]

Mackenzie was so successful in seeking out and punishing troublemakers that within a very short time the number of dissident breakouts by the Indians practically ceased. Finally, in 1875, the last band of hostile Comanches, under Quanah Parker, surrendered to Mackenzie, to the immense chagrin of Miles, and that ended the Red River War.

Then came the disastrous Battle of the Little Big Horn on June 25, 1876, which resulted in the death of Lt. Col. George Armstrong Custer (who achieved a sort of immortality) and the decimation of his 7th U.S. Cavalry Regiment (which suffered a total of 365 casualties out of about 600 officers and enlisted men engaged, including the complete and total annihilation of the five troops that had actually been with Custer). Sheridan in this emergency turned to Mackenzie, who was sent north from Texas. In June 1877, Mackenzie and his 4th Cavalry were ordered to join General George Crook in punishing the Northern Plains Indians for their part in the Little Big Horn disaster of the previous year. Mackenzie's orders were to put an end to the depredations of both the Lakota Sioux and the Northern Cheyenne.

However, shortly before leaving Fort Sill, Mackenzie had an accident. He fell out of a wagon in which he was riding, landing practically on his head, and suffered severe head injuries. He was not entirely himself for several days due to the accident. In addition, he was also suffering at the same time from the effects of his seven battle wounds and was in extreme "discomfort," which is why he had been riding in the wagon in the first place.

"He was fretful, irritable, oftentimes irascible, and pretty hard to serve with," his adjutant, Capt. Carter, said. "This was due largely to his failing to take care of himself, or his wounds.... He could not ride more than 25 or 30 miles without being in great pain...." Yet, even as he complained about Mackenzie's manner, Carter also recognized Mackenzie's effectiveness as a soldier. "He had more brains than Custer, better judgment, and he carefully planned his attacks."

When Mackenzie did arrive in the north, the very first thing he did was to go to the Spotted Tail and Red Cloud agencies in the Black Hills of Dakota Territory and proceed to count noses. His census found that there were only 4,706 Indians there, about half of the number that should have been there. Therefore, Mackenzie ordered the old and nearly blind Lakota Chief Red Cloud to move closer to the agency, both to keep a closer watch on the remaining agency Indians and to catch returning raiders. When Red Cloud refused, Mackenzie took his troopers and surrounded Red Cloud's lodge at night, taking him prisoner. Red Cloud was thereupon placed in confinement and removed as the primary spokesman for the Oglala tribe of the Lakota Sioux. Mackenzie's swift and decisive action demoralized potential hostiles among the reservation and agency Indians.

The following October, Mackenzie led a mixed column of cavalry and Indian allies, mostly Shoshonis (the Shoshonis were bitter enemies of both the Sioux and the Cheyenne), into the Powder River country, where Dull Knife and his Northern Cheyenne had based themselves after the Battle of the Little Big Horn. Mackenzie, in a surprise dawn assault, attacked Dull Knife's village. About 50 Northern Cheyenne warriors were killed and when the Indians fled the village it was totally destroyed.

Many of Dull Knife's people escaped, only to freeze to death when the temperatures dropped to 30 degrees below zero. Finally the surviving Indians who had been deprived of food, clothing, horses, and weapons by Mackenzie's successful attack gave up and surrendered. By his actions Mackenzie had significantly contributed to the final defeat of the Northern Plains Indians, who had bested Custer. "I can't commend too highly [Mackenzie's] brilliant achievements and the gallantry of the troops under his command," Crook had wired the War Department once it was all over.

With the Northern Plains Indians crushed, Mackenzie was next given command of the Department of the Nueces, with headquarters at his former post, Fort Clark, near Bracketville, Texas. He again invaded Mexico in pursuit of cattle-rustling Mexican brigands as well as Kickapoo Indian raiders. Shortly after this incident the Mexican government agreed to police the border to prevent Indian raiders and Mexican brigands from crossing into Texas.

Mackenzie, who by this time had become something of a troubleshooter for the U.S. Army, was next ordered to Colorado to stop the uprising of the White River Utes. This uprising had begun in September 1879 and had resulted in the deaths of 30 white people, with another 44 wounded. The people of the state of Colorado were demanding that the Indians be punished and expelled. The Utes, on their part, pledged to die fighting, and the attacks and resulting depredations continued on both sides. (Col. Wesley Merritt, who had been sent to Colorado, with his 5th U.S. Cavalry Regiment, had not been successful in quelling the uprising and Mackenzie and the 4th Cavalry replaced him and his regiment.)

In 1881, Mackenzie rode alone and unarmed into a council of Ute chiefs. Upon his arrival he issued them an ultimatum. He told them to decide then and there whether they would stay and fight and die, or whether they would agree to leave Colorado. The chiefs were dumbfounded by Mackenzie's sheer gall. When they had recovered their wits and had begun arguing with him, Mackenzie took out his watch and gave them 10 minutes to decide. Before the expiration of his deadline 20 of the principal Ute chiefs had capitulated. Two days later the Utes began their journey to leave Colorado on their way to a reservation in Utah.

Mackenzie was next sent to Arizona, receiving his orders on September 2, 1881. This time he was to deal with the Apaches. Mackenzie was placed in command of all field forces in Arizona, with his headquarters at Fort Apache. After a short and brilliant campaign, using Indian policemen wherever possible as spies, he was able to nip trouble in the bud, despite opposition from both the department and the division commanders.

He was then reassigned on October 30 as commandant of the District of New Mexico, with headquarters at Santa Fe, where the Apaches ignored departmental and international boundaries and where the Navajos were restless. Within a year, the army was in control and Mackenzie was promoted to the rank of brigadier general. In a military career that had spanned just over 20 years this proved to be his last service.

On November 1, 1883, Mackenzie arrived at his new headquarters at Fort Sam Houston, San Antonio, Texas, where he took command of the Department of Texas. He was 43 and his health was continuing to fail. He apparently had plans to retire soon on land he had purchased at Boerne, Texas, where he intended to take up ranching.

It was also reported that he intended to marry. At about this time he met, for the second time, Florida Tunstall, to whom he was reportedly greatly attached. Shortly after first meeting her in 1869 she had married Dr. Redford Sharpe, an army surgeon. She was now widowed and they reportedly had become engaged. However, Mackenzie's future would prove to be much darker and none of his apparent plans for his retirement and marriage would ever actually see fruition.

Mackenzie's associates for some time had been noting changes and physical deterioration in the man, as well as erratic behavior. By early December, only a month after assuming command of the Department of Texas, Mackenzie's staff became convinced that he was suffering from mental aberrations. A crisis occurred on December 18, 1883, when he went into San Antonio and became involved in a brawl with local residents. He was beaten severely and then tied to a wagon. His medical director diagnosed Mackenzie as suffering from "paralysis of the insane" and decided he was no longer fit for military command.

Mackenzie was committed to the Bloomingdale Asylum on December 29, 1883. On March 25, 1884, he was officially retired from the army. The retiring board concluded that Mackenzie's breakdown was the result of wounds and exposure incurred in his 20 plus years of military service, and that he was entitled to a full pension. Their basic diagnosis was that he was suffering from a severe case of what would become known as combat fatigue, or as it would be known today, post-traumatic stress disorder.

After his breakdown there was no more question of his getting married. Some authorities have questioned the legitimacy of Mackenzie's engagement to Florida Tunstall.[4] They have noted that there have been stories that Mackenzie may have been much more the pursued, rather than the pursuer. According to these stories Mackenzie's erstwhile fiancé may in fact have been taking advantage of his deteriorating mental condition.

There is also speculation that Mackenzie's descent into insanity may not have been caused by post-traumatic stress disorder or combat fatigue at all, but may have actually been due to syphilis.[5] Such a cause, at first glance, would seem to be out of character for Mackenzie. He did not have the reputation of being either a ladies man or personally sexually promiscuous like many of his military contemporaries, such as Hugh Judson Kilpatrick, for example. Mackenzie actually had the reputation of avoiding close personal relationships, considering them to be a distraction from his army career. It is, however, still possible (if not probable) that he could have become infected by a prostitute or through some illicit affair when he was younger, most likely while he was at college or while he was serving as a cadet at West Point.

Military physicians at West Point were well aware that cadets on their way to West Point or returning from furlough after completing their second year at the academy often arrived with venereal disease infections after being routed through New York City, where they were exposed to prostitutes. Certain of their biographers have speculated that both A.P. Hill and George A. Custer were so infected, probably with gonorrhea.

Other possible explanations could include a hereditary degenerative disease, dementia, collagen vascular disease, metabolic derangement, or peripheral vascular disease, accompanied by a stroke. Then again, the retiring board may have hit the nail exactly upon the head when they determined it was due to his wounds, long exposure to the elements, the head injuries he had suffered from the wagon accident in 1877, and even grief over the recent death of his mother.

There is also another possibility that at least one mental health professional has agreed is plausible, and that it could be very plausible. This explanation does not lie in combat fatigue, battle wounds, exposure, or physical illness. Rather, it has to do with Mackenzie's relationship with his father and his reactions to his father's quasi disgrace over the "*Somers* Affair" and his death at the age of 45.

Remember, Mackenzie was only eight years old when his father, Alexander Slidell Mackenzie, Sr., died. Even more important to be remembered is the fact that it was young Ranald who actually discovered his father's body. Therefore, as the oldest child and eldest son, it is not unusual that in order to vindicate his father's memory he chose to emulate his father and his disciplinary proclivities to such an extent that he was known to the soldiers of the 2nd Connecticut Heavy Artillery Regiment, his first command, as the "Perpetual Punisher." They hated him and his stern, harsh, and severe discipline to such a degree that some of the soldiers would plot to kill him the very first time they faced the Confederates in open battle under his command.

But in battle, the persona that he adopted to emulate his father and to vindicate his father's memory fell away and Ranald S. Mackenzie allowed his true self to emerge. He could smile and laugh at danger and inspire his soldiers to feats that they did not consider themselves capable of achieving. While he never cultivated popularity with the soldiers under his command, then or at any other time, they still accorded him their utmost respect as a fighting man among fighting men, and his soldiers, both volunteers and time-serving regulars, would gladly follow him anywhere. (The regulars recognized that while he was in charge their chances of surviving the Indian Wars were greatly increased.) Unlike Custer, Mackenzie would have no trouble at all adjusting to the peacetime army.

Custer—who despite his record at West Point became something of a martinet once he took command of the Michigan Cavalry Brigade—was loved, admired, and popular with the soldiers he led during the American Civil War, all well-motivated volunteers. They were there, fighting and dying, in the final analysis because they wanted to be there, realizing that they had a lot to lean about soldiering and that Custer's methods, although harsh, were the quickest way to obtain that teaching. After the American Civil War, the volunteers were replaced by long-serving regulars who were either immigrants or in the army because they had nowhere else to go, the army being the traditional employer of last resort. These men were not interested in glory or seeing their war through to the end but only in staying alive. Primarily for this reason Custer after the Civil War quickly went from being loved and admired to being hated by his soldiers.

Mackenzie, on the other hand, had never been worried about being popular in the first place, so he had no trouble at all adjusting to the changed conditions of the "peacetime" army.

In looking for the cause of Mackenzie's insanity, could it be that the conflict between his true nature and the persona he adopted due to his father's legacy, combined with the stress of combat, provides the best explanation of the personal calamity that ended his military career and clouded what remained of his life?

Ranald Slidell Mackenzie had only a few more years to live within the secluded shell that remained. In June 1884 he was released from the asylum and went to his boyhood home in Morristown, New Jersey, to live in the custody of his sister, Harriet. In 1886 he was moved to New Brighten, Staten Island, where he died and finally found some measure of peace.

29

Sheridan's Troubleshooter

Despite his eventual insanity, Mackenzie was the "man who proved the rule" and demonstrated the kind of military leadership that Philip H. Sheridan was seeking in his subordinates when in the final six months of the war he rejected William Woods Averell, Alfred Thomas Archimedes Torbert, and Gouverneur Kemble Warren to embrace Ranald Slidell Mackenzie.

After the war Mackenzie would go on to become one of the best, if not the best, frontier military officers and Indian fighters in the entire United States Army. However, George A. Custer, due to his dramatic death at the Battle of the Little Big Horn, would become the best known commander of the frontier regulars who confronted the Indians between the end of the American Civil War and the last engagement of the Indian Wars at the so-called Battle of Wounded Knee in 1890.

At the end of the American Civil War, Sheridan had one close friend, George C. Crook, whose friendship would eventually sour, and four protégés—Nelson A. Miles, George A. Custer, Wesley Merritt, and Ranald S. Mackenzie—who would lead the army in its final conquest of the Native Americans after over 250 years of almost constant warfare.

Crook would fail in perhaps his greatest test during the Great Sioux War at the Battle of the Rosebud only about a week prior to the Battle of the Little Big Horn. Although his casualties were relatively insignificant he would give up the campaign and go fishing, claiming that his soldiers had shot up all of their ammunition. Then there was Wesley Merritt, who maintained his Civil War reputation as always being extremely competent if so unflashy as to almost escape all notice whatsoever. Miles was Crook's great rival and was every bit as competent. However, when the situation was at its most desperate it was Mackenzie who was the man summoned to deal with the situation, whatever, or wherever, it may have been.

Another thing to remember about the great post–American Civil War Indian fighters—Crook, Miles, Merritt, Custer, and Mackenzie—was the fact that they were no more guilty of white oppression and genocide against the Indians than any other U.S. Army officers of their time. In addition, they were far less guilty than John Chivington (the Colorado volunteer and Methodist preacher who was not a regular army officer), who led the infamous Sand Creek massacre in 1864 against Indians who believed that they were under the protection of the United States government.

George C. Crook clearly saw the advantages that friendly Indian allies offered as auxiliaries in his campaigns against hostile Indians. He used Shoshonis against Paiutes in Oregon, 1866–1868; Pimas and Maricopas against Apaches in Arizona, 1872–1873; and Shoshonis and Crows against the Sioux, Northern Cheyenne, and Northern Arapaho in Wyoming and Montana, 1876–1877. Crook's allies usually fought under their own leaders and followed their own inclinations as often as the instructions of the white officers or scouts assigned to accompany them.

In addition to seeking allies from one tribe to fight another, Crook often turned to the very tribe against whom his current operations were directed.[1] The efficiency of this method lay not only in matching the Indians' special skills with those of other Indians, but also in the psychological impact of the hostile Indian finding his own people arrayed against him. In effect, Crook had become one of the earliest practitioners in the art of psychological warfare.

"To polish a diamond, there is nothing like its own dust," Crook said in explaining his methods to a reporter in 1866. "It is the same with these fellows. Nothing breaks them up like turning their own people against them. They don't fear the white soldiers, whom they easily surpass in the particular style of warfare which they force upon us, but put upon their trail an enemy of their own blood, as enemy as tireless, as foxy, and as stealthy and familiar with the country as they themselves and it breaks them all up. It is not merely a question of catching them better with Indians, but with a broader and more enduring aim — their disintegration." This strategy of divide and conquer was applied successfully by both Crook and Miles in the closing stages of the Great Sioux War in 1876–1877. It received its most intensive tests under Crook during the Apache Wars of the 1880s.

The exclusive or even major use of Indian allies to trail and fight other Indians carried with it some risk, since they were all more or less a kind of kinsmen of the people who were their targets. Good leadership could offset these risks; therefore, Crook choose his scout officers who commanded his irregular allies with great care. Young men of ambition, dedication, sensitivity, and, above all those, capable of a rapport with the Indians under their command were the best candidates. In effect, they were "Indian thinkers" rather than "Indian fighters."

Crook recognized that successful strategies against the various hostile Indian tribes or bands involved more than simple Indian fighting. He reduced it to four simple precepts as follows:

1. Make no promises that could not be kept.
2. Tell the truth, always.
3. Provide remunerated labor.
4. Be patient, be just, and fear not.

Few officers in the army and far fewer officials in the Indian Bureau actually possessed the necessary qualities to follow such a code. Crook himself — since he shared authority with civilian officials and reported to superiors who could overrule him — sometimes found that these two circumstances made it practically impossible to follow his own precepts.

The Paiute War launched Crook on a rapid rise to top rank among the U.S. Army's Indian-fighting commanders. On campaign he rarely wore a uniform, never indulging in military dash and ostentation. He was also quiet to the point of introspection, modest, unselfish, considerate, conscientious, yet he could also upon occasion (especially in his memoirs that he quietly put away and were therefore not published until well after his death) pronounce savage judgments on the character, motives, and actions of other officers (and this included his one-time close friend Philip H. Sheridan, along with his great rival, Nelson A. Miles). He possessed legendary stamina and endurance, along with the ability to meet the frontier on its own terms. He was also a student of nature, an avid hunter and fisherman (perhaps too much so), a crack shot, and an accomplished horseman (but for hard traveling he preferred a mule).

One of the reasons for Crook's success was that he studied Indians intensely. "He knew Indians better than the Indians did," claimed one aide. He shared one vital characteristic with Sheridan, when he was at war: he was as ruthless as he needed to be. But when he was at peace, he was paternalistic, humane, and solicitous when it came to his Indian allies and even to his one-time Indian foes. In fact, he became so obsessed with obtaining honest treatment for the Indians that it probably hurt his military career, particularly when his great rival, Miles, replaced him as the top field commander against the Apaches.

When he fought Indians he practiced the Indian-fighting adage of getting on a trail and staying on it until his quarry was cornered. He gave new emphasis to the techniques that became his hallmark as an Indian fighter — using Indians to fight Indians and relying on pack mules, rather than wagons, for field transportation. (However, he made sure that his mules were well trained and that his mule skinners knew what they were doing, something other officers seeking to emulate him, such as Custer in his last campaign, failed to do.) One gave him the skills he needed in Indian-style guerrilla warfare and the other gave him a mobility that was denied to those who were dependant upon mule or horse-drawn wagon trains.

Nelson A. Miles, at the end of the American Civil War, was a young and handsome military officer. He was also the proud bearer of a superb military record. He was teamed with an attractive and politically astute wife whose uncles were General William T. Sherman and his brother John, a U.S. senator from Ohio. Due to Miles naked ambition he was not well liked by most of his military contemporaries, the major exception being George A. Custer and his wife, Libbie. After the American Civil War Miles joined the ranks of the most successful Indian fighters in the U.S. Army.

His ambition, which was almost as unlimited in its ends as in its means, spurred Miles to solid achievements. That was the plus side. On the minus side it also drove him to disparage the achievements and the abilities of others, most especially those of George C. Crook. When he was forced to share the laurels with someone else it was usually done so with bad grace. In addition, he was not above exploiting any possible influence that could be brought to bear to advance his military career. His rank naked ambition was also colored by something of an inferiority complex due to his lack of a formal military education.

When the American Civil War began, Miles was nothing more than a Boston crockery clerk. But by the end of the American Civil War, through self-study, experience, and sheer raw military talent, he achieved the rank of major general, U.S. Volunteers, and corps command.

More than almost any other officer, Miles deserved the laurels and kudos for converting the disasters of the summer of 1876 into the achievements that drove Sitting Bull and his hostile Sioux across the border into Canada during the winter of 1876-1877 and resulted in the Sioux chieftain's final surrender at Fort Buford on July 19, 1881.

In part, his success against the Sioux and Northern Cheyenne had been due to the Tongue River Cantonment and Fort Keogh, both in Yellowstone country. This had given him a fixed base in the heart of Indian country, allowing him to keep his soldiers within a comparatively close striking range of the hostile Indians and greatly simplifying his logistical problems (a lesson that he had learned from his participation in the Red River War, where the Indians had managed, unintentionally, to sever his supply and communications lines), as well as undermining the morale and the resilience of the Indians.

An even larger factor in his success had been his own sheer ability. He was an excellent military commander. A *Chicago Times* correspondent, John F. Finerty, described him "as a splendid field soldier, prompt, bold, and magnetic ... always in high spirits, which is a good thing in a commanding officer. Miles was also energetic, innovative, imaginative, flexible in strategy and tactics, and inflexible in pursuit of his objectives."

Neither weather nor fatigue particularly bothered Miles (who was known among the Indians as "Bearcoat" for the way he dressed to protect himself against cold weather, and particularly since he was an expert at the winter campaign, a tactic of hunting down and hitting the Indians during the winter when they were at their most immobile and vulnerable). He also did not overestimate the capabilities of the hostile Northern Plains Indians who followed Sitting Bull and other leaders such as Crazy Horse, Gall, and Dull Knife. He pursued them until he eventually caused them to surrender. He did not let obstacles deter him.

Finally, he was an expert at applying infantry successfully against the Plains Indian tribes, who were called — for good reason — the finest light cavalry in the world. At times he would mount his infantry upon captured Indian ponies, at other times he would not bother with this particular military curlicue. At one point he even told Congress "infantry troops can walk down any band of Indians in the country in four months." In addition, like Crook, he also appreciated the benefits of Indian allies and used them extensively, although quietly.

Miles first came into prominence as an Indian fighter during the Red River War, leading one of five columns and carrying through to final victory without using unconventional methods that Crook so enjoyed. (In point of fact, Sheridan distrusted Indians and preferred not to make any use of them at all, which was why when Miles did use them he did it quietly, without any fanfare.) He employed sheer tenacity in scouring the plains through blizzards, sub-zero temperatures, and storms of all kinds.

Miles kept his soldiers out in the field constantly pushing against the hostiles, until one by one the scattered bands of fugitives were walked down and surrendered. It was this success in the Red River War that signaled the beginning of the end of the Indian Wars on the Southern Plains. It was the great rivalry between Miles and Crook that was to define the end of the Indian Wars between 1870 and 1890.

Miles was the champion grudge bearer of the entire army. Crook, on the other hand, had a tendency to think well of himself and poorly of others.[2] Crook maintained unfavorable opinions of his contemporaries in the army and he could certainly bear a grudge almost as long as Miles. Under Crook's placid exterior there was anger and resentment that began when he felt his services during the American Civil War had not been fully or completely appreciated.[3]

The feud between Crook and Miles was sparked by acclaim that was given Crook after his campaign against the Paiutes that resulted in Crook being assigned to command the Department of Arizona in his brevet grade of major general, although he was only a lieutenant colonel. Miles, a full colonel in command of the 5th Infantry at Fort Levenworth, Kansas, was miffed. After the American Civil War he commenced a single-minded campaign for fame and rank that caused him to flaunt his own genuine abilities while at the same time deriding those of others. He felt that if anyone should be assigned in his brevet rank it should be him. Miles complained about it constantly, especially when two years later he was denied command of the District of New Mexico at his own brevet rank of major general. Miles in his complaints appealed to his wife's uncles — William T. Sherman, then general-in-chief, and John Sherman, the U.S. senator — which, however, mainly tended to irritate them both.

Miles and Crook served together for the first time on the frontier during the Great Sioux War, and it was here that what had heretofore had been a minor rivalry turned into one of epic proportions. During the Centennial Campaign in 1876, Crook could do almost nothing right. A first thrust north from Fort Fetterman in March was turned back by the weather. Then there was a fight on the Powder River that was mismanaged by Crook's subordinates. Then came the three pronged thrust aimed at the Sioux, Northern Cheyenne, and Northern Arapaho. Crook commanded the largest of the three prongs, with the other two being under the command of then Brig. Gen. Alfred H. Terry (accompanied by Custer and his 7th Cavalry) and Col. John Gibbon.

On June 17, 1876, Crook was met by the Sioux under Crazy Horse in the Battle of the Rosebud. The Indians surprised Crook while his men were taking their morning coffee break and if it had not been for the quick reactions of his Shoshoni and Crow allies Crook's whole force might have been overwhelmed. (Crook was unfortunate in that he had also been surprised during the American Civil War at the Battle of Cedar Creek where his Army of West Virginia/VIII Corps almost immediately disintegrated.) During the fighting, Crook nearly lost control of his forces and afterwards, retreating back to his base, he refused to resume the offensive without heavy reinforcements and almost complete resupply. Terry, Gibbon, and Custer did not know that

Crook had quit the campaign until after the 7th Cavalry had been smashed and Custer killed at the Little Big Horn.

Miles and his 5th U.S. Infantry Regiment were among the reinforcements Sheridan rushed to the area. Terry, Crook and Miles rendezvoused on August 10, 1876, and Miles soon realized that Terry and Crook and their huge force of 4,000 men had practically no chance at all of catching up with the hostiles. Miles managed to get permission to operate independently and persevered his way to victory, while Terry and Crook both eventually gave up the campaign. (The only successes scored under Crook's command were actually achieved by Col. Wesley Merritt and his 5th Cavalry at War Bonnet Creek—which forced a powerful band of Northern Cheyenne to return to the reservation—and Col. Ranald S. Mackenzie and his 4th Cavalry when he destroyed the Northern Cheyenne village of Dull Knife, which eventually forced the capitulation of this band of hostile Indians.)

Miles hounded the hostiles throughout the autumn, winter, spring, and into the summer of 1877 and beyond (when the Great Sioux War segued practically without pause into the Nez Perce War). Miles went over both Crook's and Sheridan's heads, appealing to Sherman, seeking to have himself named supreme commander against the hostiles. He became extremely upset when Crook sent emissaries to convince most of the hostiles to surrender to him. There were a few who surrendered to Miles and the rest slipped over the Canadian border with Sitting Bull. What had before had been a relatively mild jockeying between Miles and Crook had now become personal.

The feud revived in Arizona during the 1880s when both Crook and Miles turned their hands to reining in the rampaging Apaches. Crook and his former friend, Sheridan (who had succeeded the retired Sherman in Washington), forever ended their friendship when the Apache, Geronimo, whom Crook had persuaded to surrender, jumped the reservation in 1886 and went on a rampage.

Sheridan distrusted the Indians whom Crook had been using as scouts and wanted army regulars to be used instead to bring in Geronimo. Sheridan ordered Crook to repudiate promises made to those Apaches who had remained on the reservation and to demand unconditional surrender from Geronimo. When Crook in response asked to be relieved, Sheridan replaced him with Miles.

When his own methods failed, Miles began to make use of Apache scouts himself, although he did not advertise that fact. In addition, he deported to Florida all of the Chiricahua and Warm Springs Apaches on the San Carlos Reservation in Arizona. When Geronimo was informed of what Miles had done, he surrendered.

In 1888 Crook and Miles were both being considered for a promotion to major general due to the retirement of Alfred H. Terry. President Grover Cleveland followed the rule of seniority, despite Miles' lobbying, and gave the promotion to Crook. In 1890 Crook suffered a heart attack and died. Miles again sought the promotion and when it was resisted he blamed Crook's friends and rushed to Washington, where he personally won over President Benjamin Harrison and received the promotion.

Thus it was Miles who brought the Indian Wars to an end when he succeeded in forcing the surrender of the Ghost Dancers after the tremendously one-sided so-called Battle of Wounded Knee, a confrontation that Miles, as a matter of fact, had tried (without success) to avoid. What the feud did was to highlight the vanity, pettiness, disdain for peers, hunger for applause, and obsession with rank that most eloquently epitomized all that was wrong with the Frontier Regulars.[4]

George Armstrong Custer was relatively tall, slight of build, with reddish-blonde hair habitually worn rather long, and a walrus mustache (and sometimes a goatee). During the American Civil War he had risen to fame as a hard-hitting cavalry commander. A brigadier general and a brevet-major general of volunteers in command of his own cavalry division at the age of 25, after the American Civil War he had been made a lieutenant colonel and was given effective command of the 7th U.S. Cavalry Regiment, since the colonel who was officially in command of the regiment was usually on staff assignment elsewhere. (This colonel, Samuel D. Sturgis, demonstrated his own ineptitude in Indian fighting in the immediate aftermath of the Battle of the Little Big Horn and during his involvement in the Nez Perce War in 1877.)

Custer's first experience against hostile Plains Indians had been with the 1867 Hancock Expedition. In 1868 he proved the effectiveness of Sheridan's winter campaign strategy and tactics during his successful attack upon Black Kettle's Cheyenne at the Battle of the Washita. (Although Black Kettle himself was a peace chief and had been the victim of Col. Chivington at Sand Creek in 1864, Custer had followed the trail of a Cheyenne war band that led through Black Kettle's village. In addition, evidence was found in the ruins of the village after the battle that indicated that Black Kettle's warriors were not nearly as peaceful as their chief.)

Eight years after that, Custer and five companies of his 7th Cavalry would be wiped out at the Little Big Horn. After that he would be remembered as famous or infamous, and idolized or abominated. No one, not even his biographers and other historians, has ever really been neutral about George Armstrong Custer. But could Custer really be called an effective Indian fighter?

Despite a brilliant Civil War record, Custer's tenure as an Indian fighter could only be called "erratic." Only towards the end of his career — just before the Little Big Horn, ironically — did Custer begin to understand the special demands of Indian warfare and understand Indian combat strategy.

One problem with any study of the life and career of George Armstrong Custer has been the fact that he was always a polarizing personality. His contemporaries, biographers, and American Civil War and frontier historians either loved him or hated him; there was no middle ground. But, perhaps now, about 130 years after his death, a middle ground can be found in the divide between the Custer of the American Civil War and the Custer of the Indians Wars that followed it.

George Armstrong Custer and the American Civil War were made for each other. After all, historian S.L.A. Marshall hit the nail squarely upon the head, for all the wrong reasons, when he wrote, "If there is anything truly heroic about Custer it must be read in the Civil War." A.T.A. Torbert's biographer, A.D. Slade, noted that Custer's fighting style was exactly what Sheridan liked to see in his subordinates. However, Custer's record as an Indian fighter leaves much to be desired. When he began this new career in 1867 he knew next to nothing about Indians and they proceeded to lead him by the nose so badly — that combined with his inability to cope with the difference between the wartime army and the peacetime army — it may have resulted in something of a breakdown that in turn led to a court-martial.

When he returned to the frontier, after his sentence of one year's suspension without pay (that was itself suspended through the behind the scenes action of Phil Sheridan), he had recovered his equilibrium and won the Battle of the Washita. At the Battle of the Little Big Horn there can be no denying that he personally made a number of crucial decisions and tactical mistakes that eventually led to his own personal destruction and the defeat and decimation of his regiment. However, it has also been shown by modern scholarship that he was not the only one who made "mistakes," if not outright blunders, during that failed campaign.

In addition, at least one historian has maintained that, given what Custer knew or could anticipate at each of the decisive points during his approach to the Little Big Horn battlefield and during the fighting itself, an objective observer would be hard pressed to determine what Custer ought to have done differently.[5] The biggest problem was that everyone, from Phil Sheridan, to George Crook, to John Gibbon, to Alfred Terry, to Custer himself, was almost entirely concerned with how to catch the Indians, not with how to actually fight them.

However, Custer committed one blunder that Mackenzie throughout his career studiously avoided. On the very eve of the Centennial Campaign of 1876 Custer allowed himself, for all the right reasons, to become distracted by politics—not in the sense that he was seeking to become president, which was out and out utter hogwash, but rather in the sense of being a whistle-blower who, in the end, was taken advantage of by the professional politicians. This was when Custer involved himself in one of the endemic scandals of the presidential administration of U.S. Grant. This concerned the Indian Ring, which was behind both the systematic mistreatment of Indians on the reservation and corruption involving the sale of post traderships (the precursor of the modern PX or post exchange system) at the various forts that dotted the frontier.

Custer involved himself in an undercover investigation that helped unveil the involvement of Grant's secretary of war (Belknap) and Grant's own brother in the scandal, Belknap for taking bribes and Orville Grant for acting as the "bagman" for the entire operation. Custer was summoned away from his preparations for what would become the Centennial Campaign—against the Sioux, Northern Cheyenne, and Northern Arapaho—in order to testify before Congress, which found that the bulk of his testimony was hearsay and therefore inadmissible in a court of law. This in turn brought the wrath of Grant squarely upon Custer's head at a time when Custer should have been preparing for his part in the Centennial Campaign being planned for the late spring and early summer.

Custer himself was a lifelong Democrat, and he was like a babe in the woods when it came to politics. He provided a perfect tailor-made opportunity to embarrass the Republican president of the United States and his administration, which the professional Democratic politicians who quickly surrounded Custer took full advantage of—a situation not too much different from the political shenanigans that can be found amongst professional politicians of all stripes today.

As a result, Custer lost command of one of the three prongs of the campaign and almost lost tactical command of his regiment, the 7th Cavalry. Time that Custer should have been devoting to getting the 7th Cavalry ready for this campaign was instead spent in testifying before Congress and later in trying to salvage his military career in the face of what can only be described as Grant's retaliation.

One result was that Custer's 7th Cavalry went into action with a number of recruits who barely knew how to ride a horse or fire their guns. In addition, over 100 soldiers of the 7th Cavalry did not participate in the battle for the simple reason that a totally inadequate number of remounts were made available as the regiment was preparing for the campaign. Truly this resulted in the 7th Cavalry going out on campaign with at least one hand tied quite firmly behind its back. If Custer and the other officers of the 7th Cavalry had not been distracted then perhaps these problems could have, like they should have, been corrected before the 7th Cavalry ever hit the campaign trail.

Wesley Merritt, who had risen to command of the Cavalry Corps, Army of the Potomac, directly under Phil Sheridan, was a man who did the job that he was given, no matter what. One of Merritt's problems as an Indian fighter may have been that he was simply rarely given the opportunity to shine in this role. A case in point would be just about his only major Indian encounter, the Battle of War Bonnet Creek, an almost bloodless affair that became famous due to the spectacular participation of that notorious frontier scout and western showman—one William F. "Buffalo Bill" Cody. (He and a certain James Butler "Wild Bill" Hickok had once scouted for Custer and as a frontier scout Cody received the honorary title of colonel since he was paid at the same rate as a colonel.)

As soon as Cody learned about the Battle of the Little Big Horn, he abandoned the Eastern stage (where he had been making his living since 1872) and joined the 5th U.S. Cavalry Regiment. Crook had summoned the regiment, of which Merritt had just assumed command, as soon as he had learned about the Battle of the Little Big Horn and Custer's death.

The Battle of War Bonnet Creek occurred when Merritt delayed his march to join Crook when he learned that 800 Northern Cheyenne warriors, led by a chief named Little Wolf, had left the Red Cloud Agency and were on their way to the Powder River country to join Sitting Bull. The 5th Cavalry was scouting the rolling hills along War Bonnet Creek, Nebraska, on July 17, 1876, when an advance party of Little Wolf's Northern Cheyenne on their way to join Sitting Bull collided with a group of soldiers being guided by Cody. At the time, Cody, instead of wearing a normal frontier scout's buckskin suit, was actually wearing (believe it or not) one of his theatrical costumes, a Mexican vaquero outfit of black velvet trimmed with silver buttons and lace. During the resulting skirmish Cody, in a personal demonstration of machismo, brought down in man-to-man combat the only casualty to be suffered by either side in the entire affair, a Northern Cheyenne warrior known by the ironic name of Yellow Hair (which name possibly came from one of the scalps taken by this particular Indian). Cody lifted the Indian's scalp, proclaiming that he had won the "the first scalp for Custer" and promptly returned with it back to the Eastern stage. It was not long before Cody was re-creating the Battle of the Little Big Horn in his Wild West Show.

After Cody's skirmish, Merritt and the 5th Cavalry then chased the rest of the Indians back to the Red Cloud Agency, despite Crook's irritation with Merritt for him at being late and even though Merritt had achieved one of the few out and out victories thus far in the entire campaign. (Crook may have also been getting even with Merritt due to jealousy over the fact that during the last campaign of the Army of the Potomac Merritt had been his direct superior as commander of the Cavalry Corps, Army of the Potomac.) Merritt and his 5th Cavalry also participated in the Nez Perce War in 1877, and against the Utes in Colorado in 1879. (This was the uprising that was finally terminated by Mackenzie when he delivered the dramatic ultimatum to the Ute chiefs that caused them to leave Colorado for a reservation in Utah.)

Like Custer, Merritt and the American Civil War had been made for each other. Merritt rose in rank from second lieutenant to brevet major general of volunteers and corps command.[6] One staff officer described him at that time as "tall, slender, and intellectual-looking. He had a constitution of iron, and underneath a rather passive demeanor a rather fiery ambition." But Merritt found little real chance to shine during the Indian Wars. He simply was like the vast majority of the officers during this period in the history of the United States Army in that he did his job, more or less ignored by the rest of the country, to the best of his ability.

Ranald Slidell Mackenzie remained "the most promising young officer in the army." His Indian fighting career really took fire in 1871 when he and his 4th U.S. Cavalry Regiment were assigned to Fort Richardson in Texas. Before that, the job of keeping the Indians under control in Texas had been in the lackluster hands of officers more concerned with enforcing Reconstruction than in actually fighting Indians and defending the frontier.

Mackenzie did not concern himself with Reconstruction. He was there to keep the Indians contained. At this time Mackenzie was just 31 and as one of the "boy generals" he also could boast, although he most definitely wasn't into boasting, of a brilliant record during the American Civil War, particularly in the Shenandoah Valley with Sheridan and at Five Forks and the final campaign that led to Robert E. Lee's surrender at Appomattox. At this time in both his life and his army career he was tireless, high-strung, irascible from wounds and exposure, and that severe head injury suffered in a fall from a wagon. In addition, he was always a harsh disciplinarian, the "Perpetual Punisher," well honing his 4th Cavalry into the best cavalry regiment in the army, and that included Custer's 7th Cavalry.

In the opposite way from when it could be said during the American Civil War that Hugh Judson Kilpatrick was everything George Armstrong Custer was ever accused of being and was not, it could also be said that Mackenzie and his elite 4th Cavalry were everything that Custer and his veteran 7th Cavalry were supposed to be and in actuality were not.

Custer's 7th Cavalry — although a veteran regiment, having served on the frontier since its creation in 1866 — was not a tightly knit regiment.[7] The 7th Cavalry's officer corps was divided. There was a solid core of officers who were Custer loyalists — such as Custer's brother, Thomas W. Custer, and his brother-in-law, James Calhoun, as well as a number of officers who had served with him during the American Civil War.

However, Custer's two senior subordinates, Maj. Marcus A. Reno and Capt. Frederick W. Benteen, detested him and each other. Reno, who during the American Civil War had been Torbert's chief of staff, enjoyed little respect, was socially inept, and considered weak as both an officer and a man.[8] There has also been much debate about whether or not Reno was an alcoholic and whether or not he was actually drunk during the Battle of the Little Big Horn. (There are some historians who disagree with this assessment, noting that a significant change had occurred in Reno's personality after the death of his wife.) Benteen, however, was a first-rate combat officer who was also a sour, crotchety troublemaker and both originated and circulated the vilest rumors he could imagine against Custer, his commanding officer.

It was Benteen who accused Custer of being a hypocrite, concealing his own brand of frontier fraud, while pretending on the other hand to be crusading against the Indian Ring scandal. Benteen also spread rumors that Custer's supposedly idyllic marriage with his wife, Libbie, nevertheless tolerated infidelity, on both sides.

He spread rumors that Custer had impregnated an Indian squaw who was his prisoner, that Custer had an affair with his colored cook, and that Libbie Custer and Capt. Thomas Weir had also had an affair and that Custer knew about it. Benteen spread the Libbie Custer/Thomas Weir rumor just before Weir died at a time that Weir was seeking a meeting with Libbie Custer (that never occurred due to his death) because he claimed to have had information about what happened at the Little Big Horn that led to her husband's death and he wanted her to know about it.

Concerning the large numbers of recruits and dismounted men within the 7th Cavalry before it left Fort Abraham Lincoln on it way to the Little Big Horn, Mackenzie, the "Perpetual Punisher," would never have allowed such a situation to develop in the first place and would not have tolerated it in the second.

Mackenzie was a believer in training. Before he took his troops into battle they were as ready as they possibly could be. He made sure that his soldiers knew how to ride, how to shoot, and how to survive. Before going on campaign he made sure that his troops were given specialized training to prepare them for whatever they faced in a particular campaign. As noted before, Mackenzie may not have been loved, and he certainly never sought the adulation of his soldiers, but they recognized that they had a better chance of coming back alive with him in command, so they utterly respected him.

Mackenzie has to be considered the best of the Indian fighters in the post–American Civil War army for one simple reason. He did the job, and he did it superbly. There were no disasters like the Little Big Horn, or anything more than an occasional mild setback. There were no aberrations like Crook after the Battle of the Rosebud, quitting an entire campaign and going fishing. There were also no great rivalries — like that between Crook and Miles — to get in the way of the job. Finally, Mackenzie kept his ambition strictly under control, being in fact more than willing to let his actions speak for him.

If Mackenzie had a fault it lay in what was oftentimes a simple failure to communicate with his superiors. It was something that was shared by a lot of highly competent combat commanders, a severe dislike of paperwork. As noted by historian James L. Haley, "It was Mackenzie's 'style' when given an assignment, to perform it in a magnificent manner, but in return he expected his commanders to trust in his capacity, without him being required to waste time on progress reports. Unfortunately, while no one doubted Mackenzie's ability to deliver, the lines of communications even at their best were so poor that the high command had only the vaguest and belated notion of what was transpiring in the field. Mackenzie's 'notorious' silences, therefore, if they did not create administrative chaos, certainly did nothing to alleviate the nerve-wracking infrequency of [his] field reports."[9]

Unlike Merritt and Custer, who were born for the American Civil War, Mackenzie was actually born for the Indians Wars. Although he too had a brilliant American Civil War record he was handicapped by the fact that he entered the war a year later than Merritt and Custer did and he did not have the time to rise as high as they did — Custer in the popular imagination and Merritt in reaching one of the highest levels of command, that of corps command.

In the end, he could best be described simply as Sheridan's troubleshooter. If anyone wanted to know just where the army's biggest headaches with the Indians were they could just check out Mackenzie's location. Chances were that he would be right in the middle of the problem, whatever it was, wherever it was— simply dealing with it.

Epilogue: The Method Behind Sheridan's Madness

When you compare the men who Philip H. Sheridan sacked during the final six months of the American Civil War—William W. Averell, Alfred T.A. Torbert, and Gouverneur K. Warren—to The Man Who Proved the Rule, Ranald S. Mackenzie, the contrast between them and what Sheridan was looking for in his subordinates becomes evident.

What Sheridan wanted were subordinates who could take his orders and, using their own initiative, build upon them and even go beyond them if circumstances and conditions dictated it. Sheridan, for one, realized that initiative was needed to blow away the fog of war. This was why Sheridan was generally willing to overlook anything up to and including disregarding and disobeying orders—if it succeeded in bringing about victory.

Sheridan's wrath was formidable with those who failed (or were perceived to have failed) to perform their duty, or even failed (or were perceived to have failed) to display Sheridan's zeal for combat. It was in these areas that Averell, Torbert, and Warren were all found wanting. For example, his treatment of Warren, the Gettysburg hero, was unmerciful. Warren's personal sins were to be perceived by Sheridan to have been moving his soldiers into position too slowly and displaying a quiet calm in the face of the enemy, which the much more excitable Sheridan considered to be nothing other than apathy. In Warren's case, it was not apathy, but merely the outward manifestation of his personal style of command, which was to quietly and quite calmly maintain control of his own head while everyone around him, including Sheridan, were in the process of losing theirs.

Averell, Torbert, and Warren, each of them in their own ways—and within their own individual limitations, could be an effective commander. Averell, Torbert and Warren all failed, or were perceived to have failed, in one way or another, to rise to the higher standard that Sheridan required of his subordinates. Mackenzie, on the other hand, demonstrated that he could and did rise to the level of performance that Sheridan demanded.

Averell was a superb commander of independent units, a raider. Today he would probably be considered a marvelous leader of Special Forces. His primary flaw was that he was inhibited when he had to operate under the direct eye of a superior officer. Much of the time, Averell's superiors had a tendency to confuse him. In such situations he was unable to trust his own initiative and as a result went by the book and refused to take chances. Under a superior's eye he had a tendency to play it safe. Where Mackenzie used audacity to place opponents off balance, Averell, when in doubt, stuck to the tried and true, and if his orders did not cover a situation or, as they often did, they confused him, then he simply was not able to rise to the occasion.

The editors of Averell's memoirs (which do not cover either the Chancellorsville Campaign or Sheridan's Shenandoah Valley Campaign of 1864, two of the most important incidents in his entire American Civil War career) noted, "William Averell was not a failure during the

Civil War; he was a victim of change. He was just what the army needed early in the conflict—disciplined, capable and cautious. He took untrained horsemen and molded them into a cavalry force of which any commander could be proud."

When he had no superior around to confuse him, and when he was in the mountains where communications with superiors were even more difficult and they therefore had little or no opportunity to go about confusing him from a distance with that marvelous new tool of the military micromanager, the telegraph, that was where he shined.

Therefore, in the aftermath of the Battle of Fisher's Hill, Sheridan must be faulted because he did not give Averell a clear understanding about what he wanted Averell to accomplish. He assumed that Averell would use his initiative when the opportunity arose to pursue Early's fleeing army. The problem was that Averell could only employ his initiative when he was away from the eye of a superior.

It is unknown how he would have fared if Sheridan had followed normal army procedure and named Averell to be his chief of cavalry instead of Torbert, since Averell was senior to Torbert. It is also possible that if Averell and not Torbert had led the attempt to get around Confederate Lt. Gen. Jubal Early's Valley District Army in the Luray Valley he would not have allowed an inferior enemy — whom he outnumbered at least two-to-one — to best him as Torbert had done. Who knows what the effect on the war might have been if Sheridan had destroyed Early's army at New Market Gap, as he had originally planned.

As it was, the aftermath of the Battle of Fisher's Hill became something of a failed dress rehearsal to the aftermath of the Battle of Five Forks, which led directly to Appomattox Court House and the final surrender of General Robert E. Lee and his Army of Northern Virginia. It was Torbert's failure in the Luray Valley that earned for him his first big, black, mark in Sheridan's personal ledger.

Torbert was a fine brigade and reasonably competent divisional commander. His flaw was the exact opposite of Averell's. First he was overwhelmed by corps command and he did not really have the ability, or maybe simply the initiative, or the combination of moral courage and audacity needed to successfully operate independently. Torbert excelled as a subordinate directly under his chief's eye. What he needed was at least a basic understanding of exactly what was expected of him. Who knows what might have happened in the aftermath of Fisher's Hill if he and Averell had changed places.

With Sheridan in close proximity and with subordinates like Wesley Merritt, George A. Custer, Thomas Devin, and Charles Russell Lowell urging him on, Torbert could well have pursued Early's beaten army, as he did in the aftermath of both the Third Battle of Winchester/Opequon Creek and the Battle of Cedar Creek. However, once he was out from under Sheridan's watchful eye and acting under what he perceived to be Sheridan's intentions he could still be at a loss as to how to precede, as he was just prior to the Battle of Tom's Brook, where his lack of action earned him a second big black mark as far as Sheridan was concerned. The third and final big black mark occurred during the failed Gordonsville Raid in December 1864; after that Torbert's days were numbered.

It's possible the Gordonsville Raid may have been more of a final test of Torbert than anything else. Sheridan well realized that the possibilities for a successful raid, given the weather conditions—the worst winter to hit the Shenandoah Valley in a generation, were slim. Sheridan may have been considering getting rid of Torbert ever since Fisher's Hill or Tom's Brook. Sheridan knew that the coming spring campaigning season could very well bring with it the deathblow to the Confederacy. Therefore, Sheridan may have wanted to clear away what he saw as Torbert's dead wood. But, he would first give Torbert one final chance to redeem himself. Thus, when the raid failed and when Sheridan rode out of his final winter camp, Torbert, who arrived back from furlough a day later, no longer rode with him.

Warren was a different kettle of fish entirely, for he demonstrated in 1862 and 1863 that he had the spark that Sheridan wanted, the initiative to take action without orders or prodding from higher authority. However, by 1865 Warren had mostly lost it due to the stress of corps command compounded by the effect the casualties suffered by the troops of II Corps and later V Corps had upon him. His feeling that the lives of his men were being thrown away by Grant first sparked and then aggravated their clash of personalities, which in turn caused Grant to go from considering him as a possible replacement for Meade, should that be required, to the decision that he should be removed from his command, a decision that Grant did not follow through with himself but left to Sheridan's discretion.

Warren's fits of passion — whether they were due to anger at what he saw as the waste of his soldiers' lives or despair in watching them die — his irritability, his irascibility were all symptoms that he may have been suffering from combat fatigue, or post-traumatic stress disorder. After what he went through during the Overland Campaign, 56 solid days of battle piled upon battle such as the Wilderness, Spotsylvania, Cold Harbor, and then to top it all off the Siege of Petersburg and the Battle of the Crater, it is no wonder that he was showing signs of combat fatigue. It would have been much better for Grant to have relieved Warren earlier and to have placed him in a job where he could have used his considerable engineering talents away from combat.

Major General Philip H. Sheridan, U.S. Army. By the end of the American Civil War, Sheridan had earned for himself the title bestowed upon him by historian Paul A. Hutton — Paladin of the Republic (Library of Congress).

That is exactly what Sheridan did when he kicked Torbert upstairs to take over what was left of the Middle Military Division when Sheridan moved out to rejoin Grant for the final campaign of the Army of the Potomac. In the case of Averell and Warren, Sheridan had clear mandates from Grant for the removal of both officers. In the case of Torbert there was no such mandate, so Sheridan, once he decided to get rid of Torbert, acted with circumspection.

Therefore, in the end it is clear that Sheridan did not relieve Averell or Warren merely out of spitefulness. First, Grant (for a variety of reasons) had already given him the authority to do so, without Sheridan asking or seeking it (especially in the case of Warren). Secondly, Sheridan, in the final analysis, removed both Averell and Warren because they did not display the same consuming aggressiveness that Sheridan felt, the same lust to be in at the kill when Sheridan could sense that the kill was approaching fast.

Here was the military aspect of Sheridan's temper and even cruelty, an overwhelming thirst for combat and a relentless determination to drive his enemy into the ground, which suggests that the very qualities that made Sheridan an unamiable, if not a totally obnoxious man also tended to have made him a general one cannot help but respect, however, grudgingly though that respect may be tendered.

If there was one quality that the Army of the Potomac, so often suspicious of Sheridan, most conspicuously lacked, it was the instinct for the kill, the reflex to batter a wavering enemy without mercy until he succumbed. If there was one quality that Sheridan exhibited above all the other Union generals of the war, it was that same killer's instinct. From first to last, the conspicuous central feature of Phil Sheridan's generalship was his ruthless aggressiveness. Sheridan never sought to simply defeat his opponents; he aimed at their total annihilation and destruction.

The major irony of Warren's disagreements with Grant stemmed from the fact that in their opposing positions on how the war should be fought they were both right. Grant after all did have the resources to win a war of attrition. However, Warren was right in that their own casualties should not be disregarded but reduced as much as possible. Due to the casualties among the Army of the Potomac's low and mid level leadership (as much as William F. Smith's great blunder), when it came time for decisive action, when the Army of the Potomac reached Petersburg and could have taken the town and won the war with hardly any effort at all, Grant pushed the button and nothing happened.

The same thing had happened by this time to Lee's Army of Northern Virginia. Practically none of Lee's victories from the Seven Days' in 1862 and Chancellorsville in 1863 came without great cost (with the exception of Fredericksburg, which was due mostly to Ambrose E. Burnside's incompetence and obstinacy). Then came the Battle of Gettysburg, which bled both the Confederate officer corps and the rank and file white. The Army of Northern Virginia was never quite the same afterwards, although it would remain an incredibly resourceful foe. Starting with the Battle of Spotsylvania it would fight whenever possible from behind fieldworks for the remainder of the war. The reason was that it could no longer maneuver in the open against the sheer power that Ulysses S. Grant could muster against it.

It was now that Sheridan came to the fore and his killer's instinct became invaluable to Grant. And in this area Grant gave Sheridan his complete and wholehearted support, even in the face of what can only be described as Sheridan's own insubordination.

Sylvanus Cadwallader, a newspaper correspondent who traveled with Grant's headquarters during the final year of the war, may have best described the relationship between Grant and Sheridan. "It is well known to Grant's intimates," Cadwallader said, "that he considered Sheridan incomparably to be the greatest general our Civil War produced. Other generals might be equally good under ordinary circumstances under the eyes of an able superior commander, and up to a point of a given or limited number of men. Sheridan, he [Grant] believed could be more safely trusted with an independent army than any of them; and he often said in private confidential conversation that no army would ever be raised on this continent so large that Sheridan could not competently command it."

For instance, Meade and Sheridan clashed almost immediately. Sheridan believed that the proper role of the Union cavalry was to operate as an autonomous command, acting under general orders, to oppose the Confederate cavalry. Meade, on the other hand, had a more traditional view of his cavalry. A.D. Slade, Torbert's biographer, noted that the accepted practice in the Army of the Potomac was based on Winfield Scott's premise at the beginning of the war that the cavalry would not have much of a role, particularly in the Napoleonic sense. Therefore, Meade (like McClellan, Pope, and Burnside before him, but generally not Hooker) had scattered it to guard baggage and supply trains, picket outposts, and patrol his army's communications. Sheridan considered this to be a waste of good cavalry and he knew that the Confederates had taken cavalry tactics one step further, at least in the related reconnaissance and raiding role. Sheridan was determined to emulate Confederate practice and do them one step better through the use of a combined arms approach. Meade was also particularly upset because he believed that Sheridan, shanty Irishman, westerner, and non-gentleman that he was, had violated certain rules of behavior in his protests.

In fact, when Meade protested Sheridan's attitude to Grant concerning the proper role of the cavalry, Grant backed Sheridan, unloosing his Cavalry Corps on a raid aimed at Richmond, but which in fact mainly targeted J.E.B. Stuart and his Confederate cavalry of the Army of Northern Virginia. Grant saw Sheridan's demands as part of a shared understanding of the goals of Grant's Overland Campaign. This marked the beginning of Meade's eclipse and the rise of Sheridan to what eventually amounted to co-equal status with Meade.

It also encouraged Sheridan in what was his greatest flaw as a general: his tendency towards insubordination, which he would most clearly demonstrate in the Shenandoah Valley when it came to directives or suggestions from Grant that he did not want to accept. This was particularly demonstrated whenever Grant brought up the subject of raiding the Virginia Central Railroad and then going off to join Sherman. Sheridan resisted that idea until he finally got his way. What Sheridan wanted, what Sheridan demanded, was to be in at the kill, to be the spearhead that would finally slay the dragon: Robert E. Lee and his Army of Northern Virginia.

Eric Wittenberg, a modern historian who has both studied and written about the evolution of the Union cavalry in the American Civil War, has often wondered why Grant chose to overlook and ignore Sheridan's insubordination. One possible reason may have been that Grant realized that out of all of the generals in the Union army only William T. Sherman and Sheridan fully shared Grant's vision about how the war could best be brought to an end. Therefore, because they shared this vision, Grant was willing to overlook and ignore quite a bit.

As Sherman put it, "I stood by Grant when he was drunk and Grant stood by me when I was crazy and now we both stand together." By the time Sheridan was sent to the Shenandoah Valley, he and Grant also stood together. When Grant gave Sheridan the authority to relieve Warren, American Civil War historian Bruce Catton pointed out, Grant's explanation of why he had done so was vague, to say the least. But Catton believed that what Grant was apparently trying to do was ram home the solution he had finally reached to resolve what was the greatest single command problem that had plagued the Army of the Potomac since its birth.

Time and again the Army of the Potomac had missed opportunities for victory because someone did not move fast enough, or strike with all of their strength, or came into action in a way other than they were expected to do. What Grant was aiming at was the sluggishness and excessive caution that kept happening, at some critical moment, somewhere within the army's chain of command. At Five Forks — with the time for decisive decision so clearly at hand — Grant gave Sheridan as many troops as he needed and also gave him a clear signal that he would be supported in whatever he chose to do to deal with the army's fatal flaw in order to make it absolutely certain that at this critical junction it would not rear its head again.

"This was the first time in the history of the Army of the Potomac," Catton noted, "that a ranking commander had been summarily fired for going into action tardily and inexpertly. Sheridan had been cruel and unjust — and if that cruel and unjust insistence on driving, aggressive, promptness had been the rule in this army from the beginning, the war probably would have been won two years earlier...."

Certain of Sheridan's other faults can be seen in his relationship with two of his chief subordinates. First, there is the question of Sheridan's treatment of the man who had been one of his closest friends but who had never been his protégé, George C. Crook. Crook and Sheridan had been classmates at West Point, although Crook graduated a year before Sheridan due to Sheridan's suspension after he attacked an upperclassman. The friendship became strained after Sheridan declined to share credit, in Crook's opinion, for the victories at the Third Battle of Winchester/Opequon Creek and Fisher's Hill. Crook's command had helped bring victory at Winchester when Sheridan's own battle plan was in danger of complete collapse. Furthermore, the plan that Sheridan had adopted at Fisher's Hill had been Crook's own brainstorm and in addition Crook had personally overseen its successful execution.

Sheridan and Crook's relationship may also have been affected by Crook's jealousy of George A. Custer in the aftermath of the Battle of Saylor's Creek while Crook was in command of the Second Cavalry Division after the resignation of Maj. Gen. David McMurtie Gregg. According to Crook, Custer hogged the credit for cutting off and destroying about a third of Lee's remaining strength at Saylor's Creek. In actuality there should have been enough credit to go around for both generals since they both performed superbly. Custer, like Mackenzie, Wesley Merritt, Nelson A. Miles, and Crook himself, used his initiative to take immediate action without referring everything to higher headquarters and taking the chance that a fleeting opportunity might be lost.

Second, there was what can only be referred to as the strange case of General David McMurtie Gregg. Gregg had been part of the Cavalry Corps, Army of the Potomac, since it was first formed by Joseph Hooker. He had commanded his cavalry division under George Stoneman, Alfred Pleasonton, and Sheridan. Then suddenly he resigned his commission, on January 21, 1865, and it was accepted on February 2. Gregg then went home to Pennsylvania.

Gregg's professed reasons for his resignation were the press of private duties and business. Gregg's own son apparently felt that his father's resignation was something of a puzzle and maybe even an embarrassment when he wrote, "As General Gregg himself felt there was no necessity for offering an explanation in regard to his resignation, it appears more gracious to make no effort to hunt for reasons, other than those given in the resignation itself." James H. Wilson, who for a time also commanded a division in the Cavalry Corps, noted that whether the resignation had been "due to pique or to disappointment, he was always too proud to explain."

The timing of the resignation, however, may point to a reason. It occurred just when the effective conclusion of Sheridan's Shenandoah Valley Campaign of 1864 made it likely that Sheridan would soon be returning to the Army of the Potomac and that Gregg, rather then being commander of the cavalry with the Army of the Potomac, would once again find himself under Sheridan's command.

Although Gregg had performed well under Sheridan's command at Yellow Tavern, where he made the decisive final attack against the Confederate rear, and at Trevilian Station, Haw's Shop, and Cold Harbor, he was not and never had been one of Sheridan's favorites. Another factor could have been jealousy, since, for a brief time, Gregg as the senior officer present had commanded the Cavalry Corps between the relief of Pleasonton and the advent of Sheridan.

In addition, Gregg might have recognized that the differences between him and Sheridan precluded their working harmoniously together, for Sheridan valued audacity and he could be harsh in dealing with those who—in his opinion—did not demonstrate enough of it, like Averell, Torbert, and Warren. Gregg himself was not always as audacious as he appeared to be when, during the Battle of Gettysburg on July 3, 1863, he retained Custer's brigade, on his own authority, so that he could stop Stuart and his cavalry when they attempted to turn the Union right flank while the climax of Pickett's charge was occurring at the center of the Union line (although there have been historians who have speculated that Gregg retained Custer in an effort to have a scapegoat on hand if one was needed, one too junior to really protest when Gregg attempted to claim the lion's share of the credit for turning back Stuart).[1]

Wilson also, while praising Gregg generally, noted that he was "somewhat lacking in enthusiasm and perhaps in aggressive temper." Here Wilson may have simply noted that Gregg was less audacious and less ruthless than Sheridan. Where Sheridan was one of those who waged total war, as demonstrated in the Shenandoah Valley and then during the Indian Wars, Gregg from first to last was an American military gentleman of the old school. For instance, his raids never featured the destruction that occurred in the Shenandoah.

He and his division had been the perfect choice to stay behind with the Army of the Potomac at Petersburg when Sheridan took the First and Third Cavalry Divisions to the Shenandoah. After all, he was the senior cavalry divisional commander. But perhaps he resigned because he also knew that he did not have within himself the sheer constant audacity, the cruelty, or the ruthlessness that Sheridan demanded. Therefore, perhaps for all of these reasons, Gregg simply may not have wanted to serve under Sheridan's command again.

That Sheridan was ruthless there can be no possible denial. He could also be two-faced when it came to manipulating his superiors (Grant especially) to get what he wanted. He could disregard friendships, as when he claimed full credit for the victory at Fisher's Hill even though the plan that led to the victory had been the brainstorm of his friend, George C. Crook. He could hide the fact that he had mostly failed at Trevelian Station, which he proclaimed and Grant accepted as a victory. (However, Sheridan accomplished the one thing that Grant most needed to have done, the distraction of Robert E. Lee from Grant's move from the lines of Cold Harbor, across the James River, and to the almost unmanned defenses of Petersburg. In fact, Lee did not realize what was happening until Grant's vanguard had actually reached Petersburg. Everything else Grant might have considered to be simply gravy.) And Sheridan's temper can only be described as volcanic or even thermonuclear.

Sheridan also had contrasting qualities, loyalty being the most important. He was loyal fist and foremost to the Union, to his superiors, and to his subordinates, most especially those who became his protégés. He was also scrupulously honest financially. In fact, this once got him into trouble early in the war when he refused to buy what he believed were stolen horses even though his superior needed horses and didn't care where they came from. In addition, if Sheridan had not become a soldier he would probably have made a marvelous police detective. When Halleck took over John C. Fremont's mess in St. Louis his primary assistant in cleaning it up was Sheridan. Shortly after he was promoted to brigadier general he discovered that one of Don Carlos Buell's corps commander's commission as a major general was bogus. Although he was one of the most junior brigadier generals in the army he was given command of a division, which was carefully selected with colonels commanding its brigades so that there would be no problem with seniority.

For Sheridan it was not what you know. It was not even who you know. It was more of a matter of what you know about who you know.

Ironically, perhaps, it was one of his biggest critics—Joshua Lawrence Chamberlain, the defender of both Fitz John Porter and Gouverneur K. Warren—who managed to take the full, complete, measure of Philip Henry Sheridan, both the general and the man. Chamberlain's great moment of insight occurred late in the evening of April 1, 1865, immediately after the Battle of Five Forks had been won, when the commanders of the various V Corps brigades and divisions were gathered together, discussing what had happened that day.[2] "We grouped ourselves around Griffin at the forks ... halted reclining against the gloomy tree trunks and rudely piled defenses.... Few things were said; but they were not of the history that is told," Chamberlain wrote well after the war. He continued:

> Suddenly emerged from the shadows came a compact form, with a vigorous stride, unlike the measure and mood of ours and with a voice that would have itself thrilled us had not the import thrilled us more. "Gentlemen," says Sheridan, as we have started to our feet, "I have come over to see you. I may have spoken harshly to some of you today; but I would not have it hurt you. You know how it is: We had to carry this place and I was fretted all day until it was done. You must forgive me. I know it is hard for the men, too; but we must push. There is more for us to do together. I appreciate and thank you all."
>
> And this is Phil Sheridan! A new view of him, and we liked it. In some respects it was different from ours, although this was not a case to test all qualities. We had formed some habits of fighting, too.... We went into a fight with knowledge of what it meant and what was to be done. We went at things with dogged resolution; not much show; not much flare; not much accompaniment

of brass instruments. But we could give credit to more brilliant things. We could see how this voice and vision, this swing and color, this vivid impression on the senses carried the pulse and will of us.... We had a habit, drawn from dire experience, and for which we also had Grant's quite recent sanction, when we had carried a vital point, or to hold one, to entrench.

But Sheridan does not entrench. He pushes on carrying his flank and rear with him — rushing, flashing, smashing. He transfuses into his subordinates the vitality and energy of his purpose, transforms into parts of his own mind and will. He shares the power of a commander — inspiring both confidence and fear. He commanded our admiration, but we could discriminate: we reserved room for question whether he exhibited all the qualities in a chief commander in a campaign, or even in the complicated movements of an extensive field of battle.

As a rule our corps and army commanders were men of brains rather than of magnetism. Warren was one of these. He was well capable of organizing an entire plan of battle upon a great battlefield. He would have been an admirable chief of staff of the army, where brains outweigh temperament. He could see the whole comprehensibly and adjust the parts subordinate to it. But he had a certain ardor of temperament, which, although it brought him distinction as a subordinate commander, seemed to work against him as a corps commander. It led him to go in personally with a single division or brigade, when a sharp fight came on. Doing this when one has a larger command, one takes the risk of losing grasp of the whole.

(At this particular instance Chamberlain — ironically and perhaps not actually realizing it — was echoing Grant's own major complaint with Warren, that he got so involved with the trees that he could not adequately focus his attention on the forest as a whole.)

In the final analysis it cannot be denied that Sheridan produced results at the battles of Perryville, Murfreesboro/Stone's River, Missionary Ridge, Yellow Tavern, Cold Harbor, Winchester/Opequon Creek, Fisher's Hill, Cedar Creek, Five Forks, Saylor's Creek, and Appomattox Court House. What Five Forks and the ensuing Appomattox Campaign showed was that cavalry could add considerable impetus to normal infantry operations when used in the blitzkrieg mold. The high mobility of the horsemen allowed them considerable extra freedom upon the battlefield, which tended to unsettle the more conservative American Civil War generals who were more used to the sedate pace of infantry movements. Even if they did not always get there with the "mostest" they could at least get there "firstest."

This in turn greatly multiplied the natural force of the infantry, so that when used in conjunction with each other — as at Winchester/Opequon Creek, Cedar Creek, Five Forks, Saylor's Creek, and Appomattox Court House — infantry and cavalry became far more formidable than either one could ever be on its own. Therefore, it is greatly to Sheridan's credit that he alone, out of the generals of both sides (with the possible exception of Nathan Bedford Forrest), understood this and was successful in pressing his ideas upon his more traditionally minded superiors. On the other hand, it is greatly to the discredit of so many American Civil War commanders, on both sides, that it took so long for what eventually became the modern all-arms battle group to enter their tactical thinking. This is also one reason why World War I became such a bloodbath, since most of the generals either never learned or forgot that lesson (with the possible exception of Sir Edmund Allenby).

Then there is the question of Why the North Won the American Civil War.

First of all, it must be pointed out that there was no single turning point to the American Civil War.[3] By the spring of 1862 the momentum of the war seemed to be favoring the North. In the West, George H. Thomas had smashed the right end of Albert Sidney Johnston's defensive line in Tennessee at Mill Springs, while Ulysses S. Grant had crushed the center of it at Fort Henry and Fort Donelson, and Samuel Curtis had forced back the left at Elkorn Tavern/Pea Ridge. In addition, Grant had also managed to stop Albert Sidney Johnston's attempt to recover the situation at Shiloh. David G. Farragut had taken New Orleans (in what may have been the single most important battle of the entire war) and George B. McClellan had finally launched his Peninsula Campaign in the East, which was aimed at Richmond.

But then came the first of four separate and individual turning points. Three of them were military (with political overtones) and one was political (although it too had depended upon military victories) and they included:

1. The summer of 1862 when Lee stopped McClellan during the Seven Days' and smashed Pope at Second Manassas/Bull Run, while in the West the Union ceded the initiative to the Confederates when Halleck went East to become general-in-chief. The resulting counteroffensives of Robert E. Lee (most ably assisted by Stonewall Jackson) in the East, along with those of Braxton Bragg and Edmund Kirby Smith in the West, arrested the momentum of seemingly imminent Union victory. In turn this insured that the war would be both prolonged and intensified.

2. In the fall of 1862 the Confederate counteroffensives were in turn thrown back at the battles of Antietam/Sharpsburg and Perryville. These forestalled European mediation and recognition of the Southern Confederacy and possibly prevented enough Democratic Party victories in the Northern elections of 1862 so that the Lincoln Administration's ability to carry on the war and set the stage for the issuance of the Emancipation Proclamation that enlarged the scope and purpose of the war was not inhibited.

3. In the summer and fall of 1863 came the Union victories of Gettysburg, Vicksburg, Port Hudson, and Chattanooga that turned the tide towards an ultimate Northern military victory (and which also caused the last great Confederate victory at Chickamauga to become irrelevant).

4. The final turning point came on November 8, 1864, with the reelection of Abraham Lincoln. During the summer of 1864 appalling Union casualties and the apparent lack of progress in both the Eastern and Western Theatres of Operations brought the North to the brink of repudiating Lincoln and electing a Democrat as president. But the closing of Mobile Bay by Farragut and the fall of Atlanta and Sheridan's victories in the Shenandoah Valley clinched the outcome of the election and therefore the war in the Union's favor. Then and only then did the inevitability of final Union victory seem possible and it was only then that the Southern Confederacy began an irretrievable loss of its will to fight.

But, in a larger sense, the answer of why the North won the war may simply have lain in the difference between the quality and quantity of the military leadership available to both sides.[4]

While the South had Lee, it needed at least two of him (even though Lee himself was dangerously addicted to the strategic and tactical Napoleonic offense when the best grand strategy for the South was probably a Washingtonian defense). The South was also at a great disadvantage because no one ever enumerated just what the South's grand strategy was after the cordon defense of Jefferson Davis was discredited (which had only proved Frederick the Great's dictate that "he who defends everything defends nothing"). In the North the grand strategy had at least been enumerated by the piecemeal and unofficial adoption of what became known as Winfield Scott's Anaconda Plan, with its blockade of the Southern ports and its drive down the Mississippi River. It was upon this foundation after the fall of Vicksburg and Port Hudson that Grant built his own win-the-war strategy of continuous attack and dismemberment of the Southern Confederacy.

Lee had other weaknesses, one of them being his failure to learn the lesson of his own experiences during the Mexican War. Lee as commander of the Army of Northern Virginia never insisted upon complete and adequate reconnaissance before making his moves, although he did take advantage of J.E.B. Stuart's talents is this regard; but after Stuart's death no one quite filled that void, although Hampton tried. In addition, Lee's army was not supported by an adequate engineering component like that provided to the Army of the Potomac (and most other major Union armies) as a matter of course. Furthermore, Lee relied almost exclusively upon his own audacity. By being aggressive and unpredictable he baffled his opponents between June of 1862 and the spring of 1864, sometimes winning, but always surviving. He did this by being both audacious and unorthodox and by his ability to recognize opportunities when they occurred and his willingness to exploit those opportunities when he found them.

However, all of this would change and Lee would ultimately be unable to conduct the war his way with the advent of Grant from out of the West — because Grant could be every bit as audacious as Lee himself and he simply would not allow himself to be bluffed or bullied by Lee, and, unlike Joseph Hooker, he never lost his nerve. Finally, Lee seldom, if ever, looked beyond Virginia to consider the war as a whole, leaving that entirely to President Jefferson Davis and his War Department.

Among the other Confederate army commanders, great things were expected of Albert Sidney Johnston. But on the whole his tenure in command of the Confederate Western Theatre of Operations in Department No. 1 was one of disappointment and with his death at Shiloh in the spring of 1862 there was no chance to show that he could learn from the experience. P.G.T. Beauregard, although he won the First Battle of Manassas/Bull Run, maintained Charleston, South Carolina, as the greatest single citadel in the South; he bottled up Benjamin Butler at Bermuda Hundred; and had kept Petersburg from falling. But he ultimately failed to deliver on his early promise. Joseph E. Johnston's forte was to trade space for time a la Washington, but he hardly ever seemed to realize that eventually with such a strategy there definitely does come a time to turn and fight. Braxton Bragg knew what had to be done, but knowing what has to be done and how to do it are two entirely different things. John Bell Hood, while he was an excellent brigade and division commander, simply was not capable of high command at either the corps or the army level. John Pemberton, like McClellan on the Union side, was a great little planner and organizer, but he was simply not really capable of field command. Edmund Kirby Smith was relegated to the backwater of the Trans-Mississippi, a responsibility that he guarded well, but that was all.

Of the Southern subordinate commanders only Thomas J. Jackson, Nathan Bedford Forrest, and possibly Patrick Cleiburne showed the promise that they could develop the quality of military leadership at the level needed — that of independent army command. But, Jackson, who displayed brilliance in his Shenandoah Valley Campaign of 1862, died in 1863 after the Battle of Chancellorsville, while Forrest and Cleiburne (before his own death at the Battle of Franklin) never got the chance to show whether they were capable of successful command at the highest level.

Richard Ewell, A.P. Hill, Jubal Early, and Richard H. Anderson also showed promise but never fully measured up. Their greatest failure was the fact that none of them was quite the equal of Stonewall Jackson. In the end Ewell, at Gettysburg, was unable to read between the lines of Lee's orders (one thing that Jackson excelled at) and Early made the fatal mistake of underestimating Sheridan. Hill's main problem was that he was too impatient and he was also in continuous poor health. Anderson was a superb division commander but did not rise to permanent corps command (during the siege of Petersburg) until it was too late.

Then there were Earl Van Dorn, D.H. Hill, and Sterling Price. Van Dorn had every quality needed to be a successful general except one: luck (most particularly demonstrated in the manner of his death, as he was shot in the back of the head by a supposedly jealous husband). D.H. Hill's problem was that he continuously spoke his mind and never learned the value of discretion. Hill's promotion to lieutenant general was ultimately unconfirmed and it passed to Hood. Price launched the final invasion of Northern territory when he moved into Missouri in the fall of 1864 with a mounted army on the model of Forrest. Ultimately Curtis and Alfred Pleasonton (who had been transferred to Missouri as a form of exile) smashed his command; Price was brave, resolute, and capable, but like Van Dorn he was just not very lucky.

James Longstreet is a special case. He was superb as the commander of the Army of Northern Virginia's I Corps. Lee called Longstreet his "Old War Horse," even though he preferred the tactical defense to the tactical offense and thus was sluggish at Second Manassas/Bull Run (until prodded by Lee) and Gettysburg. Although he craved an independent command, Longstreet nonetheless failed when he was given one after the Battle of Chickamauga. Longstreet was tasked by Bragg with the recapture of Knoxville, Tennessee, opposing Ambrose E. Burnside, of all people, and still did not achieve much of anything.

In contrast, where the Confederacy had Lee the Union had five generals whose combined efforts brought total victory. In order of importance they included:

- Ulysses S. Grant, due to his conquest of Vicksburg, which resulted in the final opening of the Mississippi River, and his direction of the Union armies in the final year of the war.
- George H. Thomas, one of the old school generals, who nonetheless knew what had to be done and then went out and did it, at Mill Springs, Stone's River/Murfreesboro, Chickamauga, Chattanooga, Franklin, and Nashville.
- William S. Rosecrans, who at the Battle of Stone's River/Murfreesboro validated the issuance of the Emancipation Proclamation and who created the preconditions needed for Sherman to take Atlanta, but who was removed — after one great failure in an otherwise successful career as a general — primarily due to someone else's almost intentional blunder.
- William T. Sherman, whose marches through Georgia and the Carolinas demonstrated to everyone, North and South and even overseas, that the Southern Confederacy was truly on the verge of collapse.
- And finally, Philip H. Sheridan, who through his victories at Winchester, Fisher's Hill, and Cedar Creek guaranteed the reelection of Abraham Lincoln and then delivered the coup de grace at Five Forks and Appomattox Court House.

Aside from the five generals who won the war the North also had a reservoir of other generals who supported and sustained them.

Before the advent of Grant the problem was that generals such as George B. McClellan, Henry W. Halleck, and Don Carlos Buell, who, although they were great organizers and trainers of soldiers, were too slow, too cautious, and lacking in the aggressive ruthlessness needed to drive on to final victory (although Halleck could recognize that quality when he saw it). What success they achieved before the advent of Grant (and in large part the successes achieved by Grant, Sherman, Thomas, Rosecrans, and Sheridan) was due to the military talent shown by many of their subordinates and other autonomous commanders.

These included such men as George G. Meade (before he became commander of the Army of the Potomac), James B. McPherson, John Sedgwick, Philip Kearney, John Reynolds, John Buford, Winfield Scott Hancock, Alfred Pleasonton, John Gibbon, David M. Gregg, Wesley Merritt, George A. Custer, George C. Crook, Nelson A. Miles, Ranald S. Mackenzie, Charles F. Smith, Benjamin Grierson, Gouverneur K. Warren, Joshua L. Chamberlain, and many others (even including at times Benjamin Butler and Daniel Sickles).

There was also Nathaniel Lyon, the fanatical Connecticut Yankee Unionist who at the very beginning of the war kept St. Louis from falling under the control of secessionists who included the governor of Missouri, who controlled the official state militia and forcibly kept the State of

Missouri within the Union, and was killed at the Battle of Wilson's Creek. Samuel Curtis, who succeeded in repelling Van Dorn at Elkhorn Tavern/Pea Ridge, carried on his efforts, and with Pleasonton as one of his primary field commanders first drove back and then smashed Sterling Price's invasion of Missouri.

There are those who have questioned whether or not Sheridan really belongs in this august body of Union military leadership. It has been said that Sheridan's tenure as chief of cavalry of the Army of the Potomac was devoid of positive results and that his Shenandoah Valley Campaign of 1864 was devoid of true strategic significance due primarily to the fact that Sheridan so outnumbered Early that any reasonably competent commander could have won.

Sheridan's only outright victory as commander of the cavalry of the Army of the Potomac may well have been Yellow Tavern; but he kept grinding away at the cavalry of the Army of Northern Virginia so that by Five Forks it was only a shadow of its former self. Even before Stonewall Jackson's Shenandoah Valley Campaign of 1862 the valley had been the graveyard of Union military reputations. In the valley the Confederacy had proven time and again that being outnumbered is not always completely relevant. After all, there is a difference between sheer size and combat effectiveness (even though it can also be said that quantity has a quality all its own).

All Early had to do was win once and he might have stemmed the tide of Lincoln's victory at the polls on November 8, 1864, while Sheridan had to win all the time. At Cedar Creek, Early came within an ace of that victory, although in the end Sheridan literally managed to snatch victory from defeat and thus ensured Lincoln's reelection.

Concerning Sheridan's abilities as a general, it might also be enlightening to look upon his effect on the generalship of Ulysses S. Grant. In Grant's conduct of the war it sometimes appeared as if there were two very different Grants. First there was the magnificent general at Fort Henry and Fort Donelson, Shiloh (although he did make a number of mistakes), the Vicksburg Campaign, and the battles for Chattanooga, along with the final campaign of the Army of the Potomac that led to Lee's surrender at Appomattox Court House. Then there is the general who led the strategically inspired but tactically lackluster Overland Campaign. This leads to the question of what happened to the Grant of Fort Henry and Fort Donelson, Shiloh, the Vicksburg Campaign and Chattanooga, and what it was that brought him back for the campaign that led to Lee's final surrender.

It must be remembered that the American Civil War was the first modern war and that the conduct of a modern war is and must be a team effort, not an individual one. Therefore, perhaps the answer to the question can be found in the men who were Grant's primary subordinates. At Fort Henry and Fort Donelson it was Charles F. Smith, a man that Grant deeply respected and whose death Grant greatly mourned. At Shiloh and Vicksburg it was William T. Sherman and at Chattanooga it was both Sherman and George H. Thomas. Then Grant came East and his principal subordinate became George G. Meade during the Overland Campaign. By the time the Army of the Potomac's final campaign began Sheridan had returned from the Shenandoah Valley and was given co-equal status with Meade to become Grant's spearhead, and the reconciliation of the two Grants becomes obvious. Despite all of his manifold faults and the fact that he emerged to high command only relatively late in the war, Sheridan deserves his place among the victorious quinumvirate of Union military leadership, without whom the war might well have ended differently or could have been much further prolonged.

Finally, as the *Harper Encyclopedia of Military Biography* put it, Sheridan was "intelligent, resourceful, and aggressive; his [abrasive] personality, although it earned him the enmity of many of his contemporaries, also endeared him to his troops and won the respect of his most important superiors, Lincoln, Halleck, and Grant. Finally, he was also blunt and a man who spoke his mind, to everyone." To illustrate this point, once, long after the war, he was asked, "General, how did you feel when you came out of a battle?"[5]

"Very much like a dishrag."

Notes

Prologue

1. According to T. Harry Williams in his study of the Union high command in his book, *Lincoln and His Generals*, page 3.
2. As noted by Thomas C. Buell in his book, *The Warrior Generals: Combat Leadership in the Civil War*, pages 299–300.
3. Their recollections upon the subject were included in the archives of artist James E. Kelly, which are part of the collection of the New York State Historical Society. William B. Styple edited this material and published it for the first time in his book *Generals in Bronze: Interviewing the Commanders of the Civil War*, pages 126 and 104.
4. Gabor S. Borritt noted throughout *Jefferson Davis's Generals* that Davis and almost all of his top generals clashed continuously.
5. The James E. Kelly archives provided this anecdote, page 232.
6. William C. Davis in *Look Away!* provided one of the best descriptions available of Grant's win-the-war strategy, pages 317–322.
7. According to Davis in *Look Away!*, page 317.
8. According to Maj. Gen. Frederick Maurice in his book, *Robert E. Lee: The Soldier*, pages 216–217.
9. Once again according to Gen. Maurice, pages 249–250.
10. In Gen. Maurice's view, pages 157 and 250.
11. According to Noah Andre Trudeau in his article, "I Have A Great Contempt For History."
12. Included in the James E. Kelly archives, page 232.
13. As noted by Paul A. Hutton in his article, "Paladin of the Republic." He called Sheridan's treatment of Warren in the aftermath of the victory at Five Forks as being unmerciful, particularly in light of the fact that Warren had as much or more to do with the victory, and its scope, as any other Union officer on the field.

Chapter 1

1. According to Lawrence Schiller in his article, "A Taste of Northern Steel."
2. Schiller cited Stephen Z. Starr's *The Union Cavalry in the Civil War* for challenging the assumption that the Union cavalry was never more than a mounted infantry and used horses only for transportation and mobility. Starr and Schiller maintain that, while Union cavalry troopers did most of their fighting dismounted, they never ceased to consider themselves as cavalry, while other units, such as Wilder's Lightning Brigade, actually were mounted infantry (in that they were raised as infantry and became mounted during the course of the war) and did not consider themselves to be cavalry.
3. According to Schiller's article.

Chapter 3

1. Although Eric Wittenberg, throughout his *Glory Enough for All: Sheridan's Second Raid and the Battle of Trevilian Station*, faults Sheridan for such hesitation during this particular raid.
2. Bruce Catton in his three-volume history of the Army of the Potomac collected in *Bruce Catton's Civil War*, page 348.
3. Robert Leckie, in *None Died in Vain*, concluded that Hooker folded his hand and gave up when he did not really need to do so, page 440.
4. According to Bruce Catton in his study of the campaign and battle of Chancellorsville.
5. Most particularly by Ben Fordney in his article, "Stoneman's Chancellorsville Raid: Failure or Harbinger?"
6. Catton, however, did not ignore Hooker's failings. His conclusions about Hooker's performance — in his history of the Army of the Potomac — were scathing and may have best summed up what happened (page 348):

"[Hooker] planned his campaign like a master and carried out the first half of it with great skill, and then he simple folded up: there had been no [moral] courage in him, no life, no spark; during most of the battle the army to all intents and purposes had no commander at all. With a two-to-one advantage, Hooker had let his men fight at a numerical disadvantage at every important point upon the battlefield. Howard's XI Corps had been smashed by an irresistible flank attack, but the reason for that disaster was that neither Hooker nor anyone else in authority would listen to the specific warnings, which the unhappy Dutchmen (the XI Corps consisting primarily of German immigrants) had repeatedly sent in. Thereafter while Lee and Stuart (who had temporarily succeeded the wounded Stonewall Jackson) crushed his lines between Fairview and Chancellorsville, Hooker had held back 30,000 good troops out of action, he had cowered in his trenches while Lee broke up Sedgwick's corps, and then, to cap it all off, he had hastily retreated across the river just as he was about to be given a chance to redeem the whole situation. For on the morning the army re-crossed the river, Lee had actually been planning a full-scale assault upon Hooker's lines. Those lines were strong, Hooker still had a two-to-one advantage in numbers, he had 106 [field] guns in emplacements with 140 more in reserve, and by all military logic that assault should have resulted in a Confederate defeat as bad as the one at Malvern Hill. Yet it may be that military logic had nothing to do with it. Lee had not been contending with the Yankee army at Chancellorsville. He had been contending with Joe Hooker, he was more of a man than Joe Hooker was, and Hooker knew it.... Years later when someone asked Hooker what went wrong at Chancellorsville, the general knew a rare moment of humility and remarked: 'Well to tell the truth, I just lost confidence in Joe Hooker.'"

Chapter 4

1. As noted by Eric Wittenberg in an e-mail to the author.
2. As Robert Boehm put it in his article, "The Unfortunate Averell."

Chapter 5

1. As noted by A.D. Slade in the only published biography of Torbert, *A.T.A. Torbert: Southern Gentleman in Union Blue.*

Chapter 6

1. According to Jeffry D. Wert in *From Winchester to Cedar Creek: The Shenandoah Valley Campaign of 1864,* pages 110–111.
2. Once again according to Wert, page 111.
3. Wert, in *From Winchester to Cedar Creek,* suggests that this undertaking may have been responsible for Averell's concentrating on collecting booty, rather than pursuing Early's Confederate troops, once they had been forced off the natural fortress of Fisher's Hill, page 120.

Chapter 7

1. As noted in Boehm's article, "The Unfortunate Averell."

Chapter 8

1. As noted in the only published biography of Torbert, *A.T.A. Torbert: Southern Gentleman in Union Blue* by A.D. Slade.
2. Once again according to Slade in his biography of Torbert.
3. As related by Samuel J. Martin in *Kill — Cavalry: The Life of Union General Hugh Judson Kilpatrick,* page 147.
4. As stated by Michael Phipps and John S. Peterson in their study of Buford *The Devil's to Pay: Gen. John Buford, U.S.A.*

5. Sheridan's statement is recorded in the James E. Kelly archives, page 14.
6. As noted by Victor Davis Hanson in his book, *The Soul of Battle.*
7. Gregory J.W. Urwin's *Custer Victorious* relates how these command politics were untangled, pages 124–127.

Chapter 9

1. Robert A. Williams in his article, "Haw's Shop: A Storm of Shot and Shell," detailed what happened during this relatively small engagement.
2. The complete story of this is recounted in Eric Wittenberg's *Glory Enough for All: Sheridan's Second Raid and the Battle of Trevilian Station.*
3. As noted in Urwin's *Custer Victorious,* pages 151–164.
4. Wittenberg in *Little Phil: A Reassessment of the Civil War Leadership of Gen. Philip H. Sheridan,* has disputed this claim, stating that there was no way that Sheridan could have possibly received this information, page 138.
5. In *Custer Victorious* Urwin maintained that no one was really to blame for the catastrophe that engulfed the Michigan Cavalry Brigade. Torbert went so far as to say in his dispatches, "Much credit is due to General Custer for saving his command under such trying circumstances," pages 163–164. Wittenberg saw it differently and in *Glory Enough for All* offers this evaluation:
"Sheridan persistently claimed victory in the Trevilian Raid and Grant's memoirs perpetuated this myth... Within days of the Battle of Trevilian Station, Sheridan submitted his report and claimed victory... Although Sheridan scored a tactical victory on June 11, he nevertheless failed to accomplish all [but one] of Grant's strategic objectives, negating the outcome. No matter how positive a spin Little Phil tried to put on things the Trevilian Station Raid was an unmitigated disaster for his troopers ... nothing about the Battle of Trevilian Station can be considered a Union victory.
"Sheridan failed to make the planned junction with Hunter and obviously failed to bring Hunter's army east to link with the Army of the Potomac. More important he failed to put the Virginia Central Railroad out of commission....
"If Sheridan had destroyed the railroad as ordered, Hunter's expedition to capture Lynchburg might have succeeded, because Early might have gone after Sheridan instead of Hunter. Instead Hunter declined to give battle and withdrew into West Virginia temporarily removed from action. In short, Sheridan's failure to destroy the Virginia Central Railroad likely extended the war in the east as much as six months. There were few really decisive cavalry battles in the [American] Civil War, but Hampton's victory at Trevilian Station must be counted as one because of its far reaching implications," [pages 304–306].

Chapter 11

1. According to Edward G. Longacre in his book, *Custer and His Wolverines: The Michigan Cavalry Brigade 1861–1865.*

2. Kidd expressed his bewilderment in his memoirs, *Recollections of a Cavalryman,* and in the abridged version, *A Cavalryman with Custer,* page 289.
3. As cited in Wert's *From Winchester to Cedar Creek,* pages 133–134.

Chapter 12

1. As described by Urwin in *Custer Victorious*, the description of which was taken from George Sanford's memoirs, *Fighting Rebels and Redskins,* pages 196–197.
2. Urwin recorded in *Custer Victorious* what happened next, pages 197–201.

Chapter 14

1. Wittenberg in *Little Phil* noted, "In hindsight, it is obvious that Torbert possessed neither the vision nor the ability to command an entire corps of horse soldiers," pages 83–84.
2. According to Torbert's sole biographer, A.D. Slade.

Chapter 15

1. According to Edward G. Longacre in "Gouverneur K. Warren: A Profile."

Chapter 16

1. James M. McPherson, in his *Battle Cry of Freedom,* noted that Porter was in part the victim of Radical Republican attacks on McClellan and his associates—and Porter was one of the closest of McClellan's associates. However, Porter's failure to do anything with V Corps would seem to indicate, according to McPherson, that Porter deserved some censure, page 529.
2. Once again according to McPherson, page 531.
3. According to Stephen W. Sears in his article, "The Court-Martial of Fitz John Porter."
4. Also according to Sears in this article.
5. Sears, in his article, joined McPherson in deploring Porter's basic inaction.
6. Once again according to the Sears article.
7. Sears, in his article, acknowledged that an injustice had indeed been done to Porter when he was cashiered on the particular charges brought against him by Pope. However, Sears agreed with then Captain (and later Col.) Charles Russell Lowell, who said at the time of Porter's court-martial that Porter "exhibited a frame of mind ... unofficerlike and dangerous" and that Porter, due to this frame of mind, was "better out of the army."
8. As Shelby Foote noted in his *The Stars in Their Courses,* pages 131–135.

Chapter 20

1. According to Stewart Sifakis, in his *Who Was Who in the Union,* Grant wanted "Tardy George" Sykes replaced with someone more "energetic."

2. When it became clear that the Army of the Potomac was advancing, not retreating, Grant was spontaneously cheered by Hancock's II Corps troops as he passed by, something that had not happened since the days of George McClellan, according to *Bruce Catton's Civil War,* page 514, and Grant's *Personal Memoirs,* page 440.

Chapter 21

1. According to Bruce Catton in his book *Never Call Retreat,* the end and final collapse of the Confederacy was plainly in sight, page 660.
2. Catton, in *Bruce Catton's Civil War,* inferred that neither Grant nor Meade nor Sheridan ever really took that fact into account, page 664.

Chapter 22

1. The text for this telegraph can be found only in *Pickett and His Men,* the memoir written by LaSalle Corbell Pickett, Pickett's wife. The problem was that her book glorified her husband's service and was written well after his death and is therefore considered suspect by many historians.
2. Chamberlain stated his opinion in his book, *The Passing of the Armies.*

Chapter 23

1. Chamberlain's disagreements with Grant concerning Warren were noted in Mark Perry's *Conceived in Liberty,* pages 346–347, 349, 370 and 394.
2. As noted by Perry in *Conceived in Liberty*, page 346.
3. Just prior to testifying, Chamberlain, as he noted in *The Passing of the Armies,* met and talked with both Sheridan and Winfield Scott Hancock. Chamberlain described his greeting from Sheridan as being cool and distant.

Chapter 25

1. According to Joseph P. Cullen in his article, "Sheridan Wins at Winchester."

Chapter 26

1. According to Leslie Gordon in his essay, "The Seeds of Disaster: The Generalship of George E. Pickett after Gettysburg," which is included in *Leadership and Command in the American Civil War,* pages 174–194.
2. It is reiterated that the text of this telegram appears only in *Pickett and His Men,* written by Pickett's wife, and not in the *Official Records of the Union and Confederate Armies of the War of the Rebellion.* Therefore, it is not known if the telegram actually existed or if it was invented by Pickett's widow. It is possible that Pickett simply pocketed the telegram and any copies, if they ever existed, never made their way to the Confederate War Department archives or were destroyed during the con-

fusion that resulted from the Battle of Five Forks, the evacuation of Richmond, and the final retreat and surrender at Appomattox.

Chapter 27

1. According to Ken Biven in his article, "The Fall of Richmond: Driving Dixie Down," and Brian John Murphy in his article, "When the Yankees Drove Old Dixie Down."
2. Taken from the articles "The Fall of Richmond" by Godfrey Weitzell and "The Fighting about Richmond and the Evacuation of the City" by Theodore S. Garnet, Jr., as collected in *New Annals of the Civil War* edited by Peter Cozzens and Robert I. Giradi.

Chapter 28

1. Carl W. Beihan recorded many of Mackenzie's accomplishments in his book, *Great Lawmen of the West*. Strictly speaking, Mackenzie was a soldier, not a lawman, in any true sense of the word. However, it cannot be denied that his accomplishments were vital to bringing an end to the Indian Wars and thus helped to stabilize the western frontier.
2. According to James L. Haley in *The Buffalo War*, pages 105–106.
3. Also according to Haley in *The Buffalo War*, pages 206–207.
4. This included the opinion of one of his two biographers, Michael D. Pierce, in his *The Most Promising Young Officer: A Life of Ranald Slidell Mackenzie*.
5. This speculation was primarily by Pierce in his book.

Chapter 29

1. As noted by Robert M. Utley in his book, *Frontier Regulars: The United States Army and the Indian, 1866–1890*, pages 55–66.
2. The opinion of Utley expressed in his article, "Crook and Miles: Fighting and Feuding on the Indian Frontier."
3. Utley felt that Crook's contributions to the American Civil War were modest enough; his major claim to fame was having been taken captive by Confederate guerillas in a hotel in Cumberland, MD, immediately after the end of Sheridan's Shenandoah Valley Campaign of 1864. It is probably due to his friendship with Sheridan that Crook was not quietly eased out of the army as other generals had been in quite similar circumstances. The cases of Edwin H. Stoughton and Alfred Duffie most particularly come to mind. In point of fact, Crook's efforts were highly instrumental in Sheridan's twin victories at the Third Battle of Winchester/Opequon Creek and Fisher's Hill.
4. Utley, in his article, most properly identified this as being among the most unattractive facets of the Frontier Army.
5. That would be Utley, once again, most particularly in his article, "Last Stand."
6. A.D. Slade, A.T.A. Torbert's biographer, noted that Merritt was a year younger than Torbert and that he had languished in staff positions until 1863 when he, Custer, and Elon J. Farnesworth (who was killed at the Battle of Gettysburg), were all promoted to brigadier general and were given command of brigades within the Cavalry Corps, Army of the Potomac. Slade speculated that Sheridan recognized a kindred spirit and during the course of the war he and Merritt were to become close personal friends.
7. According to Utley, in his article "Last Stand."
8. This was Utley's evaluation.
9. Included in Haley's *The Buffalo War*, pages 179 and 182–183.

Epilogue

1. According to Thomas Carhart in his book, *Lost Triumph: Lee's Real Plan at Gettysburg — and Why It Failed*. He noted that Gregg realized that the terrain and at least one country road offered an avenue that led directly to the Union rear and sought assistance by first having Custer's brigade attached to his division and later retaining it when it was reassigned. Perhaps Gregg displayed amazing foresight or, as Carhart maintains, there was another reason. Gregg placed Custer's brigade in a position where it could block any move by Stuart to get into the Union rear instead of either of his two brigades, which were then available. By doing so he had insured that the responsibility for any battlefield failure would fall on Custer's head, not on his own. In addition, Gregg, in his after-action report, seemed to indicate that Custer and his brigade, although providing support, had little to do with turning back Stuart. But the casualty figures make it clear that Custer's brigade (with losses of 219 men, including roughly 30 killed) was more heavily involved in the fighting than Gregg's division (whose casualties numbered 35, none of whom were killed), pages 189–190 and 250–254.
2. Which he wrote about in his book, *The Passing of the Armies*.
3. James M. McPherson pointed this out most eloquently in *Battle Cry of Freedom*. The conventional wisdom has been that the turning point of the war occurred on July 4, 1863, when John Pemberton surrendered Vicksburg and his Army of Mississippi to Grant, and Lee began his retreat back to Virginia from Gettysburg. McPherson argues there were four separate turning points, not just one. These occurred during the summer of 1862, the fall of 1862, the summer and fall of 1863, and, finally, upon Lincoln's reelection on November 8, 1864, pages 857–858.
4. This argument was most plausibly made in Albert Castell's article, "Why the North Won and the South Lost."
5. Included in the James E. Kelly Archives, page 11.

Bibliography

Books

Averell, William W. *Ten Years in the Saddle*. Edited by Edward K. Eckert and Nicholas J. Amato. Novato, CA: Presidio Press, 1979.

Breihan, Cark W. *Great Lawmen of the West*. South Yarmouth, MA: Curling Publishing, 1953, 1978.

Boritt, Gabor S. *Jefferson Davis's Generals*. Oxford: Oxford University Press, 1999.

Buell, Thomas B. *The Warrior Generals: Combat Leadership in the Civil War*. New York: Crown Publishers, 1997.

Calkins, Chris. *Great Campaigns: The Appomattox Campaign, March 29–April 9, 1865*. Conshohocken, PA: Combined Books, 1997.

Carhart, Tom. *Lost Triumph: Lee's Real Plan at Gettysburg — and Why It Failed*. New York: A Berkley Caliber Book, 2005.

Catton, Bruce. *Bruce Catton's Civil War — Three Volumes in One: Mr. Lincoln's Army, Glory Road, A Stillness at Appomattox*. New York: Fairfax Press, 1984.

_____. *The Centennial History of the Civil War*. Vol. 3, *Never Call Retreat*. Garden City, NY: Doubleday & Company, 1965.

_____. *The Civil War*. New York: The Fairfax Press, by arrangement with American Heritage Publishing Co., 1960, 1971.

_____. *Reflections on the Civil War*. Edited by John Leekley. New York: Berkley Books, published by arrangement with Doubleday & Company, 1982.

_____. *This Hallowed Ground: The Story of the Union Side of the Civil War*. New York: Pocket Books, by arrangement with Doubleday & Doubleday, 1955, 1956.

Chamberlain, Joshua L. *The Passing of the Armies: An Account of the Final Campaign of the Army of the Potomac, Based Upon Personal Reminiscences of the Fifth Corps*. New York, Toronto, London, Sydney, Auckland: Bantam Books, 1915, 1993.

Cooper, William J. *Jefferson Davis, American*. New York: Alfred A. Knopf, 2000.

Current, Richard N., ed. *MacMillan Information Now Encyclopedia: The Confederacy*. New York: MacMillan Reference USA and Simon & Schuster MacMillan; London, Mexico City, New Dehli, Singapore, Sydney, Toronto: Prentiss Hall International, 1993.

Davis, Burke. *To Appomattox: Nine April Days, 1865*. Short Hills, NJ: Burford Books, 1959, 2002.

Davis, William C. *Look Away!: A History of the Confederate States of America*. New York, London, Toronto, Sydney, Singapore: The Free Press, 2002.

_____. *Rebels and Yankees: The Battlefields of the Civil War*. London: Salamander Books, 1990, 1999.

_____. *Rebels and Yankees: The Commanders of the Civil War*. London: Salamander Books, 1990, 1999.

_____. *Rebels and Yankees: The Fighting Men of the Civil War*. London: Salamander Books, 1990, 1999.

Donald, David H. *Lincoln*. New York, London, Toronto, Sydney, Tokyo, Singapore: Simon & Schuster, 1995.

Donovan, Jim. *Custer and the Little Big Horn: The Man, the Mystery, the Myth*. Stillwater, MN: Voyageur Press, 2001.

Dupuy, Trevor N., Curt Johnson, and David L. Bongard. *The Harper Encyclopedia of Military Biography*. Edison, NY: Castle Books, 1992.

Early, Jubal Anderson. *Autobiographical Sketch and Narrative of the War Between the States, with notes by R.H. Early*. Philadelphia and London: J.B. Lippincott Company, 1912.

Eisenschiml, Otto. *The Celebrated Case of Fitz John Porter: An American Dreyfus Affair*. Indianapolis and New York: The Bobbs-Merrill Company, 1950.

Emerson, Edward W., ed. *Life and Letters of Charles Russell Lowell*. Port Washington, New York, London: Kennikat Press, 1907.

Foote, Shelby. *The Stars in Their Courses: The Gettysburg Campaign*. New York: The Modern Library and Random House, 1963, 1991, 1994.

Fredericks, Pierce G., ed. *The Civil War as They Knew It: Abraham Lincoln's Immortal Words and Matthew Brady's Famous Photographs*. New York, Toronto, London: Bantam Books, 1961.

Garnett, Theodore S., Jr. "The Fighting about Petersburg and the Evacuation of the City." In *The New Annals of the Civil War*. Edited by Peter Cozzens and Robert I. Giradi. Mechanicsburg, PA: Stackpole Books, 2004.

Govan, Gilbert, and James Livingwood. *A Different Valor: Joseph E. Johnston*. New York: Smithmark, 1956.

Grant, Ulysses S. *Personal Memoirs of Ulysses S. Grant*. New York: Barnes & Noble Books, 1885, 2003.

Greene, A. Wilson. *Whatever You Resolve to Be: Essays on Stonewall Jackson*. Baltimore: Butternut and Blue, 1992.

Griffith, Paddy. *Battle in the Civil War: Generalship and Tactics in America 1861–1865*. Fieldbooks, 1986.

Hale, C. Wesley. *The Tragedy of the Crater*. Petersburg, VA: Eastern National Park and Monument Association, 1938, 1975.

Haley, James L. *The Buffalo War*. Garden City, NY: Doubleday & Co., 1976.

Hanson, Victor David. *The Soul of Battle: From Ancient Times to the Present Day, How Three Great Liberators Vanquished Tyranny*. New York: Free Press, 1999.

Harwell, Richard B., ed. *The Civil War Reader: The Union Reader and the Confederate Reader*. New York: Konecky & Konecky, 1957, 1958.

Haskell, Frank A., and William C. Oates. *Gettysburg*. New York, Toronto, London, Sydney, Auckland: Bantam Books, 1992.

Isham, Asa B. *Seventh Michigan Cavalry of Custer's Wolverine Brigade*. New York and Huntington, WV: Town Topics Publishing Company, Blue Acorn Press, 2000.

Johnson, Clint. *Bull's-Eyes and Misfires: 50 People Whose Obscure Efforts Shaped the American Civil War*. Nashville, TN: Rutledge Hill Press, 2002.

Jones, Archer. *Civil War Command & Strategy: The Process of Victory and Defeat*. New York, Toronto, Oxford, Singapore, Sydney: Free Press, 1992.

Jones, Virgil Carrington. *Ranger Mosby*. Charlotte, NC: University of North Carolina Press, 1944.

Jordan, David M. *Happiness Is Not My Companion: The Life of General G.K. Warren*. Bloomington: Indiana University Press, 2001.

Kathcher, Philip. *The Army of Robert E. Lee*. London: Arms and Armour Press, 1994.

Kidd, James H. *A Cavalryman with Custer*. New York, Toronto, London, Sidney, Auckland: Bantam Books, 1991.

_____. *Reflections of a Cavalryman*. Ionia, MI: Sentinel Printing Co., 1908.

Kinsley, D.A. *Custer: Favor the Bold: A Soldier's Story*. New York: Promontory Press, 1967, 1968, 1988.

Korn, Jerry, and the editors of Time Life Books. *The Civil War: Pursuit to Appomattox: The Last Battles*. Alexandria, VA: Time Life Books, 1987.

Leckie, Robert. *None Died in Vain: The Saga of the American Civil War*. New York: Harper Collins Publishers, 1990.

Lewis, Thomas A. *The Guns of Cedar Creek*. New York, Cambridge, Philadelphia, San Francisco, London, Mexico City, Sao Paulo, Singapore, Sydney: Harper & Row, 1988.

_____, and the editors of Time Life Books. *The Civil War: The Shenandoah in Flames, the Valley Campaign of 1864*. Alexandria, VA: Time Life Books, 1987.

Longacre, Edward. *Custer and His Wolverines: The Michigan Cavalry Brigade, 1861–1865*. Coshohocken, PA: Combined Publishing, 1997.

Martin, Samuel J. *Kill-Cavalry: The Life of Union General Hugh Judson Kilpatrick*. Mechanicsville, PA: Stackpole Books, 2000.

Maurice, Maj. Gen. Sir Frederick. *Robert E. Lee the Soldier*. New York: Bonanza Books, a division of Crown Publishers, Inc., 1925.

McPherson, James M. *Battle Cry of Freedom: The Civil War Era*. Oxford, New York: Oxford University Press and Ballantine Books, 1988.

Miller, David Humphreys. *Custer's Fall: The Native American Side of the Story*. New York: Meridian (previously published in a Dutton edition), 1957, 1992.

Mitchell, Joseph B. *Decisive Battles of the Civil War*. New York: Fawcett Premier, Ballantine Books, 1955.

Mogelever, Jacob. *Death to Traitors: The Story of General Lafayette C. Baker, Lincoln's Forgotten Secret Service Chief*. Garden City, NY: Doubleday, 1960.

Morris, Roy, Jr. *Sheridan: The Life and Wars of General Phil Sheridan*. New York: Vintage Civil War Library, Vintage Books, 1992.

Mosby, John S. *Gray Ghost: The Memoirs of Col. John S. Mosby*. New York, Toronto, London, Sydney, Auckland: Bantam Books 1917, 1992.

Murfin, James V. *The Gleam of Bayonets : The Battle of Antietam and Robert E. Lee's Maryland Campaign, September 1862*. Baton Rouge and London: Louisiana State University Press, 1965.

Nofi, Albert A. *The Gettysburg Campaign: June and July, 1863*. Conshohocken, PA: Combined Books, 1986.

Nolan, Alan T. *Lee Considered: General Lee and Civil War History*. London and Chapel Hill: University of North Carolina Press, 1991.

Perry, Mark. *Conceived in Liberty: Joshua Chamberlain, William Oates, and the American Civil War*. New York: Penguin Books, 1997.

Phillips, David. *Civil War Chronicles: Crucial Land Battles*. New York: MetroBooks, 1996.

Phipps, Michael, and John S. Peterson. *The Devil's to Pay: Gen. John Buford, USA*. Gettysburg: Farnsworth Military Impressions, 1995.

Pierce, Michael D. *The Most Promising Young Officer: A Life of Ranald Slidell Mackenzie*. Norman and London: University of Oklahoma Press, 1993.

Piston, William Garrett. *Lee's Tarnished Lieutenant: James Longstreet and His Place in Southern History*. Athens, GA, and London: University of Georgia Press, 1987.

Rankin, Charles E., ed. *Legacy: New Perspectives on the Battle of the Little Big Horn*. Helena: Montana Historical Society Press, 1996.

Robertson, James I., Jr. *General A.P. Hill: The Story of a Confederate Warrior*. New York: Vintage Books, 1992.

_____. *Soldiers Blue and Gray*. Columbia: University of South Carolina Press, 1988.

_____. *Stonewall Jackson: The Man, the Soldier, the Legend*. New York: Macmillan, 1997.

Robinson, Charles M. *Bad Hand: A Biography of General Ranald S. Mackenzie*. Austin, TX: State House Press, 1993.

Sanford, George B. *Fighting Rebels and Redskins: Experiences in Army Life of Colonel George B. Sanford, 1861–1892*. Edited by E.R. Hagemann. Norman: University of Oklahoma Press, 1969.

Sears, Stephen W. *Landscape Turned Red: The Battle of Antietam*. New York: Warner Books, 1983.

Sell, Bill. *Civil War Chronicles: Leaders of the North and South*. New York: Metro Books, 1996.
Sheridan, Philip H. *General Philip Sheridan: Civil War Memoirs*. New York, Toronto, London, Sydney, Auckland: Bantam Books, 1888, 1991.
Sifakis, Stewart. *Who Was Who in the Union*. New York: Facts on File, 1988.
Simson, Jay W. *Naval Strategies of the Civil War: Confederate Innovations and Federal Opportunism*. Nashville: Cumberland House Publishing, 2001.
Sklenar, Larry. *To Hell With Honor: Custer and the Little Big Horn*. Norman: University of Oklahoma Press, 2003.
Slade, A.D. *A.T.A. Torbert: Southern Gentleman in Union Blue*. Dayton: Morningside Press, 1992.
Smith, David M., ed. *Compelled to Appear in Print: The Vicksburg Manuscript of General John C. Pemberton*. Cincinnati: Ironclad Publishing, 1999.
Starr, Stephen Z. *The Union Cavalry in the Civil War*. 3 vols. Baton Rouge: Louisiana State University Press, 1976–1985.
Stiles, T.J., ed. *In Their Own Words: Civil War Commanders*. New York: A Perigee Book, Berkley Publishing Company, 1995.
Storrick, W.C. *Gettysburg: The Place — The Battle — The Results*. Harrisburg, PA: J. Horace McFarland, 1932.
Styple, William B., ed. *Generals in Bronze: Interviewing the Commanders of the Civil War*. Kearny, NJ: Belle Grove Publishing Co., 2005.
Time Life Books. *Brother Against Brother: Time-Life Books History of the Civil War*. New York, London, Toronto, Sydney, Tokyo, Singapore: Prentiss Hall Press, 1990.
Pohanka, Brian C. *Don Troiani's Civil War*. Illustrated by Don Troiani. Mechanicsburg, PA: Stackpole Books, 1995.
Trudeau, Noah Andre. *Gettysburg: A Testing of Courage*. New York: Harper Collins Publishers, 2002.
Urwin, Gregory J.W. *Custer Victorious*. London and Toronto: Associated University Presses, 1983.
Utley, Robert M. *Custer and the Great Controversy: The Origin and Development of a Legend*. Pasadena: Westernlore Press, 1980.
_____. *Frontier Regulars: The United States Army and the Indian, 1866–1890*. New York and London: Macmillan and Collier Macmillan Publishers, 1973.
Vaill, Dudley Landon. *The County Regiment: A Sketch of the 2nd Regiment of Connecticut Heavy Artillery, Originally the Nineteenth Volunteer Infantry in the Civil War*. Litchfield County, MA: University Club, 1908.
Ward, Geoffrey C. *The Civil War: An Illustrated History*. With Ric Burns and Ken Burns. New York: Alfred A. Knopf, 1990.
Weitzel, Godfrey. "The Fall of Richmond." In *The New Annals of the Civil War*. Edited by Peter Cozzens and Robert I. Giradi. Mechanicsburg, PA: Stackpole Books, 2004.
Wert, Jeffry D. *Custer: The Controversial Life of George Armstrong Custer*. New York: Simon & Schuster, 1996.
_____. *From Winchester to Cedar Creek: The Shenandoah Campaign of 1864*. New York, London, Toronto, Sydney, Tokyo: A Touchstone Book published by Simon & Schuster, 1987.
_____. *Mosby's Rangers*. New York, London, Sydney, Tokyo, and Singapore: Simon & Schuster, 1990.
Williams, T. Harry. *Lincoln and His Generals*. New York and Toronto, Canada: Vintage Books and Alfred A. Knopf, 1952.
Williamson, James J. *Mosby Rangers: The Operations of the 43rd Battalion of Virginia Cavalry From Its Organization to the Surrender*. New York: Sturgis and Walton, 1901.
Wittenberg, Eric, ed. *One of Custer's Wolverines: The Civil War Letters of General James H. Kidd, 6th Michigan Cavalry Regiment*. London and Kent, OH: Kent State University Press, 1999.
_____. *Under Custer's Command: The Civil War Journal of James Henry Avery, Compiled by Karla Jean Husby*. Kent, OH: Kent State University Press, 1999.
Wittenberg, Eric J. *Glory Enough for All: Sheridan's Second Raid and the Battle of Trevilian Station*. Washington, DC: Brassey's, 2001.
_____. *Little Phil: A Reassessment of the Civil War Leadership of Gen. Philip H. Sheridan*. Washington, DC: Potomac Books, 2002.
Woodworth, Steven E., ed. *Leadership and Command in the American Civil War*. Campbell, CA: Savas Woodbury Publishers, 1995.
Wormser, Richard. *The Yellowlegs: The Story of the United States Cavalry*. Garden City, New York: Doubleday & Co., 1966.

Transcripts

"Proceedings, Findings, and Opinions of the Court of Inquiry convened by order of the President of the United States in Special Orders No. 277, Headquarters of the Army, Adjutant General's Office, Washington, D.C., Dec. 9, 1879. In the Case of Gouverneur K. Warren, Late Major General, U.S. Volunteers, Commanding the Fifth Army Corps in the Campaign of Five Forks, VA, 1865." In Three Parts with Maps. Washington, D.C: Government Printing Office, 1883.
"Southern Historical Society Papers, Vol. XXVII." Richmond, VA: January to December 1899.
U.S. War Department. "The War of the Rebellion: A Compilation of Official Records of the Union and Confederate Armies." 128 vols. Washington, DC: U.S. Government Printing Office, 1880–1901.

Periodical Articles

Ambrose, Stephen E. "An Appraisal of Lincoln — The Savior of His Country." *Civil War Times Illustrated* 6, No. 10 (February 1968).
_____. "Halleck — The Despised 'Old Brains.'" *Civil War Times Illustrated* 1, no. 4 (July 1962).

_____. "The War Comes to West Point." *Civil War Times Illustrated* 4, no. 5 (August 1965).
Bakeless, John. "The Mystery of Appomattox." *Civil War Times Illustrated* 9, no 3 (June 1970).
Barton, John V. "The Procurement of Horses." *Civil War Times Illustrated* 6, no. 8 (December 1967).
Bearss, Edwin C. "We Have to Save the People." *Civil War Times Illustrated* 39, no. 2 (May 2000).
Benton, Barbara. "The Antagonists of Little Round Top." *MHQ: The Quarterly Journal of Military History* 5, no. 4 (Summer 1993).
Biven, Ken. "The Fall of Richmond: Driving Dixie Down." *America's Civil War* (May 1995).
Boehm, Robert B. "The Jones-Imboden Raid through West Virginia." *Civil War Times Illustrated* 3, no. 2 (May 1964).
_____. "The Unfortunate Averell." *Civil War Times Illustrated* 5, no. 5 (August 1966).
Brennan, Patrick "The Best Cavalry in the World." *North & South* 2, no. 2 (January 1999).
Brown, D. Alexander. "Grierson's Raid: 'Most Brilliant' of the War." *Civil War Times Illustrated* 3, no. 9 (January 1965).
Bundy, Carol. "The Transcendental Chevalier: Charles Russell Lowell." *Civil War Times* 44, no. 5 (October 2005).
Carmichael, Peter S. "We Shall Never Any of Us Be the Same." *Civil War Times Illustrated* 39, no. 2 (May 2000).
Castel, Albert. "Why the North Won and the South Lost." *Civil War Times Illustrated* 39, no. 2 (May 2000).
Cheeks, Robert C. "Fire and Fury at Catherine's Furnace." *America's Civil War* (May 1995).
Cullen, Joseph P. "The Battle of Chancellorsville." *Civil War Times Illustrated* 7, no. 2 (May 1968).
_____. "The Battle of Cold Harbor." *Civil War Times Illustrated* 2, no. 7 (November 1963).
_____. "The Battle of Malvern Hill." *Civil War Times Illustrated* 5, no. 2 (May 1966).
_____. "Battle of the Wilderness." *Civil War Times Illustrated* 10, no. 1 (April 1971).
_____. "Cedar Creek." *Civil War Times Illustrated* 8, no. 8 (December 1969).
_____. "Sheridan Wins at Winchester." *Civil War Times Illustrated* 6, no. 2 (May 1967).
_____. "The Siege of Petersburg." *Civil War Times Illustrated* 9, no. 5 (August 1970).
_____. "Spotsylvania." *Civil War Times Illustrated* 10, no. 2 (May 1971).
Davis, William C. "John C. Breckinridge: A Profile." *Civil War Times Illustrated* 6, no. 3 (June 1967).
_____. "Jubilee: General Jubal A. Early." *Civil War Times Illustrated* 9, No. 8 (December 1970).
Dowdey, Clifford. "General Lee's Unsolved Problem: Its Name Was Jefferson Davis." *American Heritage Civil War Chronicles* (1993).
Faeder, Gustav. "The Best of Enemies." *Civil War Times Illustrated* 26, no. 6 (October 1987).
Fordney, Ben. "Stoneman's Chancellorsville Raid: Failure or Harbinger?" *Civil War: The Magazine of the Civil War Society* 50 (April 1995).
Gallagher, Gary W. "There is a Rancor in Our Hearts... Which You Little Dream of." *Civil War Times Illustrated* 39, no. 2 (May 2000).
Gerleman, David J. "War Horse." *North & South* 2, no. 2 (January 1999).
Griffith, Paddy. "Civil War Cavalry: Missed Opportunities." *MHQ: The Quarterly Journal of Military History* 1, no. 3 (Spring 1989).
Grimsley, Mark. "Robert E. Lee: The Life and Career of the Master General." *Civil War Times Illustrated* 24, no. 7 (November 1985).
"'Grumble' Jones: A Personality Profile." *Civil War Times Illustrated* 7, no. 3 (June 1968).
Guttman, Jon. "Beauregard Battles the Beast." *America's Civil War* (March 1998).
Hassler, William W. "The Battle of Yellow Tavern." *Civil War Times Illustrated* 5, no. 7 (November 1966).
_____. "John Pelham of the Horse Artillery." *Civil War Times Illustrated* 3, no. 5 (August 1964).
_____. "The Slaughter Pen at Bristoe Station." *Civil War Times Illustrated* 1, no. 2 (May, 1962).
Hutton, Paul A. "Paladin of the Republic." *MHQ: The Quarterly Journal of Military History* 4, no. 3 (Spring 1992).
Jones, V.C. "The Story of the Kilpatrick-Dahlgren Raid." *Civil War Times Illustrated* 4, no. 1 (April 1965).
Kimball, William J. "The Little Battle of Big Bethel." *Civil War Times Illustrated* 6, no. 3 (June 1967).
Klein, Frederic S. "Butler at Bermuda Hundred." *Civil War Times Illustrated* 6, no. 7 (November 1967).
Klein, Maury. "J.E.B. Stuart's Life: A Feature Review." *Civil War Times Illustrated* 25, no. 5 (September 1986).
Kurtz, Henry J. "Five Forks: The South's Waterloo. " *Civil War Times Illustrated* 3, no. 6 (October 1964).
LaFantasie, Glenn. "The Other Man." *MHQ: The Quarterly Journal of Military History* 5, no. 4 (Summer 1993).
"Lee Blamed Ewell and Longstreet for His Failure in the Wilderness." *Civil War Times Illustrated* 5, no. 1 (April 1966).
Longacre, Edward G. "The Blackest of All Days." *Civil War Times Illustrated* 25, no. 1 (March 1986).
_____. "First of Seven." *Civil War Times Illustrated* 25, no. 9 (January 1987).
_____. "Gouverneur K. Warren: A Profile. " *Civil War Times Illustrated* 10, no. 9 (January 1972).
_____. "John Gibbon: Cool as a Steel Knife." *Civil War Illustrated* 26, no. 7 (November 1987).
_____. "Judson Kilpatrick." *Civil War Times Illustrated* 10, no.1 (April 1971).
_____. "The Raid That Failed." *Civil War Times Illustrated* 26, no. 9 (January 1988).
_____. "The Wilson-Kautz Raid." *Civil War Times Illustrated* 9, no. 2 (May 1970).
Luvaas, Dr. Jay. "Cavalry Lessons of the Civil War." *Civil War Times Illustrated* 6, no. 9 (January 1968).
Luvaas, Dr. Jay, and Col. Wilbur S. Nye. "The Campaign That History Forgot." *Civil War Times Illustrated* 8, no. 7 (November, 1969).
Mahone, William, Major General (CSA). "On the Road to Appomattox." *Civil War Times Illustrated* 9, no. 9 (January 1971).
McChesney, James Z. "The Burning of Chambersburg." *Civil War Times Illustrated* 10, no. 7 (November 1971).

McDowell, John E. "Nathaniel Banks: Fighting Politico." *Civil War Times Illustrated* 11, no. 9 (January 1973).

Miller, William J. "The Hope of the Confederacy: A Conversation with Steven E. Woodworth." *Civil War Magazine* 57 (June 1996).

Mitchell, Joseph B. "The Battle of Saylor's Creek." *Civil War Times Illustrated* 4, no. 6 (October 1965).

Murphy, Brian John. "When the Yankees Drove Old Dixie Down." *Civil War Times* 44, no. 1 (April. 2005).

Murray, Williamson. "What Took the North So Long?" *MHQ: The Quarterly Journal of Military History* 1, no. 4 (Summer 1989).

Naisawald, L. VanLoan. "The Battle of Chantilly." *Civil War Times Illustrated* 3, no. 7 (June 1964).

_____. "The Fitz John Porter Case." *Civil War Times Illustrated* 7, no. 3 (June 1968)

_____. "Stuart as a Cavalryman's Cavalryman." *Civil War Times Illustrated* 1, no. 10 (February 1963).

Nye, Wilbur S. "James H. Wilson: A Profile." *Civil War Times Illustrated* 1, no. 2 (May 1962).

_____. "U.S. Grant — Genius or Fortune's Child?" *Civil War Times Illustrated* 4, no. 3 (June 1965).

O'Brien, Jean Getmann. "The Last Days of Jackson." *Civil War Times Illustrated* 2, no. 8 (December 1963).

Osborne, Charles C. "Early's Raid on Washington." *MHQ: The Quarterly Journal of Military History* 6, no. 1 (Autumn 1993).

Patterson, Gerald A. "George E. Pickett: A Personality Profile." *Civil War Times Illustrated* 5, no. 2 (May 1966).

Razza, Michael S. "The Man Behind the Mine." *Civil War Magazine* 57 (June 1996).

Robertson, James I., Jr. "Story of the Stonewall Brigade." *Civil War Times Illustrated* 2, no. 8 (December 1963).

Robertson, Robert S. "Into the Furnace of the Wilderness." *Civil War Times Illustrated* 8, no. 1 (April 1969).

Rose, Gideon. "The Victor." *MHQ: The Quarterly Journal of Military History* 5, no. 4 (Summer 1993).

Schiller, Lawrence D. "A Taste of Northern Steel." *North & South* 2, no. 2 (January 1999).

Sears, Stephen W. "America's Bloodiest Day: The Battle of Antietam." *Civil War Times Illustrated* 26, no. 2 (April 1987).

_____. "The Court-Martial of Fitz John Porter." *MHQ: The Quarterly Journal of Military History* 5, no. 3 (Spring 1993).

_____. "In Defense of Fighting Joe Hooker." *North & South* 1, no. 1 (November 1997).

_____. "Stonewall Jackson's Last March." *MHQ: The Quarterly Journal of Military History* 8, no. 4 (Summer 1996).

Sharra, Jeff. "Lee in the Wilderness." *Civil War Times Illustrated* 37, no. 3 (June 1998).

Steffen, Randy. "The Blakeslee Quickloader." *Civil War Times, Illustrated* 1, no. 6 (October 1962).

Stinson, Dr. Byron. "Civil War Combat Fatigue and How it was Treated." *Civil War Times Illustrated* 4, no. 7 (November 1965).

Stackpole, Edward J. "The Story of the Three Days at Gettysburg. " *Civil War Times Illustrated* 2, no. 4 (July 1963).

Taylor, John M. "The Crater." *MHQ: The Quarterly Journal of Military History* 10, no. 2 (Winter 1998).

Trudeau, Noah A. "A Frightful and Frightening Place." *Civil War Times Illustrated* 38, no. 2 (May 1999).

_____. "I Have a Great Contempt for History." *Civil War Times Illustrated* 30, no. 4 (October 1991).

_____. "Like the Lords of the World." *Civil War Times Illustrated* 39, no. 2 (May 2000).

_____. "No Brilliant Victory to Record." *America's Civil War* (May 1996).

_____. "The Walls of 1864." *MHQ: The Quarterly Journal of Military History* 6, no. 2 (Winter 1994).

Tucker, Glenn. "An Appraisal of Robert E. Lee." *Civil War Times Illustrated* 4, no. 1 (April 1965).

_____. "Longstreet: Culprit or Scapegoat?" *Civil War Times Illustrated* 1, no. 1 (April 1962).

_____. "Pickett's Report on Gettysburg." *Civil War Times Illustrated* 6, no. 6 (October 1967).

_____. "Winfield S. Hancock: A Personality Profile." *Civil War Times Illustrated* 7, No. 5 (August 1968).

Utley, Robert M. "Crook and Miles, Fighting and Feuding on the Indian Frontier." *MHQ: The Quarterly Journal of Military History* 2, no. 1 (Autumn 1989).

_____. "Last Stand." *MHQ: The Quarterly Journal of Military History* 1, no. 1 (Autumn 1988).

Weigley, Russell F. "David McMurtie Gregg: A Profile." *Civil War Times Illustrated* 1, no. 7 (November 1962).

Weigley, Russell F. "John Buford: A Personality Profile." *Civil War Times Illustrated* 5, no. 3 (June 1966).

_____. "Philip H. Sheridan: A Personality Profile." *Civil War Times Illustrated* 7, no. 4 (July 1968).

Weinert, Richard P. "Longstreet's Suffolk Campaign." *Civil War Times Illustrated* 7, no. 9 (January 1969).

_____. "Lee and His Staff." *Civil War Times Illustrated* 11, no. 4 (July 1972).

Wert, Jeffry D. "His Unhonored Service." *Civil War Times Illustrated* 24, no. 4 (June 1985).

_____. "No Retreat Was Ever Possible." *Civil War Times Illustrated* 39, no. 2 (May 2000).

Wiley, Bell I. "Jefferson Davis: An Appraisal." *Civil War Times Illustrated* 6, no. 1 (April 1967).

Williams, Robert A. "Haws Shop: A 'Storm of Shot and Shell.'" *Civil War Times Illustrated* 9, no. 9 (January 1971).

Wittenberg, Eric J. "Learning the Hard Lessons of Logistics." *North & South* 2, no. 2 (January 1999).

Young, John R. "Grant Remembers Appomattox." *Civil War Times Illustrated* 9, no. 3 (June 1970).

Special Collections

"G.K. Warren Biographical Note." *Gouverneur Kemble Warren Papers, 1848–1882*. Albany: New York State Library, 1994.

Wallace, Ernest. "Mackenzie, Ranald Slidell." *The Handbook of Texas Online*. Austin: The General Libraries of the University of Texas at Austin and the Texas State Historical Association, 2005.

"W.W. Averell Biographical Note." *William Woods Averell Papers, 1836–1910*. Albany: New York State Library, 1991.

Index

I Corps, Army of Northern Virginia, Confederate 26, 34, 90, 119, 125, 182, 221
I Corps, Army of the Potomac, Union 31, 35, 65, 109, 112, 113, 119, 121, 126, 131, 132, 133
II Corps, Army of Northern Virginia, Confederate 12, 34, 72, 90–96, 111, 119, 125, 147
II Corps, Army of the Potomac, Union 31, 65, 108, 119, 126, 127, 128, 131, 132, 133, 134, 135, 136, 137, 138, 139–140, 142, 144, 145, 150, 151, 152, 164, 176, 182, 187, 188, 189, 212
III Corps, Army of Northern Virginia, Confederate 119, 125
III Corps, Army of the Potomac, Union 23, 31, 34, 36, 65, 111, 118, 121, 126, 127, 128, 130, 132, 133, 134, 135, 137, 175
V Corps, Army of the Potomac, Union 31, 65, 111, 112, 113, 118, 121, 126, 128, 131, 132, 135, 137, 138, 140, 141, 142, 143, 145, 148, 149, 150, 151, 152, 153, 154, 155, 156, 157, 158, 159, 161, 162, 164, 165, 167, 175, 176, 182, 183, 184, 185, 187, 188, 189, 191, 212, 217
VI Corps, Army of the Potomac (Army of the Shenandoah), Union 31, 48–52, 53, 62, 65, 69, 70, 75, 78, 87, 89–96, 111, 118, 121, 124, 126, 130, 131, 135, 137, 138, 141, 142, 143, 144, 145, 148, 151, 153, 177, 178, 179, 180, 181, 188
IX Corps, Army of the Potomac, Union 74, 112, 113, 128, 139, 142, 143, 145, 148, 174, 181, 188
X Corps, Army of the James, Union 146, 149, 181
XI Corps, Army of the Potomac, Union 31, 35, 36, 109, 110, 112, 118, 121, 125
XII Corps, Army of the Potomac, Union 31, 35, 109, 110, 112, 118, 125
XVIII Corps, Army of the James, Union 145, 146, 147, 149, 181
XIX Corps, Army of the Shenandoah, Union 48–52, 53, 75–78, 87, 89–96, 178, 179, 180
XX Corps, Union 125
XXIV Corps, Army of the James, Union 149, 181, 187, 190, 191
XXV Corps, Army of the James, Union 149, 181, 187, 188

Adobe Walls 195
Alamagordo, New Mexico 193
Aldie, Battle of 120
Alleghenies 85
Allenby, Sir Edmund 218
Amelia Court House, Virginia 188, 189
Amissville, Virginia 126, 130
Anaedarko, Battle of 195
Anderson, Richard H. 33, 70, 118–119, 127–128, 140, 141–144, 150, 189, 220

Annapolis, Virginia 138
Antietam Furnace 43, 44
Antietam (Maryland) Campaign 20, 23, 62, 114, 174
Apache 192, 194, 198, 201, 202
Apache Wars 202
Appomattox Campaign 2, 29, 48, 165, 182, 185, 187–191, 218
Appomattox Court House, Virginia 187, 190, 191, 212, 218, 221, 222
Appomattox River 187, 188, 189, 190
Appomattox Station, Virginia 190, 191
Aquia Landing 130
Army of Mississippi, Confederate 97
Army of Northern Virginia, Confederate 1, 11, 12, 21, 24, 25, 26, 29–36, 37, 48, 53, 62, 68, 97, 109, 110, 112, 119, 120, 125, 129, 141, 142, 146, 149, 150, 161, 177, 183, 212, 214, 215, 219, 222
Army of Tennessee, Confederate 11, 65, 97, 125, 149
Army of the Cumberland, Union 38, 67, 125
Army of the James, Union 11, 140, 141, 142, 144, 146, 148, 149, 181, 191
Army of the Potomac, Union 1, 11, 13, 19, 20, 21, 24, 25, 26, 29–36, 54–62, 64, 65, 71, 74, 76, 94, 100, 105, 111, 118, 119, 120, 121, 125, 129, 130, 132, 137, 138, 139, 140, 141, 144, 146, 147, 148, 149, 162, 166, 174, 176, 183, 185, 191, 208, 213, 214, 215, 216, 220, 222
Army of the Shenandoah, Union 19, 40, 74, 75, 76, 87, 100, 148
Army of Virginia, Union 13, 20, 111–114
Army of West Virginia/VIII Corps, Union 11, 39, 46, 48–52, 75–78, 89–96, 178, 179, 180, 184, 204
Arnold, Benedict 116
Arthur, Chester A. 117
Ashland, Virginia 142
Atlanta, Georgia 1, 11, 12, 36, 125, 177
Atlanta Campaign 64, 177, 219, 221
Auburn, Virginia 126, 127
Augur, C.C. 163
Averell, William Woods 1, 2, 13, 15, 17, 19–23, 24–28, 29–36, 37, 40, 41–47, 48–52, 53–58, 61, 63, 74–78, 86, 120, 178, 201, 211–212, 213, 216
Ayres, R.B., 151–152, 157, 158, 162, 163, 164, 165, 166

"Bad Hand (Broken Hand)" 177
Baker, Lafayette 183
Baltimore, Maryland 108
Baltimore & Ohio Railroaded 76, 91
Banks, Nathaniel 11, 109, 111
Banks Ford 29, 30, 31, 119
Barlow, Francis 139, 143, 145
Barns, James 175
Bearcoat 203

233

Beauregard, P.G.T. 9, 143, 147, 182, 220
Beaver Dam Creek 109
Belknap, William W. 194, 207
Belle Grove Plantation 91, 93
Benteen, Frederick W. 209
Bermuda Hundred, Virginia 11, 138, 144, 147, 187, 220
Berryville, Virginia 42, 75, 76
Berryville Pike 178
Bethesda Church 145
Beverly Ford 30
Big Bethel, Battle of 106–108
Big Round Top 121, 122
Birney, David B. 140, 143
Black Kettle 206
Bloomingdale Asylum 198
Blue Ridge Mountains 75, 79, 80, 83, 85, 91, 98
Boonsborough, Maryland 76
Boydton Plank Roader 150, 151, 152, 154, 155, 163, 164, 165
Bracketville, Texas 197
Bragg, Braxton 9, 11, 53, 219, 220
Brandy Station 32, 126, 130
Brandy Station, First Battle of 68, 120
Brandy Station, Second Battle of 126
Breckinridge, John C. 7, 11, 12, 179–180
Bristoe Station, Battle of 105, 127–128, 135, 176
Bristoe Station, Virginia 126, 127, 128, 129
Broad Run 127–128
Brown's Gap 83
Buchanan, Franklin 273
Buckland, Virginia 127
Buell, Don Carlos 16, 217, 221
Buell, George C. 195
Buford, John 30, 36, 64, 74, 121, 126, 221
Buford, Napoleon Bonaparte 115
Bull Run Creek 138
Bull Run Mountains 112
Bunker Hill, Virginia 45, 46
Burkeville, Virginia 149, 190
Burnside, Ambrose E. 13, 14, 20, 21, 74, 138, 139, 143–144, 145, 148, 181, 214
Burnside's Mud March 21
Butler, Benjamin 11, 106, 107, 119, 137, 141, 142, 144, 146, 147, 148, 181, 220, 221
Butler, Matthew C. 21, 69–70
Butterfield, Dan 14, 114

Cadwallader, Sylvanus 214
Calhoun, James 209
Cameron, Simon 21
Carr, James B. 134, 137
Carter, Robert 144, 197
Cartharpin Road 139
Casey, Silas 115
Catherine Furnace 34
Catlett's Station, Virginia 127
Catton, Bruce 215
Cavalry Bureau, Union 36, 64
Cavalry Corps, Army of the Potomac, Union 20, 22, 23, 24, 29, 31, 36, 62, 63, 64, 65, 66, 68, 84, 148, 183, 207, 208, 215, 216
Cedar Creek 50, 89, 90, 91, 94
Cedar Creek, Battle of 16, 41, 89–96, 100, 177, 180, 204, 212, 218, 221, 222
Cedar Mountain 32, 111
Cedarville, Virginia 49
Cemetery Ridge 121, 175, 181
Centennial Campaign 204, 207

Centreville, Virginia 127, 129
Chamberlain, Joshua Lawrence 10, 14, 116, 122–123, 150–153, 154–160, 162–164, 167, 217–218, 221
Chambersburg, Pennsylvania 39
Chancellor House 35
Chancellorsville, Battle of 14, 29–36, 48, 118–119, 121, 174, 214, 220
Chancellorsville, Virginia 31, 33, 34, 118, 132
Chancellorsville Campaign 19, 21, 26, 27, 29–36, 37, 62, 75, 120, 211
Chantilly Mansion, Battle of 114
Charleston, South Carolina 5, 61, 220
Charlestown, West Virginia 42, 44, 76
Charlestown Road 178
Charlottesville, Virginia 71, 72, 98, 100, 142
Chase, Salmon P. 115
Chattanooga, Battles for 125, 219, 221, 222
Chattanooga, Tennessee 65, 125
Cherry Run 42, 44
Chester Gap 98, 99
Chesapeake Bay 111
Cheyenne 197, 206
Chickahominy River 70, 71, 108, 109, 144, 145, 146
Chickamauga, Battle of 11, 125, 219, 221
Chiricahua 203
Chivington, John 201, 206
The Citadel 5
City Point, Virginia 74, 141, 147
Clairborne Road 151, 152, 187
Clayton's Store 71
Cleiburne, Patrick 54, 220
Cleveland, Grover 119
Cody, William F. "Buffalo Bill" 207
Cold Harbor, Battle of 12, 68, 70–71, 75, 144–146, 175, 213, 216, 217, 218
Comanche 192, 193, 194, 195, 196
Comancheria 193
Congressional Medal of Honor 124
Corbin's Bridge 139
Couch, Darius 118–119
Craig's Meeting House 138
Crater, Battle of the 74, 148, 181, 213
Crawford, S.W. 151–152, 157, 158–159, 160, 163, 164, 166, 187
Crazy Horse 203, 204
Criglersville, Virginia 99
Crook, George C. 15, 16, 19, 39, 48–52, 53, 75, 76, 89–96, 151–152, 178, 180, 183, 185, 189, 190, 191, 196, 201–203, 204, 205, 208, 209, 215, 217, 221
Crooked Run 49
Crow 201, 204
Crump Road 163, 165
Culpeper Court House, Virginia 26, 32, 64, 120, 125, 126, 129, 131, 132
Culpeper Ford 132
Culp's Hill 121
Cumberland, Maryland 75, 76
Curtis, Samuel 218, 221, 222
Custer, Elizabeth Clift Bacon "Libbie" 203, 209
Custer, George A. 15, 42, 46, 49, 64, 65, 55, 70, 71–73, 79–83, 84–88, 92–96, 98–99, 106, 129, 131, 151–152, 156, 159, 184, 189, 191, 192, 196, 197, 198, 199, 201, 204, 205–206, 208, 209, 212, 215, 216, 221
Custer, Thomas W. 209

Dahlgren, Ulrich 63
Danville, North Carolina 189
Davidson, John W. 195
Davies, Henry E. 65, 66, 190

Davis, Jefferson 6, 9, 11, 106, 109, 119–120, 149, 188, 189, 219, 220
Deep Creek 189
Department of Texas 198
Department of the Nueces 197
Department of the Susquehanna, Union 12, 41
Department of Virginia 191
Department of Washington, Union 12, 41
Department of West Virginia, Union 12, 38, 41, 43, 74, 75, 84
Devin, Thomas 50, 52, 53, 56, 70, 71–73, 82, 100, 151–153, 156, 158, 184, 191, 212
Dinwiddie Court House, Virginia 150, 151, 152, 154, 155, 159, 161, 162, 165, 183, 184, 185
District of Vicksburg, Union 160
Duffie, Alfred 41, 43, 74–76
Dull Knife 197, 03, 205
Duryea, Abram 107

Early, Jubal 12, 33, 38, 446, 48–52, 53, 56, 70, 72, 74–78, 84, 85, 88, 89–96, 98, 131, 133, 135, 141–144, 147, 148, 177–180, 212, 220, 222
Eisenschiml, Otto 116
Elkhorn Tavern/Pea Ridge, Battle of 218, 222
Ely's Ford 31, 33, 132, 138
Emancipation Proclamation 219, 221
Emmitsburg Road 122
Emory, William H. 49, 92
Engineer Battalion, Army of the Potomac 174
Evans, Clement A. 90, 95
Ewell, Richard 52, 70, 72, 112, 119, 120, 121, 125–127, 131, 133, 138, 142–144, 147, 188, 189, 220

Fair Play, Maryland 43, 44, 76
Falling Waters, Maryland 45, 62
Falmouth, Virginia 130
Farmville, Virginia 189, 190
Farragut, David G. 2, 11, 62, 171, 177, 218, 219
Finerty, John F. 203
Fisher's Hill 47, 48–52, 56, 80, 90, 180, 212
Fisher's Hill, Battle of 48–52, 80, 82, 90, 177, 212, 215, 217, 218, 221
Five Forks 150, 151, 152, 154, 155, 156, 159, 162, 167, 182, 183, 184, 185, 186, 187
Five Forks, Battle of 2, 48, 53, 105, 154–160, 161, 162, 164, 174, 183–186, 187, 188, 208, 215, 217, 218, 221, 222
Fleetwood Heights 126
Flint Hill 50
Ford Road 187
Ford's Depot, Virginia 183
Ford's Station, Virginia 187
Forrest, Nathan Bedford 10, 22, 121, 218, 220
Fort Apache 198
Fort Bascom, New Mexico 195
Fort Buford 203
Fort Clark 194, 197
Fort Concho, San Angelo, Texas 193
Fort Dodge 195
Fort Donelson 218, 222
Fort Fetterman 204
Fort Griffin 195
Fort Henry 218, 222
Fort Keogh 203
Fort Levenworth, Kansas 204
Fort Monroe, Virginia 106, 108
Fort Richardson 208
Fort Sam Houston, San Antonio, Texas 198
Fort Sill, Oklahoma (Indian Territory) 195, 196, 197

Fort Stedman 150
Franklin, Battle of 11, 220, 221
Frederick the Great 219
Fredericksburg, Battle of 20, 21, 23, 31, 62, 117, 130, 174, 214
Fredericksburg, Virginia 130, 131, 135, 138, 141, 142
Fredericksburg, Richmond & Petersburg Railroad 135
Fredericksburg Road 144
Frémont, John C. 65, 109, 217
French, William 130, 132–135, 137
Front Royal, Virginia 45, 49, 79, 82, 98, 99, 177

Gaines Mill, Battle of 109
Gainsville, Virginia 129
Gall 203
Garfield, James 115, 117
Geraldstown, Virginia 46
German Plank Road 131
Germanna Ford 31, 33, 131, 132, 138
Geronimo 205
Getty, George W. 116, 139
Gettysburg, Battle of 21, 26, 48, 62, 63, 105, 120, 121–124, 125, 135, 162, 174, 176, 181–182, 211, 214, 216, 219, 220, 221
Gettysburg, Pennsylvania 120
Gettysburg Battlefield Park 162
Gettysburg Campaign 26, 27, 68
Ghost Dancers 205
Gibbon, John 140, 143, 145, 204, 206, 221
Gilmer, Thomas 173
Glendale, Battle of 109
Goony Run 79
Gordon, John B. 90–96, 133, 178, 180
Gordonsville, Virginia 32, 71, 72, 98, 99, 111, 130, 142
Gordonsville Raid 96, 97–99, 212
Grant, Orville 207
Grant, Ulysses S. 1, 5, 6, 8, 9, 12, 13, 14, 15, 16, 29, 40, 45, 55, 56, 64, 66, 67, 69, 70–71, 75, 84, 87, 90, 91, 100, 106, 116–117, 119, 129, 137–148, 149, 150–153, 154–156, 159, 161–166, 171, 181, 183, 185, 186, 189–191, 194, 195, 207, 213, 214, 215, 217, 219, 220, 221, 222
Grant's Indian Peace Policy 195
Gravelly Ford 187
Gravelly Run Church 156
Gravelly Run Creek 150, 153, 154, 164
Great Sioux War 201, 202
Greenwich, Virginia 126, 127
Gregg, David M. 24, 36, 64, 65, 67, 69–70, 71–73, 75, 126, 128, 133, 138, 139, 144, 151, 215–217, 221
Grierson, Benjamin H. 97, 221
Griffin, Charles 151–153, 154, 157, 159, 160, 163, 164, 166, 191, 217
Groveton, Battle of 112, 119
Guiney Station, Virginia 33

Hagerstown, Maryland 39, 40
Hainesville, Virginia 45
Haley, James L. 209–210
Halleck, Henry W. 8, 9, 64, 87, 91, 110, 111, 120–121, 129–130, 217, 219, 221, 222
Halltown, Virginia 44, 76, 177
Hampton, Frank 68
Hampton, Wade 10, 21, 26, 27, 33, 34, 68, 69–70, 71–73, 125–126, 150
Hancock, Maryland 41, 75
Hancock, Winfield Scott 121, 137, 138, 139–141–144, 145, 147, 149, 175, 176, 221
Hancock Expedition of 1867 206

Hanover Junction, Virginia 182
Hanover Station, Virginia 29, 144
Hanover Town Ford 69
Harney, William 106
Harpers Ferry, West Virginia 40, 41, 42, 45, 74, 76, 120, 177
Harrison Landing, Virginia 20, 109, 110, 111
Harrisonburg, Virginia 84
Hatcher's Run 154, 181, 187
Haw's Shop, Battle of 68, 69–70, 75, 144, 216
Hayes, Rutherford B. 49–52, 89, 100, 116–117, 162, 166, 183
Hazel Grove 35, 121
Hazel River 64
Hazlett, Charles 114, 122–123
Henry House Hill 114
Heth, Henry 119, 121, 127–128
Hickok, James B. "Wild Bill" 207
Hill, A.P. 70, 110, 119–120, 125–128, 131, 134, 138, 139–140, 188, 198, 220
Hill, D.H. 106–108, 120, 125, 143, 220
Hitchcock, Ethan Allen 115
Hood, John Bell 9, 220
Hooker, Joseph 13, 19, 20–21, 22, 24, 25, 26, 27, 29–36, 37, 62, 63, 75, 117, 118–119, 120–121, 125, 174, 214, 216, 220
Hotkiss, Jedediah 6, 90
Howard, Oliver O. 35, 119, 120
Hudson River 174
Humphreys, Andrew A. 14, 144, 149, 150, 151, 181, 187, 189, 191
Humphreys Station, Virginia 183
Hunter, David 11, 12, 39, 71, 72, 115, 137, 146, 147

Imboden, John 26, 37, 90
Indian Ring 207
Indian Territory 193, 195

Jackson, Thomas J. "Stonewall" 6, 12, 34, 35, 36, 52, 109–110, 111–113, 119, 219, 220
Jackson's Shenandoah Valley Campaign of 1862 107, 112, 220, 222
Jacob's Ford 131, 132
James River 71, 109, 111, 137, 138,m 141, 142, 144, 146, 147, 149, 166, 217
James River Canal 71, 87, 100
Jefferson, Virginia 126
Jetersville, Virginia 189, 190
Johnson, Bradley 40
Johnson, Bushrod 150, 181
Johnson, Edward 126, 133, 134
Johnston, Albert S. 218, 220
Johnston, Joseph E. 9, 11, 97, 108, 109, 149, 150, 188, 189, 191, 220
Joint Congressional Committee on the Conduct of the War 64
Jones, William E. "Grumble" 26, 37, 72

Kanawha Valley 39
Kautz, A.V. 143, 147, 181
Kearney, Philip 114, 221
Kellogg, Elisha S. 176, 177
Kelly's Ford 29, 30, 31, 32, 33
Kelly's Ford, Battle of 19, 24–28
Keogh, Myles 64
Kernstown, Second Battle of 19, 39, 75
Kershaw, Joseph 90–96, 177
Kickapoo 192, 193, 194
Kidd, James H. 81, 82, 84, 92

Kilpatrick, Hugh Judson 62, 63, 65, 66, 106, 126, 127, 129, 298, 208
Kilpatrick-Dahlgren Raid 63, 66
King, Rufus 115
Kiowa 192, 193, 194
Kitching, Howard 89, 92
Knoxville, Tennessee 38, 221

Lacey Springs, Virginia 98
Lakota Sioux 196
Langdon, Louis L. 263
Laurel Brigade, Confederate 70, 72, 85
Lee, Fitzhugh 10, 24, 26–28, 33, 34, 35, 48, 68, 72, 125–126, 150–153, 156–157, 159, 179–180, 181, 183
Lee, George Washington Custis 106
Lee, Robert E. 1, 2, 9, 11, 12, 24, 25, 26, 29–36, 37, 48, 68, 69, 70, 71, 72, 73, 90, 97, 106, 108, 109–110, 111–114, 115, 117, 118–120, 123, 125–128, 129–136, 137–148, 149–153, 156, 161, 164, 177, 181, 183, 184, 185, 186, 187–191, 212, 215, 217, 221
Lee, W.H.F. "Rooney" 26, 32, 33, 36, 68–69, 150, 152, 155–156, 159, 184
Lee's Mill 74
Leetown, Virginia 46
Leonard's Mill 189
Lewisberg, Virginia 38, 39
Liberty Mills 99
Light Division, Confederate 119
Lincoln, Abraham 1, 6, 8, 9, 10, 11, 12, 13, 21, 64, 91, 108, 109, 110, 115–116, 120, 121, 129–130, 161, 166, 190, 219, 221, 222
Lipan 192, 193, 194
Little Bethel, Virginia 106, 107
Little Big Horn, Battle of the 15, 42, 64, 191, 196, 197, 201, 206, 207, 208, 209
Little North Mountain 48, 50, 51
Little Round Top 105, 121–124, 174–175
Little Wolf 208
Littlepage's Ford 144
Llanco Estacado 193
Locust Grove 131, 132, 133, 135
Lomax, Lunsford 45, 48–52, 86–88, 90, 91, 95, 96, 98–99
Longfellow, Henry W. 171
Longstreet, James 26, 30, 33, 70, 90, 110, 112–114, 116, 119, 120, 121, 125, 138, 139–140, 141, 150, 175, 181, 182, 188, 221
Lookout Mountain, Battle of 125
Lost Valley Fight 195
Louisa Court House, Virginia 72
Lowell, Charles R. 49, 75, 76, 79–83, 88, 96, 212
Luray Valley 49, 53, 79, 80, 61, 84, 85, 88, 212
Lyman, Theodore 145
Lynchburg, Virginia 39, 71, 72, 98, 142, 145, 189, 190
Lyon, Nathaniel 221

Mackenzie, Alexander S., Jr. 171
Mackenzie, Alexander S., Sr. 171–174, 199
Mackenzie, Harriet 171, 200
Mackenzie, Morris R.S. 171
Mackenzie, Ranald S. 1, 2, 15, 66, 106, 149, 154, 156–158, 171–175, 176–180, 181–186, 187–191, 192–200, 201, 205, 207, 208–210, 211, 221
Madison Court House 99, 126
Magruder, John 106–108, 109
Mahone, William 148
Malvern Hill, Battle of 20, 109
Manassas/Bull Run, First Battle of 20, 61, 129, 220
Manassas/Bull Run, Second Battle of 13, 20, 29, 62, 94, 106, 111–117, 118, 119, 122, 129, 174, 219, 221

Manassas Gap 91
Manassas Gap Railroad 50
Manassas Junction, Virginia 112, 120, 137
March Through the Carolinas 64, 65, 150, 221
March to the Sea 64, 65, 221
Maricopa 201
Marshall, S.L.A. 206
Martinsburg, Virginia 38, 39, 41–42, 43, 44, 75, 76, 91
Marye's Heights 31
Maryland Heights 120
Massanutten Mountain 48, 49, 79
McCausland 39–40
McClellan, George B. 1, 13, 14, 20, 26, 70, 94, 108–110, 111–115, 117, 177, 214, 218, 219, 220, 221
McClellan Creek 194
McCoy's Ford 79, 80
McDowell, Irvin 20, 109, 113–117
McLaws, Lafayette 34, 35
McPherson, James B. 221
Meade, George G., 9. 13, 14, 64, 65, 75, 106, 118–119, 121–124, 125–127, 129–136, 137–148, 152–153, 154, 162–164, 166, 174–175, 176, 189, 213, 214, 215, 221, 222
Meadow Bridge 144
Mechanicsburg, Battle of 109, 144
Meigs, John F. 6, 75
Meigs, Montgomery C. 24
Merritt, Wesley 15, 41, 49, 66, 70, 71–73, 74, 76–78, 79–83, 86–88, 89–96, 98–99, 100, 106, 141, 148, 151, 154–156, 178–180, 183, 184,m 197, 201, 205, 207–208, 210, 212, 221
Mexican War 219
Michigan Cavalry Brigade, Union 65, 66, 71–73, 79, 81, 82, 84, 93, 131, 199
Middle Department, Union 12, 37, 41
Middle Military Division, Union 12, 19, 39, 40, 41, 42, 43, 44, 45, 55, 56, 74, 84, 100, 148, 177, 213
Middleburg, Battle of 120
Middletown, Virginia 88, 89
Miles, Nelson A. 15, 66, 151–152, 187, 195, 196, 201, 202, 203–205, 221
Milford, Virginia 79, 80, 81
Mill Creek 94
Mill Springs, Battle of 21, 221
Mills Gap 42
Mine Run 121, 133, 135, 138
Mine Run Campaign 64, 105, 129–136, 137, 176
Missionary Ridge, Battle of 10, 53, 65, 218
Mississippi River 105, 106, 120, 162, 193, 219, 220
Mobile, Alabama 11
Moorefield, Battle of 39, 40
Morristown, New Jersey 173, 174
Morton's Ford 131, 132
Mosby, John S. 15, 22, 181
Mott, Gershom 140, 143
Mount Jackson 53
Munford, Thomas 21, 80, 85, 150, 155, 157

Namozino Road 187, 189
Nashville, Battle of 11, 121
National Detective Police 183
New Cold Harbor 70, 71, 144, 147
New Hope Church 133, 135
New Market, Battle of 11, 137, 14
New Market, Virginia 82, 83
New Market Gap 49, 83, 212
New Market Road 182
New Orleans, Battle of 218
New Orleans, Louisiana 218
New York, New York 198

Newton, John 131, 135, 163
Newtown, Virginia 75
Nez Perce War 205, 206, 208
Norfolk & Petersburg Railroad 183
North Anna, Battle of 144
North Anna River 71, 144
Northern Cheyenne 196, 197, 201, 203, 204, 205, 207, 208

Oates, William 121–123
Office of Military Information 26
Old Cold Harbor 70, 144, 145
Old Orange Turnpike 133
Opequon Creek 177, 180
Orange & Alexandria Railroad 26, 32, 126, 131
Orange Court House 125, 138
Orange (Court House) Plank Road 138
Orange Turnpike 138
Ord, Edward O.C. 149, 181, 183, 187, 190, 191
O'Rorke, Patrick 122–123
Overall's Run 80
Overland Campaign 12, 29, 30, 66, 68, 70, 105, 137–148, 153, 175, 213, 215, 222

Paiute War 202
Paiutes 201, 202, 204
Palo Duro Canyon 195
Palo Duro Canyon, Battle of 196
Pamunkey River 32, 69, 144
Parke, John G. 148, 183
Parker, Quanah 193, 196
Parker's Store 131, 133, 138, 139
Payne, William H. 91–92
Payne's Farm, Battle of 134
Peach Orchard, the 121, 122
Pegram, John 90
Pelham, John 27
Pemberton, John 97, 220
Pender, Dorsey 119
Pendleton, Alexander S. 52
Pendleton, William 52, 119
Peninsula, the 111, 112
Peninsula Campaign 20, 23, 62, 108–110, 218
"Perpetual Punisher" 177, 199, 208
Perry, Matthew C. 171
Perry, Oliver H. 171
Perryville, Battle of 16, 67, 218, 219
Peter Principle 63, 100
Petersburg, Siege of 72, 74, 76, 87, 91, 97, 140, 147–148, 149, 175, 177, 178, 213, 220
Petersburg, Virginia 11, 12, 71, 72, 74, 76, 87, 91, 97, 143, 147, 148, 149, 150, 160, 166, 175, 177, 181, 182, 186, 187, 188, 189, 214, 217, 220
Pickett, George E. 120, 150, 151–153, 154–160, 162, 181–186
Pickett's Charge 62, 127
Pierce, Ebenezer 107
Pima 201
Piney Branch Church 141
Pinkerton, Alan 110
Pleasants, Henry 74
Pleasonton, Alfred 8, 24, 31, 36, 63, 64, 65,m 66, 120, 126, 216, 221, 222
Point of Rocks, Maryland 76
Polk Leonidas K. n9
Pope, John 13, 20, 106, 110, 111–117, 214
Port Hudson, Siege of 119, 219
Port Republic, Virginia 83, 84
Porter, Fitz John 8, 106, 109, 110, 113–117, 162, 217
Potomac River 42, 43, 76, 111

Powder River 197, 204, 208
Powell, William H. 55, 82, 84, 87, 89, 91, 92, 95, 96, 98–99
Prentiss, Benjamin 115
Price, Sterling 220–221, 222
Price, William Redwood 195
Prince, Henry 132, 134, 137
Prince Edward Court House, Virginia 190
U.S.S. *Princeton* 173
Pughtown, Virginia 46

Quaker Road 150, 163
Quaker Road, Battle of the 150

Raccoon Ford 131
Ramseur, Stephen D. 39, 43, 51, 77, 90, 95, 96, 106, 178
Rancheria 194
Rapidan River 99, 125, 126, 131, 132, 138
Rapidan Station, Virginia 32, 33, 130, 133
Rappahannock River 25, 26, 27, 30, 31, 35, 111, 112, 119, 120, 125, 126, 130, 138
Rappahannock Station, Virginia 112
Rawlins, John 147
Reams Station, Virginia 183
Reconstrruction 192, 193, 208
Red Cloud 192, 197
Red Cloud Agency 197, 208
Red River 194
Red River, Battle of 195
Red River War 195–196, 203, 204
Reno, Jesse L. 174
Reno, Marcus A. 42, 209
Reserve Brigade, Cavalry Corps, Army of the Potomac, Union 30, 76, 82, 88
Reynolds, John F. 114, 121, 122
Richmond, Virginia 11, 27, 30, 31, 32, 33, 68, 69, 70, 99, 108, 111, 120, 125, 131, 141, 142, 143, 144, 146, 147, 149, 153, 181, 186, 187, 188, 189, 218
Richmond & Danville Railroad 149, 188, 189
Richmond, Fredericksburg & Potomac Railroad 31, 32, 100, 132
Richmond Garrison 189
Ricketts, James B. 93, 115
Rienzi 94
Rio Grande River 193, 194
Roberts, Benjamin 37
Roberts Brigade, Confederate 156, 183, 184
Robertson's (Robinson's) Tavern 121, 135
Rodes, Robert E. 126, 133, 178–179
Rosebud, Battle of the 201, 204, 209
Rosecrans, William S. 221
Rosser, Thomas L. 21, 70, 72, 85–88, 90–96, 98, 106, 126, 140, 150, 152, 156, 183
Rowanty River 183
Rude's Hill 56, 82–83
Russell, D.A. 69, 77, 179

St. Louis, Missouri 65, 217, 221
San Carlos Reservation 205
San Rodrigo River 194
Sand Creek Massacre 201, 205
Sandy Grove Church 138
Sanford, George B. 74
Savage's Station, Virginia 109
Saylor's Creek, Battle of 189, 216, 218
Schenck, Robert 37
Scholfield, John M. 116
Scott, Winfield F. 5, 8, 108, 214
Scott's Anaconda Plan 219

Sedgwick, John 31, 33, 35, 118, 120, 130, 131, 134, 135, 138, 139–140, 141–144, 221
Selma, Virginia 38
Seminary Ridge 62
Semmes, Raphael 173
Senseney Road 178
Seven Days' Battle 20, 62, 109–110, 214, 219
Seven Pines/Fair Oaks, Battle of 108, 109
Sharpsburg, Maryland 42
Shenandoah Peak 98
Shenandoah River 75, 99
Shenandoah River, North Fork 48, 79
Shenandoah River, South Fork 79, 83
Shenandoah Valley 7, 11, 12, 26, 38, 71, 72, 75, 76, 84, 85, 86, 97, 98, 109, 110, 111, 112, 120, 137, 138, 144, 147, 148, 177, 208, 212, 215, 216, 217, 219, 222
Shepherdstown, Virginia 42, 44, 76
Sheridan, Philip Henry "Little Phil" 1, 2, 6, 10, 12, 13, 14, 15, 16, 19, 21, 26, 30, 37, 39, 40, 41–47, 48–52, 53–58, 63, 64, 65, 66, 67, 68–73, 74–78, 79–83, 84–88, 97–100, 105, 139, 140, 141–142, 144, 146, 148, 149–153, 154–160, 161–167, 171, 177–180, 181, 183–186, 187–191, 192, 193, 196, 201, 202, 205, 206, 207, 208, 211, 212, 213–214, 215, 216, 217–218, 219, 220, 222
Sheridan's Provisional Cavalry Corps 74, 97
Sheridan's Shenandoah Valley Campaign of 1864 19, 74, 84, 87, 91, 97, 180, 211, 216, 222
Sherman, William T. 1, 2, 8, 10, 11, 14, 16, 40, 63, 65, 91, 149, 150, 165–166, 186, 189, 203, 204, 205, 215, 221, 222
Shiloh, Battle of 218, 220, 222
Shoshonis 197, 201, 204
Sickles, Daniel 34, 35, 119, 121, 175, 221
Siegle, Franz 11, 38, 137, 144, 146
Sioux 192, 197, 203, 204, 207
Sitting Bull 203, 205
Slade, A.D. 206, 214
Slidel, John 171
Slocum, John 31, 33, 35, 118–119
Slough, James 115
Smith, Charles F. 221, 222
Smith, Edmund Kirby 11, 191, 219, 220
Smith, William F. "Baldy" 10, 12, 145, 148, 211
Smithfield, West Virginia 42, 76
U.S.S. *Somers* 172, 173
Somers Affair 171–174
Southern Arapaho 192, 193, 194
Southern Cheyenne 192, 193, 194, 196
Southside Railroad 149, 150, 154, 183
Southwestern Mountain 99
Spencer, John C. 171–172
Sperryville, Virginia 126, 130
Spotsylvania, Battle of 69, 141–144, 213, 214
Spotsylvania, Virginia 132, 141, 141, 143
Spotted Tail Agency 197
Staked Plains 193, 194
Stanton, Edmund M. 21, 64, 88, 91, 115, 129
Staunton, Virginia 39, 71, 84, 98
Stevensburg, Virginia 32, 132
Stevenson's Depot 46, 77, 178, 179
Stockton, Robert F. 62
Stoneman, George 22–23, 24, 26, 29–36, 63, 64, 120, 216
Stoneman, John 203, 204
Stoneman Raid 19, 29–36
Stone's River/Murfreesboro, Battle of 218, 221
Stonewall Brigade, Confederate 111
Strasbourg, Virginia 50
Strong, George Templeton 116

Stuart, James Ewell Brown "J.E.B." 10, 19, 20, 21, 22, 23, 24, 26, 27, 31, 33, 34, 35, 68, 109, 112, 119, 120, 125–128, 129, 131, 135, 142, 153, 215, 219
Sturgis, Samuel D. 208
Sulphur Springs, Virginia 126
Summit Point, Virginia 42, 44, 75, 76
Sumner, Edwin V. 108, 174
C.S.S. Sumter 173
Sutherland's Depot, Virginia 187
Sykes, George 122, 131–134, 137, 175, 176

Tabernacle Church 118
Taylor Ford 144
Terrell, William 16
Terry, Alfred H. 116, 204, 205, 206
Terrytown, New York 174
Texas Rangers (Frontier Battalion) 193, 195
Thoburn, Joseph 49–52, 89, 92
Thomas, George H. 218, 221, 222
Three Sisters 48, 49, 50,m 56
Three Top Mountain 86, 87
Timberville, Virginia 82
Todd's Tavern 139, 141
Tom's Brook, Battle of 86–87, 88, 90, 98, 212
Tongue River Cantonment 203
Torbert, Alfred T.A. 1, 2, 13, 15, 41, 43, 44, 45, 46, 49, 53, 55, 61–67, 68–73, 74–78, 79–83, 84–88, 89,m 93–94, 97–101, 138, 144, 178, 180, 201, 206, 211, 212, 213, 214, 216
Totopotomy, Virginia 145
Trans-Mississippi Department, Confederate 191, 220
Trevilian Station, Battle of 68, 75, 97, 147, 216, 217
Trevilian Station, Virginia 71, 72
Tumbling Run 48, 50
Tuntstall, Florida 198
Tyler, John 172

Upperville, Battle of 120
Upton, Emory 77, 142–143, 179
U.S. Army Corps of Engineers 117, 174, 192
U.S. Army of Topographical Engineers 105, 117, 174
U.S. Military Academy, West Point 5, 19, 22, 61, 63, 75, 105, 106, 123, 174, 176, 191, 198, 199, 215
U.S. Naval Academy, Annapolis, Maryland 173

Vaill, Theodore 176
Valley District, Confederate 74, 75, 90
Valley District Army, Confederate 39, 48–52, 53, 76, 84, 87, 178, 180, 212
Valley Pike 178
Van Dorn, Earl 220, 222
Varina Station, Virginia 183
Vicksburg Campaign 99, 119, 221, 222
Vincent, Strong 122–123, 175
Virginia & Tennessee Railroad 38
Virginia Campaign of 1863 126, 128
Virginia Central Railroad 29, 31, 32, 33, 71, 87, 89, 97, 98, 99, 100, 111, 215
Virginia Military Institute 5, 128

Wadsworth, James 139
War Bonnet Creek, Battle of 205, 207
Warm Springs 205
Warren, Gouverneur K. 1, 2, 13, 14, 15, 16, 105–110, 111–117, 118–124, 125, 127–128, 129–137, 137–148, 149–153, 154–160, 161–169, 174–175, 176, 183–186, 201, 211, 212, 214, 215, 216, 217, 221
Warren Court of Inquiry 161–168, 184, 185
Warrenton Junction, Virginia 126, 127, 129, 138
Washington, D.C. 12, 16, 37, 64, 65, 74, 88, 91, 100, 106, 109, 110, 111, 120, 125, 129, 130, 132, 162, 177, 178
Washington, George 8
Washington Raid 74
Washita, Battle of the 206
Waterloo, Virginia 126
Waynesboro, Battle of 100, 148
Weed, Stephen H. 122–123
Weir, Thomas 209
Weitzel, Godfrey 181, 187, 188
Weldon Railroad 148
Wharton, Gabriel 90–96, 98–99
Wheeler, Joseph 106
Wheeling, West Virginia 55
White House, Virginia 144, 149
White Oak Road 150, 151, 152, 153, 154, 155, 156, 157, 158, 159, 162, 164, 184, 187
White Oak Swamp Road 156, 184
White River Utes 197–198, 208
Wickham, Williams C. 48, 53, 68, 70, 78, 79–83, 85
The Wilderness 21, 34, 119, 132, 138
Wilderness, Battle of the 69, 94, 138–140, 213
Wilderness Tavern 138
Wilder's Lightning Brigade, Union 38
Williamsport, Maryland 42, 43
Wilson, James H. 10, 46, 49, 64, 65, 67, 71, 75–78, 79–80, 82, 84, 138, 139, 144, 178–179, 215, 216
Wilson's Creek, Battle of 222
Winchester, Second Battle of 120
Winchester, Virginia 16, 39, 42, 44, 45, 46, 76, 77, 78, 94, 99, 100, 120, 177
Winchester/Opequan Creek, Third Battle of 45, 46–47, 48, 54, 76, 77–78, 82, 90, 100, 177–180, 212, 215, 218, 221
Wittenberg, Eric 215
Woodstock, Virginia 53, 55, 56
Wool, John E. 5
World War I 146, 218
World War II 146
Wounded Knee, Battle of 205
Wright, Horatio G., 4Winchester, Virginia 16, 39, 42, 44, 45, 46, 76, 77, 78, 94, 99, 100, 120, 177
Wytheville, Virginia 39

Yellow Hair 208
Yellow Tavern, Battle of 68, 69, 142, 153, 216, 218, 222
Yorktown, Siege of 62, 108

www.ingramcontent.com/pod-product-compliance
Ingram Content Group UK Ltd.
Pitfield, Milton Keynes, MK11 3LW, UK
UKHW050533150426
5217IPUK00026B/1915